Book
of the
Dead

and other Egyptian Papyri and Tablets

Devoted Publsihing
Woodstock, Ontario, Canada 2017

Book of the Dead and other Egyptian Papyri and Tablets

Orginally published as: *Egyptian Literature Comprising Egyptian Tales, Hymns, Litanies, Invocations, The Book Of The Dead, And Cuneiform Writings*

By: Various Translators
Edited By: Anthony Uyl

This edition published by Devoted Publishing, a division of 2165467 Ontario Inc.
Originally published by: The Co-Operative Publication Society, Copyright, 1901, The Colonial Press in New York And London

The text of Book of the Dead and other Egyptial Papyri and Tablets is all in the Public Domain.

Contact us at: devotedpub@hotmail.com
Visit us on Facebook: @DevotedPublishing
Visit our website: www.devotedpublishing.com

Published in Woodstock, Ontario, Canada 2017.

ISBN: 978-1-77356-127-1

Table of Contents

SPECIAL INTRODUCTION 6
THE BOOK OF THE DEAD 8
A Hymn To The Setting Sun 8
Hymn And Litany To Osiris 9
Litany 10
Hymn To Ra 11
Hymn To The Setting Sun 13
Hymn To The Setting Sun 15
The Chapter Of The Chaplet Of Victory . 16
The Chapter Of The Victory Over Enemies. 17
The Chapter Of Giving A Mouth To The Overseer 18
The Chapter Of Giving A Mouth To Osiris Ani 19
Opening The Mouth Of Osiris 20
The Chapter Of Bringing Charms To Osiris 21
The Chapter Of Memory 22
The Chapter Of Giving A Heart To Osiris 23
The Chapter Of Preserving The Heart 24
The Chapter Of Preserving The Heart 25
The Chapter Of Preserving The Heart 26
The Chapter Of Preserving The Heart 27
The Heart Of Carnelian 28
Preserving The Heart 29
Preserving The Heart 30
Preserving The Heart 31
Rubric 32
Beating Back The Crocodile 33
Beating Back The Crocodile 34
Repulsing Serpents 35
Against Snakes 36
Against Serpents 37
Driving Away Apshait 38
Driving Back The Merti 39
Living By Air 40
Living By Air 41
Driving Back Rerek 42
Repulsing The Eater Of The Ass 43
Abolishing The Slaughterings 44
Abolishing The Slaughterings 45
Air And Water 47
Dominion Over Elements 48
Dominion Over Elements 49
Dominion Over Elements 50
Preservation Of The Soul 51
Of Drinking Water 52
Of Drinking Water 53
Preservation From Scalding 54
On Coming Forth By Day 55
Chapter Of Knowledge 57
Of Gaining Mastery Over Enemies 59
Victory Over Enemies 60
Coming Forth By Day 61
Opening The Underworld 62
Coming Forth By Day 63
Coming Forth By Day 64
Coming Forth By Day 65
Coming Forth By Day 66
Coming Forth By Day 67
Of Lifting Up The Feet 68
Of Journeying To Annu 69
Of Transformation 70
Of Performing Transformations 71
Of Transformation Into A Hawk 72
Of Transformation Into A Governor 74
Of Transformation Into A God 75
Transformation Into A Lotus 76
Transformation Into A Lotus 77
Transformation Into Ptah 78
Transformation Into A Bennu Bird 79
Transformation Into A Heron 80
Of The Living Soul 81
Of The Swallow 82
The Serpent Sata 83
Of The Crocodile 84
Soul And Body 85
Of Evil Recollections 86

Of Rescue	87
Of Opening The Tomb	88
Of Not Sailing To The East	89
Of The Ink-Pot And Palette	90
Of Being Nigh Unto Thoth	91
Of Being Nigh Unto Thoth	92
Of Bringing A Boat Along In Heaven	93
Of Bringing The Makhent Boat	94
Of Entering The Boat Of Ra	96
Of Protecting The Boat Of Ra	97
Of Going Into The Boat Of Ra	98
Of Knowing The Souls Of The East	99
Of Sekhet-Hetepet	100
Of Knowing The Souls Of Pe	102
Of Knowing The Souls Of Nekhen	103
Of Knowing The Souls Of Khemennu	104
Of Coming Forth From Heaven	105
Of Knowing The Souls Of Khemennu	106
Of Receiving Paths	107
Of Coming Forth From Re-Stau	108
Of Coming Forth From Re-Stau	109
Of Going About In The Underworld	110
Of Entering Into The Great House	111
Of Entering The Presence	112
The Introduction To Maati	113
The Introduction To Maati	114
The Negative Confession	115
Address To The Gods Of The Underworld	117
Of The Hour Apes(109)	119
Of The Praise Of The Gods	120
Adoration Of The Gods Of The Qerti	121
Hymn Of Praise To Osiris	122
Of Making Perfect The Khu	123
Of Living Nigh Unto Ra	125
Of Bringing Men Back To Earth	126
Of Making Perfect The Khu	127
Of Making Perfect The Khu	128
For The New Moon	129
Of Travelling In The Boat Of Ra	130
Of Making Perfect The Khu	131
Sailing In The Great Boat	132
Of The Four Flames	133
EGYPTIAN TALES	134
The Taking Of Joppa	134
The Doomed Prince	136
Anpu And Bata	138
Setna And The Magic Book	142
Ahura's Tale	142
Tales Of The Magicians	147
Khafra's Tale	147
Bau-F-Ra's Tale	148
Hordedef's Tale	148
The Peasant And The Workman	151
The Shipwrecked Sailor	154
The Adventures Of Sanehat	156
Petition To The King Of Egypt	158
Copy Of The Answer To This Order	159
THE TELL AMARNA TABLETS	161
The Hittite Invasion Of Damascus	161
The Amorite Treachery	165
The War In Phœnicia	169
RIBADDA'S LETTERS FROM GEBAL	171
SUBANDI'S LETTERS	182
Northern Palestine	183
LETTERS FROM BEIRUT	183
LETTER FROM SIDON	184
LETTERS FROM TYRE	185
LETTERS FROM ACCHO	188
LETTERS FROM HAZOR	189
Southern Palestine	190
LETTERS FROM JOPPA	190
LETTERS FROM ASCALON	191
LETTERS FROM MAKKEDAH	192
LETTERS FROM GEZER	195
LETTERS FROM JERUSALEM	197
SUYARDATA'S LETTERS FROM (Keilah?)(357)	200
LETTERS OF THE LADY BASMATH	201
OTHER LETTERS FROM THE SOUTH OF PALESTINE	202

LETTERS FROM UNCERTAIN SITES 203	The Solemn Festal Dirge Of The Egyptians 236
Royal Letters 205	Hymns To Amen 238
DUSRATTA'S LETTERS 205	Hymn To Pharaoh 240
RIMMON NIRARI'S LETTER 212	The Song Of The Harper 241
CALLIMMASIN'S LETTERS 213	Hymn To Amen-Ra 243
ASSURUBALID'S LETTER 215	Hymn To Ra-Harmachis 248
LETTERS FROM BURNABURIAS 216	The Lamentations Of Isis And Nephthys 251
LETTERS FROM ALASIYA 219	The Litany Of Ra 255
CUNEIFORM INSCRIPTIONS AND HIERATIC PAPYRI 221	CHAPTER I 255
The Great Tablet Of Rameses II At Abu-Simbel 221	CHAPTER II 258
	CHAPTER III 259
Hymn To Osiris 224	CHAPTER IV 260
Travels Of An Egyptian In The Fourteenth Century B.C. 227	The Book Of Respirations 263
Dirge Of Menephtah 231	THE EPIC OF PENTA-OUR 268
Hymn To The Nile 232	FOOTNOTES 270

SPECIAL INTRODUCTION.

The wonders of Egyptian archæology are the latest and most precious harvest of scholars and explorers. From Belzoni to Flinders Petrie there has been a succession of discoveries in the valley of the Nile with which it is hard for ordinary students to keep pace. Our knowledge of Egyptian life to-day is far clearer and more complete than Bentley's or Porson's acquaintance with the antiquities of Greece and Rome, and we have far more complete access to the treasures of Egyptian literature than Dante or Thomas Aquinas had to the remains of Attic poets and mystics. We know exactly how an Egyptian of the twelfth dynasty dressed; what was the position of women in Egypt; and what uniform was worn by the Egyptian soldiers who took part in the campaign against Khitasis. We can see Rameses II riding in his war-chariot; we know the very names of the horses by whose side his tame lion is running and thirsting for the blood of his master's foes. We know all about the domestic animals, the funeral customs, the trades, the gods, the agriculture of the Nile valley thirty centuries ago. We see the whole many-sided civilization portrayed in the brightest colors in the poetry, the books of ritual, the hieratic inscriptions, the tablets, papyri, and hieroglyphics which day by day come to light in exhaustless abundance from the mounds and ruins of that fertile plain that stretches from Thebes to the Mareotic lake.

For instance, we can learn exact particulars about the mode in which Rameses II made war, from the poem of Penta-Our, a Theban writer of the fourteenth century B.C. It is only by a figure of speech that this poem can be called an epic; it is rather a historical narrative couched in terms of poetic exaggeration with the object of flattering the royal vanity of Pharaoh.

The campaign in which Rameses then engaged was directed against Kadesh, a city built on an island in the Orontes. It is, according to Penta-Our, inhabited by a people known as Khita, whose spies are brought into the tent of Rameses and questioned as to the whereabouts of the King of Kadesh. The spies are forced by blows to answer, and they tell the Egyptian monarch that the King of the Khita "is powerful with many soldiers, and with chariot soldiers, and with their harness, as many as the sand of the seashore, and they are ready to fight behind Kadesh."

The King is very angry; for he had been deceived by false news to the effect that his enemy had fled in terror to Khilibu. "The fault is great," he cries, "that the governors of the land and the vassal princes of Pharaoh have committed, in neglecting to watch the movements of the Khita." He sends to bring back the legions he had sent away, and meanwhile the approach of the enemy is announced. The camp of Rameses is surprised by the Asiatics; many foot-soldiers are killed before they can seize their weapons, but a faithful band rallies in front of the royal quarters. Suddenly a cry is heard; Rameses has quickly put on his armor, seized his lance, ordered his war lion to be loosed, and dashed into the fight. Pharaoh with his master of the horse, Menni, is soon hemmed in by foes. "My Lord, O generous King!" cries Menni, "Egypt's great protector in the day of battle! behold we stand alone in the midst of the enemy, for the archers and the chariots have left us. Let us return, that our lives may be saved. Save us, O my Lord, Rameses Miamun!" Then Rameses called upon Amen, his god, and under his protection charged the enemy, and "his hand devoured them in the space of an instant." Five times he rushed upon them, and five times they repulsed him. The sixth time he breaks their ranks and regains his own lines. Then the legions of Ptah, which had returned to the camp, join the battle, and the Asiatics are routed. The first care of Rameses is to refresh his brave horses, Victory-in-Thebes and Maut-is-Satisfied. Neither they nor Rameses and his lion are wounded, though all stained with blood and dust, while the head-plumes of the team are torn and tattered and their caparison broken.

This is a brief account of the main incident in this Egyptian epic, which is written with life-like detail and animation. The war concludes with a treaty, and the marriage of Rameses with the daughter of the King of Kadesh, so that henceforth "the people of Egypt were of one mind with the princes of Khita, which had not been the case since the god Rā."

The Egyptians have always been deeply impressed by the fact of human mortality, and much of their religious belief and religious ritual is taken up with the rites of burial, and detailed doctrines as to the experience of the soul after parting from the body. Their elaborate embalming of the dead springs from the desire to keep the mortal tenement prepared for the soul's return to it. In their Book of the Dead is a full series of prayers, songs, and incantations to be employed at funerals, and by the individual in his journey beyond the tomb. The funeral procession was a very noisy company; lamentations were heard through its whole length, but the burden of the hymns was always, "To the West." This was enlarged upon, "To the West, the dwelling of Osiris; O Chief, as thou goest to the West, the Gods themselves lament, as thou goest to the West."

Osiris is the judge who weighs the souls, and allots them happiness or misery, according to their deserts. "The Book of the Dead" is interesting because it teaches how clearly and dogmatically the solemn and precise Egyptian stated his views and held his convictions concerning the unknown country. Four parts of man, it was said, survive after death, namely, the soul, the spirit, the shadow, and the double. The double remains in the tomb, and only leaves it in search of food. Sometimes it feels its loneliness and avenges itself upon near relations who have forsaken it. But the soul hurries to the bar of Osiris, where Thoth weighs the heart in the scales, and the innocent are admitted into the Field of Beans, a realm of fertility, where wheat grows seven cubits high. Immortality is spent in feasting, singing, conversation, and games. But the whole of this wonderful book is well worth studying. It shows how what Addison calls "this longing after immortality" led an ancient and deeply religious people to attempt in their burial rites to rob even the grave of its terrors, and conjured up out of the shadows of the tomb a clear and distinct vision of future life, wherein man in his complete individuality survived to all eternity.

Among the most important results of recent Egyptian exploration must be reckoned the discovery of the tablets of Tell Amarna. Tell Amarna is a village in Upper Egypt, and in a pit at the foot of the mountain, at the base of which it stands, were discovered hundreds of these relics, which have since been distributed among the museums of London, Berlin, and Gizeh. The writing on these tablets is cuneiform, and the matter is of profound historic importance, illustrating, as it does, the relations between Egypt and western Asia in the fifteenth century B.C. While the existence of these tablets proves that cuneiform writing was common to Palestine and Syria as well as the Euphrates Valley, yet curiously enough the manuscripts of Tell Amarna are different from any of the same kind that have been found elsewhere, and the language resembles somewhat the Hebrew of the Old Testament.

While most of these tablets are letters and despatches from friendly powers in Syria, and from vassal princes in Palestine, others contain interesting legends. The letters are addressed to the Pharaohs known as Amenophis III and Amenophis IV, who reigned in the sixteenth and fifteenth centuries B.C.

The Egyptians employed what practically were three alphabets—the hieroglyphic, the hieratic, and the demotic. The hieroglyph is a symbol, denoting something without letters or syllables; as, pictures of a bee stand for king. The hieratic handwriting was a transition from symbols to primitive letters; the papyrus reed, cut in slices and gummed together, was used as paper for this writing, much of which is very beautifully executed in black and red inks. These papyri are constantly being discovered, but perhaps the earliest "find" of importance was that at Thebes in 1846, when a number of literary compositions were brought to light which must have been executed during the twelfth dynasty, about twenty-five centuries B.C.

The Egyptian Tales are works written in a lighter vein than the literature we have already described. They will be read with delight, and none the less so because they show that the Egyptians, who are the Chinese of the Mediterranean, possess that saving quality in literary and political life, namely, a sense of humor.

(signed) Epiphanius Wilson

THE BOOK OF THE DEAD

According to the Theban Recension

Translated by E. A. Wallis Budge, Litt.D., D.Lit., F.S.A.

A Hymn To The Setting Sun

A HYMN OF PRAISE TO RA WHEN HE RISETH UPON THE HORIZON, AND WHEN HE SETTETH IN THE LAND OF LIFE. Osiris, the scribe Ani, saith:

"Homage to thee, O Rā, when thou risest [as] Tem-Heru-khuti (Tem-Harmachis). Thou art adored [by me when] thy beauties are before mine eyes, and [when thy] radiance [falleth] upon [my] body. Thou goest forth to thy setting in the Sektet boat with [fair] winds, and thy heart is glad; the heart of the Mātet boat rejoiceth. Thou stridest over the heavens in peace, and all thy foes are cast down; the never-resting stars sing hymns of praise unto thee, and the stars which rest, and the stars which never fail glorify thee as thou sinkest to rest in the horizon of Manu,(1) O thou who art beautiful at morn and at eve, O thou lord who livest and art established, O my lord!

"Homage to thee, O thou who art Rā when thou risest, and Tem when thou settest [in] beauty. Thou risest and shinest on the back of thy mother [Nut], O thou who art crowned king of the gods! Nut doeth homage unto thee, and everlasting and never-changing order(2) embraceth thee at morn and at eve. Thou stridest over the heaven, being glad of heart, and the Lake of Testes is content [thereat]. The Sebau Fiend hath fallen to the ground; his arms and his hands have been hacked off, and the knife hath severed the joints of his body. Rā hath a fair wind; the Sektet boat goeth forth and sailing along it cometh into port. The gods of the south and of the north, of the west and of the east, praise thee, O thou divine substance, from whom all forms of life come into being. Thou sendest forth the word, and the earth is flooded with silence, O thou only One, who didst dwell in heaven before ever the earth and the mountains came into existence. O Runner, O Lord, O only One, thou maker of things which are, thou hast fashioned the tongue of the company of the gods, thou hast produced whatsoever cometh forth from the waters, and thou springest up from them over the flooded land of the Lake of Horus. Let me snuff the air which cometh forth from thy nostrils, and the north wind which cometh forth from thy mother [Nut]. Oh, make thou to be glorious my shining form (khu), O Osiris, make thou to be divine my soul (ba)! Thou art worshipped [in] peace (or [in] setting), O lord of the gods, thou art exalted by reason of thy wondrous works. Shine thou with thy rays of light upon my body day by day, [upon me], Osiris the scribe, the teller of the divine offerings of all the gods, the overseer of the granary of the lords of Abtu (Abydos), the royal scribe in truth who loveth thee; Ani, victorious in peace."

Hymn And Litany To Osiris

[From the Papyrus of Ani (British Museum No. 10,470, sheet 19).]

"Praise be unto thee, O Osiris, lord of eternity, Unnefer, Heru-khuti (Harmachis), whose forms are manifold, and whose attributes are majestic, Ptah-Seker-Tem in Annu (Heliopolis), the lord of the hidden place, and the creator of Het-ka-Ptah (Memphis) and of the gods [therein], the guide of the underworld, whom [the gods] glorify when thou settest in Nut. Isis embraceth thee in peace, and she driveth away the fiends from the mouth of thy paths. Thou turnest thy face upon Amentet, and thou makest the earth to shine as with refined copper. Those who have lain down (i.e., the dead) rise up to see thee, they breathe the air and they look upon thy face when the Disk riseth on its horizon; their hearts are at peace inasmuch as they behold thee, O thou who art Eternity and Everlastingness!"

Litany

"Homage to thee, [O lord of] starry deities in Annu, and of heavenly beings in Kher-āba; thou god Unti, who art more glorious than the gods who are hidden in Annu; oh grant(3) thou unto me a path whereon I may pass in peace, for I am just and true; I have not spoken lies wittingly, nor have I done aught with deceit."

"Homage to thee, O An in Antes, (?) Heru-khuti (Harmachis), with long strides thou stridest over heaven, O Heru-khuti. Oh, grant thou unto me a path whereon I may pass in peace, for I am just and true; I have not spoken lies wittingly, nor have I done aught with deceit."

"Homage to thee, O Soul of everlastingness, thou Soul who dwellest in Tattu, Unnefer, son of Nut; thou art lord of Akert. Oh, grant thou unto me a path wherein I may pass in peace, for I am just and true; I have not spoken lies wittingly, nor have I done aught with deceit."

"Homage to thee in thy dominion over Tattu; the Ureret crown is established upon thy head; thou art the One who maketh the strength which protecteth himself, and thou dwellest in peace in Tattu. Oh, grant thou unto me a path whereon I may pass in peace, for I am just and true; I have not spoken lies wittingly, nor have I done aught with deceit."

"Homage to thee, O lord of the Acacia tree, the Seker boat is set upon its sledge; thou turnest back the Fiend, the worker of evil, and thou causest the Utchat to rest upon its seat. Oh, grant thou unto me a path whereon I may pass in peace, for I am just and true; I have not spoken lies wittingly, nor have I done aught with deceit."

"Homage to thee, O thou who art mighty in thine hour, thou great and mighty Prince, dweller in An-rut-f,(4) lord of eternity and creator of everlastingness, thou art the lord of Suten-henen (Heracleopolis Magna). Oh, grant thou unto me a path whereon I may pass in peace, for I am just and true; I have not spoken lies wittingly, nor have I done aught with deceit."

"Homage to thee, O thou who restest upon Right and Truth, thou art the lord of Abtu (Abydos), and thy limbs are joined unto Ta-tchesertet; thou art he to whom fraud and guile are hateful. Oh, grant thou unto me a path whereon I may pass in peace, for I am just and true; I have not spoken lies wittingly, nor have I done aught with deceit."

"Homage to thee, O thou who art within thy boat, thou bringest Hāpi (i.e., the Nile) forth from his source; the light shineth upon thy body and thou art the dweller in Nekhen.(5) Oh, grant thou unto me a path whereon I may pass in peace, for I am just and true; I have not spoken lies wittingly, nor have I done aught with deceit."

"Homage to thee, O creator of the gods, thou King of the North and of the South, O Osiris, victorious one, ruler of the world in thy gracious seasons; thou art the lord of the celestial world.(6) Oh, grant thou unto me a path whereon I may pass in peace, for I am just and true; I have not spoken lies wittingly, nor have I done aught with deceit."

Hymn To Rā

[From the Papyrus of Ani (British Museum No. 10,470, sheet 20).]

A HYMN OF PRAISE TO RĀ WHEN HE RISETH IN THE EASTERN PART OF HEAVEN. Those who are in his train rejoice, and lo! Osiris Ani, victorious, saith:

"Hail, thou Disk, thou lord of rays, who risest on the horizon day by day! Shine thou with thy beams of light upon the face of Osiris Ani, who is victorious; for he singeth hymns of praise unto thee at dawn, and he maketh thee to set at eventide with words of adoration. May the soul of Osiris Ani, the triumphant one, come forth with thee into heaven, may he go forth in the Mātet boat. May he come into port in the Sektet boat, and may he cleave his path among the never-resting stars in the heavens."

Osiris Ani, being in peace and in triumph, adoreth his lord, the lord of eternity, saying: "Homage to thee, O Heru-khuti (Harmachis), who art the god Khepera, the self-created; when thou risest on the horizon and sheddest thy beams of light upon the lands of the North and of the South, thou art beautiful, yea beautiful, and all the gods rejoice when they behold thee, the King of heaven. The goddess Nebt-Unnut is stablished upon thy head; and her uræi of the South and of the North are upon thy brow; she taketh up her place before thee. The god Thoth is stablished in the bows of thy boat to destroy utterly all thy foes. Those who are in the Tuat (underworld) come forth to meet thee, and they bow in homage as they come toward thee, to behold [thy] beautiful Image. And I have come before thee that I may be with thee to behold thy Disk every day. May I not be shut up in [the tomb], may I not be turned back, may the limbs of my body be made new again when I view thy beauties, even as [are those of] all thy favored ones, because I am one of those who worshipped thee [whilst I lived] upon earth. May I come in unto the land of eternity, may I come even unto the everlasting land, for behold, O my lord, this hast thou ordained for me."

And lo, Osiris Ani triumphant in peace, the triumphant one, saith: "Homage to thee, O thou who risest in thy horizon as Rā, thou reposest upon law [which changeth not nor can it be altered]. Thou passest over the sky, and every face watcheth thee and thy course, for thou hast been hidden from their gaze. Thou dost shew thyself at dawn and at eventide day by day. The Sektet boat, wherein is thy Majesty, goeth forth with might; thy beams [shine] upon [all] faces; [the number] of thy red and yellow rays cannot be known, nor can thy bright beams be told. The lands of the gods, and the eastern lands of Punt(7) must be seen, ere that which is hidden [in thee] may be measured. Alone and by thyself thou dost manifest thyself [when] thou comest into being above Nu (i.e., the sky). May Ani advance, even as thou dost advance; may he never cease [to go forward], even as thy Majesty ceaseth not [to go forward], even though it be for a moment; for with strides dost thou in one little moment pass over the spaces which would need hundreds of thousands and millions of years [for man to pass over; this] thou doest, and then dost thou sink to rest. Thou puttest an end to the hours of the night, and thou dost count them, even thou; thou endest them in thine own appointed season, and the earth becometh light. Thou settest thyself before thy handiwork in the likeness of Rā; thou risest in the horizon."

Osiris, the scribe Ani, triumphant, declareth his praise of thee when thou shinest, and when thou risest at dawn he crieth in his joy at thy birth: "Thou art crowned with the majesty of thy beauties; thou mouldest thy limbs as thou dost advance, and thou bringest them forth without birth-pangs in the form of Rā, as thou dost rise up into the upper air. Grant thou that I may come unto the heaven which is everlasting, and unto the mountain where dwell thy favored ones. May I be joined unto those shining beings, holy and perfect, who are in the underworld; and may I come forth with them to behold thy beauties when thou shinest at eventide and goest to thy mother Nu. Thou dost place thyself in the west, and my two hands are [raised] in adoration [of thee] when thou settest as a living being. Behold, thou art the maker of eternity, and thou art adored [when] thou settest in the heavens. I have given my heart unto thee without wavering, O thou who art mightier than the gods."

Osiris Ani, triumphant, saith: "A hymn of praise to thee, O thou who risest like unto gold, and who dost flood the world with light on the day of thy birth. Thy mother giveth thee birth upon [her] hand, and thou dost give light unto the course of the Disk. O thou great Light, who shinest in the heavens, thou dost strengthen the generations of men with the Nile-flood, and thou dost cause gladness in all lands, and in all cities, and in all the temples. Thou art glorious by reason of thy splendors, and thou makest strong thy ka (i.e., Double) with hu and tchefau foods. O thou who art the mighty one of victories, thou who art the Power of [all] powers, who dost make strong thy throne against evil fiends; who art glorious in majesty in the Sektet boat, and who art exceeding mighty in the Atet boat, make thou glorious Osiris Ani with victory in the underworld; grant thou that in the netherworld he may be without evil. I pray thee to put away [his] faults behind thee: grant thou that he may be one of thy venerable servants who are with the shining ones; may he be joined unto the souls which are in Ta-tchesertet; and may he journey into the Sekhet-Aaru by a prosperous and happy decree, he the Osiris, the scribe, Ani, triumphant."

And the god saith:

"Thou shalt come forth into heaven, thou shalt pass over the sky, thou shalt be joined into the starry deities. Praises shall be offered unto thee in thy boat, thou shalt be hymned in the Atet boat, thou shalt behold Rā within his shrine, thou shalt set together with his Disk day by day, thou shalt see the Ant fish when it springeth into being in the waters of turquoise, and thou shalt see the Abtu fish in his hour. It shall come to pass that the Evil One shall fall when he layeth a snare to destroy thee, and the joints of his neck and of his back shall be hacked asunder. Rā [saileth] with a fair wind, and the Sektet boat draweth on and cometh into port. The mariners of Rā rejoice, and the heart of Nebt-ānkh(8) is glad, for the enemy of her lord hath fallen to the ground. Thou shalt behold Horus on the standing-place of the pilot of the boat, and Thoth and Maāt shall stand one upon each side of him. All the gods shall rejoice when they behold Rā coming in peace to make the hearts of the shining ones to live, and Osiris Ani, victorious, the scribe of the divine offerings of the lords of Thebes, shall be along with them!"

Hymn To The Setting Sun

[From the Papyrus of Mut-hetep (British Museum No, 10,010, sheet 5).]

[ANOTHER CHAPTER OF] THE MYSTERY OF THE TUAT (UNDERWORLD) AND OF PASSING THROUGH THE UNSEEN NETHERWORLD, and of seeing the Disk when he setteth in Amentet, [when] he is adored by the gods and by the Khus in the underworld, and [when] the Soul which dwelleth in Rā is made perfect. He is made mighty before Tem; he is made great before Osiris; he setteth his terror before the company of the gods who are the guides of the netherworld; he maketh long (?) his steps and he maketh his face to enter (?) [with that of] the great god. Now every Khu, for whom these words shall have been said, shall come forth by day in any form which he is pleased to take; he shall gain power among the gods of the Tuat (underworld), and they shall recognize him as one of themselves; and he shall enter in at the hidden gate with power.

    The lady Mut-hetep, victorious, singeth hymns of praise to thee [saying]: "O Rā-Tem, in thy splendid progress thou risest, and thou settest as a living being in the glories of the western horizon; thou settest in thy territory which is in Manu.(9) Thy uræus is behind thee, thy uræus is behind thee. Homage to thee, O thou who art in peace, homage to thee, O thou who art in peace. Thou art joined unto the Eye of Tem, and it chooseth its powers of protection [to place] behind thy members. Thou goest forth through heaven, thou travellest over the earth, and thou journeyest onward. O Luminary, the northern and southern halves of heaven come to thee and they bow low in adoration, and they pay homage unto thee, day by day. The gods of Amentet rejoice in thy beauties and the unseen places sing hymns of praise unto thee. Those who dwell in the Sektet boat go round about thee, and the Souls of the East pay homage to thee, and when they meet thy Majesty they cry: 'Come, come in peace!' There is a shout of welcome to thee, O lord of heaven and governor of Amentet! Thou art acknowledged by Isis who seeth her son in thee, the lord of fear, the mighty one of terror. Thou settest as a living being in the hidden place. Thy father [Ta-]tunen raiseth thee up and he placeth both his hands behind thee; thou becomest endowed with divine attributes in [thy] members of earth; thou wakest in peace and thou settest in Manu.(10) Grant thou that I may become a being honored before Osiris, and that I may come to thee, O Rā-Tem! I have adored thee, therefore do thou for me that which I wish. Grant thou that I may be victorious in the presence of the company of the gods. Thou are beautiful, O Rā, in thy western horizon of Amentet, thou lord of Maāt, thou mighty one of fear, thou whose attributes are majestic, O thou who art greatly beloved by those who dwell in the Tuat (underworld); thou shinest with thy beams upon the beings that are therein perpetually, and thou sendest forth thy light upon the path of Re-stau. Thou openest up the path of the double Lion-god, thou settest the gods upon [their] thrones, and the Khus in their abiding places. The heart of Naarerf(11) is glad [when] Rā setteth, the heart of Naarerf is glad when Rā setteth."

    "Hail, O ye gods of the land of Amentet who make offerings and oblations unto Rā-Tem, ascribe ye glory [unto him when] ye meet him. Grasp ye your weapons and overthrow ye the fiend Seba on behalf of Rā, and repulse the fiend Nebt on behalf of Osiris. The gods of the land of Amentet rejoice and lay hold upon the cords of the Sektet boat, and they come in peace; the gods of the hidden place who dwell in Amentet triumph."

    "Hail, Thoth, who didst make Osiris to triumph over his enemies, make thou Mut-hetep, victorious, to triumph over her enemies in the presence of the great divine sovereign chiefs who live with Osiris, the lord of life. The great god who dwelleth in his Disk cometh forth, that is, Horus the avenger of his father Unnefer-Rā. Osiris setteth, and the Khus who are in the Tuat (underworld) say: Homage to thee, O thou who comest as Tem, and who comest into being as the creator of the gods. Homage to thee, O thou who comest as the holy Soul of souls, who dwellest in the horizon. Homage to thee who art more glorious than [all] the gods and who illuminest the Tuat with thine Eye. Homage to thee who sailest in thy glory and who goest round about it in thy Disk."

    The following variant of the above hymn is translated from the text in the Papyrus of Nekhtu-Amen (Naville, "Todtenbuch," Bd. II. p. 23).

ANOTHER CHAPTER OF THE MYSTERY OF THE TUAT (UNDERWORLD) AND OF TRAVERSING THE UNSEEN PLACES OF THE UNDERWORLD, of seeing the Disk when he setteth in Amentet, [when] he is adored by the gods and by the Khus of the Tuat (underworld), and [when] the divine Khu which dwelleth within Rā is made perfect. He setteth his might before Rā, he setteth his power before Tem, [he setteth his strength] before Khenti-Amentet, and he setteth his terror before the company of the gods. The Osiris of the gods goeth as leader through the Tuat (underworld), he crasheth through mountains, he bursteth through rocks, he maketh glad (?) the heart of every Khu. This composition shall be recited by the deceased when he cometh forth and when he goeth in with the gods, among whom he findeth no opposition; then shall he come forth by day in all the manifold and exceedingly numerous forms which he may be pleased to take. [The Osiris ... saith:]

"A hymn of praise to Rā at eventide [when] he setteth as a living being in Baakha.(12) The great god who dwelleth in his Disk riseth in his two eyes(13) and all the Khus of the underworld receive him in his horizon of Amentet; they shout praises unto Heru-khuti (Harmachis) in his form of Tem, and they sing hymns of joy to Rā when they have received him at the head of his beautiful path of Amentet."

He (i.e., the deceased) saith: "Praise be unto thee, O Rā, praise be unto thee, O Tem, in thy splendid progress. Thou hast risen and thou hast put on strength, and thou settest like a living being amid thy glories in the horizon of Amentet, in thy domain which is in Manu. Thy uræus-goddess is behind thee; thy uræus-goddess is behind thee. Hail to thee, in peace; hail to thee, in peace. Thou joinest thyself unto the Eye of Horus, and thou hidest thyself within its secret place; it destroyeth for thee all the convulsions of thy face, it maketh thee strong with life, and thou livest. It bindeth its protecting amulets behind thy members. Thou sailest forth over heaven, and thou makest the earth to be stablished; thou joinest thyself unto the upper heaven, O Luminary. The two regions of the East and West make adoration unto thee, bowing low and paying homage unto thee, and they praise thee day by day; the gods of Amentet rejoice in thy splendid beauties. The hidden places adore thee, the aged ones make offerings unto thee, and they create for thee protecting powers. The divine beings who dwell in the eastern and western horizons transport thee, and those who are in the Sektet boat convey thee round and about. The Souls of Amentet cry out unto thee and say unto thee when they meet thy majesty (Life, Health, Strength!), 'All hail, all hail!' When thou comest forth in peace there arise shouts of delight to thee, O thou lord of heaven, thou Prince of Amentet. Thy mother Isis embraceth thee, and in thee she recognizeth her son, the lord of fear, the mighty one of terror. Thou settest as a living being within the dark portal. Thy father Tatunen lifteth thee up and he stretcheth out his two hands behind thee; thou becomest a divine being in the earth. Thou wakest as thou settest, and thy habitation is in Manu. Grant thou that I may be venerated before Osiris, and come thou [to me], O Rā-Tem. Since thou hast been adored [by me] that which I wish thou shalt do for me day by day. Grant thou victory [unto me] before the great company of the gods, O Rā who art doubly beautiful in thy horizon of Amentet, thou lord of Maāt who dwellest in the horizon. The fear of thee is great, thy forms are majestic, and the love of thee is great among those who dwell in the underworld."

Hymn To The Setting Sun

[From a Papyrus of the nineteenth dynasty preserved at Dublin (see Naville, "Todtenbuch," Bd. I. Bl. 19).]

A HYMN OF PRAISE TO RA-HERU-KHUTI (RA-HARMACHIS) WHEN HE SETTETH IN THE WESTERN PART OF HEAVEN. He (i.e., the deceased) saith:

"Homage to thee, O Rā [who] in thy sitting art Tem-Heru-khuti (Tem-Harmachis), thou divine god, thou self-created being, thou primeval matter [from which all things were made]. When [thou] appearest in the bows of [thy] bark men shout for joy at thee, O maker of the gods! Thou didst stretch out the heavens wherein thy two eyes(14) might travel, thou didst make the earth to be a vast chamber for thy Khus, so that every man might know his fellow. The Sektet boat is glad, and the Mātet boat rejoiceth; and they greet thee with exaltation as thou journeyest along. The god Nu is content, and thy mariners are satisfied; the uræus-goddess hath overthrown thine enemies, and thou hast carried off the legs of Apep. Thou art beautiful, O Rā, each day, and thy mother Nut embraceth thee; thou settest in beauty, and thy heart is glad in the horizon of Manu, and the holy beings therein rejoice. Thou shinest there with thy beams, O thou great god, Osiris, the everlasting Prince. The lords of the zones of the Tuat in their caverns stretch out their hands in adoration before thy Ka (double), and they cry out to thee, and they all come forth in the train of thy form shining brilliantly. The hearts of the lords of the Tuat (underworld) are glad when thou sendest forth thy glorious light in Amentet; their two eyes are directed toward thee, and they press forward to see thee, and their hearts rejoice when they do see thee. Thou hearkenest unto the acclamations of those that are in the funeral chest,(15) thou doest away with their helplessness and drivest away the evils which are about them. Thou givest breath to their nostrils and they take hold of the bows of thy bark in the horizon of Manu. Thou art beautiful each day, O Rā, and may thy mother Nut embrace Osiris ...,(16) victorious."

The Chapter Of The Chaplet Of Victory

[From Lepsius "Todtenbuch," Bl. 13.]

THE CHAPTER OF THE CHAPLET OF VICTORY. Osiris Auf-ānkh, victorious, born of Sheret-Amsu, victorious, saith:

"Thy father Tem hath woven for thee a beautiful chaplet of victory [to be placed] on [thy] living brow, O thou who lovest the gods, and thou shalt live forever. Osiris-khent-Amentet(17) hath made thee to triumph over thine enemies, and thy father Seb hath decreed for thee all his inheritance. Come, therefore, O Horus, son of Isis, for thou, O son of Osiris, sittest upon the throne of thy father Rā to overthrow thine enemies, for he hath ordained for thee the two lands to their utmost limits. Atem hath [also] ordained this, and the company of the gods hath confirmed the splendid power of the victory of Horus the son of Isis and the son of Osiris forever and forever. And Osiris Auf-ānkh shall be victorious forever and ever. O Osiris-khent-Amentet, the whole of the northern and southern parts of the heavens, and every god and every goddess, who are in heaven and who are upon earth [will] the victory of Horus, the son of Isis and the son of Osiris, over his enemies in the presence of Osiris-khent-Amentet who will make Osiris Auf-ānkh, victorious, to triumph over his enemies in the presence of Osiris-khent-Amentet, Un-nefer, the son of Nut, on the day of making him to triumph over Set and his fiends in the presence of the great sovereign chiefs who are in Annu (Heliopolis); on the night of the battle and overthrow of the Seba-fiend in the presence of the great sovereign princes who are in Abtu; on the night of making Osiris to triumph over his enemies make thou Osiris Auf-ānkh, triumphant, to triumph over his enemies in the presence of the great sovereign princes, who are in the horizon of Amentet; on the day of the festival of Haker in the presence of the great sovereign princes who are in Tattu; on the night of the setting up of the Tet in Tattu in the presence of the great sovereign princes who are in the ways of the damned; on the night of the judgment of those who shall be annihilated in the presence of the great sovereign princes who are in Sekhem (Letopolis); on the night of the 'things of the altars in Sekhem' in the presence of the great sovereign princes who are in Pe and Tepu; on the night of the stablishing of the inheriting by Horus of the things of his father Osiris in the presence of the great sovereign princes who are at the great festival of the ploughing and turning up of the earth in Tattu, or (as others say), [in] Abtu; on the night of the weighing of words," or (as others say), "weighing of locks in the presence of the great sovereign princes who are in An-rut-f on its place; on the night when Horus receiveth the birth-chamber of the gods in the presence of the great sovereign princes who are in the lands of Rekhti(?); on the night when Isis lieth down to watch [and] to make lamentation for her brother in the presence of the great sovereign princes who are in Re-stau; on the night of making Osiris to triumph over all his enemies."

"Horus repeated [these] words four times, and all his enemies fell headlong and were overthrown and were cut to pieces; and Osiris Auf-ānkh, triumphant, repeated [these] words four times, therefore let all his enemies fall headlong, and be overthrown and cut to pieces. Horus the son of Isis and son of Osiris celebrated in turn millions of festivals, and all his enemies fell headlong, and were overthrown and cut to pieces. Their habitation hath gone forth to the block of the East, their heads have been cut off; their necks have been destroyed; their thighs have been cut off; they have been given over to the Great Destroyer who dwelleth in the valley of the grave; and they shall never come forth from under the restraint of the god Seb."

THIS CHAPTER SHALL BE RECITED OVER THE DIVINE CHAPLET WHICH IS LAID UPON THE FACE OF THE DECEASED, AND THOU SHALT CAST INCENSE INTO THE FIRE ON BEHALF OF OSIRIS AUF-ANKH, TRIUMPHANT, BORN OF SHERET-AMSU, TRIUMPHANT; THUS SHALT THOU CAUSE HIM TO TRIUMPH OVER HIS ENEMIES, DEAD OR ALIVE, AND HE SHALL BE AMONG THE FOLLOWERS OF OSIRIS; AND A HAND SHALL BE STRETCHED OUT TO HIM WITH MEAT AND DRINK IN THE PRESENCE OF THE GOD. [THIS CHAPTER] SHALL BE SAID BY THEE TWICE AT DAWN—NOW IT IS A NEVER-FAILING CHARM—REGULARLY AND CONTINUALLY.

The Chapter Of The Victory Over Enemies.

[From the Papyrus of Nebseni (British Museum No. 9,900, sheet 12).]

"Hail, Thoth, who didst make Osiris to triumph over his enemies, snare thou the enemies of Osiris, the scribe Nebseni, the lord of piety, in the presence of the great sovereign princes of every god and of every goddess; in the presence of the great sovereign princes who are in Annu (Heliopolis) on the night of the battle and of the overthrow of the Sebau-fiend in Tattu; on the night of making to stand up the double Tet in Sekhem (Letopolis); on the night of the things of the night in Sekhem, in Pe, and in Tepu;(18) on the night of the stablishing of Horus in the heritage of the things of his father in the double land of Rekhti(?); on the night when Isis maketh lamentation at the side of her brother Osiris in Abtu (Abydos); on the night of the Haker festival of the distinguishing [between] the dead (i.e., the damned) and the Khus on the path of the dead (i.e., the damned); on the night of the judgment of those who are to be annihilated at the great [festival of] the ploughing and the turning up of the earth in Naare-rut-f(19) in Re-stau; and on the night of making Horus to triumph over his enemies. Horus is mighty, the northern and southern halves of heaven rejoice, Osiris is content thereat and his heart is glad. Hail, Thoth, make thou to triumph Osiris, the scribe Nebseni, over his enemies in the presence of the sovereign princes of every god and every goddess, and in the presence of you, ye sovereign princes who passed judgment on Osiris behind the shrine."

In the Saïte Recension this chapter has no vignette, but it has the title "Another Chapter of the Chaplet of Victory," and is arranged in tabular form. The words, "Hail, Thoth, make Osiris Auf-ānkh, triumphant, to triumph over his enemies even as thou didst make Osiris to triumph over his enemies," which are written in two horizontal lines, are to be repeated before each column of text. The "great sovereign princes" invoked are those of: (1) Annu (Heliopolis), (2) Tattu, (3) Sekhem (Letopolis), (4) Pe and Tep, (5) An-arut-f, (6) the double land of Rekhti, (7) Re-stau, (8) Abtu, (9) the paths of the dead, (10) the ploughing festival in Tattu, (11) Kher-āba, (12) Osiris, (13) heaven and earth, (14) every god and every goddess. The rubric reads:

IF THIS CHAPTER BE RECITED REGULARLY AND ALWAYS BY A MAN WHO HATH PURIFIED HIMSELF IN WATER OF NATRON, HE SHALL COME FORTH BY DAY AFTER HE HATH COME INTO PORT (I.E., IS DEAD), AND HE SHALL PERFORM ALL THE TRANSFORMATIONS WHICH HIS HEART SHALL DICTATE, AND HE SHALL COME FORTH FROM EVERY FIRE.

The Chapter Of Giving A Mouth To The Overseer

THE CHAPTER OF GIVING A MOUTH TO THE OVERSEER OF THE HOUSE, NU, TRIUMPHANT, IN THE UNDERWORLD. He saith:

"Homage to thee, O thou lord of brightness, thou who art at the head of the Great House, prince of the night and of thick darkness. I have come unto thee being a pure khu. Thy two hands are behind thee, and thou hast thy lot with [thy] ancestors. Oh, grant thou unto me my mouth that I may speak therewith; and guide thou to me my heart at the season when there is cloud and darkness."

The Chapter Of Giving A Mouth To Osiris Ani

[From the Papyrus of Ani (British Museum No. 10,470, sheet 6).]

THE CHAPTER OF GIVING A MOUTH TO OSIRIS ANI, THE SCRIBE AND TELLER OF THE HOLY OFFERINGS OF ALL THE GODS, TRIUMPHANT, IN THE UNDERWORLD. He saith:

"I rise out of the egg in the hidden land. May my mouth be given unto me that I may speak therewith in the presence of the great god, the lord of the Tuat (underworld). May my hand and my arm not be forced back in the presence of the sovereign princes of any god. I am Osiris, the lord of Re-stau; may I, Osiris the scribe Ani, triumphant, have a portion with him who is on the top of the steps (i.e., Osiris). According to the desire of my heart, I have come from the Pool of Fire, and I have quenched the fire."

Opening The Mouth Of Osiris

[From the Papyrus of Ani (British Museum No. 10,470, sheet 15).]

THE CHAPTER OF OPENING THE MOUTH OF OSIRIS. The scribe Ani, triumphant, saith:

"May the good Ptah open my mouth, and may the god of my city loose the swathings, even the swathings which are over my mouth. Moreover, may Thoth, being filled and furnished with charms, come and loose the bandages, even the bandages of Set which fetter my mouth; and may the god Tem hurl them at those who would fetter [me] with them, and drive them back. May my mouth be opened, may my mouth be unclosed by Shu with his iron knife wherewith he opened the mouths of the gods. I am the goddess Sekhet, and I sit upon [my] place in the great wind(?) of heaven. I am the great goddess Sah who dwelleth among the Souls of Annu (Heliopolis). Now as concerning every charm and all the words which may be spoken against me, may the gods resist them, and may each and every one of the company of the gods withstand them."

The Chapter Of Bringing Charms To Osiris

[From the Papyrus of Ani (British Museum No. 10,470, sheet 15).]

THE CHAPTER OF BRINGING CHARMS UNTO OSIRIS ANI [IN THE UNDERWORLD]. He saith:

"I am Tem-Khepera, who brought himself into being upon the thigh of his divine mother. Those who are in Nu (i.e., the sky) are made wolves, and those who are among the sovereign princes are become hyenas. Behold, I gather together the charm [from every place where] it is, and from every man with whom it is, swifter than greyhounds and quicker than light. Hail, thou who towest along the Mākhent boat of Rā, the stays of thy sails and of thy rudder are taut in the wind as thou sailest up the Pool of Fire in the underworld. Behold, thou gatherest together the charm from every place where it is, and from every man with whom it is, swifter than greyhounds and quicker than light, [the charm] which created the forms of being from the ... mother, and which either createth the gods or maketh them silent, and which giveth the heat of fire unto the gods. Behold, the charm is given unto me, from wherever it is [and from him with whom it is], swifter than greyhounds and quicker than light," or (as others say) "quicker than a shadow."

The Chapter Of Memory

[From the Papyrus of Nu (British Museum No, 10,477, sheet 5).]

THE CHAPTER OF MAKING A MAN TO POSSESS MEMORY IN THE UNDERWORLD. The chancellor-in-chief, Nu, triumphant, the overseer of the palace, the son of the chief chancellor Amen-hetep, saith:

"May my name be given to me in the Great House, and may I remember my name in the House of Fire on the night of counting the years and of telling the number of the months. I am with the Divine One, and I sit on the eastern side of heaven. If any god whatsoever should advance unto me, let me be able to proclaim his name forthwith."

The Chapter Of Giving A Heart To Osiris

[From the Papyrus of Ani (British Museum No. 10,470, sheet 15).]

THE CHAPTER OF GIVING A HEART TO OSIRIS ANI IN THE UNDERWORLD. He saith:

"May my heart (ab)(20) be with me in the House of Hearts! May my heart (hat) be with me in the House of Hearts! May my heart be with me, and may it rest there, [or] I shall not eat of the cakes of Osiris on the eastern side of the Lake of Flowers, neither shall I have a boat wherein to go down the Nile, nor another wherein to go up, nor shall I be able to sail down the Nile with thee. May my mouth [be given] to me that I may speak therewith, and my two legs to walk therewith, and my two hands and arms to overthrow my foe. May the doors of heaven be opened unto me; may Seb, the Prince(21) of the gods, open wide his two jaws unto me; may he open my two eyes which are blindfolded; may he cause me to stretch apart my two legs which are bound together; and may Anpu (Anubis) make my thighs firm so that I may stand upon them. May the goddess Sekhet make me to rise so that I may ascend unto heaven, and may that be done which I command in the House of the foreign (double) of Ptah (i.e., Memphis). I understand with my heart. I have gained the mastery over my heart, I have gained the mastery over my two hands, I have gained the mastery over my legs, I have gained the power to do whatsoever my ka (double) pleaseth. My soul shall not be fettered to my body at the gates of the underworld; but I shall enter in peace and I shall come forth in peace."

The Chapter Of Preserving The Heart

[From the Papyrus of Ani (British Museum No. 10,470, sheets 15 and 16).]

THE CHAPTER OF NOT LETTING THE HEART (HATI) OF A MAN BE TAKEN FROM HIM IN THE UNDERWORLD.(22) Saith Osiris Ani:

"Hail, ye who carry away hearts! [Hail,] ye who steal [hearts, and who make the heart of a man to go through its transformations according to his deeds, let not what he hath done harm him before you].(23) Homage to you, O ye lords of eternity, ye possessors of everlastingness, take ye not this heart of Osiris Ani into your grasp, this heart of Osiris, and cause ye not words of evil to spring up against it; because this is the heart of Osiris Ani, triumphant, and it belongeth unto him of many names (i.e., Thoth), the mighty one whose words are his limbs, and who sendeth forth his heart to dwell in his body. The heart of Osiris Ani is triumphant, it is made new before the gods, he hath gained power over it, he hath not been spoken to [according to] what he hath done. He hath gotten power over his own members. His heart obeyeth him, he is the lord thereof, it is in his body, and it shall never fall away therefrom. I, Osiris, the scribe Ani, victorious in peace, and triumphant in the beautiful Amenta and on the mountain of eternity, bid thee to be obedient unto me in the underworld."

The Chapter Of Preserving The Heart

[From the Papyrus of Nu (British Museum No. 10,477, sheet 5).]

THE CHAPTER OF NOT LETTING THE HEART OF THE OVERSEER OF THE PALACE, THE CHANCELLOR-IN-CHIEF, NU, TRIUMPHANT, BE CARRIED AWAY FROM HIM IN THE UNDERWORLD. He saith:

"Hail, thou Lion-god! I am the Flower Bush (Unb). That which is an abomination unto me is the divine block. Let not this my heart (hāti) be carried away from me by the fighting gods in Annu. Hail, thou who dost wind bandages round Osiris and who hast seen Set! Hail, thou who returnest after smiting and destroying him before the mighty ones! This my heart (ab) [sitteth] and weepeth for itself before Osiris; it hath made supplication for me. I have given unto him and I have decreed unto him the thoughts of the heart in the House of the god Usekh-hra,(24) and I have brought to him sand (sic) at the entry to Khemennu (Hermopolis Magna). Let not this my heart (hāti) be carried away from me! I make thee to dwell(?) upon this throne, O thou who joinest together hearts (hātu) [in Sekhet-hetep (with) years] of strength against all things that are an abomination unto thee, and to carry off food from among the things which belong unto thee, and are in thy grasp by reason of thy twofold strength. And this my heart (hāti) is devoted to the decrees of the god Tem who leadeth me into the dens of Suti, but let not this my heart which hath done its desire before the sovereign princes who are in the underworld be given unto him. When they find the leg and the swathings they bury them."

The Chapter Of Preserving The Heart

[From the Papyrus of Ani (British Museum No. 10,470, sheet 15).]

THE CHAPTER OF NOT LETTING THE HEART OF A MAN BE TAKEN AWAY FROM HIM IN THE UNDERWORLD. Osiris Ani, triumphant, saith:

"Turn thou back, O messenger of every god! Is it that thou art come [to carry away] this my heart which liveth? But my heart which liveth shall not be given unto thee. [As I] advance, the gods hearken unto my offerings, and they all fall down upon their faces in their own places."

The Chapter Of Preserving The Heart

[From the Papyrus of Amen-hetep (Naville, "Todtenbuch," Bd. I. Bl. 40).]

THE CHAPTER OF NOT ALLOWING THE HEART OF AMEN-HETEP, TRIUMPHANT, TO BE CARRIED AWAY DEAD IN THE UNDERWORLD. The deceased saith:

"My heart is with me, and it shall never come to pass that it shall be carried away. I am the lord of hearts, the slayer of the heart. I live in right and truth (Maāt) and I have my being therein. I am Horus, the dweller in hearts, who is within the dweller in the body. I live in my word, and my heart hath being. Let not my heart be taken away from me, let it not be wounded, and may neither wounds nor gashes be dealt upon me because it hath been taken away from me. Let me have my being in the body of [my] father Seb, [and in the body of my] mother Nut. I have not done that which is held in abomination by the gods; let me not suffer defeat there, [but let me be] triumphant."

The Heart Of Carnelian

[From the Papyrus of Ani (British Museum No. 10,470, sheet 33).]

THE CHAPTER OF A HEART OF CARNELIAN. Osiris Ani, triumphant, saith:

"I am the Bennu, the soul of Rā, and the guide of the gods in the Tuat (underworld). Their divine souls come forth upon earth to do the will of their kas; let, therefore, the soul of Osiris Ani come forth to do the will of his ka."

Preserving The Heart

[From Lepsius, "Todtenbuch," Bl. 16.]

THE CHAPTER OF NOT LETTING THE HEART OF A MAN BE DRIVEN AWAY FROM HIM IN THE UNDERWORLD. Osiris Auf-ānkh, triumphant, born of Sheret-Amsu, triumphant, saith:

"My heart, my mother; my heart, my mother! My heart of my existence upon earth. May naught stand up to oppose me in judgment; may there be no opposition to me in the presence of the sovereign princes; may [no evil] be wrought against me in the presence of the gods; may there be no parting [of thee] from me in the presence of the great god, the lord of Amentet. Homage to thee, O thou heart of Osiris-khent-Amentet! Homage to you, O my reins! Homage to you, O ye gods who dwell in the divine clouds, and who are exalted (or holy) by reason of your sceptres! Speak ye fair words for the Osiris Auf-ānkh, and make ye him to prosper before Nehebka. And behold, though I be joined unto the earth, and am in the mighty innermost part of heaven, let me remain on the earth and not die in Amentet, and let me be a khu therein forever and ever."

THIS [CHAPTER] SHALL BE RECITED OVER A BASALT SCARAB, WHICH SHALL BE SET IN A GOLD SETTING, AND IT SHALL BE PLACED INSIDE THE HEART OF THE MAN(25) FOR WHOM THE CEREMONIES OF "OPENING THE MOUTH" AND OF ANOINTING WITH UNGUENT HAVE BEEN PERFORMED. AND THERE SHALL BE RECITED BY WAY OF A MAGICAL CHARM THE WORDS: "MY HEART, MY MOTHER; MY HEART, MY MOTHER! MY HEART OF TRANSFORMATIONS."

Preserving The Heart

[From the Papyrus of Nu (British Museum No. 10,477, sheet 5).]

THE CHAPTER OF NOT LETTING THE HEART OF THE OVERSEER OF THE PALACE, THE CHANCELLOR-IN-CHIEF, NU, TRIUMPHANT, BE DRIVEN AWAY FROM HIM IN THE UNDERWORLD. He Saith:

"O my heart, my mother; O my heart, my mother! O my heart of my existence upon earth. May naught stand up to oppose me in judgment in the presence of the lords of the trial; let it not be said of me and of that which I have done, 'He hath done deeds against that which is right and true'; may naught be against me in the presence of the great god, the lord of Amentet. Homage to thee, O my heart! Homage to thee, O my heart! Homage to you, O my reins! Homage to you, O ye gods who dwell in the divine clouds, and who are exalted (or holy) by reason of your sceptres! Speak ye [for me] fair things to Rā, and make ye me to prosper before Nehebka. And behold me, even though I be joined to the earth in the mighty innermost parts thereof, let me remain upon the earth and let me not die in Amentet, but become a Khu therein."

Preserving The Heart

[From the Papyrus of Ani (British Museum No. 10,470, sheet 15).]

THE CHAPTER OF NOT LETTING THE HEART OF OSIRIS, THE SCRIBE OF THE HOLY OFFERINGS OF ALL THE GODS, ANI, TRIUMPHANT, BE DRIVEN FROM HIM IN THE UNDERWORLD. He saith:

"My heart, my mother; my heart, my mother! My heart whereby I came into being! May naught stand up to oppose me at [my] judgment; may there be no opposition to me in the presence of the sovereign princes (Tchatcha); may there be no parting of thee from me in the presence of him that keepeth the Balance! Thou art my ka, the dweller in my body; the god Khnemu who knitteth and strengtheneth my limbs. Mayest thou come forth into the place of happiness whither we go. May the Shenit (i.e., the divine officers of the court of Osiris), who form the conditions of the lives of men, not cause my name to stink. [Let it be satisfactory unto us, and let the listening be satisfactory unto us, and let there be joy of heart unto us at the weighing of words. Let not that which is false be uttered against me before the great god, the lord of Amentet. Verily how great shalt thou be when thou risest in triumph!]"(26)

Rubric

[From the Papyrus of Amen-hetep (see Naville, "Todtenbuch," Bd. II. p. 99).]

THESE WORDS ARE TO BE SAID OVER A SCARAB OF GREEN STONE ENCIRCLED WITH A BAND OF REFINED COPPER AND [HAVING] A RING OF SILVER, WHICH SHALL BE PLACED ON THE NECK OF THE KHU.

THIS CHAPTER WAS FOUND IN THE CITY OF KHEMENNU (HERMOPOLIS MAGNA) UNDER THE FEET OF [THE STATUE OF] THIS GOD. [IT WAS INSCRIBED] UPON A SLAB OF IRON OF THE SOUTH, IN THE WRITING OF THE GOD HIMSELF, IN THE TIME OF THE MAJESTY OF THE KING OF THE NORTH AND OF THE SOUTH, MEN-KAU-RA,(27) TRIUMPHANT, BY THE ROYAL SON HERU-TA-TA-F, WHO DISCOVERED IT WHILE HE WAS ON HIS JOURNEY TO MAKE AN INSPECTION OF THE TEMPLES AND OF THEIR ESTATES.

Beating Back The Crocodile

[From the Papyrus of Nu (British Museum No. 10,477, sheet 5).]

THE CHAPTER OF BEATING BACK THE CROCODILE THAT COMETH TO CARRY AWAY THE CHARM FROM NU, THE OVERSEER OF THE PALACE, THE CHANCELLOR-IN-CHIEF, TRIUMPHANT, THE SON OF THE OVERSEER OF THE PALACE, AMEN-HETEP, TRIUMPHANT, IN THE UNDERWORLD. He saith:

"Get thee back, return, get thee back, thou crocodile-fiend Sui; thou shalt not advance to me, for I live by reason of the magical words which I have by me. I do not utter that name of thine to the great god who will cause thee to come to the two divine envoys; the name of the one is Betti,(28) and the name of the other is 'Hra-k-en-Maāt.'(29) Heaven hath power over its seasons, and the magical word hath power over that which is in its possession, let therefore my mouth have power over the magical word which is therein. My front teeth are like unto flint knives, and my jaw-teeth are like unto the Nome of Tutef.(30) Hail thou that sittest with thine eyeball upon these my magical words! Thou shalt not carry them away, O thou crocodile that livest by means of magical words!"

[In the Turin Papyrus (Lepsius, op. cit., Bl. 16) the following lines are added to this chapter:]

"I am the Prince in the field. I, even I, am Osiris, who hath shut in his father Seb together with his mother Nut on the day of the great slaughter. My father is Seb and my mother is Nut. I am Horus, the first-born of Rā, who is crowned. I am Anpu (Anubis) on the day of reckoning. I, even I, am Osiris the prince who goeth in and declareth the offerings which are written down. I am the guardian of the door of Osiris, even I. I have come, I have become glorious (or a Khu), I have been reckoned up, I am strong, I have come and I avenge mine own self. I have sat in the birth-chamber of Osiris, and I was born with him, and I renew my youth along with him. I have laid hold upon the Thigh which was by Osiris, and I have opened the mouth of the gods therewith, I sit upon the place where he sitteth, and I write down the number [of the things] which make strong(?) the heart, thousands of loaves of bread, thousands of vases of beer, which are upon the altars of his father Osiris, [numbers of] jackals, wolves, oxen, red fowl, geese and ducks. Horus hath done away with the sacrifices of Thoth. I fill the office of priest in the regions above, and I write down there [the things] which make strong the heart. I make offerings (or offerings are made to me) at the altars of the Prince of Tattu, and I have my being through the oblations [made to] him. I snuff the wind of the East by his head, and I lay hold upon the breezes of the West thereby.... I go round about heaven in the four quarters thereof, I stretch out my hand and grasp the breezes of the south [which] are upon its hair. Grant unto me air among the venerable beings and among those who eat bread."

IF THIS CHAPTER BE KNOWN BY [THE DECEASED] HE SHALL COME FORTH BY DAY, HE SHALL RISE UP TO WALK UPON THE EARTH AMONG THE LIVING, AND HE SHALL NEVER FAIL AND COME TO AN END, NEVER, NEVER, NEVER.

Beating Back The Crocodile

[From Lepsius, "Todtenbuch," Bll. 16 and 17.]

THE CHAPTER OF BEATING BACK THE CROCODILE THAT COMETH TO CARRY AWAY THE MAGICAL WORDS FROM THE KHU IN THE UNDERWORLD. Osiris Auf-ānkh, triumphant, saith:

"The Mighty One fell down upon the place where he is, or (as others say), upon his belly, but the company of the gods caught him and set him up again. [My] soul cometh and it speaketh with its father, and the Mighty One delivereth it from these eight(31) crocodiles. I know them by their names and [what] they live upon, and I am he who hath delivered his father from them."

"Get thee back, O Crocodile that dwellest in the West, thou that livest upon the stars which never rest, for that which is an abomination unto thee is in my belly, O thou that hast eaten the forehead of Osiris. I am Set."

"Get thee back, O Crocodile that dwellest in the West, for the serpent-fiend Nāau is in my belly, and I will give him unto thee; let not thy flame be against me."

"Get thee back, O Crocodile that dwellest in the East, who feedest upon those who eat their own filth, for that which is an abomination unto thee is in my belly; I advance, I am Osiris."

"Get thee back, O Crocodile that dwellest in the East, the serpent-fiend Nāau is in my belly, and I will give [him] unto thee; let not thy flame be against me."

"Get thee back, O Crocodile that dwellest in the South, who feedest upon filth, and waste, and dirt, for that which is an abomination unto thee is in my belly; shall not the flame be on thy hand? I am Sept."

"Get thee back, O Crocodile that dwellest in the South, for I am safe by reason of my charm; my fist is among the flowers and I will not give it unto thee."

"Get thee back, O Crocodile that dwellest in the North, who feedest upon what is offered(?) within the hours, for that which thou abominatest is in my belly; let [not] thy venom be upon my head, for I am Tem."

"Get thee back, O Crocodile that dwellest in the North, for the goddess Serqet is in my belly and I have not yet brought her forth. I am Uatch-Maati (or Merti)."

"The things which are created are in the hollow of my hand, and those which have not yet come into being are in my body. I am clothed and wholly provided with thy magical words, O Rā, the which are in heaven above me and in the earth beneath me. I have gained power, and exaltation, and a full-breathing throat in the abode of my father Ur (i.e., the Mighty One), and he hath delivered unto me the beautiful Amentet which destroyeth living men and women; but strong is its divine lord, who suffereth from weakness," or (as others say) "exhaustion twofold, therein day by day. My face is open, my heart is upon its seat, and the crown with the serpent is upon me day by day. I am Rā, who is his own protector, and nothing shall ever cast me to the ground."

Repulsing Serpents

[From the Papyrus of Nu (British Museum No. 10,477, sheet 6).]

THE CHAPTER OF REPULSING SERPENTS (OR WORMS). Nu, the overseer of the palace, the chancellor-in-chief, triumphant, saith:

"Hail, thou serpent Rerek, advance not hither. Behold Seb and Shu. Stand still now, and thou shalt eat the rat which is an abominable thing unto Rā, and thou shalt crunch the bones of the filthy cat."

Against Snakes

[From the Papyrus of Nu (British Museum No. 10,477, sheet 6).]

THE CHAPTER OF NOT [LETTING] OSIRIS NU, TRIUMPHANT, BE BITTEN BY SNAKES (OR WORMS) IN THE UNDERWORLD. He saith:

"O Serpent! I am the flame which shineth upon the Opener(?) of hundreds of thousands of years, and the standard of the god Tenpu," or (as others say) "the standard of young plants and flowers. Depart ye from me, for I am the divine Mäftet."(32)

Against Serpents

[From the Papyrus of Nu (British Museum No. 10,477, sheet 6).]

THE CHAPTER OF NOT [LETTING] NU, THE CHANCELLOR-IN-CHIEF, TRIUMPHANT, BE DEVOURED BY SERPENTS IN THE UNDERWORLD. He saith:

"Hail, thou god Shu! Behold Tattu! Behold Shu! Hail Tattu! [Shu] hath the head-dress of the goddess Hathor. They nurse Osiris. Behold the twofold being who is about to eat me! Alighting from the boat I depart(?), and the serpent-fiend Seksek passeth me by. Behold sām and aaqet flowers are kept under guard(?). This being is Osiris, and he maketh entreaty for his tomb. The eyes of the divine prince are dropped, and he performeth the reparation which is to be done for thee; [he] giveth [unto thee thy] portion of right and truth according to the decision concerning the states and conditions [of men]."

Driving Away Apshait

[From the Papyrus of Nu (British Museum No. 10,477, sheet 8).]

THE CHAPTER OF DRIVING AWAY APSHAIT. Osiris Nu, the chancellor-in-chief, triumphant, saith:

"Depart from me, O thou that hast lips which gnaw, for I am Khnemu, the lord of Peshennu,(33) and [I] bring the words of the gods to Rā, and I report [my] message to the lord thereof."(34)

Driving Back The Merti

[From the Papyrus of Nu (British Museum No. 10,477, sheet 8).]

THE CHAPTER OF DRIVING BACK THE TWO MERTI GODDESSES. Nu, the chancellor-in-chief, triumphant, saith:

"Homage to you, ye two Rekht goddesses,(35) ye two Sisters, ye two Mert goddesses, I bring a message to you concerning my magical words. I shine from the Sektet boat, I am Horus the son of Osiris, and I have come to see my father Osiris."

Living By Air

[From the Papyrus of Nebseni (British Museum No. 9,900, sheet 12).]

THE CHAPTER OF LIVING BY AIR IN THE UNDERWORLD. The scribe Nebseni, the lord to whom veneration is paid, saith:

"[I am the god Tem], who cometh forth out of Nu into the watery abyss. I have received [my habitation of Amentet, and have given commands] with my words to the [Khus] whose abiding-places are hidden, to the Khus and to the double Lion-god. I have made journeys round about and I have sung hymns of joy in the boat of Khepera. I have eaten therein, I have gained power therein, and I live therein through the breezes [which are there]. I am the guide in the boat of Rā, and he openeth out for me a path; he maketh a passage for me through the gates of the god Seb. I have seized and carried away those who live in the embrace of the god Ur (i.e., Mighty One); I am the guide of those who live in their shrines, the two brother-gods Horus and Set; and I bring the noble ones with me. I enter in and I come forth, and my throat is not slit; I go into the boat of Maāt, and I pass in among those who live in the Atet boat, and who are in the following of Rā, and are nigh unto him in his horizon. I live after my death day by day, and I am strong even as is the double Lion-god. I live, and I am delivered after my death, I, the scribe Nebseni, the lord of piety, who fill the earth and come forth like the lily of mother-of-emerald, of the god Hetep of the two lands."

Living By Air

[From the Papyrus of Nu (British Museum No. 10,477, sheet 12).]

THE CHAPTER OF LIVING BY AIR IN THE UNDERWORLD. Nu, the overseer of the palace, the chancellor-in-chief, triumphant, the son of the overseer of the palace, the chancellor-in-chief, Amen-hetep, triumphant, saith:

"I am the double Lion-god, the first-born of Rā and Tem of Ha-khebti(?), [the gods] who dwell in their divine chambers. Those who dwell in their divine abodes have become my guides, and they make paths for me as they revolve in the watery abyss of the sky by the side of the path of the boat of Tem. I stand upon the timbers(?) of the boat of Rā, and I recite his ordinances to the beings who have knowledge, and I am the herald of his words to him whose throat stinketh. I set free my divine fathers at eventide. I close the lips of my mouth, and I eat like unto a living being. I have life in Tattu, and I live again after death like Rā day by day."

Driving Back Rerek

[From the Papyrus of Mes-em-neter (see Naville, op. cit., Bd. I. Bl. 53).]

THE CHAPTER OF DRIVING BACK THE SERPENT REREK IN THE UNDERWORLD. Osiris Mes-em-neter saith:

"Get thee back, depart, retreat(?) from [me], O Aāapef, withdraw, or thou shalt be drowned at the Pool of Nu, at the place where thy father hath ordered that thy slaughter shall be performed. Depart thou from the divine place of birth of Rā wherein is thy terror. I am Rā who dwelleth in his terror. Get thee back, Fiend, before the darts of his beams. Rā hath overthrown thy words, the gods have turned thy face backward, the Lynx hath torn open thy breast, the Scorpion hath cast fetters upon thee; and Maāt hath sent forth thy destruction. Those who are in the ways have overthrown thee; fall down and depart, O Apep, thou Enemy of Rā! O thou that passest over the region in the eastern part of heaven with the sound of the roaring thunder-cloud, O Rā who openest the gates of the horizon straightway on thy appearance, [Apep] hath sunk helpless under [thy] gashings. I have performed thy will, O Rā, I have performed thy will; I have done that which is fair, I have done that which is fair, I have labored for the peace of Rā. [I] have made to advance thy fetters, O Rā, and Apep hath fallen through thy drawing them tight. The gods of the south and of the north, of the west and of the east have fastened chains upon him, and they have fettered him with fetters; the god Rekes hath overthrown him and the god Hertit hath put him in chains. Rā setteth, Rā setteth; Rā is strong at [his] setting. Apep hath fallen, Apep, the enemy of Rā, departeth. Greater is the punishment [which hath been inflicted on] thee than the sting(?) which is in the Scorpion goddess, and mightily hath she, whose course is everlasting, worked it upon thee and with deadly effect. Thou shalt never enjoy the delights of love, thou shalt never fulfil thy desire, O Apep, thou Enemy of Rā! He maketh thee to go back, O thou who art hateful to Rā; he looketh upon thee, get thee back! [He] pierceth [thy] head, [he] cutteth through thy face, [he] divideth [thy] head at the two sides of the ways, and it is crushed in his land; thy bones are smashed in pieces, thy members are hacked off thee, and the god [A]ker hath condemned thee, O Apep, thou enemy of Rā! Thy mariners are those who keep the reckoning for thee, [O Rā, as thou] advancest, and thou restest there wherein are the offerings made to thee [As thou] advancest, [as thou] advancest toward the House the advance which thou hast made toward the House is a prosperous advance; let not any baleful obstacle proceed from thy mouth against me when thou workest on my behalf. I am Set who let loose the storm-clouds and the thunder in the horizon of heaven even as [doth] the god Netcheb-ab-f."

" 'Hail,' saith the god Tem, 'make strong your faces, O soldiers of Rā, for I have driven back the god Nentchā in the presence of the divine sovereign princes.' 'Hail,' saith the god Seb, 'make ye firm those who are upon their seats which are in the boat of Khepera, take ye your ways, [grasping] your weapons of war in your hands.' 'Hail,' saith Hathor, 'take ye your armor.' 'Hail,' saith Nut, 'come and repulse the god Tchā who pursueth him that dwelleth in his shrine and who setteth out on his way alone, namely, Neb-er-tcher, who cannot be repulsed.' 'Hail,' say those gods who dwell in their companies and who go round about the Turquoise Pool, 'come, O mighty One, we praise and we will deliver the Mighty One [who dwelleth in] the divine Shrine, from whom proceeds the company of the gods, let commemorations be made for him, let praise be given to him, let words [of praise] be recited before him by you and by me.' 'Hail,' saith Nut to thy Sweet One. 'Hail,' say those who dwell among the gods, 'he cometh forth, he findeth [his] way, he maketh captives among the gods, he hath taken possession of the goddess Nut, and Seb standeth up.' Hail, thou terrible one, the company of the gods is on the march. Hathor quaketh with terror, and Rā hath triumphed over Apep."

Repulsing The Eater Of The Ass

[From the Papyrus of Rā (see Naville, op. cit., Bd. I. Bl. 54) and from the Papyrus of Nu (British Museum No. 10,477, sheet 8).]

THE CHAPTER OF DRIVING BACK THE EATER OF THE ASS. Osiris Rā, triumphant, saith:

I. "Get thee back, Hai, thou impure one, thou abomination of Osiris! Thoth hath cut off thy head, and I have performed upon thee all the things which the company of the gods ordered concerning thee in the matter of the work of thy slaughter. Get thee back, thou abomination of Osiris, from the Neshmet boat ... which advanceth with a fair wind. Ye are holy, O all ye gods, and [ye] have cast down headlong the enemies of Osiris; the gods of Ta-ur shout for joy. Get thee back, O thou Eater of the Ass, thou abomination of the god Haas who dwelleth in the underworld. I know thee, I know thee, I know thee, I know thee. Who art thou? I am..."

II. "On thy face [O fiend], and devour me not, for I am pure, and I am with the time which cometh of itself. Thou shalt not come to me, O thou that comest(36) without being invoked, and whose [time of coming] is unknown. I am the lord of thy mouth, get thee back, thou and thy desires(?). Hail, Haas, with his stone [knife] Horus hath cut asunder thy members, and thou art destroyed within thy company, and thy bend (or dwelling-place) is destroyed for thee by the company of thy gods who dwell in the cities of Pe and Tep. He that slayeth [thee] there is in the form of the Eye of Horus, and I have driven thee away as thou wast advancing, and I have vanquished thee by the winds of my mouth. O thou Eater of those who commit sins, who dost plunder and spoil, I have [committed] no sin; therefore, let my palette and the writings with hostile charges [against me upon them] be given unto me. I have done no wrong in the presence of the sovereign princes, therefore shoot not thy [venom] at me. I give, do thou take according to what I order; snatch me not away, and eat me not, for I am the lord of life, the Prince (Life, Health, Strength!) of the horizon."

Abolishing The Slaughterings

[From the Papyrus of Nebseni, sheet 25.]

THE CHAPTER OF DRIVING AWAY THE SLAUGHTERINGS WHICH ARE PERFORMED IN THE UNDERWORLD. Nebseni, the scribe and designer in the Temples of Upper and Lower Egypt, he to whom fair veneration is paid, the son of the scribe and artist Thena, triumphant, saith:

"Hail, Tem, I have become glorious (or a Khu) in the presence of the double Lion-god, the great god, therefore open thou unto me the gate of the god Seb. I smell the earth (i.e., I bow down so that my nose toucheth the ground) of the great god who dwelleth in the underworld, and I advance into the presence of the company of the gods who dwell with the beings who are in the underworld. Hail, thou guardian of the divine door of the city of Beta, thou [god] Neti(?) who dwellest in Amentet, I eat food, and I have life through the air, and the god Atch-ur leadeth me with [him] to the mighty boat of Khepera. I hold converse with the divine mariners at eventide, I enter in, I go forth, and I see the being who is there; I lift him up, and I say that which I have to say unto him, whose throat stinketh [for lack of air]. I have life, and I am delivered, having lain down in death. Hail, thou that bringest offerings and oblations, bring forward thy mouth and make to draw nigh the writings (or lists) of offerings and oblations. Set thou Right and Truth firmly upon their throne, make thou the writings to draw nigh, and set thou up the goddesses in the presence of Osiris, the mighty god, the Prince of everlastingness, who counteth his years, who hearkeneth unto those who are in the islands (or pools), who raiseth his right shoulder, who judgeth the divine princes, and who sendeth [Osiris] into the presence of the great sovereign princes who live in the underworld."

Abolishing The Slaughterings

[From the Papyrus of Nu (British Museum No. 10,477, sheet 6).]

THE CHAPTER OF DRIVING BACK THE SLAUGHTERINGS WHICH ARE PERFORMED IN SUTEN-HENEN. Osiris Nu, triumphant, saith:

"O thou land of the sceptre! (literally, wood) O thou white crown of the divine form! O thou resting-place of the boat! I am the Child, I am the Child, I am the Child, I am the Child. Hail, Abu-ur, thou sayest day by day: 'The slaughter-block is made ready as thou knowest, and thou hast come to decay.' I am Rā, the stablisher of those who praise [him]. I am the knot of the god within the Aser tree, the doubly beautiful one, who is more splendid than yesterday (say four times). I am Rā, the stablisher of those who praise [him]. I am the knot of the god within the Aser tree, and my going forth is the going forth [of Rā] on this day."

"My hair is the hair of Nu. My face is the face of the Disk. My eyes are the eyes of Hathor. My ears are the ears of Ap-uat. My nose is the nose of Khenti-khas. My lips are the lips of Anpu. My teeth are the teeth of Serqet. My neck is the neck of the divine goddess Isis. My hands are the hands of Ba-neb-Tattu. My forearms are the forearms of Neith, the Lady of Sais. My backbone is the backbone of Suti. My phallus is the phallus of Osiris. My reins are the reins of the Lords of Kher-āba. My chest is the chest of the Mighty one of Terror. My belly and back are the belly and back of Sekhet. My buttocks are the buttocks of the Eye of Horus. My hips and legs are the hips and legs of Nut. My feet are the feet of Ptah. [My fingers] and my leg-bones are the [fingers and] leg-bones of the Living Gods. There is no member of my body which is not the member of some god. The god Thoth shieldeth my body altogether, and I am Rā day by day. I shall not be dragged back by my arms, and none shall lay violent hold upon my hands. And shall do me hurt neither men, nor gods, nor the sainted dead, nor those who have perished, nor any one of those ancient times, nor any mortal, nor any human being. I am he who cometh forth, advancing, whose name is unknown. I am Yesterday, and Seer of millions of years is my name. I pass along, I pass along the paths of the divine celestial judges. I am the lord of eternity, and I decree and I judge like the god Khepera. I am the lord of the Ureret crown. I am he who dwelleth in the Utchat [and in the Egg, in the Utchat and in the Egg, and it is given unto me to live [with] them. I am he that dwelleth in the Utchat when it closeth, and I exist by the strength thereof. I come forth and I shine; I enter in and I come to life. I am in the Utchat],(37) my seat is upon my throne, and I sit in the abode of splendor(?) before it. I am Horus and (I) traverse millions of years. I have given the decree [for the stablishing of] my throne and I am the ruler thereof; and in very truth, my mouth keepeth an even balance both in speech and in silence. In very truth, my forms are inverted. I am Un-nefer, from one season even unto another, and what I have is within me; [I am] the only One, who proceedeth from an only One who goeth round about in his course. I am he who dwelleth in the Utchat, no evil thing of any form or kind shall spring up against me, and no baleful object, and no harmful thing, and no disastrous thing shall happen unto me. I open the door in heaven, I govern my throne, and I open up [the way] for the births [which take place] on this day. I am (?) the child who marcheth along the road of Yesterday. [I am] To-day for untold nations and peoples. I am he who protecteth you for millions of years, and whether ye be denizens of the heavens, or of the earth, or of the south, or of the north, or of the east, or of the west, the fear of me is in your bodies. I am he whose being has been moulded in his eye, and I shall not die again. My moment is in your bodies, but my forms are in my place of habitation. I am he who cannot be known, but the Red Ones have their faces directed toward me. I am the unveiled one. The season wherein [the god] created the heavens for me and enlarged the bounds of the earth and made great the progeny thereof cannot be found out; but they fail and are not united [again]. My name setteth itself apart from all things [and from] the great evil [which is in] the mouths [of men] by reason of the speech which I address unto you. I am he who riseth and shineth, the wall which cometh out of a wall, an only One who proceedeth from an only One. There is never a day that passeth without the things which appertain unto him being therein; passing, passing, passing, passing. Verily I say unto thee, I am the Sprout which cometh forth from Nu, and my Mother is Nut. Hail, O my Creator, I am he who hath no power to walk, the great Knot who is within yesterday. The might of my strength is within my hand. I myself am not known, but I am he who knoweth thee. I cannot be held with the hand, but I am he who can hold thee in his hand. Hail, O Egg! Hail, O Egg! I am Horus who lives for millions of years, whose flame shineth upon you and bringeth your hearts to me. I have the command of my throne and I advance at this season, I have opened a path, and I have delivered myself from all evil things. I am the dog-headed ape of gold three palms and two fingers [high], which hath neither arms nor legs and dwelleth in Het-ka-Ptah (Memphis), and I go forth as goeth forth the dog-headed ape that dwelleth in Het-ka-Ptah."

Air And Water

[From the Papyrus of Nu (British Museum No. 10,477, sheet 12).]

THE CHAPTER OF SNUFFING THE AIR AND OF HAVING THE MASTERY OVER THE WATER IN THE UNDERWORLD. The overseer of the palace, the chancellor-in-chief, Nu, triumphant, saith:

"Hail, Hāp-ur, god of heaven, in thy name of 'Divider of heaven,' grant thou unto me that I may have dominion over the water, even as the goddess Sekhet had power over Osiris on the night of the storms and floods. Grant thou that I may have power over the divine princes who have their habitations in the place of the god of the inundation, even as they have power over their own holy god of whose name they are ignorant; and may they let me have power even as [he hath let them have power]."

"My nostrils are opened in Tattu," or (as others say), "My mouth and my nostrils are opened in Tātāu, and I have my place of peace in Annu, which is my house; it was built for me by the goddess Sesheta, and the god Khnemu set it up for me upon its walls. If to this heaven it cometh by the north, I sit at the south; if to this heaven it cometh by the south, I sit at the north; if to this heaven it cometh by the west, I sit at the east; and if to this heaven it cometh by the east, I sit at the west. I draw the hair of my nostrils, and I make my way into every place in which I wish to sit."

In the Papyrus of Nefer-uben-f (see Naville, op. cit., Bd. I. Bl. 70) this chapter ends quite differently, and reads:

"I am strong in my mouth and in my nostrils, for behold Tem has stablished them; behold, O ye gods and Khus. Rest thou, then, O Tem. Behold the staff which blossometh, and which cometh forth when a man crieth out in your names. Behold, I am Tem, the tree (?) of the gods in [their] visible forms. Let me not be turned back.... I am the Am-khent, Nefer-uben-f, triumphant. Let neither my flesh nor my members be gashed with knives, let me not be wounded by knives by you. I have come, I have been judged, I have come forth therein, [I] have power with my father, the Old man, Nu. He hath granted that I may live, he hath given strength unto me, and he hath provided me with the inheritance of my father therein."

Dominion Over Elements

[From the Papyrus of Ani (British Museum No. 10,470, sheet 16).]

THE CHAPTER OF BREATHING THE AIR AND OF HAVING DOMINION OVER THE WATER IN THE UNDERWORLD. Osiris Ani saith:

"Open to me." Who art thou? Whither goest thou? What is thy name? "I am one of you." Who are those with thee? "The two serpent goddesses Merti. Separate thou from him, head from head, when [thou] goest into the divine Mesqen chamber. He letteth me set out for the temple of the gods who have found their faces. 'Assembler of Souls' is the name of my boat; 'Making the hair to stand on end' is the name of the oars; 'Goad' is the name of the hold; 'Making straight for the middle' is the name of the rudder; likewise [the boat] is a type of my being borne onward in the pool. Let there be given unto me vessels of milk, together with cakes, and loaves of bread, and cups of drink, and flesh in the Temple of Anpu."

IF HE (I.E., THE DECEASED) KNOWETH THIS CHAPTER, HE SHALL GO INTO, AFTER COMING FORTH FROM, THE UNDERWORLD OF THE [BEAUTIFUL AMENTET].

Dominion Over Elements

[From the Papyrus of Ani (British Museum No. 10,470, sheet 16).]

THE CHAPTER OF SNUFFING THE AIR, AND OF HAVING DOMINION OVER THE WATERS IN THE UNDERWORLD. Osiris Ani saith:

"Hail, thou sycamore tree of the goddess Nut! Grant thou to me of [the water and of] the air which dwell in thee. I embrace the throne which is in Unnu (Hermopolis), and I watch and guard the egg of Nekek-ur (i.e., the Great Cackler). It groweth, I grow; it liveth, I live; it snuffeth the air, I snuff the air, I the Osiris Ani, in triumph."

Dominion Over Elements

[From Lepsius, "Todtenbuch," Bl. 23.]

ANOTHER CHAPTER. Osiris Auf-ānkh, triumphant, saith:

"Let the gates of heaven be opened for me by the god [Thoth] and by Hāpi, and let me pass through the doors of Ta-qebh(38) into the great heaven," or (as others say), "at the time," [or (as others say)], "with the strength(?) of Rā. Grant ye, [O Thoth and Hāpi,] that I may have power over the water, even as Set had power over his enemies on the day when there were storms and rain upon the earth. Let me have power over the divine beings who have mighty arms in their shoulders, even as the god who is apparelled in splendor and whose name is unknown had power over them; and may I have power over the beings whose arms are mighty."

Preservation Of The Soul

[From the Papyrus of Ani (British Museum No. 10,470, sheet 15).]

THE CHAPTER OF NOT LETTING THE SOUL OF A MAN BE TAKEN FROM HIM IN THE UNDERWORLD. Osiris, the Scribe Ani, saith:

"I, even I, am he who came forth from the water-flood which I make to overflow, and which becometh mighty as the river [Nile]."

Of Drinking Water

[From the Papyrus of Nebseni (British Museum No. 9,900, sheet 4).]

THE CHAPTER OF DRINKING WATER IN THE UNDERWORLD. The scribe Nebseni ... saith:

"May be opened [to me] the mighty flood by Osiris, and may the abyss of water be opened [to me] by Tehuti-Hāpi, the lord of the horizon, in my name of 'Opener.' May there be granted [to me] mastery over the water-courses as over the members of Set. I go forth into heaven. I am the Lion-god Rā. I am the Bull. [I] have eaten the Thigh, and I have divided the carcass. I have gone round about among the islands (or lakes) of Sekhet-Aaru. Indefinite time, without beginning and without end, hath been given to me; I inherit eternity, and everlastingness hath been bestowed upon me."

The last three chapters, with a single vignette, are grouped in one in the Papyrus of Nefer-uben-f (see Naville, op. cit., Bd. I. Bl. 72); but the order of them as there given is 61, 60, 62. In the Turin Papyrus (Lepsius, op. cit., Bl. 23) the vignette of each is the same, i.e., the deceased holding a sail in his left hand.

Of Drinking Water

[From the Papyrus of Nu (British Museum No. 10,477, sheet 7).]

THE CHAPTER OF DRINKING WATER AND OF NOT BEING BURNT BY FIRE [IN THE UNDERWORLD]. The overseer of the palace, the chancellor-in-chief, Nu, triumphant, saith:

"Hail, Bull of Amentet! I am brought unto thee, I am the oar of Rā wherewith he ferried over the divine aged ones; let me neither be burnt up nor destroyed by fire. I am Bet, the first-born son of Osiris, who doth meet every god within his Eye in Annu. I am the divine Heir, the exalted one(?), the Mighty One, the Resting One. I have made my name to germinate, I have delivered [it], and thou shalt live through me day by day."

Preservation From Scalding

[From the Papyrus of Nu (British Museum No. 10,477, sheet 12).]

THE CHAPTER OF NOT BEING SCALDED WITH WATER. The overseer of the palace, the chancellor-in-chief, Nu, triumphant, saith:

"I am the oar made ready for rowing, wherewith Rā transported the boat containing the divine ancestors, and lifted up the moist emanations of Osiris from the Lake of Fire, and he was not burned. I lie down like a divine Khu, [and like] Khnemu who dwelleth among lions. Come, break away the restraints from him that passeth by the side of this path, and let me come forth by it."

On Coming Forth By Day

[From the Papyrus of Nebseni (British Museum No. 9,900, sheets 23 and 24).]

THE CHAPTER OF COMING FORTH BY DAY IN THE UNDERWORLD. Nebseni, the lord of reverence, saith:

"I am Yesterday, To-day, and To-morrow, [and I have] the power to be born a second time; [I am] the divine hidden Soul who createth the gods, and who giveth sepulchral meals unto the denizens of the Tuat (underworld), Amentet, and heaven. [I am] the rudder of the east, the possessor of two divine faces wherein his beams are seen. I am the lord of the men who are raised up; [the lord] who cometh forth from out of the darkness, and whose forms of existence are of the house wherein are the dead. Hail, ye two hawks who are perched upon your resting-places, who hearken unto the things which are said by him, who guide the bier to the hidden place, who lead along Rā, and who follow [him] into the uppermost place of the shrine which is in the celestial heights! [Hail,] lord of the shrine which standeth in the middle of the earth. He is I, and I am he, and Ptah hath covered his sky with crystal. [Hail] Rā, thou who art content, thy heart is glad by reason of thy beautiful law of the day; thou enterest in by Khemennu(?) and comest forth at the east, and the divine first-born beings who are in [thy] presence cry out with gladness [unto thee]. Make thou thy roads glad for me, and make broad for me thy paths when I shall set out from earth for the life in the celestial regions. Send forth thy light upon me, O Soul unknown, for I am [one] of those who are about to enter in, and the divine speech is in [my] ears in the Tuat (underworld), and let no defects of my mother be [imputed] unto me; let me be delivered and let me be safe from him whose divine eyes sleep at eventide, when [he] gathereth together and finisheth [the day] in night. I flood [the land] with water, and 'Qem-ur' is my name, and the garment wherewith I am clothed is complete. Hail, thou divine prince Ati-she-f, cry out unto those divine beings who dwell in their hair at the season when the god is [lifted upon] the shoulder, saying: 'Come thou who [dwellest] above thy divine abyss of water, for verily the thigh [of the sacrifice] is tied to the neck, and the buttocks are [laid] upon the head of Amentet.' May the Ur-urti goddesses (i.e., Isis and Nephthys) grant [such] gifts unto me when my tears start from me as I see myself journeying with the divine Tena in Abydos, and the wooden fastenings which fasten the four doors above thee are in thy power within thy garment. Thy face is like that of a greyhound which scenteth with his nose the place whither I go on my feet. The god Akau transported me to the chamber(?), and [my] nurse is the divine double Lion-god himself. I am made strong and I come forth like him that forceth a way through the gate, and the radiance which my heart hath made is enduring; 'I know the abysses' is thy name. I work for you, O ye Khus—4,000,000, 600,000, 1,000, and 200 are they—concerning the things which are there. [I am] over their affairs working for hours and days in setting straight the shoulders of the twelve Sah gods, and joining the hands of their company, each to each; the sixth who is at the head of the abyss is the hour of the defeat of the Fiends. [I] have come there in triumph, and [I am] he who is in the halls (or courtyards) of the underworld, and I am he who is laid under tribute to Shu. I rise as the Lord of Life through the beautiful law of this day, and it is their blood and the cool water of [their] slaughter which make the union of the earth to blossom. I make a way among the horns of all those who make themselves strong against me, and [among] those who in secret make themselves adversaries unto me, and who are upon their bellies. I have come as the envoy of my Lord of lords to give counsel [concerning] Osiris; the eye shall not absorb(39) its tears. I am the divine envoy(?) of the house of him that dwelleth in his possessions, and I have come from Sekhem to Annu to make known to the Bennu bird therein concerning the events of the Tuat (underworld). Hail, thou Aukert (i.e., underworld) which hidest thy companion who is in thee, thou divine creator of forms of existence like the god Khepera, grant thou that Nebseni, the scribe and designer to the temples of the South and of the North, may come forth to see the Disk, and that his journeyings forth(?) may be in the presence of the great god, that is to say, Shu, who dwelleth in everlastingness. Let me journey on in peace; let me pass over the sky; let me adore the radiance of the splendor [which is in] my sight; let me soar like a bird to see the companies(?) of the Khus in the presence of Rā day by day, who vivifieth every human being that walketh upon the regions which are upon the earth. Hail, Hemti (i.e., Runner); Hail, Hemti; who carriest away the shades of the dead and the Khus from earth, grant thou unto me a prosperous way to the Tuat (underworld), such as is made for the favored ones [of the god], because [I am] helpless to gather together the emanations which come from me. Who art thou, then, who consumest in its hidden place? I am the Chief in Re-stau, and 'He that goeth in in his own name and cometh forth in that of Hehi(?), the lord of millions of years, and of the earth,' is my name. The pregnant goddess hath deposited [upon the earth] her load, and hath given birth to Hit straightway; the closed door which is by the wall is overthrown, it is turned upside down and I rejoice thereat. To the Mighty One hath his eye been given, and it sendeth forth light from his face when the earth becometh light (or at daybreak). I shall not become corrupt, but I shall come into being in the form of the Lion-god and like the blossoms of Shu; I am the being who is never overwhelmed in the waters. Happy, yea happy is he that looked upon the funeral couch which hath come to its place of rest, upon the happy day of the god whose heart resteth, who maketh his place of alighting [thereon]. I am he who cometh forth by day; the lord of the bier which giveth life in the presence of Osiris. In very truth the things which are thine are stable each day, O scribe, artist, child of the Seshet chamber, Nebseni, lord of veneration. I clasp the sycamore tree, I myself am joined unto the sycamore tree, and its arm[s] are opened unto me graciously. I have come and I have clasped the Utchat, and I have caused it to be seated in peace upon its throne. I have come to see Rā when he setteth, and I absorb into myself the winds [which arise] when he cometh forth, and both my hands are clean to adore him. I have gathered together [all my members], I have gathered together [all my members]. I soar like a bird and I descend upon the earth, and mine eye maketh me to walk thereon in my footsteps. I am the child of yesterday, and the Akeru gods of the earth have made me to come into being, and they have made me strong for my moment [of coming forth]. I hide with the god Aba-āāiu who will walk behind me, and my members shall germinate, and my khu shall be as an amulet for my body and as one who watcheth [to protect] my soul and to defend it and to converse therewith; and the company of the gods shall hearken unto my words."

IF THIS CHAPTER BE KNOWN [BY THE DECEASED] HE SHALL BE VICTORIOUS BOTH UPON EARTH AND IN THE UNDERWORLD. HE SHALL DO WHATSOEVER A MAN DOETH WHO IS UPON THE EARTH, AND HE SHALL PERFORM ALL THE DEEDS WHICH THOSE DO WHO ARE [ALIVE]. NOW IT IS A GREAT PROTECTION [GIVEN] BY THE GOD. THIS CHAPTER WAS FOUND IN THE CITY OF KHE-MENNU INSCRIBED UPON THE BLOCK OF IRON IN LETTERS OF LAPIS-LAZULI WHICH WAS UNDER THE FEET OF THIS GOD.

In the rubric to this chapter as found in the Papyrus of Mes-em-neter, the chapter is said to have been "discovered in the foundations of the shrine of the divine Hennu boat by the chief mason in the time of the King of the North and of the South, Hesepti,(40) triumphant," and it is there directed that it shall be recited by one who is ceremonially pure and clean, and who hath not touched women, and who hath not eaten flesh of animals or fish.

Chapter Of Knowledge

[From the Papyrus of Nu (British Museum No. 10,477, sheet 13).]

THE CHAPTER OF KNOWING THE "CHAPTERS OF COMING FORTH BY DAY" IN A SINGLE CHAPTER. The overseer of the palace, the chancellor-in-chief, Osiris Nu, triumphant, begotten of the overseer of the palace, Amen-hetep, triumphant, saith:

"I am Yesterday and To-morrow; and I have the power to be born a second time. [I am] the divine hidden Soul, who createth the gods, and who giveth sepulchral meals to the divine hidden beings [in the Tuat (underworld)], in Amenti, and in heaven. [I am] the rudder of the east, the possessor of two divine faces wherein his beams are seen. I am the lord of those who are raised up, [the lord] who cometh forth from out of the darkness. [Hail,] ye two divine Hawks who are perched upon your resting-places, and who hearken unto the things which are said by him, the thigh [of the sacrifice] is tied to the neck, and the buttocks [are laid] upon the head of Amentet. May the Ur-urti goddesses (i.e., Isis and Nephthys) grant such gifts unto me when my tears start from me as I look on. 'I know the abysses' is thy name. [I] work for [you], O ye Khus, who are in number [four] millions, [six] hundred, and 1,000, and 200, and they are [in height] twelve cubits. [Ye] travel on joining the hands, each to each, but the sixth [hour], which belongeth at the head of the Tuat (underworld), is the hour of the overthrow of the Fiend. [I] have come there in triumph, and [I am] he who is in the hall (or courtyard) of the Tuat; and the seven(?) come in his manifestations. The strength which protecteth me is that which hath my Khu under its protection, [that is] the blood, and the cool water, and the slaughterings which abound(?). I open [a way among] the horns of all those who would do harm unto me, who keep themselves hidden, who make themselves adversaries unto me, and those who are upon their bellies. The Eye shall not eat (or absorb) the tears of the goddess Aukert. Hail, goddess Aukert, open thou unto me the enclosed place, and grant thou unto me pleasant roads whereupon I may travel. Who art thou, then, who consumest in the hidden places? I am the Chief in Re-stau, and [I] go in and come forth in my name of 'Hehi, the lord of millions of years [and of] the earth'; [I am] the maker of my name. The pregnant one hath deposited [upon the earth] her load. The door by the wall is shut fast, and the things of terror are overturned and thrown down upon the backbone(?) of the Bennu bird by the two Samait goddesses. To the Mighty One hath his Eye been given, and his face emitteth light when [he] illumineth the earth, [my name is his name].(41) I shall not become corrupt, but I shall come into being in the form of the Lion-god; the blossoms of Shu shall be in me. I am he who is never overwhelmed in the waters. Happy, yea happy, is the funeral couch of the Still-heart; he maketh himself to alight upon the pool(?), and verily he cometh forth [therefrom]. I am the lord of my life. I have come to this [place], and I have come forth from Re-āa-urt the city of Osiris. Verily the things which are thine are with the Sariu deities. I have clasped the sycamore tree and I have divided(?) it; I have opened a way for myself [among] the Sekhiu gods of the Tuat. I have come to see him that dwelleth in his divine uræus, face to face and eye to eye, and [I] draw to myself the winds [which rise] when he cometh forth. My two eyes(?) are weak in my face, O Lion[-god], Babe, who dwellest in Utent. Thou art in me and I am in thee; and thy attributes are my attributes. I am the god of the Inundation (Bāh), and 'Qem-ur-she' is my name. My forms are the forms of the god Khepera, the hair of the earth of Tem, the hair of the earth of Tem. I have entered in as a man of no understanding, and I shall come forth in the form of a strong Khu, and I shall look upon my form which shall be that of men and women forever and forever."

I.(42) [IF THIS CHAPTER BE KNOWN] BY A MAN HE SHALL COME FORTH BY DAY, AND HE SHALL NOT BE REPULSED AT ANY GATE OF THE TUAT (UNDERWORLD), EITHER IN GOING IN OR IN COMING OUT. HE SHALL PERFORM [ALL] THE TRANSFORMATIONS WHICH HIS HEART SHALL DESIRE FOR HIM AND HE SHALL NOT DIE; BEHOLD, THE SOUL OF [THIS] MAN SHALL FLOURISH. AND MOREOVER, IF [HE] KNOW THIS CHAPTER HE SHALL BE VICTORIOUS UPON EARTH AND IN THE UNDERWORLD, AND HE SHALL PERFORM EVERY ACT OF A LIVING HUMAN BEING. NOW IT IS A GREAT PROTECTION WHICH [HATH BEEN GIVEN] BY THE GOD. THIS CHAPTER WAS FOUND IN THE FOUNDATIONS OF THE SHRINE OF HENNU BY THE CHIEF MASON DURING THE REIGN OF HIS MAJESTY THE KING OF THE NORTH AND OF THE SOUTH, HESEPTI, TRIUMPHANT,

WHO CARRIED [IT] AWAY AS A MYSTERIOUS OBJECT WHICH HAD NEVER [BEFORE] BEEN SEEN OR LOOKED UPON. THIS CHAPTER SHALL BE RECITED BY A MAN WHO IS CEREMONIALLY CLEAN AND PURE, WHO HATH NOT EATEN THE FLESH OF ANIMALS OR FISH, AND WHO HATH NOT HAD INTERCOURSE WITH WOMEN.

II.(43) IF THIS CHAPTER BE KNOWN [BY THE DECEASED] HE SHALL BE VICTORIOUS BOTH UPON EARTH AND IN THE UNDERWORLD, AND HE SHALL PERFORM EVERY ACT OF A LIVING HUMAN BEING. NOW IT IS A GREAT PROTECTION WHICH [HATH BEEN GIVEN] BY THE GOD.

THIS CHAPTER WAS FOUND IN THE CITY OF KHEMENNU, UPON A BLOCK OF IRON OF THE SOUTH, WHICH HAD BEEN INLAID [WITH LETTERS] OF REAL LAPIS-LAZULI, UNDER THE FEET OF THE GOD DURING THE REIGN OF HIS MAJESTY, THE KING OF THE NORTH AND OF THE SOUTH, MEN-KAU-RA (MYCERINUS) TRIUMPHANT, BY THE ROYAL SON HERU-TA-TA-F,(44) TRIUMPHANT; HE FOUND IT WHEN HE WAS JOURNEYING ABOUT TO MAKE AN INSPECTION OF THE TEMPLES. ONE NEKHT(?) WAS WITH HIM WHO WAS DILIGENT IN MAKING HIM TO UNDERSTAND(?) IT, AND HE BROUGHT IT TO THE KING AS A WONDERFUL OBJECT WHEN HE SAW THAT IT WAS A THING OF GREAT MYSTERY, WHICH HAD NEVER [BEFORE] BEEN SEEN OR LOOKED UPON.

THIS CHAPTER SHALL BE RECITED BY A MAN WHO IS CEREMONIALLY CLEAN AND PURE, WHO HATH NOT EATEN THE FLESH OF ANIMALS OR FISH, AND WHO HATH NOT HAD INTERCOURSE WITH WOMEN. AND BEHOLD, THOU SHALT MAKE A SCARAB OF GREEN STONE, WITH A RIM PLATED(?) WITH GOLD, WHICH SHALL BE PLACED IN THE HEART OF A MAN, AND IT SHALL PERFORM FOR HIM THE "OPENING OF THE MOUTH." AND THOU SHALT ANOINT IT WITH ANTI UNGUENT, AND THOU SHALT RECITE OVER IT [THESE] ENCHANTMENTS:(45)

Of Gaining Mastery Over Enemies

[From the Papyrus of Nu (British Museum No. 10,477, sheet 15).]

THE CHAPTER OF COMING FORTH BY DAY AND OF GAINING THE MASTERY OVER ENEMIES. The chancellor-in-chief, Nu, saith:

"Rā sitteth in his habitation of millions of years, and he hath gathered together the company of the gods, with those divine beings, whose faces are hidden, who dwell in the Temple of Khepera, who eat the god Bāh, and who drink the drink-offerings which are brought into the celestial regions of light; and conversely. Grant that I may take possession of the captives of Osiris, and never let me have my being among the fiends of Suti! Hail, let me sit upon his folds in the habitation of the god User-ba (i.e., he of the strong Soul)! Grant thou that I may sit upon the throne of Rā, and let me have possession of my body before the god Seb. Grant thou that Osiris may come forth triumphant over Suti [and over] the night-watchers of Suti, and over the night-watchers of the Crocodile, yea the night-watchers of the Crocodile, whose faces are hidden and who dwell in the divine Temple of the King of the North in the apparel of the gods on the sixth day of the festival, whose snares are like unto everlastingness and whose cords are like unto eternity. I have seen the god Abet-ka placing the cord; the child is laid in fetters, and the rope of the god Ab-ka is drawn tight(?) ... Behold me. I am born, and I come forth in the form of a living Khu, and the human beings who are upon the earth ascribe praise [unto me]. Hail, Mer, who doest these things for me, and who art put an end to by the vigor of Rā, grant thou that I may see Rā; grant thou that I may come forth against my enemies; and grant thou that I may be victorious over them in the presence of the sovereign princes of the great god who are in the presence of the great god. If, repulsing [me], thou dost not allow me to come forth against my Enemy and to be victorious over him before the sovereign princes, then may Hāpi—who liveth upon law and order—not come forth into heaven—now he liveth by Maāt—and may Rā—who feedeth upon fish—not descend into the waters! And then, verily shall Rā—who feedeth upon right and order—come forth into heaven, and then, verily, shall Hāpi—who feedeth upon fish—descend into the waters; and then, verily, the great day upon the earth shall not be in its season. I have come against my Enemy, he hath been given unto me, he hath come to an end, and I have gotten possession [of him] before the sovereign princes."

Victory Over Enemies

[From Lepsius, "Todtenbuch," Bl. 25.]

THE CHAPTER OF COMING FORTH BY DAY AND OF GAINING THE MASTERY OVER ENEMIES.

"Hail, [thou] who shinest from the Moon and who sendest forth light therefrom, thou comest forth among thy multitudes, and thou goest round about, let me rise," or (as others say), "let me be brought in among the Khus, and let the underworld be opened [unto me]. Behold, I have come forth on this day, and I have become a Khu (or a shining being); therefore shall the Khus let me live, and they shall cause my enemies to be brought to me in a state of misery in the presence of the divine sovereign princes. The divine ka (double) of my mother shall rest in peace because of this, and I shall stand upon my feet and have a staff of gold," or (as others say), "a rod of gold in my hand, wherewith I shall inflict cuts on the limbs [of mine enemy] and shall live. The legs of Sothis are stablished, and I am born in their state of rest."

Coming Forth By Day

[From the Papyrus of Amen-em-heb (Naville, op. cit., Bd. I. Bl. 78).]

THE CHAPTER OF COMING FORTH BY DAY. The scribe Māhu saith:

"I have knowledge. I was conceived by the goddess Sekhet, and the goddess Neith gave birth to me; I am Horus, and [I have] come forth from the Eye of Horus. I am Uatchit who came forth from Horus. I am Horus and I fly up and perch myself upon the forehead of Rā in the bows of his boat which is in heaven."

Opening The Underworld

[From the Papyrus of Nu (British Museum No. 10,477, sheet 15).]

THE CHAPTER OF OPENING THE UNDERWORLD. The overseer of the palace, the chancellor-in-chief, Nu, triumphant, saith:

"The chamber of those who dwell in Nu is opened, and the footsteps of those who dwell with the god of Light are set free. The chamber of Shu is opened, and he cometh forth; and I shall come forth outside, and I shall advance from my territory(?), I shall receive ... and I shall lay firm hold upon the tribute in the House of the Chief of his dead. I shall advance to my throne which is in the boat of Rā. I shall not be molested, and I shall not suffer shipwreck from my throne which is in the boat of Rā, the mighty one. Hail thou that shinest and givest light from Hent-she!"

Coming Forth By Day

[From the Papyrus of Nu (British Museum No. 10,477, sheet 7).]

THE CHAPTER OF COMING FORTH BY DAY. The overseer of the palace, the chancellor-in-chief, Nu, triumphant, saith:

"The doors of heaven are opened for me, the doors of earth are opened for me, the bars and bolts of Seb are opened for me, and the first temple hath been unfastened for me by the god Petra. Behold, I was guarded and watched, [but now] I am released; behold, his hand had tied cords round me and his hand had darted upon me in the earth. Re-hent hath been opened for me and Re-hent hath been unfastened before me, Re-hent hath been given unto me, and I shall come forth by day into whatsoever place I please. I have gained the mastery over my heart; I have gained the mastery over my breast(?); I have gained the mastery over my two hands; I have gained the mastery over my two feet; I have gained the mastery over my mouth; I have gained the mastery over my whole body; I have gained the mastery over sepulchral offerings; I have gained the mastery over the waters; I have gained the mastery over the air; I have gained the mastery over the canal; I have gained the mastery over the river and over the land; I have gained the mastery over the furrows; I have gained the mastery over the male workers for me; I have gained the mastery over the female workers for me in the underworld; I have gained the mastery over [all] the things which were ordered to be done for me upon the earth, according to the entreaty which ye spake for me [saying], 'Behold, let him live upon the bread of Seb.' That which is an abomination unto me, I shall not eat; [nay] I shall live upon cakes [made] of white grain, and my ale shall be [made] of the red grain of Hāpi (i.e., the Nile). In a clean place shall I sit on the ground beneath the foliage of the date-palm of the goddess Hathor, who dwelleth in the spacious Disk as it advanceth to Annu (Heliopolis), having the books of the divine words of the writings of the god Thoth. I have gained the mastery over my heart; I have gained the mastery over my heart's place (or breast); I have gained the mastery over my mouth; I have gained the mastery over my two hands; I have gained the mastery over the waters; I have gained the mastery over the canal; I have gained the mastery over the river; I have gained the mastery over the furrows; I have gained the mastery over the men who work for me; I have gained the mastery over the women who work for me in the underworld; I have gained the mastery over [all] the things which were ordered to be done for me upon earth and in the underworld. I shall lift myself up on my left side, and I shall place myself on my right side; I shall lift myself up on my right side, and I shall place myself [on my left side]. I shall sit down, I shall stand up, and I shall place myself in [the path of] the wind like a guide who is well prepared."

IF THIS COMPOSITION BE KNOWN [BY THE DECEASED] HE SHALL COME FORTH BY DAY, AND HE SHALL BE IN A POSITION TO JOURNEY ABOUT OVER THE EARTH AMONG THE LIVING. AND HE SHALL NEVER SUFFER DIMINUTION, NEVER, NEVER.

Coming Forth By Day

[From the Papyrus of Mes-em-neter (Naville, op. cit., Bd. I. Bl. 81).]

ANOTHER CHAPTER.

"I am the Fire-god, the divine brother of the Fire-god, and [I am] Osiris the brother of Isis. My divine son, together with his mother Isis, hath avenged me on mine enemies. My enemies have wrought every [kind of] evil, therefore their arms, and hands, and feet, have been fettered by reason of their wickedness which they have wrought upon me. I am Osiris, the first-born of the divine womb, the first-born of the gods, and the heir of my father Osiris-Seb(?). I am Osiris, the lord of the heads that live, mighty of breast and powerful of back, with a phallus which goeth to the remotest limits [where] men and women [live]. I am Sah (Orion) who travelleth over his domain and who journeyeth along before the stars of heaven, [which is] the belly of my mother Nut; she conceived me through her love, and she gave birth to me because it was her will so to do. I am Anpu (Anubis) on the day of the god Sepa. I am the Bull at the head of the meadow. I, even I, am Osiris who imprisoned his father together with his mother on the day of making the great slaughter; now, [his] father is Seb, and [his] mother is Nut. I am Horus, the first-born of Rā of the risings. I am Anpu (Anubis) [on the day of] the god Sepa. I, even I, am the lord Tem. I am Osiris. Hail, thou divine first-born, who dost enter and dost speak before the divine Scribe and Doorkeeper of Osiris, grant that I may come. I have become a khu, I have been judged, I have become a divine being, I have come, and I have avenged mine own body. I have taken up my seat by the divine birth-chamber of Osiris, and I have destroyed the sickness and suffering which were there. I have become mighty, and I have become a divine being by the side of the birth-chamber of Osiris, I am brought forth with him, I renew my youth, I renew my youth, I take possession of my two thighs which are in the place where is Osiris, and I open the mouth of the gods therewith, I take my seat by his side, and Thoth cometh forth, and [I am] strengthened in heart with thousands of cakes upon the altars of my divine father, and with my beasts, and with my cattle, and with my red feathered fowl, and with my oxen, and with my geese, and with my ducks, for Horus my Chieftain, and with the offerings which I make to Thoth, and with the sacrifices which I offer up to An-heri-ertaitsa."

Coming Forth By Day

[From the Papyrus of Mes-em-neter (Naville, op. cit., Bd. I. Bl. 82).]

ANOTHER CHAPTER.

"I have sacrificed unto An-heri-ertaitsa, and I am decreed to be strengthened in heart, for I have made offerings at the altars of my divine father Osiris; I rule in Tattu and I lift myself up over his land. I sniff the wind of the east by its hair; I lay hold upon the north wind by its hair, I seize and hold fast to the west wind by its body, and I go round about heaven on its four sides; I lay hold upon the south wind by its eye, and I bestow air upon the venerable beings [who are in the underworld] along with the eating of cakes."

IF THIS COMPOSITION BE KNOWN [BY THE DECEASED] UPON EARTH HE SHALL COME FORTH BY DAY, AND HE SHALL HAVE THE FACULTY OF TRAVELLING ABOUT AMONG THE LIVING, AND HIS NAME SHALL NEVER PERISH.

Coming Forth By Day

[From the Papyrus of Nebseni (British Museum No. 9,900, sheet 16).]

THE CHAPTER OF COMING FORTH BY DAY. The libationer, the lord of reverence, Nebseni, saith:

"Hail, thou hawk who risest in heaven, thou lord of the goddess Meh-urt! Strengthen thou me according as thou hast strengthened thyself, and show thyself upon the earth, O thou that returnest and withdrawest thyself, and let thy will be done."

"Behold the god of One Face is with me. [I am] the hawk which is within the shrine; and I open that which is upon the hangings thereof. Behold Horus, the son of Isis."

"[Behold] Horus the son of Isis! Strengthen thou me, according as thou hast strengthened thyself, and show thyself upon earth, O thou that returnest and withdrawest thyself, and let thy will be done."

"Behold, the god of One Face is with me. [I am] the hawk in the southern heaven, and [I am] Thoth in the northern heaven; I make peace with the raging fire and I bring Maāt to him that loveth her."

"Behold Thoth, even Thoth! Strengthen thou me according as thou hast strengthened thyself, and show thyself upon earth, O thou that returnest and withdrawest thyself, and let thy will be done."

"Behold the god of One Face is with me. I am the Plant of the region where nothing sprouteth, and the Blossom of the hidden horizon."

"Behold Osiris, yea Osiris! Strengthen thou me according as thou hast strengthened thyself, and show thyself upon earth, O thou that returnest and withdrawest thyself, and let thy will be done."

"Behold, the god of One Face is with me. Hail, thou who [standest] upon thy legs, in thine hour," or (as others say), "Hail, thou who art victorious upon thy legs in thine hour, thou lord of the two divine Tchafi,(46) who livest [in] the two divine Tchafi, strengthen thou me according as thou hast strengthened thyself, and show thyself upon earth, O thou that returnest and withdrawest thyself, and let thy will be done."

"Behold, the god of One Face is with me. Hail, thou Nekhen who art in thine egg, thou lord of the goddess Meh-urt, strengthen thou me according as thou hast strengthened thyself, and show thyself upon earth, O thou that returnest and withdrawest thyself, and let thy will be done."

"Behold, the god of One Face is with me. The god Sebek hath stood up within his ground, and the goddess Neith hath stood up within her plantation, O thou that returnest and withdrawest thyself, show thyself upon earth and let thy will be done."

"Behold, the god of One Face is with me. Hail, ye seven beings who make decrees, who support the Scales on the night of the judgment of the Utchat, who cut off heads, who hack necks in pieces, who take possession of hearts by violence and rend the places where hearts are fixed, who make slaughterings in the Lake of Fire, I know you and I know your names, therefore know ye me even as I know your names. I come forth to you, therefore come ye forth to me, for ye live in me and I would live in you. Make ye me to be vigorous by means of that which is in your hands, that is to say, by the rod of power which is in your hands. Decree ye for me life by [your] speech year by year; give me multitudes of years over and above my years of life, and multitudes of months over and above my months of life, and multitudes of days over and above my days of life, and multitudes of nights over and above my nights of life; and grant that I may come forth and shine upon my statue; and [grant me] air for my nose, and let my eyes have the power to see among those divine beings who dwell in the horizon on the day when evil-doing and wrong are justly assessed."

IF THIS CHAPTER BE RECITED FOR THE DECEASED HE SHALL BE STRONG UPON EARTH BEFORE RA, AND HE SHALL HAVE A COMFORTABLE BURIAL (OR TOMB) WITH OSIRIS, AND IT SHALL BE OF GREAT BENEFIT TO A MAN IN THE UNDERWORLD. SEPULCHRAL BREAD SHALL BE GIVEN UNTO HIM, AND HE SHALL COME FORTH INTO THE PRESENCE [OF RA] DAY BY DAY, AND EVERY DAY, REGULARLY, AND CONTINUALLY.(47)

Coming Forth By Day

[From the Papyrus of Nebseni (British Museum No. 9,900, sheet 3).]

THE CHAPTER OF COMING FORTH BY DAY AND OF OPENING UP A WAY THROUGH THE AMMEHET. Behold the scribe Nebseni, triumphant, who saith:

"Homage to you, O ye lords of Kas, ye who are without sin and who live for the limitless and infinite æons of time which make up eternity, I have opened up a way for myself to you! I have become a khu in my forms, I have gained the mastery over my enchantments, and I am decreed to be a khu; therefore deliver ye me from the crocodile [which liveth in] this country of right and truth. Grant ye to me my mouth that I may speak therewith, and cause that my sepulchral meals be placed in my hands in your presence, for I know you, and I know your names, and I know also the name of the mighty god, before whose nose ye set your tchefau food; and his name is 'Tekem.' [When] he openeth up his path in the eastern horizon of heaven, and [when] he fluttereth down in the western horizon of heaven, may he carry me along with him and may I be safe and sound! Let not the Mesqet make an end of me, let not the Fiend gain the mastery over me, let me not be turned back at your portals, and let not your doors be shut in my face, because my cakes are in the city of Pe and my ale is in the city of Tep. And there, in the celestial mansions of heaven which my divine father Tem hath stablished, let my hands lay hold upon the wheat and the barley which shall be given unto me therein in abundant measure, and may the son of mine own body make [ready] for me my food therein. And grant ye unto me therein sepulchral meals, and incense, and wax, and all the beautiful and pure things whereon the god liveth, in very deed forever in all the transformations which it pleaseth me [to perform]; and grant me the power to float down and to sail up the stream in Sekhet-Aarru [and may I reach Sekhet-hetep!]. I am the double Lion-god."

IF THIS CHAPTER(48) BE KNOWN [BY THE DECEASED] UPON EARTH, [OR IF IT BE DONE] IN WRITING UPON [HIS] COFFIN, HE SHALL COME FORTH BY DAY IN ALL THE FORMS WHICH HE IS PLEASED [TO TAKE], AND HE SHALL ENTER IN TO [HIS] PLACE AND SHALL NOT BE DRIVEN BACK. AND CAKES, AND ALE, AND JOINTS OF MEAT UPON THE ALTAR OF OSIRIS SHALL BE GIVEN UNTO HIM; AND HE SHALL ENTER IN PEACE INTO SEKHET-AARRU TO KNOW THE DECREE OF HIM WHO DWELLETH IN TATTU; THERE SHALL WHEAT AND BARLEY BE GIVEN UNTO HIM; THERE SHALL HE FLOURISH AS HE DID UPON EARTH; AND HE SHALL DO WHATSOEVER IT PLEASETH HIM TO DO, EVEN AS THE COMPANY OF THE GODS WHICH IS IN THE UNDERWORLD, CONTINUALLY, AND REGULARLY, FOR MILLIONS OF TIMES.

Of Lifting Up The Feet

[From the Papyrus of Nu (British Museum No. 10,477, sheet 6).]

THE CHAPTER OF LIFTING UP THE FEET AND OF COMING FORTH UPON THE EARTH. The chancellor-in-chief, Nu, triumphant, saith:

"Perform thy work, O Seker, perform thy work, O Seker, O thou [who dwellest in thy house], and who [standest] on [thy] feet in the underworld! I am the god who sendeth forth rays of light over the Thigh of heaven, and I come forth to heaven and I sit myself down by the God of Light (Khu). Hail, I have become helpless! Hail, I have become helpless! but I go forward. I have become helpless, I have become helpless in the regions of those who plunder in the underworld."

Of Journeying To Annu

[From the Papyrus of Nu (British Museum No. 10,477, sheet 13).]

THE CHAPTER OF JOURNEYING TO ANNU (HELIOPOLIS) AND OF RECEIVING A THRONE THEREIN. The chancellor-in-chief, Nu, triumphant, saith:

"I have come forth from the uttermost parts of the earth, and [I have] received my apparel(?) at the will(?) of the Ape. I penetrate into the holy habitations of those who are in [their] shrines (or coffins), I force my way through the habitations of the god Remren, and I arrive in the habitations of the god Akhsesef, I travel on through the holy chambers, and I pass into the Temple of the god Kemken. The Buckle hath been given unto me, it [hath placed] its hands upon me, it hath decreed [to my service] its sister Khebent, and its mother Kehkehet. It placeth me in [the eastern part of heaven wherein Rā riseth and is exalted every day; and I rise therein and travel onward, and I become a spiritual body (sāh) like the god, and they set me](49) on that holy way on which Thoth journeyeth when he goeth to make peace between the two Fighting-gods (i.e., Horus and Set). He journeyeth, he journeyeth to the city of Pe, and he cometh to the city of Tepu."

Of Transformation

[From the Papyrus of Nu (British Museum No. 10,477, sheet 9).]

THE CHAPTER OF A MAN TRANSFORMING HIMSELF INTO WHATEVER FORM HE PLEASETH. The chancellor-in-chief, Nu, triumphant, saith:

"I have come into the House of the King by means of the mantis (abit) which led me hither. Homage to thee, O thou who fliest into heaven, and dost shine upon the son of the white crown, and dost protect the white crown, let me have my existence with thee! I have gathered together the great god[s], I am mighty, I have made my way and I have travelled along thereon."

Of Performing Transformations

[From the Papyrus of Nu (British Museum No. 10,477, sheet 10).]

THE CHAPTER OF PERFORMING THE TRANSFORMATION INTO A HAWK OF GOLD. The chancellor-in-chief, Nu, triumphant, saith:

"I have risen, I have risen like the mighty hawk [of gold] that cometh forth from his egg; I fly and I alight like the hawk which hath a back four cubits wide, and the wings of which are like unto the mother-of-emerald of the south. I have come forth from the interior of the Sektet boat, and my heart hath been brought unto me from the mountain of the east. I have alighted upon the Atet boat, and those who were dwelling in their companies have been brought unto me, and they bowed low in paying homage unto me and in saluting me with cries of joy. I have risen, and I have gathered myself together like the beautiful hawk of gold, which hath the head of a Bennu bird, and Rā entereth in day by day to hearken unto my words; I have taken my seat among those first-born gods of Nut. I am stablished, and the divine Sekhet-hetep is before me, I have eaten therein, I have become a khu therein, I have an abundance therein—as much as I desire—the god Nepra hath given to me my throat, and I have gained the mastery over that which guardeth (or belongeth to) my head."

Of Transformation Into A Hawk

[From the Papyrus of Nu (British Museum No. 10,477, sheets 13 and 14).]

THE CHAPTER OF MAKING THE TRANSFORMATION INTO A DIVINE HAWK. The chancellor-in-chief, Nu, triumphant, saith:

"Hail, Great God, come now to Tattu! Make thou smooth for me the ways and let me go round about [to visit] my thrones; I have renewed(?) myself, and I have raised myself up. O grant thou that I may be feared, and make thou me to be a terror. Let the gods of the underworld be afraid of me, and may they fight for me in their habitations which are therein. Let not him that would do me harm draw nigh unto me, or injure(?) me, in the House of Darkness, that is, he that clotheth and covereth the feeble one, and whose [name] is hidden; and let not the gods act likewise toward me. [Hail], ye gods, who hearken unto [my] speech! Hail, ye rulers, who are among the followers of Osiris! Be ye therefore silent, O ye gods, when one god speaketh unto another, for he hearkeneth unto right and truth; and what I speak unto [him] do thou also speak for me then, O Osiris. Grant thou that I may journey round about [according to] that which cometh forth from thy mouth concerning me, and grant that I may see thine own Form (or forms), and the dispositions of thy Souls. Grant thou that I may come forth, and that I may have power over my legs, and that I may have my existence there like unto that of Neb-er-tcher who is over [all]. May the gods of the underworld fear me, and may they fight for me in their habitations. Grant thou that I may move along therein together with the divine beings who journey onward, and may I be stablished upon my resting-place like the Lord of Life. May I be joined unto Isis the divine lady, and may she protect me from him that would do an injury unto me; and let not anyone come to see the divine one naked and helpless. May I journey on, may I come into the uttermost parts of heaven. I exchange speech with the god Seb, I make supplication for divine food from Neb-er-tcher; the gods of the underworld have fear of me, and they fight for me in their habitations when they see that thou hast provided me with food, both of the fowl of the air and of the fish of the sea. I am one of those Khus who dwell with the divine Khu, and I have made my form like unto his divine Form, when he cometh forth and maketh himself manifest in Tattu. [I am] a spiritual body (sāh) and possess my soul, and will speak unto thee the things which concern me. O grant thou that I may be feared, and make thou me to be a terror; let the gods of the underworld be afraid of me, and may they fight for me in their habitations. I, even I, am the Khu who dwelleth with the divine Khu, whom the god Tem himself hath created, and who hath come into being from the blossom (i.e., the eyelashes) of his eye; he hath made to have existence, and he hath made to be glorious (i.e., to be Khus), and he hath made mighty thereby those who have their existence along with him. Behold, he is the only One in Nu, and they sing praises (or do homage) unto him [when] he cometh forth from the horizon, and the gods and the Khus who have come into being along with him ascribe [the lordship of] terror unto him."

"I am one of those worms(?) which the eye of the Lord, the only One, hath created. And behold, when as yet Isis had not given birth to Horus, I had germinated, and had flourished, and I had become aged, and I had become greater than those who dwelt with the divine Khu, and who had come into being along with him. And I had risen up like the divine hawk, and Horus made for me a spiritual body containing his own soul, so that I might take possession of all that belonged unto Osiris in the underworld. The double Lion-god, the governor of the things which belong to the Temple of the nemmes crown, who dwelleth in his secret abode, saith [unto me]: 'Get thee back to the uttermost parts of heaven, for behold, inasmuch as through thy form of Horus thou hast become a spiritual body, (sāh) the nemmes crown is not for thee; but behold, thou hast the power of speech even to the uttermost parts of heaven.' And I, the guardian, took possession of the things of Horus [which belonged] unto Osiris in the underworld, and Horus told aloud unto me the things which his divine father Osiris spake unto him in years [gone by] on the day of his own burial. I have given unto thee(50) the nemmes crown through the double Lion-god that thou mayest pass onward and mayest come to the heavenly path, and that those who dwell in the uttermost parts of the horizon may see thee, and that the gods of the underworld may see thee and may fight for thee in their habitations. And of them is the Auhet.(51) The gods, each and all of them, who are the warders of the shrine of the Lord, the only One, have fallen before my words. Hail!

He that is exalted upon his tomb is on my side, and he hath bound [upon my head] the nemmes crown, by the decree of the double Lion-god on my behalf, and the god Auhet hath prepared a way for me. I, even I, am exalted in my tomb, and the double Lion-god hath bound the nemmes crown upon my [head], and he hath also given unto me the double hairy covering of my head. He hath stablished my heart through his own backbone, he hath stablished my heart through his own great and exceeding strength, and I shall not fall through Shu. I make my peace with the beautiful divine Brother, the lord of the two uræi, adored be he! I, even I, am he who knoweth the roads through the sky, and the wind thereof is in my body. The bull which striketh terror [into men] shall not drive me back, and I shall pass on to the place where lieth the shipwrecked mariner on the border of the Sekhet-neheh (i.e., Field of illimitable time), and I shall journey on to the night and sorrow of the regions of Amenti. O Osiris, I shall come each day into the House of the double Lion-god, and I shall come forth therefrom into the House of Isis, the divine lady. I shall behold sacred things which are hidden, and I shall be led on to the secret and holy things, even as they have granted unto me to see the birth of the Great God. Horus hath made me to be a spiritual body through his soul, [and I see what is therein. If I speak near the mighty ones of Shu they repulse my opportunity. I am the guardian and I] take possession of the things which Horus had from Osiris in the underworld. I, even I, am Horus who dwelleth in the divine Khu. [I] have gained power over his crown, I have gained power over his radiance, and I have travelled over the remote, illimitable parts of heaven. Horus is upon his throne, Horus is upon his royal seat. My face is like unto that of the divine hawk, my strength is like unto that of the divine hawk, and I am one who hath been fully equipped by his divine Lord. I shall come forth to Tattu, I shall see Osiris, I shall pay homage to him on the right hand and on the left, I shall pay homage unto Nut, and she shall look upon me, and the gods shall look upon me, together with the Eye of Horus who is without sight(?). They (i.e., the gods) shall make their arms to come forth unto me. I rise up [as] a divine Power, and [I] repulse him that would subject me to restraint. They open unto me the holy paths, they see my form, and they hear that which I speak. [Down] upon your faces, ye gods of the Tuat (underworld), who would resist me with your faces and oppose me with your powers, who lead along the stars which never rest, and who make the holy paths unto the Hemati abode [where is] the Lord of the exceedingly mighty and terrible Soul. Horus hath commanded that ye lift up your faces so that I may look upon you. I have risen up like the divine hawk, and Horus hath made for me a spiritual body, through his own soul, to take possession of that which belongeth to Osiris in the Tuat (underworld). I have bound up the gods with divine tresses, and I have travelled on to those who ward their Chambers, and who were on both sides of me. I have made my roads and I have journeyed on and have reached those divine beings who inhabit their secret dwellings, and who are warders of the Temple of Osiris. I have spoken unto them with strength, and have made them to know the most mighty power of him that is provided with two horns [to fight] against Suti; and I make them to know concerning him that hath taken possession of the divine food, and who is provided with the Might of Tem. May the gods of the underworld [order] a prosperous journey for me! O ye gods who inhabit your secret dwellings, and who are warders of the Temple of Osiris, and whose numbers are great and multitudinous, grant ye that I may come unto you. I have bound up and I have gathered together the powers of Kesemu-enenet," or (as others say), "Kesemiu-enenet; and I have made holy the Powers of the paths of those who watch and ward the roads of the horizon, and who are the guardians of the horizon of Hemati which is in heaven. I have stablished habitations for Osiris, I have made the ways holy for him, I have done that which hath been commanded, I have come forth to Tattu, I have seen Osiris, I have spoken unto him concerning the matters of his first-born son whom he loveth and concerning the wounding of the heart of Suti, and I have seen the divine one who is without life. Yea, I have made them to know concerning the counsels of the gods which Horus carried out while his father Osiris was not [with him]. Hail, Lord, thou most mighty and terrible Soul! Verily, I, even I, have come, look thou upon me, and do thou make me to be exalted. I have made my way through the Tuat (underworld), and I have opened up the paths which belong to heaven and also those which belong to earth, and I have suffered no opposition therein. Exalted [be thou] upon thy throne, O Osiris! Thou hast heard fair things, O Osiris! Thy strength is vigorous, O Osiris. Thy head is fastened unto thee, O Osiris. Thy brow is stablished, O Osiris. Thy heart is glad, [O Osiris]. Thy speech(?) is stablished, [O Osiris], and thy princes rejoice. Thou art stablished like the Bull of Amentet. Thy son Horus hath risen like the sun upon thy throne, and all life is with him. Millions of years minister unto him, and millions of years hold him in fear; the company of the gods are his servants, and the company of the gods hold him in fear. The god Tem, the Governor and only One of the gods, hath spoken [these things], and his word passeth not away. Horus is both the divine food and the sacrifice. [He] hath passed on(?) to gather together [the members of] his divine father; Horus is [his] deliverer, Horus is [his] deliverer. Horus hath sprung from the water of his divine father and [from his] decay. He hath become the Governor of Egypt. The gods labor for him, and they toil for him for millions of years; and he hath made to live millions of years through his Eye, the only One of its Lord (or Neb-s), Nebt-er-tcher."

Of Transformation Into A Governor

[From the Papyrus of Nu (British Museum No. 10,477, sheets 8 and 9).]

THE CHAPTER OF BEING TRANSFORMED INTO THE GOVERNOR OF THE SOVEREIGN PRINCES. The chancellor-in-chief, Nu, triumphant, saith:

"I am the god Tem, the maker of heaven, the creator of things which are, who cometh forth from the earth, who maketh to come into being the seed which is sown, the lord of things which shall be, who gave birth to the gods; [I am] the great god who made himself, the lord of life, who maketh to flourish the company of the gods. Homage to you, O ye lords of divine things (or of creation), ye pure beings whose abodes are hidden! Homage to you, O ye everlasting lords, whose forms are hidden and whose shrines are hidden in places which are unknown! Homage to you, O ye gods, who dwell in the Tenait(?)! Homage to you, O ye gods of the circuit of the flooded lands of Qebhu! Homage to you, O ye gods who live in Amentet! Homage to you, O ye company of the gods who dwell in Nut! Grant ye that I may come unto you, for I am pure, I am divine, I am a khu, I am strong, I am endowed with a soul (or I am mighty), and I have brought unto you incense, and sweet-smelling gums, and natron; I have made an end of the spittle which floweth from your mouth upon me. I have come, and I have made an end of the evil things which are in your hearts, and I have removed the faults which ye kept [laid up against me]. I have brought to you the things which are good, and I make to come into your presence Right and Truth. I, even I, know you, and I know your names, and I know your forms, which are unknown, and I come into being along with you. My coming is like unto that of the god who eateth men and who liveth upon the gods. I am mighty with you like the god who is exalted upon his resting-place; the gods come to me in gladness, and goddesses make supplication unto me when they see me. I have come unto you, and I have risen like your two divine daughters. I have taken my seat in the horizon, and I receive my offerings upon my tables, and I drink drink-offerings at eventide. My coming is [received] with shouts of joy, and the divine beings who dwell in the horizon ascribe praises unto me, the divine spiritual body (Sāh), the lord of divine beings. I am exalted like the holy god who dwelleth in the Great Temple, and the gods rejoice when they see me in my beautiful coming forth from the body of Nut, when my mother Nut giveth birth unto me."

Of Transformation Into A God

[From the Papyrus of Ani (British Museum No. 10,470, sheet 28).]

[THE CHAPTER OF] MAKING THE TRANSFORMATION INTO THE GOD WHO GIVETH LIGHT [IN] THE DARKNESS. Saith Osiris, the scribe Ani, triumphant:

"I am the girdle of the robe of the god Nu, which shineth and sheddeth light upon that which belongeth to his breast, which sendeth forth light into the darkness, which uniteth the two fighting deities who dwell in my body through the mighty spell of the words of my mouth, which raiseth up him that hath fallen—for he who was with him in the valley of Abtu (Abydos) hath fallen—and I rest. I have remembered him. I have taken possession of the god Hu in my city, for I found him therein, and I have led away captive the darkness by my might. I have rescued the Eye [of the Sun] when it waned at the coming of the festival of the fifteenth day, and I have weighed Sut in the celestial houses against the Aged one who is with him. I have endowed Thoth [with what is needful] in the Temple of the Moon-god for the coming of the fifteenth day of the festival. I have taken possession of the Ureret crown; Maāt (i.e., right and truth) is in my body; its mouths are of turquoise and rock-crystal. My homestead is among the furrows which are [of the color of] lapis-lazuli. I am Hem-Nu(?) who sheddeth light in the darkness. I have come to give light in the darkness, which is made light and bright [by me]. I have given light in the darkness, and I have overthrown the destroying crocodiles. I have sung praises unto those who dwell in the darkness, I have raised up those who wept, and who had hidden their faces and had sunk down in wretchedness; and they did not look then upon me. [Hail, then,] ye beings, I am Hem-Nu(?), and I will not let you hear concerning the matter. [I] have opened [the way], I am Hem-Nu(?), [I] have made light the darkness, I have come, having made an end of the darkness, which hath become light indeed."

Transformation Into A Lotus

[From the Papyrus of Nu (British Museum No. 10,477, sheet 11).]

THE CHAPTER OF MAKING THE TRANSFORMATION INTO A LOTUS. The overseer of the palace, the chancellor-in-chief, Nu, saith:

"I am the pure lotus which springeth up from the divine splendor that belongeth to the nostrils of Rā. I have made [my way], and I follow on seeking for him who is Horus. I am the pure one who cometh forth out of the Field."

Transformation Into A Lotus

[From the Papyrus of Paqrer (see Naville, op. cit., Bd. I. Bl. 93).]

THE CHAPTER OF MAKING THE TRANSFORMATION INTO A LOTUS. Saith Osiris Paqrer:

"Hail, thou lotus, thou type of the god Nefer-Temu! I am the man that knoweth you, and I know your names among [those of] the gods, the lords of the underworld, and I am one of you. Grant ye that [I] may see the gods who are the divine guide in the Tuat (underworld), and grant ye unto me a place in the underworld near unto the lords of Amentet. Let me arrive at a habitation in the land of Tchesert, and receive me, O all ye gods, in the presence of the lords of eternity. Grant that my soul may come forth whithersoever it pleaseth, and let it not be driven away from the presence of the great company of the gods."

Transformation Into Ptah

[From the Papyrus of Nu (British Museum No. 10,477, sheets 9 and 10).]

THE CHAPTER OF MAKING THE TRANSFORMATION INTO PTAH, OF EATING CAKES, AND OF DRINKING ALE, AND OF UNFETTERING THE STEPS, AND OF BECOMING A LIVING BEING IN ANNU (Heliopolis). The chancellor-in-chief, Nu, triumphant, saith:

"I fly like a hawk, I cackle like the smen goose, and I perch upon that abode of the underworld (aat) on the festival of the great Being. That which is an abomination unto me, that which is an abomination unto me, I have not eaten; filth is an abomination unto me and I have not eaten thereof, and that which is an abomination unto my ka hath not entered into my belly. Let me, then, live upon that which the gods and the Khus decree for me; let me live and let me have power over cakes; let me eat them before the gods and the Khus [who have a favor] unto me; let me have power over [these cakes] and let me eat of them under the [shade of the] leaves of the palm tree of the goddess Hathor, who is my divine Lady. Let the offering of the sacrifice, and the offering of cakes, and vessels of libations be made in Annu; let me clothe myself in the taau garment [which I shall receive] from the hand of the goddess Tait; let me stand up and let me sit down wheresoever I please. My head is like unto that of Rā, and [when my members are] gathered together [I am] like unto Tem; the four [sides of the domain] of Rā, and the width of the earth four times. I come forth. My tongue is like unto that of Ptah and my throne is like unto that of the goddess Hathor, and I make mention of the words of Tem, my father, with my mouth. He it is who constraineth the handmaid, the wife of Seb, and before him are bowed [all] heads, and there is fear of him. Hymns of praise are repeated for [me] by reason of [my] mighty acts, and I am decreed to be the divine Heir of Seb, the lord of the earth and to be the protector therein. The god Seb refresheth me, and he maketh his risings to be mine. Those who dwell in Annu bow down their heads unto me, for I am their lord and I am their bull. I am more powerful than the lord of time, and I shall enjoy the pleasures of love, and shall gain the mastery over millions of years."

Transformation Into A Bennu Bird

[From the Papyrus of Nu (British Museum No. 10,477, sheet 10).]

[THE CHAPTER OF MAKING THE TRANSFORMATION INTO A BENNU BIRD.] The chancellor-in-chief, Nu, triumphant, saith:

"I came(52) into being from unformed matter. I came into existence like the god Khepera, I have germinated like the things which germinate (i.e., plants), and I have dressed myself like the Tortoise.(53) I am [of] the germs of every god. I am Yesterday of the four [quarters of the world] and of those seven Uræi which came into existence in Amentet, that is to say, [Horus, who emitteth light from his divine body. He is] the god [who] fought against Suti, but the god Thoth cometh between them through the judgment of him that dwelleth in Sekhem, and of the Souls who are in Annu, and there is a stream between them. I have come by day, and I have risen in the footsteps of the gods. I am the god Khensu, who driveth back all that oppose him."

[IF] THIS CHAPTER [BE KNOWN BY THE DECEASED] HE SHALL COME FORTH PURE BY DAY AFTER HIS DEATH, AND HE SHALL PERFORM WHATSOEVER TRANSFORMATIONS HIS HEART DESIRETH. HE SHALL BE IN THE FOLLOWING OF UN-NEFER, AND HE SHALL BE SATISFIED WITH THE FOOD OF OSIRIS AND WITH SEPULCHRAL MEALS. [HE] SHALL SEE THE DISK, [HE] SHALL BE IN GOOD CASE UPON EARTH BEFORE RA, AND HE SHALL BE TRIUMPHANT BEFORE OSIRIS, AND NO EVIL THING WHATSOEVER SHALL HAVE DOMINION OVER HIM FOREVER AND EVER.

Transformation Into A Heron

[From the Papyrus of Nu (British Museum No. 10,477, sheet 10).]

[THE CHAPTER OF MAKING THE TRANSFORMATION INTO A HERON. The chancellor-in-chief, Nu, triumphant, saith:]

"[I] have gotten dominion over the beasts that are brought for sacrifice, with the knives which are [held] at their heads, and at their hair, and at their ... [Hail], Aged ones [hail,] Khus, who are provided with the opportunity, the chancellor-in-chief, the overseer of the palace, Nu, triumphant, is upon the earth, and what he hath slaughtered is in heaven; and what he hath slaughtered is in heaven and he is upon the earth. Behold, I am strong, and I work mighty deeds to the very heights of heaven. I have made myself pure, and [I] make the breadth of heaven [a place for] my footsteps [as I go] into the cities of Aukert; I advance, and I go forward into the city of Unnu (Hermopolis). I have set the gods upon their paths, and I have roused up the exalted ones who dwell in their shrines. Do I not know Nu? Do I not know Tatunen? Do I not know the beings of the color of fire who thrust forward their horns? Do I not know [every being having] incantations unto whose words I listen? I am the Smam bull [for slaughter] which is written down in the books. The gods crying out say: 'Let your faces be gracious to him that cometh onward.' The light is beyond your knowledge, and ye cannot fetter it; and times and seasons are in my body. I do not utter words to the god Hu, [I do not utter words of] wickedness instead of [words of] right and truth, and each day right and truth come upon my eyebrows. At night taketh place the festival of him that is dead, the Aged One, who is in ward [in] the earth."

Of The Living Soul

[From the Papyrus of Nu (British Museum No. 10,477, sheet 9).]

THE CHAPTER OF MAKING THE TRANSFORMATION INTO A LIVING SOUL, AND OF NOT ENTERING INTO THE CHAMBER OF TORTURE; whosoever knoweth [it] shall not see corruption. The chancellor-in-chief, Nu, triumphant, saith:

"I am the divine Soul of Rā proceeding from the god Nu; that divine soul which is God, [I am] the creator of the divine food, and that which is an abomination unto me is sin whereon I look not. I proclaim right and truth, and I live therein. I am the divine food, which is not corrupted in my name of Soul: I gave birth unto myself together with Nu in my name of Khepera in whom I come into being day by day. I am the lord of light, and that which is an abomination unto me is death; let me not go into the chamber of torture which is in the Tuat (underworld). I ascribe honor [unto] Osiris, and I make to be at peace the heart[s] of those beings who dwell among the divine things which [I] love. They cause the fear of me [to abound], and they create awe of me in those beings who dwell in their divine territories. Behold, I am exalted upon my standard, and upon my seat, and upon the throne which is adjudged [to me]. I am the god Nu, and the workers of iniquity shall not destroy me. I am the firstborn god of primeval matter, that is to say, the divine Soul, even the Souls of the gods of everlastingness, and my body is eternity. My Form is everlastingness, and is the lord of years and the prince of eternity. [I am] the creator of the darkness who maketh his habitation in the uttermost parts of the sky, [which] I love, and I arrive at the confines thereof. I advance upon my feet, I become master of my vine, I sail over the sky which formeth the division [betwixt heaven and earth], [I] destroy the hidden worms that travel nigh unto my footsteps which are toward the lord of the two hands and arms. My soul is the Souls of the souls of everlastingness, and my body is eternity. I am the divine exalted being who is the lord of the land of Tebu. 'I am the Boy in the city and the Young man in the plain' is my name; 'he that never suffereth corruption' is my name. I am the Soul, the creator of the god Nu who maketh his habitation in the underworld: my place of incubation is unseen and my egg is not cracked. I have done away with all my iniquity, and I shall see my divine Father, the lord of eventide, whose body dwelleth in Annu. I travel(?) to the god of night(?), who dwelleth with the god of light, by the western region of the Ibis (i.e., Thoth)."

Of The Swallow

[From the Papyrus of Nu (British Museum No. 10,477, sheet 10).]

THE CHAPTER OF MAKING THE TRANSFORMATION INTO A SWALLOW. The chancellor-in-chief, Nu, triumphant, saith:

"I am a swallow, I am a swallow. I am the Scorpion, the daughter of Rā. Hail, ye gods, whose scent is sweet; hail, ye gods, whose scent is sweet! [Hail,] Flame, which cometh forth from the horizon! Hail, thou who art in the city, I have brought the Warden of his Bight therein. Oh, stretch out unto me thy hand so that I may be able to pass my days in the Pool of Double Fire, and let me advance with my message, for I have come with words to tell. Oh, open [thou] the doors to me and I will declare the things which have been seen by me. Horus hath become the divine prince of the Boat of the Sun, and unto him hath been given the throne of his divine father Osiris, and Set, that son of Nut, [lieth] under the fetters which he had made for me. I have made a computation of what is in the city of Sekhem, I have stretched out both my hands and arms at the word(?) of Osiris, I have passed on to judgment, and I have come that [I] may speak; grant that I may pass on and declare my tidings. I enter in, [I am] judged, and [I] come forth worthy at the gate of Neb-er-tcher. I am pure at the great place of the passage of souls, I have done away with my sins, I have put away mine offences, and I have destroyed the evil which appertained unto my members upon earth. Hail, ye divine beings who guard the doors, make ye for me a way, for, behold, I am like unto you. I have come forth by day, I have journeyed on on my legs, I have gained the mastery over my footsteps [before] the God of Light, I know the hidden ways and the doors of the Sekhet-Aaru, verily I, even I, have come, I have overthrown mine enemies upon earth, and yet my perishable body is in the grave!"

IF THIS CHAPTER BE KNOWN [BY THE DECEASED], HE SHALL COME FORTH BY DAY, HE SHALL NOT BE TURNED BACK AT ANY GATE IN THE UNDERWORLD, AND HE SHALL MAKE HIS TRANSFORMATION INTO A SWALLOW REGULARLY AND CONTINUALLY.

The Serpent Sata

[From the Papyrus of Nu (British Museum No. 10,477, sheet 11).]

THE CHAPTER OF MAKING THE TRANSFORMATION INTO THE SERPENT SATA. The chancellor-in-chief, Nu, triumphant, saith:

"I am the serpent Sata whose years are many.(54) I die and I am born again each day. I am the serpent Sata which dwelleth in the uttermost parts of the earth. I die, and I am born again, and I renew myself, and I grow young each day."

Of The Crocodile

[From the Papyrus of Nu (British Museum No. 10,477, sheet 11).]

THE CHAPTER OF MAKING THE TRANSFORMATION INTO A CROCODILE. The chancellor-in-chief, Nu, triumphant, saith:

"I am the divine crocodile which dwelleth in his terror, I am the divine crocodile, and I seize [my prey] like a ravening beast. I am the great and Mighty Fish which is in the city of Qem-ur. I am the lord to whom bowing and prostrations [are made] in the city of Sekhem."

Soul And Body

[From the Papyrus of Ani (British Museum No. 10,470, sheet 17).]

THE CHAPTER OF CAUSING THE SOUL TO BE UNITED TO ITS BODY IN THE UNDERWORLD. The Osiris Ani, triumphant, saith:

"Hail, thou god Anniu (i.e., Bringer)! Hail, thou god Pehrer (i.e., Runner), who dwellest in thy hall! [Hail,] great God! Grant thou that my soul may come unto me from wheresoever it may be. If [it] would tarry, then let my soul be brought unto me from wheresoever it may be, for thou shalt find the Eye of Horus standing by thee like unto those beings who are like unto Osiris, and who never lie down in death. Let not the Osiris Ani, triumphant, lie down in death among those who lie down in Annu, the land wherein souls are joined unto their bodies even in thousands. Let me have possession of my ba (soul), and of my khu, and let me triumph therewith in every place wheresoever it may be. [Observe these things which [I] speak, for it hath staves with it];(55) observe then, O ye divine guardians of heaven, my soul [wheresoever it may be].(56) If it would tarry, do thou make my soul to look upon my body,(57) for thou shalt find the Eye of Horus standing by thee like those [beings who are like unto Osiris]."

"Hail, ye gods, who tow along the boat of the lord of millions of years, who bring [it] above the underworld and who make it to travel over Nut, who make souls to enter into [their] spiritual bodies, whose hands are filled with your ropes and who clutch your weapons tight, destroy ye the Enemy; thus shall the boat of the sun be glad and the great God shall set out on his journey in peace. And behold, grant ye that the soul of Osiris Ani, triumphant, may come forth before the gods and that it may be triumphant along with you in the eastern part of the sky to follow unto the place where it was yesterday; [and that it may have] peace, peace in Amentet. May it look upon its material body, may it rest upon its spiritual body; and may its body neither perish nor suffer corruption forever."

[THESE] WORDS ARE TO BE SAID OVER A SOUL OF GOLD INLAID WITH PRECIOUS STONES AND PLACED ON THE BREAST OF OSIRIS.

Of Evil Recollections

[From the Papyrus of Nu (British Museum No. 10,477, sheet 8).]

THE CHAPTER OF DRIVING EVIL RECOLLECTIONS FROM THE MOUTH. The overseer of the palace, the chancellor-in-chief, Nu, triumphant, the son of the overseer of the palace, the chancellor-in-chief, Amen-hetep, triumphant, saith:

"Hail, thou that cuttest off heads, and slittest brows, thou being who puttest away the memory of evil things from the mouth of the Khus by means of the incantations which they have within them, look not upon me with the [same] eyes with which thou lookest upon them. Go thou round about on thy legs, and let thy face be [turned] behind thee so that thou mayest be able to see the divine slaughterers of the god Shu who are coming up behind thee to cut off thy head, and to slit thy brow by reason of the message of violence [sent] by thy lord, and to see(?) that which thou sayest. Work thou for me so that the memory of evil things shall dart from my mouth; let not my head be cut off; let not my brow be slit; and let not my mouth be shut fast by reason of the incantations which thou hast within thee, according to that which thou doest for the Khus through the incantations which they have within themselves. Get thee back and depart at the [sound of] the two speeches which the goddess Isis uttered when thou didst come to cast the recollection of evil things into the mouth of Osiris by the will of Suti his enemy, saying, 'Let thy face be toward the privy parts, and look upon that face which cometh forth from the flame of the Eye of Horus against thee from within the Eye of Tem,' and the calamity of that night which shall consume thee. And Osiris went back, for the abomination of thee was in him; and thou didst go back, for the abomination of him is in thee. I have gone back, for the abomination of thee is in me; and thou shalt go back, for the abomination of me is in thee. Thou wouldst come unto me, but I say that thou shalt not advance to me so that I come to an end, and [I] say then to the divine slaughterers of the god Shu, 'Depart.'"

Of Rescue

[From the Papyrus of Nu (British Museum No. 10,477, sheet 6).]

THE CHAPTER OF NOT LETTING THE SOUL OF NU, TRIUMPHANT, BE CAPTIVE IN THE UNDERWORLD. He saith:

"Hail, thou who art exalted! [Hail,] thou who art adored! O thou mighty one of Souls, thou divine Soul, thou possessor of terrible power, who dost put the fear of thyself into the gods, thou who art crowned upon thy throne of majesty, I pray thee to make a way for the ba (soul), and for the khu, and for the khaibit (shade) of the overseer of the palace, the chancellor-in-chief, Nu, triumphant [and let him be] provided therewith. I am a perfect khu, and I have made [my] way unto the place wherein dwell Rā and Hathor."

IF THIS CHAPTER BE KNOWN [BY THE DECEASED] HE SHALL BE ABLE TO TRANSFORM HIMSELF INTO A KHU PROVIDED [WITH HIS SOUL AND WITH HIS SHADE] IN THE UNDERWORLD, AND HE SHALL NEVER BE HELD CAPTIVE AT ANY DOOR IN AMENTET, IN ENTERING IN OR IN COMING OUT.(58)

Of Opening The Tomb

[From the Papyrus of Nebseni (British Museum No. 9,900, sheet 6).]

THE CHAPTER OF OPENING THE TOMB TO THE SOUL [AND] TO THE SHADE OF OSIRIS the scribe Nebseni, the lord of reverence, born of the lady of the house Mut-restha, triumphant, SO THAT HE MAY COME FORTH BY DAY AND HAVE DOMINION OVER HIS FLEET. [He saith:]

"That which was shut fast hath been opened, that is to say, he that lay down in death [hath been opened]. That which was open hath been shut to my soul through the command of the Eye of Horus, which hath strengthened me and which maketh to stand fast the beauties which are upon the forehead of Rā, whose strides are long as [he] lifteth up [his] legs [in journeying]. I have made for myself a way, my members are mighty and are strong. I am Horus the avenger of his divine father. I am he who bringeth along his divine father, and who bringeth along his mother by means of his sceptre(?). And the way shall be opened unto him who hath gotten dominion over his feet, and he shall see the Great God in the Boat of Rā, [when] souls are counted therein at the bows, and when the years also are counted up. Grant that the Eye of Horus, which maketh the adornments of light to be firm upon the forehead of Rā, may deliver my soul for me, and let there be darkness upon your faces, O ye who would hold fast Osiris. Oh, keep not captive my soul, Oh, keep not ward over my shade, but let a way be opened for my soul [and] for my shade, and let [them] see the Great God in the shrine on the day of the judgment of souls, and let [them] recite the utterances of Osiris, whose habitations are hidden, to those who guard the members of Osiris, and who keep ward over the Khus, and who hold captive the shades of the dead who would work evil against me, so that they shall [not] work evil against me. May a way for thy double (ka) along with thee and along with [thy] soul be prepared by those who keep ward over the members of Osiris, and who hold captive the shades of the dead. Heaven shall [not] keep thee, the earth shall [not] hold thee captive, thou shalt not have thy being with the divine beings who make slaughter, but thou shalt have dominion over thy legs, and thou shalt advance to thy body straightway in the earth [and to] those who belong to the shrine and guard the members of Osiris."

Of Not Sailing To The East

[From the Papyrus of Nu (British Museum No. 10,477, sheet 6).]

THE CHAPTER OF NOT SAILING TO THE EAST IN THE UNDERWORLD. The chancellor-in-chief, Nu, triumphant, saith:

"Hail, phallus of Rā, who departest from thy calamity [which ariseth] through opposition(?), the cycles have been without movement for millions of years. I am stronger than the strong, I am mightier than the mighty. If I sail away or if I be snatched away to the east through the two horns," or (as others say), "if any evil and abominable thing be done unto me at the feast of the devils, the phallus of Rā shall be swallowed up, [along with] the head of Osiris. And behold me, for I journey along over the fields wherein the gods mow down those who make reply unto [their words]; now verily the two horns of the god Khepera shall be thrust aside; and verily pus shall spring into being in the eye of Tem along with corruption if I be kept in restraint, or if I have gone toward the east, or if the feast of devils be made in my presence, or if any malignant wound be inflicted upon me."(59)

Of The Ink-Pot And Palette

[From the Papyrus of Nu (British Museum No. 10,477, sheet 12).]

THE CHAPTER OF PRAYING FOR AN INK-POT AND FOR A PALETTE. The chancellor-in-chief, Nu, triumphant, saith:

"Hail, aged god, who dost behold thy divine father and who art the guardian of the book of Thoth, [behold I have come; I am endowed with glory, I am endowed with strength, I am filled with might, and I am supplied with the books of Thoth], and I have brought [them to enable me] to pass through the god Aker who dwelleth in Set. I have brought the ink-pot and the palette as being the objects which are in the hands of Thoth; hidden is that which is in them. Behold me in the character of a scribe! I have brought the offal of Osiris, and I have written thereon. I have made (i.e., copied) the words of the great and beautiful god each day fairly. O Heru-khuti, thou didst order me and I have made (i.e., copied) what is right and true, and I do bring it unto thee each day."

Of Being Nigh Unto Thoth

[From the Papyrus of Nu (British Museum No. 10,477, sheet 7).]

THE CHAPTER OF BEING NIGH UNTO THOTH. The chancellor-in-chief, Nu, triumphant, saith:

"I am he who sendeth forth terror into the powers of rain and thunder, and I ward off from the great divine lady the attacks of violence. [I have smitten like the god Shāt (i.e., the god of slaughter), and I have poured out libations of cool water like the god Ashu, and I have worked for the great divine lady [to ward off] the attacks of violence], I have made to flourish [my] knife along with the knife which is in the hand of Thoth in the powers of rain and thunder."

Of Being Nigh Unto Thoth

[From the Papyrus of Nu (British Museum No. 10,477, sheets 19 and 20).]

THE CHAPTER OF BEING NIGH UNTO THOTH AND OF GIVING GLORY UNTO A MAN IN THE UNDERWORLD. The chancellor-in-chief, Nu, triumphant, saith:

"I am the god Her-ab-maat-f (i.e., 'he that is within his eye'), and I have come to give right and truth to Rā; I have made Suti to be at peace with me by means of offerings made to the god Aker and to the Tesheru deities, and by [making] reverence unto Seb."

"[The following] words are to be recited in the Sektet boat: [Hail,] sceptre of Anubis, I have made the four Khus who are in the train of the lord of the universe to be at peace with me, and I am the lord of the fields through their decree. I am the divine father Bāh (i.e., the god of the water-flood), and I do away with the thirst of him that keepeth ward over the Lakes. Behold ye me, then, O great gods of majesty who dwell among the Souls of Annu, for I am lifted up over you. I am the god Menkh (i.e., Gracious one) who dwelleth among you. Verily I have cleansed my soul, O great god of majesty, set not before me the evil obstacles which issue from thy mouth, and let not destruction come round about me, or upon me. I have made myself clean in the Lake of making to be at peace, [and in the Lake of] weighing in the balance, and I have bathed myself in Netert-utchat, which is under the holy sycamore tree of heaven. Behold [I am] bathed, [and I have] triumphed [over] all [mine enemies] straightway who come forth and rise up against right and truth. I am right and true in the earth. I, even I, have spoken(?) with my mouth [which is] the power of the Lord, the Only one, Rā the mighty, who liveth upon right and truth. Let not injury be inflicted upon me, [but let me be] clothed on the day of those who go forward(?) to every [good] thing."

Of Bringing A Boat Along In Heaven

[From the Papyrus of Nu (British Museum No. 10,477, sheet 9).]

THE CHAPTER OF BRINGING ALONG A BOAT IN HEAVEN. The chancellor-in-chief, triumphant, saith:

"Hail to thee, O thou Thigh which dwellest in the northern heaven in the Great Lake, which art seen and which diest not. I have stood up over thee when thou didst rise like a god. I have seen thee, and I have not lain down in death; I have stood over thee, and I have risen like a god. I have cackled like a goose, and I have alighted like the hawk by the divine clouds and by the great dew. I have journeyed from the earth to heaven. The god Shu hath [made] me to stand up, the god of Light hath made me to be vigorous by the two sides of the ladder, and the stars which never rest set [me] on [my] way and bring [me] away from slaughter. I bring along with me the things which drive back calamities as I advance over the passage of the god Pen; thou comest, how great art thou, O god Pen! I have come from the Pool of Flame which is in the Sekhet-Sasa (i.e., the Field of Fire). Thou livest in the Pool of Flame in Sekhet-Sasa, and I live upon the staff of the holy [god]. Hail, thou god Kaa, who dost bring those things which are in the boats by the ... I stand up in the boat and I guide myself [over] the water; I have stood up in the boat and the god hath guided me. I have stood up. I have spoken. [I am master of the] crops. I sail round about as I go forward, and the gates which are in Sekhem (Letopolis) are opened unto me, and fields are awarded unto me in the city of Unnu (Hermopolis), and laborers(?) are given unto me together with those of my own flesh and bone."

Of Bringing The Makhent Boat

[From the Papyrus of Nu (British Museum No. 10,477, sheets 21 and 22).]

THE CHAPTER OF BRINGING ALONG A BOAT IN THE UNDERWORLD. The chancellor-in-chief, Nu, triumphant, saith:

"Hail, ye who bring along the boat over the evil back [of Apepi], grant that I may bring the boat along, and coil up [its] ropes in peace, in peace. Come, come, hasten, hasten, for I have come to see my father Osiris, the lord of the ansi garment, who hath gained the mastery with joy of heart. Hail, lord of the rain-storm, thou Male, thou Sailor! Hail, thou who dost sail over the evil back of Apep! Hail, thou that dost bind up heads and dost stablish the bones of the neck when thou comest forth from the knives. Hail, thou who art in charge of the hidden boat, who dost fetter Apep, grant that I may bring along the boat, and that I may coil up the ropes and that I may sail forth therein. This land is baleful, and the stars have overbalanced themselves and have fallen upon their faces therein, and they have not found anything which will help them to ascend again: their path is blocked by the tongue of Rā. Antebu [is] the guide of the two lands. Seb is stablished [through] their rudders. The power which openeth the Disk. The prince of the red beings, I am brought along like him that hath suffered shipwreck; grant that my Khu, my brother, may come to me, and that [I] may set out for the place whereof thou knowest."

"Tell me my name," saith the wood whereat I would anchor; "Lord of the two lands who dwellest in the Shrine," is thy name.

"Tell me my name," saith the Rudder; "Leg of Hāpiu" is thy name.

"Tell me my name," saith the Rope; "Hair with which Anpu (Anubis) finisheth the work of my embalment" is thy name.

"Tell us our name," say the Oar-rests; "Pillars of the underworld" is your name.

"Tell me my name," saith the Hold; "Akar" is thy name.

"Tell me my name," saith the Mast; "He who bringeth back the great lady after she hath gone away" is thy name.

"Tell me my name," saith the Lower deck; "Standard of Ap-uat" is thy name.

"Tell me my name," saith the Upper post; "Throat of Mestha" is thy name.

"Tell me my name," saith the Sail; "Nut" is thy name.

"Tell us our name," say the Pieces of leather; "Ye who are made from the hide of the Mnevis Bull, which was burned by Suti," is your name.

"Tell us our name," say the Paddles; "Fingers of Horus the first-born" is your name.

"Tell me my name," saith the Mātchabet; "The hand of Isis, which wipeth away the blood from the Eye of Horus," is thy name.

"Tell us our names," say the Planks which are in its hulk; "Mesthi, Hāpi, Tuamāutef, Qebh-sennuf, Haqau (i.e., he who leadeth away captive), Thet-em-āua (i.e., he who seizeth by violence), Maa-an-tef (i.e., he who seeth what the father bringeth), and Ari-nef-tchesef (i.e., he who made himself)," are your names.

"Tell us our name," say the Bows; "He who is at the head of his nomes" is your name.

"Tell me my name," saith the Hull; "Mert" is thy name.

"Tell me my name," saith the Rudder; "Aqa" (i.e., true one) is thy name, O thou who shinest from the water, hidden beam(?) is thy name.

"Tell me my name," saith the Keel; "Thigh (or Leg) of Isis, which Rā cut off with the knife to bring blood into the Sektet boat," is thy name.

"Tell me my name," saith the Sailor; "Traveller" is thy name.

"Tell me my name," saith the Wind by which thou art borne along; "The North Wind which cometh from Tem to the nostrils of Khenti-Amenti"(60) is thy name.

"Tell me my name," saith the River, "if thou wouldst travel upon me;" "Those which can be seen," is thy name.

"Tell us our name," say the River-Banks; "Destroyer of the god Au-ā (i.e., he of the specious hand) in the water-house" is thy name.

"Tell me my name," saith the Ground, "if thou wouldst walk upon me;" "The Nose of heaven which proceedeth from the god Utu, who dwelleth in the Sekhet-Aaru, and who cometh forth with rejoicing therefrom," is thy name.

THEN SHALL BE RECITED BEFORE THEM THESE WORDS:

"Hail to you, O ye divine beings with splendid Kas, ye divine lords of things, who exist and who live forever, and [whose] double period of an illimitable number of years is eternity, I have made a way unto you, grant ye me food and sepulchral meals for my mouth, [and grant that] I may speak therewith, and that the goddess Isis [may give me] loaves and cakes in the presence of the great god. I know the great god before whose nostrils ye place tchefau food, and his name is Thekem; both when he maketh his way from the eastern horizon of heaven and when he journeyeth into the western horizon of heaven may his journey be my journey, and his going forth my going forth. Let me not be destroyed at the Mesqet chamber, and let not the devils gain dominion over my members. I have my cakes in the city of Pe, and I have my ale in the city of Tepu, and let the offerings [which are given unto you] be given unto me this day. Let my offerings be wheat and barley; let my offerings be ānti unguent and linen garments; let my offerings be for life, strength, and health: let my offerings be a coming forth by day in any form whatsoever in which it may please me to appear in Sekhet-Aarru."

IF THIS CHAPTER BE KNOWN [BY THE DECEASED] HE SHALL COME FORTH INTO SEKHET-AARRU, AND BREAD, AND WINE, AND CAKES SHALL BE GIVEN UNTO HIM AT THE ALTAR OF THE GREAT GOD, AND FIELDS, AND AN ESTATE [SOWN] WITH WHEAT AND BARLEY, WHICH THE FOLLOWERS OF HORUS SHALL REAP FOR HIM. AND HE SHALL EAT OF THAT WHEAT AND BARLEY, AND HIS LIMBS SHALL BE NOURISHED THEREWITH, AND HIS BODY SHALL BE LIKE UNTO THE BODIES OF THE GODS, AND HE SHALL COME FORTH INTO SEKHET-AARRU IN ANY FORM WHATSOEVER HE PLEASETH, AND HE SHALL APPEAR THEREIN REGULARLY AND CONTINUALLY.

Of Entering The Boat Of Ra

[From the Papyrus of Nu (British Museum No. 10,477, sheets 27 and 28).]

THE BOOK OF MAKING PERFECT THE KHU AND OF CAUSING HIM TO GO FORTH INTO THE BOAT OF RA ALONG WITH THOSE WHO ARE IN HIS FOLLOWING(?). The overseer of the palace, the chancellor-in-chief, Nu, triumphant, saith:

"I have brought the divine Bennu to the east, and Osiris to the city of Tattu. I have opened the treasure-houses of the god Hāp, I have made clean the roads of the Disk, and I have drawn the god Sekeri along upon his sledge. The mighty and divine Lady hath made me strong at her hour. I have praised and glorified the Disk, and I have united myself unto the divine apes who sing at the dawn, and I am a divine Being among them. I have made myself a counterpart of the goddess Isis, and her power (Khu) hath made me strong. I have tied up the rope, I have driven back Apep, I have made him to walk backward. Rā hath stretched out to me both his hands, and his mariners have not repulsed me; my strength is the strength of the Utchat, and the strength of the Utchat is my strength. If the overseer of the house, the chancellor-in-chief, Nu, triumphant, be separated [from the boat of Rā], then shall he (i.e., Rā) be separated from the Egg and from the Abtu fish."

[THIS CHAPTER] SHALL BE RECITED OVER THE DESIGN WHICH HATH BEEN DRAWN ABOVE, AND IT SHALL BE WRITTEN UPON PAPYRUS WHICH HATH NOT BEEN WRITTEN UPON, WITH [INK MADE OF] GRAINS OF GREEN ABUT MIXED WITH ANTI WATER, AND THE PAPYRUS SHALL BE PLACED ON THE BREAST OF THE DECEASED; IT SHALL NOT ENTER IN TO (I.E., TOUCH) HIS MEMBERS. IF THIS BE DONE FOR ANY DECEASED PERSON HE SHALL GO FORTH INTO THE BOAT OF RA IN THE COURSE OF THE DAY EVERY DAY, AND THE GOD THOTH SHALL TAKE ACCOUNT OF HIM AS HE COMETH FORTH FROM AND GOETH IN THE COURSE OF THE DAY EVERY DAY, REGULARLY AND CONTINUALLY, [INTO THE BOAT OF RA] AS A PERFECT KHU. AND HE SHALL SET UP THE TET AND SHALL STABLISH THE BUCKLE, AND SHALL SAIL ABOUT WITH RA INTO ANY PLACE HE WISHETH.

Of Protecting The Boat Of Ra

[From the Papyrus of Nu (British Museum No. 10,477, sheet 27).]

[THE CHAPTER OF PROTECTING THE BOAT OF RA.](61)

"O thou that cleavest the water as thou comest forth from the stream and dost sit upon thy place in thy boat, sit thou upon thy place in thy boat as thou goest forth to thy station of yesterday, and do thou join the Osiris, the overseer of the palace, the chancellor-in-chief, Nu, triumphant, the perfect Khu, unto thy mariners, and let thy strength be his strength. Hail, Rā, in thy name of Rā, if thou dost pass by the eye of seven cubits, which hath a pupil of three cubits, then verily do thou strengthen the Osiris, Nu, triumphant, the perfect Khu, [and let him be among] thy mariners, and let thy strength be his strength. Hail, Rā, in thy name of Rā, if thou dost pass by those who are overturned in death then verily do thou make the Osiris, Nu, triumphant, the perfect soul, to stand up upon his feet, and may thy strength be his strength. Hail, Rā, in thy name of Rā, if the hidden things of the underworld are opened unto thee and thou dost gratify(?) the heart of the cycle of thy gods, then verily do thou grant joy of heart unto the chancellor-in-chief, Nu, triumphant, and let thy strength be his strength. Thy members, O Rā, are established by (this) Chapter(?)."

[THIS CHAPTER] SHALL BE RECITED OVER A BANDLET OF THE FINE LINEN OF KINGS [UPON WHICH] IT HATH BEEN WRITTEN WITH ANTI, WHICH SHALL BE LAID UPON THE NECK OF THE PERFECT KHU ON THE DAY OF THE BURIAL. IF THIS AMULET BE LAID UPON HIS NECK HE SHALL DO EVERYTHING WHICH HE DESIRETH TO DO EVEN LIKE THE GODS; AND HE SHALL JOIN HIMSELF UNTO THE FOLLOWERS OF HORUS; AND HE SHALL BE STABLISHED AS A STAR FACE TO FACE WITH SEPTET (SOTHIS); AND HIS CORRUPTIBLE BODY SHALL BE AS A GOD ALONG WITH HIS KINSFOLK FOREVER; AND THE GODDESS MENQET SHALL MAKE PLANTS TO GERMINATE UPON HIS BODY; AND THE MAJESTY OF THE GOD THOTH LOVINGLY SHALL MAKE THE LIGHT TO REST UPON HIS CORRUPTIBLE BODY AT WILL, EVEN AS HE DID FOR THE MAJESTY OF THE KING OF THE NORTH AND OF THE SOUTH, THE GOD OSIRIS, TRIUMPHANT.

Of Going Into The Boat Of Ra

[From the Papyrus of Nu (British Museum No. 10,477, sheet 28).]

THE CHAPTER OF GOING INTO THE BOAT OF RA. The chancellor-in-chief, Nu, triumphant, saith:

"Hail, thou Great God who art in thy boat, bring thou me into thy boat. [I have come forward to thy steps], let me be the director of thy journeyings and let me be among those who belong to thee and who are among the stars which never rest. The things which are an abomination unto thee and the things which are an abomination unto me I will not eat, that which is an abomination unto me, that which is an abomination unto me is filth and I will not eat thereof; but sepulchral offerings and holy food [will I eat], and I shall not be overthrown thereby. I will not draw nigh unto filth with my hands, and I will not walk thereon with my sandals, because my bread [is made] of white barley, and my ale [is made] of red barley; and behold, the Sektet boat and the Atet boat have brought these things and have laid the gifts(?) of the lands upon the altar of the Souls of Annu. Hymns of praise be to thee, O Ur-arit-s, as thou travellest through heaven! Let there be food [for thee], O dweller in the city of Teni (This), and when the dogs gather together let me not suffer harm. I myself have come, and I have delivered the god from the things which have been inflicted upon him, and from the grievous sickness of the body of the arm, and of the leg. I have come and I have spit upon the body, I have bound up the arm, and I have made the leg to walk. [I have] entered [the boat] and [I] sail round about by the command of Rā."

Of Knowing The Souls Of The East

[From the Papyrus of Nu (British Museum No. 10,477, sheet 12).]

THE CHAPTER OF KNOWING THE SOULS OF THE EAST. The chancellor-in-chief, Nu, triumphant, saith:

"I, even I, know the eastern gate of heaven—know its southern part is at the Lake of Kharu and its northern part is at the canal of the geese—whereout Rā cometh with winds which make him to advance. I am he who is concerned with the tackle(?) [which is] in the divine bark, I am the sailor who ceaseth not in the boat of Rā. I, even I, know the two sycamores of turquoise between which Rā showeth himself when he strideth forward over the supports of Shu(62) toward the gate of the lord of the East through which Rā cometh forth. I, even I, know the Sektet-Aarru of Rā, the walls of which are of iron. The height of the wheat therein is five cubits, of the ears thereof two cubits, and of the stalks thereof three cubits. The barley therein is [in height] seven cubits, the ears thereof are three cubits, and the stalks thereof are four cubits. And behold, the Khus, each one of whom therein is nine cubits in height, reap it near the divine Souls of the East. I, even I, know the divine Souls of the East, that is to say, Heru-khuti (Harmachis), and the Calf of the goddess Khera, and the Morning Star(63) [daily. A divine city hath been built for me, I know it, and I know the name thereof; 'Sekhet-Aarru' is its name]."(64)

Of Sekhet-Hetepet

[From the Papyrus of Nebseni (British Museum No. 9,900, sheet 17).]

HERE BEGIN THE CHAPTERS OF SEKHET-HETEPET, AND THE CHAPTERS OF COMING FORTH BY DAY; OF GOING INTO AND OF COMING OUT FROM THE UNDERWORLD; OF COMING TO SEKHET-AARU; OF BEING IN SEKHET-HETEPET, THE MIGHTY LAND, THE LADY OF WINDS; OF HAVING POWER THERE; OF BECOMING A KHU THERE; OF PLOUGHING THERE; OF REAPING THERE; OF EATING THERE; OF DRINKING THERE; OF MAKING LOVE THERE; AND OF DOING EVERYTHING EVEN AS A MAN DOETH UPON EARTH. Behold the scribe and artist of the Temple of Ptah, Nebseni, who saith:

"Set hath taken possession of Horus, who looked with the two eyes upon the building(?) round Sekhet-hetep, but I have unfettered Horus [and taken him from] Set, and Set hath opened the ways of the two eyes [which are] in heaven. Set hath cast(?) his moisture to the winds upon the soul [that hath] his day (or his eye) and who dwelleth in the city of Mert, and he hath delivered the interior of the body of Horus from the gods of Akert. Behold me now, for I make this mighty boat to travel over the Lake of Hetep, and I brought it away with might from the palace of Shu; the domain of his stars groweth young and reneweth its former strength. I have brought the boat into the lakes thereof so that I may come forth into the cities thereof, and I have sailed into their divine city Hetep. And behold, it is because I, even I, am at peace with his seasons, and with his guidance, and with his territory, and with the company of the gods who are his first-born. He maketh the two divine fighters (i.e., Horus and Set) to be at peace with those who watch over the living ones whom he hath created in fair form, and he bringeth peace [with him]; he maketh the two divine fighters to be at peace with those who watch over them. He cutteth off the hair from the divine fighters, he driveth away storm from the helpless, and he keepeth away harm from the Khus. Let me gain dominion within that Field, for I know it, and I have sailed among its lakes so that I might come into its cities. My mouth is strong; and I am equipped [with weapons to use] against the Khus; let them not have dominion over me. Let me be rewarded with thy fields, O thou god Hetep; that which is thy wish, shalt thou do, O lord of the winds. May I become a khu therein, may I eat therein, may I drink therein, may I plough therein, may I reap therein, may I fight therein, may I make love therein, may my words be mighty therein, may I never be in a state of servitude therein, but may I be in authority therein. Thou hast made strong(?) the mouth and the throat(?) of the god Hetep; Qetetbu is its(?) name. He is stablished upon the watery supports(?) of the god Shu, and is linked unto the pleasant things of Rā. He is the divider of years, he is hidden of mouth, his mouth is silent, that which he uttereth is secret, he fulfilleth eternity and taketh possession of everlastingness of existence as Hetep, the lord Hetep. The god Horus maketh himself to be strong like unto the Hawk which is one thousand cubits in length and two thousand [cubits in width] in life; he hath equipments with him, and he journeyeth on and cometh where the seat of his heart wisheth in the Pools thereof and in the cities thereof. He was begotten in the birth-chamber of the god of the city, he hath offerings [made unto him] of the food of the god of the city, he performeth that which it is meet to do therein, and the union thereof, in the matter of everything of the birth-chamber of the divine city. When [he] setteth in life like crystal he performeth everything therein, and these things are like unto the things which are done in the Lake of double Fire, wherein there is none that rejoiceth, and wherein are all manner of evil things. The god Hetep goeth in, and cometh out, and goeth backward [in] that Field which gathereth together all manner of things for the birth-chamber of the god of the city. When he setteth in life like crystal he performeth all manner of things therein which are like unto the things which are done in the Lake of double Fire, wherein there is none that rejoiceth, and wherein are no evil things whatsoever. [Let me] live with the god Hetep, clothed and not despoiled by the lords of the north(?), and may the lords of divine things bring food unto me; may he make me to go forward and may I come forth, and may he bring my power to me there, and may I receive it, and may my equipment be from the god Hetep. May I gain the mastery over the great and mighty word which is in my body in this my place, and by it I will remember and I will forget. Let me go forward on my journey, and let me plough. I am at peace in the divine city,(65) and I know the waters, cities, nomes, and lakes which are in Sekhet-hetep. I exist therein, I am strong therein, I become a khu therein, I eat therein, I sow seed therein, I reap the harvest therein, I plough therein, I make love therein, I am at peace with the god Hetep therein. Behold I scatter seed therein, I sail about among its Lakes and I come forward to the cities thereof, O divine Hetep. Behold, my mouth is equipped with my horns [for teeth], grant me an overflowing supply of the food whereon the kas and khus [live]. I have passed the judgment of Shu upon him that knoweth him, so that I may go forth to the cities thereof, and may sail about among its lakes and may walk about in Sekhet-hetep; and behold, Rā is in heaven, and behold, the god Hetep is its double offering. I have come onward to its land, I have put on my girdle(?), I have come forth so that the gifts which are about to be given unto me may be given, I have made gladness for myself. I have laid hold upon my strength which the god Hetep hath greatly increased for me. O Unen-em-hetep,(66) I have entered in to thee and my soul followeth after me, and my divine food is upon both my hands, O Lady of the two lands,(67) who stablishest my word whereby I remember and forget; I would live without injury, without any injury [being done] unto me, oh, grant to me, oh, do thou grant to me, joy of heart. Make thou me to be at peace, bind thou up my sinews and muscles, and make me to receive the air. O Un[en]-em-hetep, thou Lady of the winds, I have entered in to thee and I have opened (i.e., shown) my head. Rā falleth asleep, but I am awake, and there is the goddess Hast at the gate of heaven by night. Obstacles have been set before me, but I have gathered together what he hath emitted. I am in my city. O Nut-urt,(68) I have entered into thee and I have counted my harvest, and I go forward to Uakh.(69) I am the Bull enveloped in turquoise, the lord of the Field of the Bull, the lord of the divine speech of the goddess Septet (Sothis) at her hours. O Uakh, I have entered into thee, I have eaten my bread, I have gotten the mastery over choice pieces of the flesh of oxen and of feathered fowl, and the birds of Shu have been given unto me; I follow after the gods and [I come after] the divine kas. O Tchefet,(70) I have entered in to thee. I array myself in apparel, and I gird myself with the sa garment of Rā; now behold, [he is] in heaven, and those who dwell therein follow Rā, and [I] follow Rā in heaven. O Unen-em-hetep, lord of the two lands, I have entered in to thee, and I have plunged into the lakes of Tchesert; behold me, for all filth hath departed from me. The Great God groweth therein, and behold, I have found [food therein]; I have snared feathered fowl and I feed upon the finest [of them]. O Qenqentet,(71) I have entered into thee, and I have seen the Osiris [my father], and I have gazed upon my mother, and I have made love. I have caught the worms and serpents, and I am delivered. And I know the name of the god who is opposite to the goddess Tchesert, and who hath straight hair and is equipped with two horns; he reapeth, and I both plough and reap. O Hast, I have entered in to thee, I have driven back those who would come to the turquoise [sky], and I have followed the winds of the company of the gods. The Great God hath given my head unto me, and he who hath bound on me my head is the Mighty one who hath turquoise(?) eyes, namely, Ari-en-ab-f (i.e., he doeth as he pleaseth). O Usert,(72) I have come into thee at the head of the house wherein divine food is brought for me. O Smam,(73) I have come into thee. My heart watcheth, my head is equipped with the white crown, I am led into celestial regions, and I make to flourish terrestrial objects, and there is joy of heart for the Bull, and for celestial beings, and for the company of the gods. I am the god who is the Bull, the lord of the gods, as he goeth forth from the turquoise [sky]. O divine nome of wheat and barley, I have come unto thee, I have come forward to thee and I have taken up that which followeth me, namely, the best of the libations of the company of the gods. I have tied up my boat in the celestial lakes, I have lifted up the post at which to anchor, I have recited the prescribed words with my voice, and I have ascribed praises unto the gods who dwell in Sekhet-hetep."

Of Knowing The Souls Of Pe

[From the Papyrus of Nu (British Museum No. 10,477, sheet 18).]

ANOTHER CHAPTER OF KNOWING THE SOULS OF PE. The overseer of the palace, the chancellor-in-chief, Nu, triumphant, saith:

"[Hail,] Khat, who dwellest in Khat, in Anpet,(74) and in the nome of Khat! [Hail,] ye goddesses of the chase who dwell in the city of Pe, ye celestial lands(?), ye stars, and ye divine beings, who give cakes and ale(?), do ye know for what reason the city of Pe hath been given unto Horus? I, even I, know though ye know it not. Behold, Rā gave the city unto him in return for the injury in his eye, for which cause Rā said to Horus, 'Let me see what is coming to pass in thine eye,' and forthwith he looked thereat. Then Rā said to Horus, 'Look at that black pig,' and he looked, and straightway an injury was done unto his eye, [namely,] a mighty storm [took place]. Then said Horus unto Rā, 'Verily, my eye seems as if it were an eye upon which Suti had inflicted a blow;' [and thus saying] he ate his heart.(75) Then said Rā to those gods, 'Place ye him in his chamber, and he shall do well.' Now the black pig was Suti who had transformed himself into a black pig, and he it was who had aimed the blow of fire which was in the eye of Horus. Then said Rā unto those gods, 'The pig is an abominable thing unto Horus; oh, but he shall do well although the pig is an abomination unto him.' Then the company of the gods, who were among the divine followers of Horus when he existed in the form of his own child, said, 'Let sacrifices be made [to the gods] of his bulls, and of his goats, and of his pigs.' Now the father of Mesthi, Hāpi, Tuamāutef and Qebhsennuf is Horus, and their mother is Isis. Then said Horus to Rā, 'Give me two divine brethren in the city of Pe and two divine brethren in the city of Nekhen, who [have sprung] from my body and who shall be with me in the guise of everlasting judges, then shall the earth blossom and thunder-clouds and rain be blotted out.' And the name of Horus became 'Her-uatch-f' (i.e., Prince of his emerald stone). I, even I, know the Souls of Pe, namely, Horus, Mesthi, and Hāpi."

Of Knowing The Souls Of Nekhen

[From the Papyrus of Nu (British Museum No. 10,477, sheet 18).]

THE CHAPTER OF KNOWING THE SOULS OF NEKHEN. The overseer of the palace, the chancellor-in-chief, Nu, triumphant, saith:

"I know the hidden things of the city of Nekhen, that is to say, the things which the mother of Horus did for him, and how she [made her voice to go forth] over the waters, saying, 'Speak ye unto me concerning the judgment which is upon me, [and shew me] the path behind you, and let me discover [it];' and how Rā said, 'This son of Isis hath perished;' and what the mother of Horus did for him [when] she cried out, saying, 'Sebek, the lord of the papyrus swamp, shall be brought to us.' [And Sebek] fished for them and he found them, and the mother of Horus made them to grow in the places to which they belonged. Then Sebek, the lord of his papyrus swamp, said, 'I went and I found the place where they had passed with my fingers on the edge of the waters, and I enclosed them in [my] net: and strong was that net.' And Rā said, 'So then, there are fish with the god Sebek, and [he] hath found the hands and arms of Horus for him in the land of fish;' and [that] land became the land of the city of Remu (i.e., Fish). And Rā said, 'A land of the pool, a land of the pool to this net.' Then were the hands of Horus brought to him at the uncovering of his face at the festivals of the month and half month in the Land of Remu. And Rā said, 'I give the city of Nekhen to Horus for the habitation of his two arms and hands, and his face shall be uncovered before his two hands and arms in the city of Nekhen; and I give into his power the slaughtered beings who are in them at the festivals of the month and half month.' Then Horus said, 'Let me carry off Tuamāutef and Qebhsennuf, and let them watch over my body; and if they are allowed to be there, then shall they be subservient to the god of the city of Nekhen.' And Rā said, 'It shall be granted unto thee there and in the city, of Senket (i.e., Sati), and there shall be done for them what hath been done for those who dwell in the city of Nekhen, and verily they shall be with thee.' And Horus said, 'They have been with thee and [now] they shall be with me, and shall hearken unto the god Suti when he calleth upon the Souls of Nekhen.' Grant to me [that I, even I, may pass on to the Souls of Nekhen, and that I may unloose the bonds of Horus]. I, even I, know the Souls of Nekhen, namely, Horus, Tuamāutef, and Qebhsennuf."

Of Knowing The Souls Of Khemennu

[From the Papyrus of Nebseni (British Museum No. 9,900, sheet 7).]

THE CHAPTER OF KNOWING THE SOULS OF KHEMENNU (Hermopolis).

"The goddess Maāt is carried by the arm at the shining of the goddess Neith in the city of Mentchat, and at the shining of the Eye when it is weighed. I am carried over by it and I know what it bringeth from the city of Kesi,(76) and I will neither declare it unto men nor tell it unto the gods. I have come, being the envoy of Rā, to stablish Maāt upon the arm at the shining of Neith in the city of Mentchat and to adjudge the eye to him that shall scrutinize it. I have come as a power through the knowledge of the Souls of Khemennu (Hermopolis) who love to know what ye love. I know Maāt, which hath germinated, and hath become strong, and hath been judged, and I have joy in passing judgment upon the things which are to be judged. Homage to you, O ye Souls of Khemennu, I, even I, know the things which are unknown on the festivals of the month and half month. Rā knoweth the hidden things of the night, and know ye that it is Thoth who hath made me to have knowledge. Homage to you, O ye Souls of Khemennu, since I know you each day."

Of Coming Forth From Heaven

[From the Papyrus of Nu (British Museum No. 10,477, sheet 18).]

THE CHAPTER OF COMING FORTH FROM HEAVEN, AND OF MAKING A WAY THROUGH THE AMMEHET, AND OF KNOWING THE SOULS OF ANNU (HELIOPOLIS). The chancellor-in-chief, Nu, triumphant, saith:

"I have passed the day since yesterday among the great divine beings, and I have come into being along with the god Khepera. [My] face is uncovered before the Eye, the only One, and the orbit of the night hath been opened. I am a divine being among you. I know the Souls of Annu. Shall not the god Ur-ma pass over it as [he] journeyeth forward with vigor? Have I not overcome(?), and have I not spoken to the gods? Behold, he that is the heir of Annu hath been destroyed. I, even I, know for what reason was made the lock of hair of the Man. Rā spake unto the god Ami-haf, and an injury was done unto his mouth, that is to say, he was wounded in [that] mouth. And Rā spake unto the god Ami-haf, saying, 'O heir of men, receive [thy] harpoon;' and the harpoon-house came into being. Behold, O god Ami-haf, two divine brethren have come into being, [that is to say], Senti-Rā came into being, and Setem-ansi-f came into being. And his hand stayed not, and he made his form into that of a woman with a lock of hair which became the divine lock in Annu, and which became the strong and mighty one in this temple; and it became the strong one of Annu, and it became the heir of the heir of Ur-maat-f (i.e., the mighty one of the two eyes), and it became before him the god Urma of Annu. I know the Souls of Annu, namely, Rā, Shu, and Tefnut."

Of Knowing The Souls Of Khemennu

[From the Papyrus of Nu (British Museum No. 10,477, sheet 18).]

ANOTHER CHAPTER OF KNOWING THE SOULS OF KHEMENNU (HERMOPOLIS). The chancellor-in-chief, Nu, triumphant, saith:

"The goddess Neith shineth in Matchat, and the goddess Maāt is carried by the arm of him who eateth the Eye, and who is its divine judge, and the Sem priest carrieth me over upon it. I will not declare it unto men, and I will not tell it unto the gods; I will not declare it unto men, and I will not tell it unto the gods. I have entered in being an ignorant man, and I have seen the hidden things. Homage to you, O ye gods who dwell in Khemennu, ye know me even as I know the goddess Neith, and [ye give] to the Eye the growth which endureth. There is joy [to me] at the judgment of the things which are to be judged. I, even I, know the Souls of Annu; they are great at the festival of the month, and are little at the festival of the half month. They are Thoth the Hidden one, and Sa, and Tem."

IF THIS CHAPTER BE KNOWN [BY THE DECEASED] OFFAL SHALL BE AN ABOMINATION UNTO HIM, AND HE SHALL NOT DRINK FILTHY WATER.

Of Receiving Paths

[From the Papyrus of Nu (British Museum No. 10,477, sheet 9).]

THE CHAPTER OF RECEIVING PATHS [WHEREON TO WALK] IN RE-STAU. The chancellor-in-chief, Nu, triumphant, saith:

"The paths which are above me [lead] to Re-stau. I am he who is girt about with his girdle and who cometh forth from the [goddess of] the Ureret crown. I have come, and I have stablished things in Abtu (Abydos), and I have opened out paths in Re-stau. The god Osiris hath eased my pains. I am he who maketh the waters to come into being, and who setteth his throne [thereon], and who maketh his path through the funeral valley and through the Great Lake. I have made my path, and indeed I am [Osiris].
"[Osiris was victorious over his enemies, and the Osiris Nebqet is victorious over his enemies. He hath become as one of yourselves, [O ye gods], his protector is the Lord of eternity, he walketh even as ye walk, he standeth even as ye stand, he sitteth even as ye sit, and he talketh even as ye talk in the presence of the Great God, the Lord of Amentet.]"(77)

Of Coming Forth From Re-Stau

[From the Papyrus of Nu (British Museum No. 10,477, sheet 9).]

THE CHAPTER OF COMING FORTH FROM RE-STAU. The chancellor-in-chief, Nu, triumphant, saith:

"I was born in Re-stau, and splendor hath been given unto me by those who dwell in their spiritual bodies (sāhu) in the habitation where libations are made unto Osiris. The divine ministers who are in Re-stau shall receive [me] when Osiris is led into the twofold funeral region of Osiris; oh, let me be a divine being whom they shall lead into the twofold funeral region of Osiris."

Of Coming Forth From Re-Stau

[From the Papyrus of Nu (British Museum No. 10,477, sheet 9).]

THE CHAPTER OF COMING FORTH FROM RE-STAU.(78) The chancellor-in-chief, Nu, triumphant, saith:

"I am the Great God who maketh his light. I have come to thee, O Osiris, and I offer praise unto thee. [I am] pure from the issues which are carried away from thee. Thy name is made in Re-stau, and thy power is in Abtu (Abydos). Thou art raised up, then, O Osiris, and thou goest round about through heaven with Rā, and thou lookest upon the generations of men, O thou One who circlest, thou Rā. Behold, verily, I have said unto thee, O Osiris, 'I am the spiritual body of the God,' and I say, 'Let it come to pass that I shall never be repulsed before thee, O Osiris.' "

The following is the chapter in a fuller form:(79)

THE CHAPTER OF KNOWING THE NAME OF OSIRIS AND OF ENTERING INTO AND OF GOING OUT FROM RE-STAU [IN ALL THE FORMS WHEREIN HE WILLETH TO COME FORTH].(80) The scribe Mes-em-neter, triumphant, saith:

"I am the Great Name who maketh his light. I have come to thee, O Osiris, and I offer praise unto thee. I am pure from the issues which are carried away from thee. [Thy] name hath been made in Re-stau when it hath fallen therein. Homage to thee, O Osiris, in thy strength and in thy power, thou hast obtained the mastery in Re-stau. Thou art raised up, O Osiris, in thy might and in thy power, thou art raised up, O Osiris, and thy might is in Re-stau, and thy power is in Abtu (Abydos). Thou goest round about through heaven, and thou sailest before Rā, and thou lookest upon the generations of men, O thou Being who circlest, thou Rā. Behold, verily, I have said unto thee, O Osiris, 'I am the spiritual body of the God,' and I say, 'Let it come to pass that I shall never be repulsed before thee, O Osiris.' "

Of Going About In The Underworld

[From the Papyrus of Nu (British Museum No. 10,477, sheet 9).]

THE CHAPTER OF GOING IN AFTER COMING FORTH [FROM THE UNDERWORLD]. The overseer of the palace, the chancellor-in-chief, Nu, triumphant, saith:

"Open unto me? Who then art thou? Whither goest thou? What is thy name? I am one of you, 'Assembler of Souls' is the name of my boat; 'Making the hair to stand on end' is the name of the oars; 'Watchful one' is the name of its bows; 'Evil is it' is the name of the rudder; 'Steering straight for the middle' is the name of the Mātchabet; so likewise [the boat] is a type of my sailing onward to the pool. Let there be given unto me vessels of milk, together with cakes, and loaves of bread, and cups of drink, and pieces of meat in the Temple of Anpu," or (as others say), "Grant thou me [these things] wholly. Let it be so done unto me that I may enter in like a hawk, and that I may come forth like the Bennu bird, [and like] the Morning Star. Let me make [my] path so that [I] may go in peace into the beautiful Amentet, and let the Lake of Osiris be mine. Let me make my path, and let me enter in, and let me adore Osiris, the Lord of life."

Of Entering Into The Great House

From the Papyrus of Nu (British Museum No. 10,477, sheet 10).]

THE CHAPTER OF ENTERING INTO THE GREAT HOUSE. The overseer of the palace, the chancellor-in-chief, Nu, triumphant, saith:

"Homage to thee, O Thoth. I am Thoth, who have weighed the two divine Fighters (i.e., Horus and Set), I have destroyed their warfare and I have diminished their wailings. I have delivered the Atu fish in his turning back, and I have performed that which thou didst order concerning him, and afterward I lay down within my eye. [I am he who hath been without opposition. I have come; do thou look upon me in the Temple of Nem-hra (or Uhem-hra).] I give commands in the words of the divine aged ones, and, moreover, I guide for thee the lesser deities."

Of Entering The Presence

[From the Papyrus of Nu (British Museum No. 10,477, sheet 10).]

THE CHAPTER OF GOING INTO THE PRESENCE OF THE DIVINE SOVEREIGN PRINCES OF OSIRIS. The overseer of the palace, the chancellor-in-chief, Nu, triumphant, saith:

"My soul hath built for me a habitation in the city of Tattu; I sow seed in the city of Pe, and I plough my field with my laborers(?), and for this reason my palm tree is like Amsu. That which is an abomination unto me, that which is an abomination unto me I shall not eat. That which is an abomination unto me, that which is an abomination unto me is filth. I shall not eat thereof; by sepulchral meals and food I shall not be destroyed. [The abominable thing] I shall not take into my hands, I shall not walk upon it in my sandals, because my cakes are [made] of white grain, and my ale is [made] of red grain, and behold, the Sektet boat and the Mātet boat bring them to me, and I eat [thereof] under the branches of [the trees], the beautiful arms [of which] I know. Oh, let splendor be prepared for me with the white crown which is lifted up upon me by the uræi-goddesses. Hail, thou guardian of the divine doors of the god Sehetep-taui (i.e., 'he who maketh the world to be at peace'), bring [thou] to me that of which they make sepulchral meals; grant thou that I may lift up the branches(?). May the god of light open to me his arms, and may the company of the gods keep silence while the denizens of heaven talk with the chancellor-in-chief, Nu, triumphant. I am the leader of the hearts of the gods which strengthen me, and I am a mighty one among the divine beings. If any god or any goddess shall come forth against me he shall be judged by the ancestors of the year who live upon hearts and who make(?) cakes(?) for me, and Osiris shall devour him at [his] coming forth from Abtu (Abydos). He shall be judged by the ancestors of Rā, and he shall be judged by the God of Light who clotheth heaven among the divine princes. I shall have bread in my mouth at stated seasons, and I shall enter in before the gods Ahiu. He shall speak with me, and I shall speak with the followers of the gods. I shall speak with the Disk and I shall speak with the denizens of heaven. I shall put the terror of myself into the blackness of night which is in the goddess Meh-urt, [who is near] him that dwelleth in might. And behold, I shall be there with Osiris. My condition of completeness shall be his condition of completeness among the divine princes. I shall speak unto him [with] the words of men, and he shall repeat unto me the words of the gods. A khu who is equipped [with power] shall come.(81) I am a khu who is equipped [with power]; I am equipped [with the power] of all the khus, [being the form of the Sāhu (i.e., spiritual bodies) of Annu, Tattu, Suten-henen, Abtu, Apu, and Sennu.(82) The Osiris Auf-ānkh is victorious over every god and every goddess who are hidden in Neter-khertet]."(83)

The Introduction To Maati

[From the Papyrus of Ani (British Museum No. 10,470, sheet 30).]

THE CHAPTER OF ENTERING INTO THE HALL OF DOUBLE MAĀTI; A HYMN OF PRAISE TO OSIRIS, THE GOVERNOR OF AMENTET. Osiris, the scribe Ani, triumphant, saith:

"I have come, and [I] have drawn nigh to see thy beauties; my hands [are raised] in adoration of thy name 'Right and Truth.' I came and I drew nigh unto [the place where] the acacia-tree groweth not, where the tree thick with leaves existeth not, and where the ground yieldeth neither herb nor grass. Then I entered into the hidden place, and I spake with the god Set, and my protector(?) advanced to me, and his face was clothed (or covered), and [he] fell upon the hidden things. He entered into the Temple of Osiris, and he looked upon the hidden things which were therein; and the sovereign chiefs of the pylons [were] in the form of khus. And the god Anpu spake [to those who were on] both sides of him with the speech of a man [as he] came from Ta-mera;(84) he knoweth our paths and our cities. I make offerings(?), and I smell the odor of him as if he were one among you, and I say unto him, I am Osiris, the scribe Ani, triumphant in peace, triumphant! I have come, and (I) have drawn nigh to see the great gods, and I feed upon the offerings which are among their food. I have been to the borders [of the territory of] Ba-neb-Tettet (i.e., the 'Soul, the lord of Tattu,' or Osiris), and he hath caused me to come forth like a Bennu bird, and to utter words. I have been in the water of the stream, and I have made offerings of incense. I have guided myself to the Shentet tree of the [divine] children. I have been in Abu (or Abu, i.e., Elephantine[?]) in the Temple of the goddess Satet. I have submerged the boat of mine enemies [while] I myself have sailed over the Lake in the Neshmet boat. I have seen the Sāhu (i.e., the spiritual bodies) [in] the city of Qem-ur. I have been in the city of Tattu, and I have brought myself to silence [therein]. I have caused the god to have the mastery over his two feet. I have been in the Temple of Tep-tu-f (i.e., 'he that is on his hill,' or Anubis), and I have seen him that is lord of the divine temple. I have entered into the Temple of Osiris, and I have arrayed myself in the apparel of him that is therein. I have entered into Re-stau, and I have seen the hidden things which are therein. I was shrouded [therein], but I found a way for myself. I have gone into the city of An-aarret-f (i.e., the place where nothing groweth), and I covered my nakedness with the garments which were therein. There was given unto me the ānti unguent [such as] women [use], along with the powder of human beings. Verily Sut(?) hath spoken unto me the things which concern himself, and I said, 'Let thy weighing be in(?) us.' "

"The Majesty of the god Anpu saith, 'Knowest thou the name of this door so as to declare it unto me?' And Osiris, the scribe Ani, triumphant in peace, triumphant! saith, 'Destroyer of the god Shu' is the name of this door. The Majesty of the god Anpu saith, 'Knowest thou the name of the upper leaf and of the lower leaf?' 'Lord of Maāt upon his two feet' is the name of the upper leaf, and 'Lord of twofold strength, the subduer of cattle,' [is the name of the lower leaf. The Majesty of the god Anpu saith], 'Since thou knowest pass on, O Osiris the scribe, the teller of the divine offerings of all the gods of Thebes, Ani, triumphant, the lord of reverence.' "

The Introduction To Maati

[From the Papyrus of Nu (British Museum No. 10477, sheet 22).]

[THE FOLLOWING] SHALL BE SAID WHEN THE OVERSEER OF THE PALACE, THE CHANCELLOR-IN-CHIEF, NU, TRIUMPHANT, COMETH FORTH INTO THE HALL OF DOUBLE MAĀTI(85) SO THAT HE MAY BE SEPARATED FROM EVERY SIN WHICH HE HATH DONE AND MAY BEHOLD THE FACES OF THE GODS. The Osiris Nu, triumphant, saith:

"Homage to thee, O Great God, thou Lord of Double Maāti, I have come to thee, O my Lord, and I have brought myself hither that I may behold thy beauties. I know thee, and I know thy name, and I know the name[s] of the two and forty gods who exist with thee in this Hall of double Maāti, who live as warders of sinners and who feed upon their blood on the day when the lives of men are taken into account in the presence of the god Un-nefer; in truth 'Rekhti-merti-neb-Maāti' (i.e., 'twin-sisters with two eyes, ladies of double Maāti') is thy name. In truth I have come to thee, and I have brought Maāt (i.e., right and truth) to thee, and I have destroyed wickedness for thee. [I have not done evil to] mankind. I have not oppressed the members of my family, I have not wrought evil in the place of right and truth. I have had no knowledge of worthless men. I have not wrought evil. I have not made to be the first [consideration] of each day that excessive labor should be performed for me. [I have] not brought forward my name for [exaltation] to honors. I have not ill-treated servants. [I have not thought scorn of God.] I have not defrauded the oppressed one of his property.(86) I have not done that which is an abomination unto the gods. I have not caused harm to be done to the servant by his chief. I have not caused pain. I have made no man to suffer hunger. I have made no one to weep. I have done no murder. I have not given the order for murder to be done for me. I have not inflicted pain upon mankind. I have not defrauded the temples of their oblations. I have not purloined the cakes of the gods. I have not carried off the cakes offered to the khus. I have not committed fornication. I have not polluted myself [in the holy places of the god of my city],(87) nor diminished from the bushel. I have neither added to nor filched away land. I have not encroached upon the fields [of others]. I have not added to the weights of the scales [to cheat the seller]. I have not misread the pointer of the scales [to cheat the buyer]. I have not carried away the milk from the mouths of children. I have not driven away the cattle which were upon their pastures. I have not snared the feathered fowl of the preserves of the gods. I have not caught fish [with bait made of] fish of their kind. I have not turned back the water at the time [when it should flow]. I have not cut a cutting in a canal of running water. I have not extinguished a fire (or light) when it should burn. I have not violated the times(88) [of offering] the chosen meat-offerings. I have not driven off the cattle from the property of the gods. I have not repulsed God in his manifestations. I am pure. I am pure. I am pure. I am pure. My purity is the purity of that great Bennu which is in the city of Suten-henen (Heracleopolis), for, behold, I am the nose of the God of the winds, who maketh all mankind to live on the day when the Eye (Utchat) of Rā is full in Annu (Heliopolis) at the end of the second month(89) of the season Pert (i.e., the season of growing) [in the presence of the divine lord of this earth].(90) I have seen the Eye of Rā when it was full in Annu, therefore let not evil befall me in this land and in this Hall of double Maāti, because I, even I, know the name[s] of these gods who are therein [and who are the followers of the great god]."(91)

The Negative Confession

[From the Papyrus of Nebseni (British Museum No. 9,900, sheet 30).]

The scribe Nebseni, triumphant, saith:
   1. "Hail, thou whose strides are long, who comest forth from Annu (Heliopolis), I have not done iniquity.
   2. "Hail, thou who art embraced by flame, who comest forth from Kher-āba,(92) I have not robbed with violence.
   3. "Hail, thou divine Nose (Fenti), who comest forth from Khemennu (Hermopolis), I have not done violence [to any man].
   4. "Hail, thou who eatest shades, who comest forth from the place where the Nile riseth,(93) I have not committed theft.
   5. "Hail, Neha-hāu,(94) who comest forth from Re-stau, I have not slain man or woman.
   6. "Hail, thou double Lion-god, who comest forth from heaven, I have not made light the bushel.
   7. "Hail, thou whose two eyes are like flint,(95) who comest forth from Sekhem (Letopolis), I have not acted deceitfully.
   8. "Hail, thou Flame, who comest forth as [thou] goest back, I have not purloined the things which belong unto God.
   9. "Hail, thou Crusher of bones, who comest forth from Suten-henen (Heracleopolis), I have not uttered falsehood.
   10. "Hail, thou who makest the flame to wax strong, who comest forth from Het-ka-Ptah (Memphis), I have not carried away food.
   11. "Hail, Qerti, (i.e., the two sources of the Nile), who come forth from Amentet, I have not uttered evil words.
   12. "Hail, thou whose teeth shine, who comest forth from Ta-she (i.e., the Fayyûm), I have attacked no man.
   13. "Hail, thou who dost consume blood, who comest forth from the house of slaughter, I have not killed the beasts [which are the property of God].
   14. "Hail, thou who dost consume the entrails, who comest forth from the mābet chamber, I have not acted deceitfully.
   15. "Hail, thou god of Right and Truth, who comest forth from the city of double Maāti, I have not laid waste the lands which have been ploughed(?).
   16. "Hail, thou who goest backward, who comest forth from the city of Bast (Bubastis), I have never pried into matters [to make mischief].
   17. "Hail, Aati, who comest forth from Annu (Heliopolis), I have not set my mouth in motion [against any man].
   18. "Hail, thou who art doubly evil, who comest forth from the nome of Ati,(96) I have not given way to wrath concerning myself without a cause.
   19. "Hail, thou serpent Uamemti, who comest forth from the house of slaughter, I have not defiled the wife of a man.
   20. "Hail, thou who lookest upon what is brought to him, who comest forth from the Temple of Amsu, I have not committed any sin against purity.
   21. "Hail, Chief of the divine Princes, who comest forth from the city of Nehatu,(97) I have not struck fear [into any man].
   22. "Hail, Khemiu (i.e., Destroyer), who comest forth from the Lake of Kaui, I have not encroached upon [sacred times and seasons].
   23. "Hail, thou who orderest speech, who comest forth from Urit, I have not been a man of anger.
   24. "Hail, thou Child, who comest forth from the Lake of Heq-āt,(98) I have not made myself deaf to the words of right and truth.
   25. "Hail, thou disposer of speech, who comest forth from the city of Unes,(99) I have not stirred up strife.
   26. "Hail, Basti, who comest forth from the Secret city, I have made [no man] to weep.
   27. "Hail, thou whose face is [turned] backward, who comest forth from the Dwelling, I have not committed acts of impurity, neither have I lain with men.

28. "Hail, Leg of fire, who comest forth from Akhekhu, I have not eaten my heart.(100)

29. "Hail, Kenemti, who comest forth from [the city of] Kenemet, I have abused [no man].

30. "Hail, thou who bringest thine offering, who comest forth from the city of Sau (Saïs), I have not acted with violence.

31. "Hail, thou god of faces, who comest forth from the city of Tchefet, I have not judged hastily.

32. "Hail, thou who givest knowledge, who comest forth from Unth, I have not ... and I have not taken vengeance upon the god.

33. "Hail, thou lord of two horns, who comest forth from Satiu, I have not multiplied [my] speech overmuch.

34. "Hail, Nefer-Tem, who comest forth from Het-ka-Ptah (Memphis), I have not acted with deceit, and I have not worked wickedness.

35. "Hail, Tem-Sep, who comest forth from Tattu, I have not uttered curses [on the king].

36. "Hail, thou whose heart doth labor, who comest forth from the city of Tebti, I have not fouled(?) water.

37. "Hail, Ahi of the water, who comest forth from Nu, I have not made haughty my voice.

38. "Hail, thou who givest commands to mankind, who comest forth from [Sau(?)], I have not cursed the god.

39. "Hail, Neheb-nefert, who comest forth from the Lake of Nefer(?), I have not behaved with insolence.

40. "Hail, Neheb-kau, who comest forth from [thy] city, I have not sought for distinctions.

41. "Hail, thou whose head is holy, who comest forth from [thy] habitations, I have not increased my wealth, except with such things as are [justly] mine own possessions.

42. "Hail, thou who bringest thine own arm, who comest forth from Aukert (underworld), I have not thought scorn of the god who is in my city."

Address To The Gods Of The Underworld

[From the Papyrus of Nu (British Museum No. 10,477, sheet 24).]

[THEN SHALL THE HEART WHICH IS RIGHTEOUS AND SINLESS SAY:](101)

The overseer of the palace, the chancellor-in-chief, Nu, triumphant, saith:

"Homage to you, O ye gods who dwell in the Hall of double Maāti, I, even I, know you, and I know your names. Let me not fall under your knives of slaughter, and bring ye not forward my wickedness unto the god in whose train ye are; and let not evil hap come upon me by your means. Oh, declare ye me right and true in the presence of Neb-er-tcher, because I have done that which is right and true in Ta-mera (Egypt). I have not cursed God, and let not evil hap come upon me through the king who dwelleth in my day. Homage to you, O ye gods, who dwell in the Hall of double Maāti, who are without evil in your bodies, and who live upon right and truth, and who feed yourselves upon right and truth in the presence of the god Horus, who dwelleth in his divine Disk: deliver ye me from the god Baba who feedeth upon the entrails of the mighty ones upon the day of the great judgment. Oh, grant ye that I may come to you, for I have not committed faults, I have not sinned, I have not done evil, I have not borne false witness; therefore let nothing [evil] be done unto me. I live upon right and truth, and I feed upon right and truth. I have performed the commandments of men [as well as] the things whereat are gratified the gods, I have made the gods to be at peace [with me by doing] that which is his will. I have given bread to the hungry man, and water to the thirsty man, and apparel to the naked man, and a boat to the [shipwrecked] mariner. I have made holy offerings to the gods, and sepulchral meals to the Khus. Be ye then my deliverers, be ye then my protectors, and make ye not accusation against me in the presence of [the great god]. I am clean of mouth and clean of hands; therefore let it be said unto me by those who shall behold me, 'Come in peace; come in peace,' for I have heard that mighty word hich the spiritual bodies (sāhu)(102) spake unto the Cat in the House of Hapt-re. I have been made to give evidence before the god Hra-f-ha-f (i.e., he whose face is behind him), and he hath given a decision [concerning me]. I have seen the things over which the persea tree spreadeth [its branches] within Re-stau. I am he who hath offered up prayers to the gods and who knoweth their persons. I have come and I have advanced to make the declaration of right and truth, and to set the balance upon what supporteth it within the region of Aukert. Hail, thou who art exalted upon thy standard, thou lord of the Atefu crown, whose name is proclaimed as 'Lord of the winds,' deliver thou me from thy divine messengers who cause dire deeds to happen, and who cause calamities to come into being, and who are without coverings for their faces, for I have done that which is right and true for the Lord of right and truth. I have purified myself and my breast with libations, and my hinder parts with the things which make clean, and my inner parts have been in the Pool of Right and Truth. There is no single member of mine which lacketh right and truth. I have been purified in the Pool of the South, and I have rested in the northern city which is in the Field of the Grasshoppers, wherein the divine sailors of Rā bathe at the second hour of the night and at the third hour of the day. And the hearts of the gods are gratified(?) after they have passed through it, whether it be by night, or whether it be by day, and they say unto me, 'Let thyself come forward.' And they say unto me, 'Who, then, art thou?' And they say unto me, 'What is thy name?' 'I am he who is equipped under the flowers [and I am] the dweller in his olive-tree,' is my name. And they say unto me straightway, 'Pass thou on'; and I passed on by thy city to the north of the olive-tree. What, then, didst thou see there? The leg and the thigh. What, then, didst thou say unto them? Let me see rejoicings in those lands of the Tenkhu.(103) And what did they give unto thee? A flame of fire and a tablet (or sceptre) of crystal. What, then, didst thou do therewith? I buried them by the furrow of Mānāat as 'things for the night.' What, then, didst thou find by the furrow of Mānāat? A sceptre of flint, the name of which is 'Giver of winds.' What, then, didst thou do to the flame of fire and the tablet (or sceptre) of crystal after thou hadst buried them? I uttered words over them in the furrow, [and I dug them out therefrom];(104) I extinguished the fire, and I broke the tablet (or sceptre), and I created a pool of water. 'Come, then,' [they say,] 'and enter in through the door of this Hall of double Maāti, for thou knowest us.' "

"'We will not let thee enter in through us,' say the bolts of the door, 'unless thou tellest [us] our names;' 'Tongue [of the Balance] of the place of right and truth' is your name. 'I will not let thee enter in by me,' saith the [right] lintel of the door, 'unless thou tellest [me] my name;' 'Balance of the support of right and truth' is thy name. 'I will not let thee enter in by me,' saith the [left] lintel of the door, 'unless thou tellest [me] my name;' ['Balance of] wine' is thy name. 'I will not let thee pass over me,' saith the threshold of this door, 'unless thou tellest [me] my name;' 'Ox of the god Seb' is thy name. 'I will not open unto thee,' saith the fastening of this door, 'unless thou tellest [me] my name;' 'Flesh of his mother' is thy name. 'I will not open unto thee,' saith the socket of the fastening of the door, 'unless thou tellest me my name;' 'Living eye of the god Sebek, the lord of Bakhau,' is thy name. 'I will not open unto thee [and I will not let thee enter in by me,' saith the guardian of the leaf of] this door, 'unless thou tellest [me] my name;' 'Elbow of the god Shu when he placeth himself to protect Osiris' is thy name. 'We will not let thee enter in by us,' say the posts of this door, 'unless thou tellest us our names;' 'Children of the uræi-goddesses' is your name.(105) 'Thou knowest us,' [they say,] 'pass on, therefore, by us.'

" 'I will not let thee tread upon me,' saith the floor of the Hall of double Maāti, 'because I am silent and I am holy, and because I do not know the name[s] of thy two feet wherewith thou wouldst walk upon me; therefore tell them to me.' 'Traveller(?) of the god Khas' is the name of my right foot, and 'Staff of the goddess Hathor' is the name of my left foot. 'Thou knowest me,' [it saith,] 'pass on therefore over me.' "

" 'I will not make mention of thee,' saith the guardian of the door of this Hall of double Maāti, 'unless thou tellest [me] my name;' 'Discerner of hearts and searcher of the reins' is thy name. 'Now will I make mention of thee [to the god]. But who is the god that dwelleth in his hour? Speak thou it' (i.e., his name). Māau-Taui (i.e., he who keepeth the record of the two lands) [is his name]. 'Who then is Māau-Taui?' He is Thoth. 'Come,' saith Thoth. 'But why hast thou come?' I have come, and I press forward that I may be mentioned. What now is thy condition? I, even I, am purified from evil things, and I am protected from the baleful deeds of those who live in their days; and I am not among them. 'Now will I make mention of thee [to the god].'(106) '[Tell me now,] who is he(107) whose heaven is of fire, whose walls [are surmounted by] living uræi, and the floor of whose house is a stream of water? Who is he? I say.' It is Osiris. 'Come forward, then: verily thou shalt be mentioned [to him]. Thy cakes [shall come] from the Eye of Rā, and thine ale [shall come] from the Eye of Rā, and the sepulchral meals [which shall be brought to thee] upon earth [shall come] from the Eye of Rā. This hath been decreed for the Osiris the overseer of the palace, the chancellor-in-chief, Nu, triumphant.' "

(THE MAKING OF THE REPRESENTATION OF WHAT SHALL HAPPEN IN THIS HALL OF DOUBLE MAATI.) THIS CHAPTER SHALL BE SAID [BY THE DECEASED] AFTER HE HATH BEEN CLEANSED AND PURIFIED, AND WHEN HE IS ARRAYED IN APPAREL, AND IS SHOD WITH WHITE LEATHER SANDALS, AND HIS EYES HAVE BEEN PAINTED WITH ANTIMONY, AND [HIS BODY] HATH BEEN ANOINTED WITH UNGUENT OF ANTI, AND WHEN HE OFFERETH OXEN, AND FEATHERED FOWL, AND INCENSE, AND CAKES, AND ALE, AND GARDEN HERBS. AND, BEHOLD, THOU SHALT DRAW A REPRESENTATION OF THIS IN COLOR UPON A NEW TILE MOULDED FROM EARTH UPON WHICH NEITHER A PIG NOR OTHER ANIMALS HAVE TRODDEN. AND IF [THOU] DOEST THIS BOOK UPON IT [IN WRITING, THE DECEASED] SHALL FLOURISH, AND HIS CHILDREN SHALL FLOURISH, AND [HIS NAME] SHALL NEVER FALL INTO OBLIVION, AND HE SHALL BE AS ONE WHO FILLETH (I.E., SATISFIETH) THE HEART OF THE KING AND OF HIS PRINCES, AND BREAD, AND CAKES, AND SWEETMEATS, AND WINE, AND PIECES OF FLESH SHALL BE GIVEN UNTO HIM UPON THE ALTAR OF THE GREAT GOD; AND HE SHALL NOT BE TURNED BACK AT ANY DOOR IN AMENTET, AND HE SHALL BE BROUGHT IN ALONG WITH THE KINGS OF UPPER AND LOWER EGYPT, AND HE SHALL BE IN THE TRAIN OF OSIRIS(108) CONTINUALLY AND REGULARLY FOREVER.

Of The Hour Apes(109)

[From the Papyrus of Nu (British Museum No. 10,477, sheet 24).]

The overseer of the palace, the chancellor-in-chief, Nu, triumphant, the son of the overseer of the palace, the chancellor-in-chief, Amen-hetep, triumphant, saith:

"Hail, ye four apes who sit in the bows of the boat of Rā, who convey right and truth to Neb-er-tcher, who sit in judgment on my misery and on my strength, who make the gods to rest contented by means of the flame of your mouths, who offer holy offerings to the gods and sepulchral meals to the khus, who live upon right and truth, and who feed upon right and truth of heart, who are without deceit and fraud, and to whom wickedness is an abomination, do ye away with my evil deeds, and put ye away my sin [which deserved stripes upon earth, and destroy ye any evil whatsoever that belongeth unto me],(110) and let there be no obstacle whatsoever on my part toward you. Oh, grant ye that I may make my way through the underworld (ammehet), let me enter into Re-stau, let me pass through the hidden pylons of Amentet. Oh, grant that there may be given to me cakes, and ale, and sweetmeats(?), even as [they are given] to the living khus, and grant that I may enter in and come forth from Re-stau."

"[The four apes make answer, saying], 'Come, then, for we have done away with thy wickedness, and we have put away thy sin, along with the [sin deserving of] stripes which thou [didst commit] upon earth, and we have destroyed [all] the evil which belonged to thee upon the earth. Enter, therefore, into Re-stau, and pass thou through the hidden pylons of Amentet, and there shall be given unto thee cakes, and ale, and sweetmeats(?), and thou shalt come forth and thou shalt enter in at thy desire, even as do those khus who are favored [of the god], and thou shalt be proclaimed (or called) each day in the horizon.' "

Of The Praise Of The Gods

[From the Tomb of Rameses IV (see Naville, op. cit., Bd. I. Bl. 141; Lefébure, "Tombeau de Ramsès IV," Plate 13).]

THE BOOK OF THE PRAISE OF THE GODS OF THE QERTI(111) WHICH A MAN SHALL RECITE WHEN HE COMETH FORTH BEFORE THEM TO ENTER IN TO SEE THE GOD IN THE GREAT TEMPLE OF THE UNDERWORLD. And he shall say:

"Homage to you, O ye gods of the Qerti, ye divine dwellers in Amentet! Homage to you, O ye guardians of the doors of the underworld, who keep ward over the god, who bear and proclaim [the names of those who come] into the presence of the god Osiris, and who hold yourselves ready, and who praise [him], and who destroy the Enemies of Rā. Oh, send ye forth your light and scatter ye the darkness [which is about] you, and behold ye the holy and divine Mighty One, O ye who live even as he liveth, and call ye upon him that dwelleth within his divine Disk. Lead ye the King of the North and of the South, (Usr-Maāt-Rā-setep-en-Amen), the son of the Sun, (Rā-meses-meri-Amen-Rā-heq-Maāt), through your doors, may his divine soul enter into your hidden places, [for] he is one among you, and he hath shot forth calamities upon the serpent fiend Apep, and he hath beaten down the obstacles [which Apep set up] in Amentet. Thy word hath prevailed mightily over thine enemies, O great God, who livest in thy divine Disk; thy word hath prevailed mightily over thine enemies, O Osiris, Governor of Amentet; thy word hath prevailed mightily over thine enemies in heaven and in earth, O thou King of the North and of the South, (Usr-Maāt-Rā-setep-en-Amen), the son of the Sun, (Rā-meses-meri-Amen-Rā-heq-Maāt), and over the sovereign princes of every god and of every goddess, O Osiris, Governor of Amentet; he hath uttered words in the presence [of the god in] the valley of the dead, and he hath gained the mastery over the mighty sovereign princes. Hail, ye doorkeepers(?), hail, ye doorkeepers, who guard your gates, who punish souls, who devour the bodies of the dead, who advance over them at their examination in the places of destruction, who give right and truth to the soul and to the divine khu, the beneficent one, the mighty one, whose throne is holy in Akert, who is endowed with soul like Rā and who is praised like Osiris, lead ye along the King of the North and of the South, (Usr-Maāt-Rā-setep-en-Amen), the son of the Sun, (Rā-meses-meri-Amen-Rā-heq-Maāt), unbolt ye for him the doors, and open [ye] the place of his Qerti for him. Behold, make ye his word to triumph over his enemies, and indeed let meat-offerings and drink-offerings be made unto him by the god of the double door, and let him put on the nemmes crown of him that dwelleth in the great and hidden shrine. Behold the image of Heru-khuti (Harmachis), who is doubly true, and who is the divine Soul and the divine and perfect Khu; he hath prevailed with his hands. The two great and mighty gods cry out to the King of the North and South (Usr-Maāt-Rā-setep-en-Amen), the son of the Sun, (Rā-meses-meri-Amen-Rā-heq-Maāt), they rejoice with him, they sing praises to him [and clap] their hands, they accord him their protection, and he liveth. The King of the North and South (Usr-Maāt-Rā-setep-en-Amen), the son of the Sun, (Rā-meses-meri-Amen-Rā-heq-Maāt), riseth like a living soul in heaven. He hath been commanded to make his transformations, he hath made himself victorious before the divine sovereign chiefs, and he hath made his way through the gates of heaven, and of earth, and of the underworld, even as hath Rā. The King of the North and South, (Usr-Maāt-Rā-setep-en-Amen), the son of the Sun, (Rā-meses-meri-Amen-Rā-heq-Maāt), saith, 'Open unto me the gate[s] of heaven, and of earth, and of the underworld, for I am the divine soul of Osiris and I rest in him, and let me pass through their halls. Let [the gods] sing praises unto me [when] they see me; let me enter and let favor be shown unto me; let me come forth and let me be beloved; and let me go forward, for no defect or failure hath been found clinging unto me.'"

Adoration Of The Gods Of The Qerti

[From the Papyrus of Ptah-mes (Naville, op. cit., Bd. I. Bl. 142).]

A CHAPTER TO BE RECITED ON COMING BEFORE THE DIVINE SOVEREIGN CHIEFS OF OSIRIS TO OFFER PRAISE UNTO THE GODS WHO ARE THE GUIDES OF THE UNDERWORLD. Osiris, the chief scribe and draughtsman, Ptah-mes, triumphant, saith:

"Homage to you, O ye gods who dwell in the Qerti, ye gods who dwell in Amentet, who keep ward over the gates of the underworld and are the guardians [thereof], who bear and proclaim [the names of those who come] into the presence of Osiris, who praise him and who destroy the enemies of Rā. Oh, send forth your light and scatter ye the darkness [which is about] you, and look upon the face of Osiris, O ye who live even as he liveth, and praise [ye] him that dwelleth in his Disk, and lead [ye] me away from your calamities. Let me come forth and let me enter in through your secret places, for I am a mighty prince among you, for I have done away with evil there, and I have beaten down the obstacles(?) [which have been set up] in Amentet. Thou hast been victorious over thine enemies, O thou that dwellest in thy Disk; thou hast been victorious over thine enemies, O Thoth, who producest(?) statutes; thou hast been victorious over thine enemies, O Osiris, the chief scribe and draughtsman, Ptah-mes, triumphant; thou hast been triumphant over thine enemies, O Osiris, thou Governor of Amentet, in heaven and upon earth in the presence of the divine sovereign chiefs of every god and of every goddess; and the food(?) of Osiris, the Governor of Amentet, is in the presence of the god whose name is hidden before the great divine sovereign chiefs. Hail ye guardians of the doors, ye [gods] who keep ward over their habitations(?), who keep the reckoning and who commit [souls] to destruction, who grant right and truth to the divine soul which is stablished, who are without evil in the abode of Akert, who are endowed with soul even as is Rā, and who are ... as is Osiris, guide ye Osiris the chief scribe, the draughtsman, Ptah-mes, triumphant, open ye unto him the gates of the underworld, and the uppermost part of his estate and his Qert. Behold, make [ye him] to be victorious over his enemies, provide [ye him] with the offerings of the god of the underworld, make noble the divine being who dwelleth in the nemmes crown, the lord of the knowledge of Akert. Behold, stablish ... this soul in right and truth, [and let it become] a perfect soul that hath gained the mastery with its two hands. The great and mighty gods cry out, 'He hath gotten the victory,' and they rejoice in him, and they ascribe praise unto him with their hands, and they turn unto him their faces. The living one is triumphant, and is even like a living soul dwelling in heaven, and he hath been ordered to perform [his] transformations. Osiris triumphed over his enemies, and Osiris, the chief scribe and draughtsman, Ptah-mes, triumphant, hath gained the victory over his enemies in the presence of the great divine sovereign chiefs who dwell in heaven, and in the presence of the great divine sovereign chiefs who dwell upon the earth."

Hymn Of Praise To Osiris

[From Lepsius, "Todtenbuch," Bl. 51.]

A HYMN OF PRAISE TO OSIRIS. The Osiris Auf-ānkh, triumphant, saith:

"Homage to thee, O Osiris Un-nefer, triumphant, thou son of Nut, thou first-born son of Seb, thou mighty one who comest forth from Nut, thou King in the city of Nifu-ur,(112) thou Governor of Amentet, thou lord of Abtu (Abydos), thou lord of souls, thou mighty one of strength, thou lord of the atef crown in Suten-henen, thou lord of the divine form in the city of Nifu-ur, thou lord of the tomb, thou mighty one of souls in Tattu, thou lord of [sepulchral] offerings, thou whose festivals are many in Tattu. The god Horus exalteth his father in every place (or shrine), and he uniteth [himself] unto the goddess Isis and unto the goddess Nephthys; and the god Thoth reciteth for him the mighty glorifyings which are within him, [and which] come forth from his mouth, and the heart of Horus is stronger than that of all the gods. Rise up, then, O Horus, thou son of Isis, and avenge thy father Osiris. Hail, O Osiris, I have come unto thee; I am Horus and I have avenged thee, and I feed this day upon the sepulchral meals of oxen, and feathered fowl, and upon all the beautiful things [offered] unto Osiris. Rise up, then, O Osiris, for I have struck down for thee all thine enemies, and I have taken vengeance upon them for thee. I am Horus upon this beautiful day of thy fair rising in thy Soul which exalteth thee along with itself on this day before thy divine sovereign princes. Hail, O Osiris, thy ka hath come unto thee and is with thee, and thou restest therein in thy name of Ka-Hetep. I maketh thee glorious in thy name of Khu, and it maketh thee like unto the Morning Star in thy name of Pehu, and it openeth for thee the ways in thy name of Ap-uat. Hail, O Osiris, I have come unto thee and I have set thine enemies under [thy feet] in every place, and thou art triumphant in the presence of the company of the gods and of the divine sovereign chiefs. Hail, O Osiris, thou hast received thy sceptre and the place whereon thou art to rest, and thy steps are under thee. Thou bringest food to the gods, and thou bringest sepulchral meals unto those who dwell in their tombs. Thou hast given thy might unto the gods and thou hast created the Great God; thou hast thy existence with them in their spiritual bodies, thou gatherest thyself unto all the gods, and thou hearest the word of right and truth on the day when offerings to this god are ordered on the festivals of Uka."

Of Making Perfect The Khu

[From the Papyrus of Nu (British Museum No. 10,477, sheet 17).]

ANOTHER CHAPTER OF MAKING PERFECT THE KHU, WHICH IS [TO BE RECITED ON] THE BIRTHDAY OF OSIRIS, AND OF MAKING TO LIVE THE SOUL FOREVER.(113) The chancellor-in-chief, Nu, triumphant, saith:

"The heavens are opened, the earth is opened, the West is opened, the East is opened, the southern half of heaven is opened, the northern half of heaven is opened, the doors are opened, and the gates are thrown wide open to Rā [as] he cometh forth from the horizon. The Sektet boat openeth for him the double doors and the Mātet boat bursteth open [for him] the gates; he breatheth, and the god Shu(114) [cometh into being], and he createth the goddess Tefnut. Those who are in the following of Osiris follow in his train, and the overseer of the palace, the chancellor-in-chief, Nu, triumphant, followeth on in the train of Rā. He taketh his iron weapon and he forceth open the shrine even as doth Horus, and pressing onward he advanceth unto the hidden things of his habitation with the libations of his divine shrine; the messenger of the god that loveth him. The Osiris Nu, the overseer of the palace, the chancellor-in-chief, triumphant, bringeth forth the right and the truth, and he maketh to advance the going forward(115) of Osiris. The Osiris Nu, the overseer of the palace, the chancellor-in-chief, triumphant, taketh in [his] hand[s] the cordage and he bindeth fast the shrine. Storms are the things which he abominateth. Let no water-flood be nigh unto him, let not the Osiris Nu, the overseer of the palace, the chancellor-in-chief, triumphant, be repulsed before Rā, and let him not be made to turn back; for, behold, the Eye is in his two hands. Let not the Osiris Nu, the overseer of the palace, the chancellor-in-chief, triumphant, walk in the valley of darkness, let him not enter into the Lake of those who are evil, and let him have no existence among the damned, even for a moment. Let not the Osiris Nu fall headlong among those who would lead him captive, and let not [his] soul go in among them. Let his divine face take possession of the place behind the block, the block of the god Septu."

"Hymns of praise be unto you, O ye divine beings of the Thigh, the knives of God [work] in secret, and the two arms and hands of God cause the light to shine; it is doubly pleasant unto him to lead the old unto him along with the young at his season. Now, behold, the god Thoth dwelleth within his hidden places, and he performeth the ceremonies of libation unto the god who reckoneth millions of years, and he maketh a way through the firmament, and he doeth away with storms and whirlwinds from his stronghold, and the Osiris Nu, the overseer of the palace, the chancellor-in-chief, triumphant, arriveth in the places of his habitations. [O ye divine beings of the Thigh], do ye away with his sorrow, and his suffering, and his pain, and may the sorrow of the Osiris Nu be altogether put away. Let the Osiris Nu, the overseer of the palace, the chancellor-in-chief, triumphant, gratify Rā, let him make a way into the horizon of Rā, let his boat be made ready for him, let him sail on happily, and let Thoth put light into [his] heart; then shall the Osiris Nu, triumphant, praise and glorify Rā, and Rā shall hearken unto his words, and he shall beat down the obstacles which come from his enemies. I have not been shipwrecked, I have not been turned back in the horizon, for I am Rā-Osiris, and the Osiris Nu, the overseer of the palace, the chancellor-in-chief, shall not be shipwrecked in the Great Boat. Behold him whose face is in the god of the Thigh, because the name of Rā is in the body of the Osiris Nu, the overseer of the palace, the chancellor-in-chief, and his honor is in his mouth; he shall speak unto Rā, and Rā shall hearken unto his words."

"Hymns of praise unto thee, O Rā, in the horizon, and homage unto thee, O thou that purifiest with light the denizens of heaven, O thou who hast sovereign power over heaven at that supreme moment when the paddles of thine enemies move with thee! The Osiris Nu, the overseer of the palace, the chancellor-in-chief, triumphant, cometh with the ordering of right and truth, for there is an iron firmament in Amentet which the fiend Apep hath broken through with his storms before the double Lion-god, and this will the Osiris Nu set in order; O hearken ye, ye who dwell upon the top of the throne of majesty. The Osiris Nu shall come in among thy divine sovereign chiefs, and Rā shall deliver him from Apep each day so that he may not come nigh unto him, and he shall make himself vigilant. The Osiris Nu shall have power over the things which are written, he shall receive sepulchral meals, and the god Thoth shall provide him with the things which should be prepared for him. The Osiris Nu maketh right and truth to go round about the bows in the Great Boat, and hath triumph among the divine sovereign chiefs, and he establisheth [it] for millions of years. The divine chiefs guide him and give unto him a passage in the boat with joy and gladness; the first ones among the company of the sailors of Rā are behind him, and he is happy. Right and truth are exalted, and they have come unto their divine lord, and praises have been ascribed unto the god Neb-er-tcher. The Osiris Nu, the overseer of the palace, the chancellor-in-chief, triumphant, hath taken in his hands the weapon and he hath made his way through heaven therewith; the denizens thereof have ascribed praises unto him as [unto] a divine being who standeth up and never sinketh to rest. The god Rā exalteth him by reason of what he hath done, and he causeth him to make of none effect the whirlwind and the storm; he looketh upon his splendors, and he stablisheth his oars, and the boat saileth round about in heaven, rising like the sun in the darkness. Thoth, the mighty one, leadeth the Osiris Nu within his eye, and he sitteth [upon his] thigh[s] in the mighty boat of Khepera; he cometh into being, and the things which he saith come to pass. The Osiris Nu advanceth, and he journeyeth round about heaven unto Amentet, the fiery deities stand up before him, and the god Shu rejoiceth exceedingly, and they take in their hands the bows [of the boat] of Rā along with his divine mariners. Rā goeth round about and he looketh upon Osiris. The Osiris Nu is at peace, the Osiris Nu is at peace. He hath not been driven back, the flame of thy moment hath not been taken away from him, [O Rā,] the whirlwind and storm of thy mouth have not come forth against him, he hath not journeyed upon the path of the crocodile—for he abominateth the crocodile—and it hath not drawn nigh unto him. The Osiris Nu embarked in thy boat, O Rā, he is furnished with thy throne, and he receiveth thy spiritual form. The Osiris Nu travelleth over the paths of Rā at daybreak to drive back the fiend Nebt; [he] cometh upon the flame of thy boat, [O Rā,] upon that mighty Thigh. The Osiris Nu knoweth it, and he attaineth unto thy boat, and behold he [sitteth] therein; and he maketh sepulchral offerings."

[THIS CHAPTER SHALL BE] RECITED OVER A BOAT OF THE GOD RA WHICH HATH BEEN PAINTED IN COLORS IN A PURE PLACE. AND BEHOLD THOU SHALT PLACE A FIGURE OF THE DECEASED IN THE BOWS THEREOF, AND THOU SHALT PAINT A SEKTET BOAT UPON THE RIGHT SIDE THEREOF, AND AN ATET BOAT UPON THE LEFT SIDE THEREOF, AND THERE SHALL BE MADE UNTO THEM OFFERINGS OF BREAD, AND CAKES, AND WINE, AND OIL, AND EVERY KIND OF FAIR OFFERING UPON THE BIRTHDAY OF OSIRIS. IF THESE CEREMONIES BE PERFORMED HIS SOUL SHALL HAVE EXISTENCE, AND SHALL LIVE FOREVER, AND SHALL NOT DIE A SECOND TIME.

The following is from the rubric to this chapter in the Saïte Recension (see Lepsius, op. cit., Bl. 53):

"[He shall know] the hidden things of the underworld, he shall penetrate the hidden things in Neter-khertet (the underworld)."

"[This chapter] was found in the large hall(?) of the Temple under the reign of his Majesty Hesepti, triumphant, and it was found in the cavern of the mountain which Horus made for his father Osiris Un-nefer, triumphant. Now since Rā looketh upon this deceased in his own flesh, he shall look upon him as the company of the gods. The fear of him shall be great, and the awe of him shall be mighty in the heart of men, and gods, and Khus, and the damned. He shall be with his soul and shall live forever; he shall not die a second time in the underworld; and on the day of weighing of words no evil hap shall befall him. He shall be triumphant over his enemies, and his sepulchral meals shall be upon the altar of Rā in the course of each day, day by day."

Of Living Nigh Unto Ra

[From the Papyrus of Nu (British Museum No. 10,477, sheets 17 and 18).]

THE CHAPTER OF HAVING EXISTENCE NIGH UNTO RĀ.(116) The overseer of the palace, the chancellor-in-chief, Nu, triumphant, saith:

"I am that god Rā who shineth in the night. Every being who followeth in his train shall have life in the following of the god Thoth, and he shall give unto him the risings of Horus in the darkness. The heart of Osiris Nu, the overseer of the palace, the chancellor-in-chief, triumphant, is glad because he is one of those beings, and his enemies have been destroyed by the divine princes. I am a follower of Rā, and [I have] received his iron weapon. I have come unto thee, O my father Rā, and I have advanced to the god Shu. I have cried unto the mighty goddess, I have equipped the god Hu, and I alone have removed the Nebt god from the path of Rā. I am a Khu, and I have come to the divine prince at the bounds of the horizon. I have met and I have received the mighty goddess. I have raised up thy soul in the following of thy strength, and my soul [liveth] through thy victory and thy mighty power; it is I who give commands in speech to Rā, in heaven. Homage to thee, O great god in the east of heaven, let me embark in thy boat, O Rā, let me open myself out in the form of a divine hawk, let me give my commands in words, let me do battle in my Sekhem (?), let me be master under my vine. Let me embark in thy boat, O Rā, in peace, and let me sail in peace to the beautiful Amentet. Let the god Tem speak unto me, [saying], 'Wouldst [thou] enter therein?' The lady, the goddess Mehen, is a million of years, yea, two million years in extent, and dwelleth in the House of Urt and Nif-urt [and in] the Lake of a million years; the whole company of the gods move about among those who are at the side of him who is the lord of divisions of places(?). And I say, 'On every road and among these millions of years is Rā the lord, and his path is in the fire, and they go round about behind him, and they go round about behind him.'"

Of Bringing Men Back To Earth

[From the Papyrus of Ani (British Museum No. 10,470, sheet 18).]

THE CHAPTER OF CAUSING A MAN TO COME BACK TO SEE HIS HOUSE UPON EARTH.(117) The Osiris Ani saith:

"I am the Lion-god coming forth with extended strides. I have shot arrows and I have wounded the prey; I have shot arrows and I have wounded the prey. I am the Eye of Horus, and I pass through the Eye of Horus at this season. I have arrived at the furrows; let the Osiris Ani advance in peace."(118)

Of Making Perfect The Khu

[From the Papyrus of Nu (British Museum No. 10,477, sheet 16).]

THE BOOK OF MAKING PERFECT THE KHU, WHICH IS TO BE RECITED ON THE DAY OF THE MONTH. The Osiris Nu, the overseer of the palace, the chancellor-in-chief, triumphant, saith:

"Rā riseth in his horizon, and his company of the gods follow after him. The god cometh forth out of his hidden habitations, and food falleth out of the eastern horizon of heaven at the word of the goddess Nut who maketh plain the paths of Rā, whereupon straightway the Prince goeth round about. Lift up then thyself, O thou Rā, who dwellest in thy divine shrine, draw thou into thyself the winds, inhale the north wind, swallow thou the skin(?) of thy net on the day wherein thou breathest right and truth. Thou separatest the divine followers, and thou sailest in [thy] boat to Nut; the divine princes march onward at thy word. Thou takest count of thy bones, thou gatherest together thy members, thou settest thy face toward the beautiful Amentet, and thou comest, being renewed each day. Behold, thou art that Image of gold, and thou dost possess the splendors of the disks of heaven and art terrible; thou comest, being renewed each day. Hail, the horizon rejoiceth, and there are shouts of joy in the rigging [of thy boat]; when the gods who dwell in the heavens see the Osiris Nu, the overseer of the palace, the chancellor-in-chief, triumphant, they ascribe unto him as his due praises which are like unto those ascribed unto Rā. The Osiris Nu, the overseer of the palace, the chancellor-in-chief, triumphant, is a divine prince and he seeketh(?) the ureret crown of Rā, and he, the only one, is strong in good fortune (?) in that supreme body which is of those divine beings who are in the presence of Rā. The Osiris Nu is strong both upon earth and in the underworld; and the Osiris Nu is strong like unto Rā every day. The Osiris Nu shall not tarry, and he shall not lie without motion in this land forever. Being doubly beautiful [he] shall see with his two eyes, and he shall hear with his two ears; rightly and truly, rightly and truly. The Osiris Nu is like unto Rā, and he setteth in order the oars [of his boat] among those who are in the train of Nu. He doth not tell that which he hath seen, and he doth not repeat that which he hath heard in the secret places. Hail, let there be shouts of joy to the Osiris Nu, who is of the divine body of Rā, as he journeyeth over Nu, and who propitiateth the KA of the god with that which he loveth. The Osiris Nu, the overseer of the palace, the chancellor-in-chief, is a hawk, the transformations of which are mighty (or manifold)."(119)

[THIS CHAPTER SHALL BE] RECITED OVER A BOAT FOUR(120) CUBITS IN ITS LENGTH AND MADE OF GREEN PORCELAIN [ON WHICH HAVE BEEN PAINTED] THE DIVINE SOVEREIGN CHIEFS OF THE CITIES; AND A HEAVEN WITH ITS STARS SHALL [ALSO] BE MADE, AND THIS THOU SHALT HAVE MADE CEREMONIALLY PURE BY MEANS OF NATRON AND INCENSE. AND, BEHOLD, THOU SHALT MAKE AN IMAGE OF RA IN YELLOW(?) COLOR UPON A NEW PLAQUE AND SET IT AT THE BOWS OF THE BOAT. AND BEHOLD, THOU SHALT PLACE AN IMAGE OF THE KHU WHICH THOU DOST WISH TO MAKE PERFECT [AND PLACE IT] IN THIS BOAT, AND THOU SHALT MAKE IT TO TRAVEL ABOUT IN THE BOAT [WHICH SHALL BE MADE IN THE FORM OF THE BOAT] OF RA; AND HE SHALL SEE THE GOD RA HIMSELF THEREIN. LET NOT THE EYE OF ANY MAN WHATSOEVER LOOK UPON IT WITH THE EXCEPTION OF THINE OWN SELF, OR THY FATHER,(121) OR THY SON, AND GUARD [THIS] WITH GREAT CARE.(122) [NOW THESE THINGS] SHALL MAKE THE KHU PERFECT IN THE HEART OF RA, AND IT SHALL GIVE UNTO HIM POWER WITH THE COMPANY OF THE GODS; AND THE GODS SHALL LOOK UPON HIM AS A DIVINE BEING LIKE UNTO THEMSELVES; AND MANKIND AND THE DEAD SHALL LOOK UPON HIM AND SHALL FALL DOWN UPON THEIR FACES, AND HE SHALL BE SEEN IN THE UNDERWORLD IN THE FORM OF THE RADIANCE OF RA.

Of Making Perfect The Khu

[From the Papyrus of Nu (British Museum No. 10,477, sheet 17).]

ANOTHER CHAPTER OF MAKING PERFECT THE KHU.(123) The Osiris Nu, the overseer of the palace, the chancellor-in-chief, triumphant, saith:

"Homage to thee, O thou who art within thy divine shrine, who shinest with rays of light and sendest forth radiance from thyself, who decreest joy for millions of years unto those who love him, who givest their hearts'desire unto mankind, thou god Khepera within thy boat who hast overthrown Apep. O ye children of the god Seb, overthrow ye the enemies of Osiris Nu, the overseer of the palace, the chancellor-in-chief, triumphant, and destroy ye them from the boat of Rā; and the god Horus shall cut off their heads in heaven [where they are] in the form of feathered fowl, and their hind parts shall be on the earth in the form of animals and in the Lake in the form of fishes. Every male fiend and every female fiend shall the Osiris Nu, the overseer of the palace, the chancellor-in-chief, destroy, whether he descendeth from the heaven, or whether he cometh forth from the earth, or whether they come upon the waters, or whether they advance toward the stars, the god Thoth, the son of Aner, coming forth from the Anerti, shall hack them in pieces. The Osiris Nu is silent and dumb(?); cause ye this god, the mighty one of slaughter, the being greatly to be feared, to make himself clean in your blood and to bathe himself in your gore, and ye shall certainly be destroyed by him from the boat of his father Rā. The Osiris Nu is the god Horus to whom his mother the goddess Isis hath given birth, and whom the goddess Nephthys hath nursed and dandled, even like Horus when [he] repulsed the fiends of the god Suti; and when they see the ureret crown stablished upon his head they fall down upon their faces and they glorify [him]. Behold, when men, and gods, and Khus, and the dead see the Osiris Nu in the form of Horus with the ureret crown stablished upon his head, they fall down upon their faces. And the Osiris Nu, the overseer of the palace, the chancellor-in-chief, triumphant, is victorious over his enemies in the heights of heaven, and in the depths thereof, and before the divine sovereign chiefs of every god and of every goddess."

[THIS CHAPTER] SHALL BE RECITED OVER A HAWK STANDING AND HAVING THE WHITE CROWN UPON HIS HEAD, [AND OVER FIGURES OF] TEM, SHU, TEFNUT, SEB, NUT, OSIRIS, ISIS, SUTI, AND NEPHTHYS PAINTED IN YELLOW COLOR UPON A NEW PLAQUE, WHICH SHALL BE PLACED IN [A MODEL OF] THE BOAT [OF THE SUN], ALONG WITH A FIGURE OF THE DECEASED WHOM THOU WOULDST MAKE PERFECT. THESE SHALT THOU ANOINT WITH CEDAR OIL, AND INCENSE SHALL BE OFFERED UP TO THEM ON THE FIRE, AND FEATHERED FOWL SHALL BE ROASTED. IT IS AN ACT OF PRAISE TO RA AS HE JOURNEYETH, AND IT SHALL CAUSE A MAN TO HAVE HIS BEING ALONG WITH RA DAY BY DAY, WHITHERSOEVER THE GOD VOYAGETH; AND IT SHALL DESTROY THE ENEMIES OF RA IN VERY TRUTH REGULARLY AND CONTINUALLY.

For The New Moon

[From Lepsius "Todtenbuch," Bl. 55.]

ANOTHER CHAPTER TO BE RECITED WHEN THE MOON RENEWETH ITSELF ON THE DAY OF THE MONTH. The Osiris Auf-ānkh, triumphant, saith:

"Osiris unfettereth," or, as others say, "openeth the storm cloud [in] the body of heaven, and is unfettered himself; Horus is made strong happily each day. He whose transformations are great (or many) hath offerings made unto him at the moment, and he hath made an end of the storm which is in the face of the Osiris Auf-ānkh, triumphant. Verily he cometh, and he is Rā in [his] journeying, and he is the four celestial gods in the heavens above. The Osiris Auf-ānkh, triumphant, cometh forth in his day, and he embarketh among the tackle of the boat."

IF THIS CHAPTER BE KNOWN BY THE DECEASED HE SHALL BECOME A PERFECT KHU IN THE UNDERWORLD, AND HE SHALL NOT DIE THEREIN A SECOND TIME, AND HE SHALL EAT HIS FOOD SIDE BY SIDE WITH OSIRIS. IF THIS CHAPTER BE KNOWN BY HIM UPON EARTH HE SHALL BE LIKE UNTO THOTH, AND HE SHALL BE ADORED BY THE LIVING ONES; HE SHALL NOT FALL HEADLONG AT THE MOMENT OF ROYAL FLAME OF THE GODDESS BAST, AND THE MIGHTY PRINCESS SHALL MAKE HIM TO ADVANCE HAPPILY.

Of Travelling In The Boat Of Ra

[From the Papyrus of Nu (British Museum No. 10,477, sheet 28).]

ANOTHER CHAPTER OF TRAVELLING IN THE GREAT BOAT OF RA. The Osiris Nu, the overseer of the palace, the chancellor-in-chief, triumphant, saith:

"Behold now, O ye luminaries in Annu, ye people in Kher-āba, the god Kha(?) hath been born; his cordage hath been completed, and the instrument wherewith he maketh his way hath [he] grasped firmly. I have protected the implements of the gods, and I have delivered the boat Kha(?) for him. I have come forth into heaven, and I have travelled therein with Rā in the form of an ape, and have turned back the paths of Nut at the staircase of the god Sebek."

Of Making Perfect The Khu

[From the Papyrus of Nu (British Museum No. 10,477, sheet 16).]

ANOTHER CHAPTER OF MAKING PERFECT THE Khu; [it shall be recited] on the festival of Six. The Osiris Nu, the overseer of the palace, the chancellor-in-chief, triumphant, saith:

"Behold now, O ye luminaries in Annu (Heliopolis), ye people in Kher-āba, the god hath been born; his cordage(?) hath been completed, and the instrument wherewith he maketh his way he hath grasped firmly; and the Osiris Nu is strong with them to direct the implement of the gods. The Osiris Nu hath delivered the boat of the sun therewith ... and he cometh forth into heaven. The Osiris Nu sailed round about in heaven, he travelleth therein unto Nut, he journeyeth along with Rā, and he voyageth therein in the form of apes; [he] turneth back the water-flood which is over the Thigh of the goddess Nut at the staircase of the god Sebaku. The hearts of Seb and Nut are glad and repeat the name which is new. Un-neferu reneweth [his] youth, Rā is in his splendors of light, Unti hath his speech, and lo, the god of the Inundation is Prince among the gods. The taste of sweetness hath forced a way into the heart of the destitute one, and the lord of thy outcries hath been done away with, and the oars(?) of the company of the gods are in vigorous motion. Adored be thou, O divine Soul, who art endowed more than the gods of the South and North [in] their splendors! Behold, grant thou that the Osiris Nu may be great in heaven even as thou art great among the gods; deliver thou him from every evil and murderous thing which may be wrought upon him by the Fiend, and fortify thou his heart. Grant thou, moreover, that the Osiris Nu may be stronger than all the gods, all the Khus, and all the dead. The Osiris Nu is strong and is the lord of powers. The Osiris Nu is the lord of right and truth which the goddess Uatchit worketh. The strength which protects the Osiris Nu is the strength which protects the god Rā in heaven. O god Rā, grant thou that the Osiris Nu may travel on in thy boat in peace, and do thou prepare a road whereon [thy] boat may journey onward; for the force which protecteth Osiris is the force which protecteth thee. The Osiris Nu driveth back the Crocodile from Rā day by day. The Osiris Nu cometh even as doth Horus in the splendors(?) of the horizon of heaven, and he directeth Rā through the mansions of the sky; the gods rejoice greatly when the Osiris Nu repulseth the Crocodile. The Osiris Nu hath the amulet(?) of the god, and the cloud of Nebt shall not come nigh unto him, and the divine guardians of the mansions of the sky shall not destroy him. The Osiris Nu is a divine being whose face is hidden, and he dwelleth within the Great House [as] chief of the Shrine of the god. The Osiris Nu carrieth the words of the gods to Rā, and he cometh and maketh supplication unto the divine lord with the words of his message. The Osiris Nu is strong of heart, and he maketh his offering at the moment among those who perform the ceremonies of sacrifice."

[THIS CHAPTER] SHALL BE SAID OVER A FIGURE OF THE DECEASED WHICH SHALL BE PLACED IN [A MODEL OF] THE BOAT OF THE SUN, AND BEHOLD, [HE THAT RECITETH IT] SHALL BE WASHED, AND SHALL BE CEREMONIALLY PURE, AND HE SHALL HAVE BURNT INCENSE BEFORE RA, AND SHALL HAVE OFFERED WINE, AND CAKES, AND ROASTED FOWL FOR THE JOURNEY [OF THE DECEASED] IN THE BOAT OF RA. NOW, EVERY KHU FOR WHOM SUCH THINGS ARE DONE SHALL HAVE AN EXISTENCE AMONG THE LIVING ONES, AND HE SHALL NEVER PERISH, AND HE SHALL HAVE A BEING LIKE UNTO THAT OF THE HOLY GOD; NO EVIL THING WHATSOEVER SHALL ATTACK HIM. AND HE SHALL BE LIKE UNTO A HAPPY KHU IN AMENTET, AND HE SHALL NOT DIE A SECOND TIME. HE SHALL EAT AND HE SHALL DRINK IN THE PRESENCE OF OSIRIS EACH DAY; HE SHALL BE BORNE ALONG WITH THE KINGS OF THE NORTH AND OF THE SOUTH EACH AND EVERY DAY; HE SHALL QUAFF WATER AT THE FOUNTAIN-HEAD; HE SHALL COME FORTH BY DAY EVEN AS DOTH HORUS; HE SHALL LIVE AND SHALL BECOME LIKE UNTO GOD; AND HE SHALL BE HYMNED BY THE LIVING ONES, EVEN AS IS RA EACH AND EVERY DAY CONTINUALLY AND REGULARLY FOREVER.

Sailing In The Great Boat

[From the Papyrus of Nu (British Museum No. 10,477, sheet 28).]

THE CHAPTER OF SAILING IN THE GREAT BOAT OF RĀ TO PASS OVER THE CIRCLE OF BRIGHT FLAME. The Osiris Nu, the overseer of the palace, the chancellor-in-chief, triumphant, saith:

"[Hail], ye bright and shining flames that keep your place behind Rā, and which slay behind him, the boat of Rā is in fear of the whirlwind and the storm; shine ye forth, then, and make [ye yourselves] visible. I have come [daily] along with the god Sek-hra from the bight of his holy lake, and I have seen the Maāt [goddesses] pass along, and the lion-gods who belong unto them. Hail, thou that dwellest in the coffer who hast multitudes of plants(?), I have seen [what is] there. We rejoice, and their princes rejoice greatly, and their lesser gods(?) are glad. I have made a way in front of the boat of Rā, I have lifted myself up into his divine Disk, I shine brightly through his splendors; he hath furnished himself with the things which are his, taking possession thereof as the lord of right and truth. And behold, O ye company of the gods, and thou ancestor of the goddess Isis,(124) grant ye that he may bear testimony to his father, the lord of those who are therein. I have weighed the ... in him [as] chief, and I have brought to him the goddess Tefnut and he liveth. Behold, come, come, and declare before him the testimony of right and truth of the lord Tem. I cry out at eventide and at his hour, saying, Grant ye unto me that I may come. I have brought unto him the jaws of the passages of the tomb; I have brought unto him the bones which are in Annu (Heliopolis); I have gathered together for him his manifold parts; I have driven back for him the serpent fiend Apep; I have spit upon his gashes for him; I have made my road and I have passed in among you. I am he who dwelleth among the gods, come, let [me] pass onward in the boat, the boat of the lord Sa. Behold, O Heru-ur, there is a flame, but the fire hath been extinguished. I have made [my] road, O ye divine fathers and your divine apes! I have entered upon the horizon, and I have passed on to the side of the divine princes, and I have borne testimony unto him that dwelleth in his divine boat. I have gone forward over the circle of bright flame which is behind the lord of the lock of hair which moveth round about. Behold, ye who cry out over yourselves, ye worms in [your] hidden places, grant ye that I may pass onward, for I am the mighty one, the lord of divine strength, and I am the spiritual body (sāh) of the lord of divine right and truth made by the goddess Uatchit. His strength which protecteth is my strength which protecteth, which is the strength which protecteth Rā. [Grant ye that I may be in the following of Rā], and grant ye that I may go round about with him in Sekhet-hetep [and in] the two lands. [I am] a great god, and [I have been] judged by the company of his gods; grant that divine, sepulchral meals may be given unto me."

Of The Four Flames

[From the Papyrus of Nu (British Museum No. 10,477, sheet 26).]

THE CHAPTER OF THE FOUR BLAZING FLAMES WHICH ARE MADE FOR THE KHU. Behold, thou shalt make four square troughs of clay, whereon thou shalt scatter incense, and thou shalt fill them with the milk of a white cow, and by means of these thou shalt extinguish the flame. The Osiris Nu, the overseer of the palace, the chancellor-in-chief, triumphant, saith:

"The fire cometh to thy KA, O Osiris, governor of Amenti; the fire cometh to thy KA, O Osiris Nu, the overseer of the palace, the chancellor-in-chief, triumphant. He that ordereth the night cometh after the day. [The flame cometh to thy KA, O Osiris, governor of those in Amenti](125) and the two sisters(?) of Rā come likewise. Behold, [the flame] riseth in Abtu (Abydos) and it cometh; and I cause it to come [to] the Eye of Horus. It is set in order upon thy brow, O Osiris, governor of Amenti,(126) and it is fixed within thy shrine and riseth upon thy brow; it is set in order upon thy breast, O Osiris Nu, and it is fixed upon thy brow. The Eye of Horus is protecting thee, O Osiris, governor of Amenti, and it keepeth thee in safety; it casteth down headlong all thine enemies for thee and all thine enemies have fallen headlong before thee. O Osiris Nu, the Eye of Horus protecteth thee, it keepeth thee in safety, and it casteth down headlong all thine enemies. Thine enemies have fallen down headlong before thy KA, O Osiris, governor of Amenti, the Eye of Horus protecteth thee, it keepeth thee in safety, and it hath cast down headlong all thine enemies. Thine enemies have fallen down headlong before thy Ka, O Osiris Nu, the overseer of the palace, the chancellor-in-chief, triumphant, the Eye of Horus protecteth thee, it keepeth thee in safety, it hath cast down headlong for thee all thine enemies, and thine enemies have fallen down headlong before thee. The Eye of Horus cometh, it is sound and well, and it sendeth forth rays like unto Rā in the horizon; it covereth over with darkness the powers of Suti, it taketh possession thereof and it bringeth its flame against him upon [its] feet(?). The Eye of Horus is sound and well, thou eatest the flesh(?) of thy body by means thereof, and thou givest praise(?) thereto. The four flames enter into thy KA, O Osiris, governor of Amenti, the four flames enter into thy ka, O Osiris Nu, the overseer of the palace, the chancellor-in-chief, triumphant. Hail, ye children of Horus, Mesthi, Hāpi, Tuamāutef and Qebhsennuf, ye have given your protection unto your divine Father Osiris, the governor of Amenti, grant ye your protection to the Osiris Nu, triumphant. Now, therefore, inasmuch as ye have destroyed the opponent[s] of Osiris, the governor of Amenti, he liveth with the gods, and he hath smitten Suti, with his hand and arm since light dawned upon the earth, and Horus hath gotten power, and he hath avenged his divine Father Osiris himself; and inasmuch as your divine father hath been made vigorous through the union which ye have effected for him with the Ka of Osiris, the governor of Amenti—now the Eye of Horus hath avenged him, and it hath protected him, and it hath cast down headlong for him all his enemies, and all his enemies have fallen down before him—even so do ye destroy the opponent[s] of the Osiris Nu, the overseer of the palace, the chancellor-in-chief, triumphant. Let him live with the gods, let him smite down his enemy, let him destroy [him] when light dawneth upon the earth, let Horus gain power and avenge the Osiris Nu, let the Osiris Nu have vigor through the union which ye have effected for him with his ka. O Osiris Nu, the Eye of Horus hath avenged thee, it hath cast down headlong all thine enemies for thee, and all thine enemies have fallen down headlong before thee. Hail, Osiris, governor of Amenti, grant thou light and fire to the happy soul which is in Sutenhenen (Heracleopolis); and [O ye children of Horus] grant ye power unto the living soul of the Osiris Nu within his flame. Let him not be repulsed and let him not be driven back at the doors of Amentet; oh let his offerings of bread and of linen garments be brought unto him among [those of] the lords of funeral oblations, oh, offer ye praises as unto a god, to the Osiris Nu, destroyer of his opponent[s] in his form of right and truth and in his attributes of a god of right and truth."

EGYPTIAN TALES

Translated from the Papyri

Edited by Wm. Flinders Petrie, Hon. D.C.L., LL.D., Edwards Professor of Egyptology, University College, London.

The Taking Of Joppa

There was once in the time of King Men-kheper-ra a revolt of the servants of his Majesty who were in Joppa; and his Majesty said, "Let Tahutia go with his footmen and destroy this wicked Foe in Joppa." And he called one of his followers, and said moreover, "Hide thou my great cane, which works wonders, in the baggage of Tahutia that my power may go with him."

Now when Tahutia came near to Joppa, with all the footmen of Pharaoh, he sent unto the Foe in Joppa, and said, "Behold now his Majesty, King Men-kheper-ra, has sent all this great army against thee; but what is that if my heart is as thy heart? Do thou come, and let us talk in the field, and see each other face to face." So Tahutia came with certain of his men; and the Foe in Joppa came likewise, but his charioteer that was with him was true of heart unto the King of Egypt. And they spoke with one another in his great tent, which Tahutia had placed far off from the soldiers. But Tahutia had made ready 200 sacks, with cords and fetters, and had made a great sack of skins with bronze fetters, and many baskets: and they were in his tent, the sacks and the baskets, and he had placed them as the forage for the horses is put in baskets. For while the Foe in Joppa drank with Tahutia, the people who were with him drank with the footmen of Pharaoh, and made merry with them. And when their bout of drinking was past, Tahutia said to the Foe in Joppa, "If it please thee, while I remain with the women and children of thy own city, let one bring of my people with their horses, that they may give them provender, or let one of the Apuro run to fetch them." So they came, and hobbled their horses, and gave them provender, and one found the great cane of Men-kheper-ra (Tahutmes III), and came to tell of it to Tahutia. And thereupon the Foe in Joppa said to Tahutia: "My heart is set on examining the great cane of Men-kheper-ra, which is named '... tautnefer.' By the ka of the King Men-kheper-ra it will be in thy hands to-day; now do thou well and bring thou it to me." And Tahutia did thus, and he brought the cane of King Men-kheper-ra. And he laid hold on the Foe in Joppa by his garment, and he arose and stood up, and said, "Look on me, O Foe in Joppa; here is the great cane of King Men-kheper-ra, the terrible lion, the son of Sekhet, to whom Amen his father gives power and strength." And he raised his hand and struck the forehead of the Foe in Joppa, and he fell helpless before him. He put him in the sack of skins and he bound with gyves the hands of the Foe in Joppa, and put on his feet the fetters with four rings. And he made bring the 200 sacks which he had cleaned, and made to enter into them 200 soldiers, and filled the hollows with cords and fetters of wood, he sealed them with a seal, and added to them their rope-nets and the poles to bear them. And he put every strong footman to bear them, in all 600 men, and said to them, "When you come into the town you shall open your burdens, you shall seize on all the inhabitants of the town, and you shall quickly put fetters upon them."

Then one went out and said unto the charioteer of the Foe in Joppa, "Thy master is fallen; go, say to thy mistress, 'A pleasant message! For Sutekh has given Tahutia to us, with his wife and his children; behold the beginning of their tribute,' that she may comprehend the two hundred sacks, which are full of men and cords and fetters." So he went before them to please the heart of his mistress, saying, "We have laid hands on Tahutia." Then the gates of the city were opened before the footmen: they entered the city, they opened their burdens, they laid hands on them of the city, both small and great, they put on them the cords and fetters quickly; the power of Pharaoh seized upon that city. After he had rested Tahutia sent a message to Egypt to the King Men-kheper-ra his lord, saying: "Be pleased, for Amen thy good father has given to thee the Foe in Joppa, together with all his people, likewise also his city. Send, therefore, people to take them as captives that thou mayest fill the house of thy father Amen Ra, king of the gods, with men-servants and maid-servants, and that they may be overthrown beneath thy feet for ever and ever."

The Doomed Prince

There once was a king to whom no son was born; and his heart was grieved, and he prayed for himself unto the gods around him for a child. They decreed that one should be born to him. And his wife, after her time was fulfilled, brought forth a son. Then came the Hathors to decree for him a destiny; they said, "His death is to be by the crocodile, or by the serpent, or by the dog." Then the people who stood by heard this, and they went to tell it to his Majesty. Then his Majesty's heart sickened very greatly. And his Majesty caused a house to be built upon the desert; it was furnished with people and with all good things of the royal house, that the child should not go abroad. And when the child was grown, he went up upon the roof, and he saw a dog; it was following a man who was walking on the road. He spoke to his page, who was with him, "What is this that walks behind the man who is coming along the road?" He answered him, "This is a dog." The child said to him, "Let there be brought to me one like it." The page went to repeat it to his Majesty. And his Majesty said, "Let there be brought to him a little pet dog, lest his heart be sad." And behold they brought to him the dog.

Then when the days increased after this, and when the child became grown in all his limbs, he sent a message to his father saying, "Come, wherefore am I kept here? Inasmuch as I am fated to three evil fates, let me follow my desire. Let God do what is in his heart." They agreed to all he said, and gave him all sorts of arms, and also his dog to follow him, and they took him to the east country, and said to him, "Behold, go thou whither thou wilt." His dog was with him, and he went northward, following his heart in the desert, while he lived on all the best of the game of the desert. He went to the chief of Naharaina.

And behold there had not been any born to the chief of Naharaina, except one daughter. Behold, there had been built for her a house; its seventy windows were seventy cubits from the ground. And the chief caused to be brought all the sons of the chiefs of the land of Khalu, and said to them, "He who reaches the window of my daughter, she shall be to him for a wife."

And many days after these things, as they were in their daily task, the youth rode by the place where they were. They took the youth to their house, they bathed him, they gave provender to his horses, they brought all kinds of things for the youth, they perfumed him, they anointed his feet, they gave him portions of their own food; and they spake to him, "Whence comest thou, goodly youth?" He said to them, "I am son of an officer of the land of Egypt; my mother is dead, and my father has taken another wife. And when she bore children, she grew to hate me, and I have come as a fugitive from before her." And they embraced him, and kissed him.

And after many days were passed, he said to the youths, "What is it that ye do here?" And they said to him: "We spend our time in this: we climb up, and he who shall reach the window of the daughter of the chief of Naharaina, to him will be given her to wife." He said to them, "If it please you, let me behold the matter, that I may come to climb with you." They went to climb, as was their daily wont: and the youth stood afar off to behold; and the face of the daughter of the chief of Naharaina was turned to them. And another day the sons came to climb, and the youth came to climb with the sons of the chiefs. He climbed, and he reached the window of the daughter of the chief of Naharaina. She kissed him, she embraced him in all his limbs.

And one went to rejoice the heart of her father, and said to him, "One of the people has reached the window of thy daughter." And the prince inquired of the messenger, saying, "The son of which of the princes is it?" And he replied to him, "It is the son of an officer, who has come as a fugitive from the land of Egypt, fleeing from before his stepmother when she had children." Then the chief of Naharaina was exceeding angry; and he said: "Shall I indeed give my daughter to the Egyptian fugitive? Let him go back whence he came." And one came to tell the youth, "Go back to the place thou camest from." But the maiden seized his hand; she swore an oath by God, saying, "By the being of Ra Harakhti, if one takes him from me, I will not eat, I will not drink, I shall die in that same hour." The messenger went to tell unto her father all that she said. Then the prince sent men to slay the youth, while he was in his house. But the maiden said: "By the being of Ra, if one slay him I shall be dead ere the sun goeth down. I will not pass an hour of life if I am parted from him." And one went to tell her father. Then the prince made them bring the youth with the maiden. The youth was seized with fear when he came before the prince. But he embraced him, he kissed him all over, and said: "Oh, tell me who thou art; behold, thou art to me as a son." He said to him: "I am a son of an officer of the land of Egypt; my mother died, my father took to him a second wife; she came to hate me, and I fled a fugitive from before her." He then gave to him his daughter to wife; he gave also to him a house, and serfs, and fields, also cattle and all manner of good things.

But after the days of these things were passed, the youth said to his wife, "I am doomed to three fates—a crocodile, a serpent, and a dog." She said to him, "Let one kill the dog which belongs to thee." He replied to her, "I am not going to kill my dog, which I have brought up from when it was small." And she feared greatly for her husband, and would not let him go alone abroad.

And one went with the youth toward the land of Egypt, to travel in that country. Behold the crocodile of the river, he came out by the town in which the youth was. And in that town was a mighty man. And the mighty man would not suffer the crocodile to escape. And when the crocodile was bound, the mighty man went out and walked abroad. And when the sun rose the mighty man went back to the house; and he did so every day, during two months of days.

Now when the days passed after this, the youth sat making a good day in his house. And when the evening came he lay down on his bed, sleep seized upon his limbs; and his wife filled a bowl of milk, and placed it by his side. Then came out a serpent from his hole, to bite the youth; behold his wife was sitting by him, she lay not down. Thereupon the servants gave milk to the serpent, and he drank, and was drunk, and lay upside down. Then his wife made it to perish with the blows of her dagger. And they woke her husband, who was astonished; and she said unto him: "Behold thy God has given one of thy dooms into thy hand; he will also give thee the others." And he sacrificed to God, adoring him, and praising his spirits from day to day.

And when the days were passed after these things, the youth went to walk in the fields of his domain. He went not alone, behold his dog was following him. And his dog ran aside after the wild game, and he followed the dog. He came to the river, and entered the river behind his dog. Then came out the crocodile, and took him to the place where the mighty man was. And the crocodile said to the youth, "I am thy doom, following after thee...."

(Here the papyrus breaks off.)

Anpu And Bata

Once there were two brethren, of one mother and one father; Anpu was the name of the elder, and Bata was the name of the younger. Now, as for Anpu he had a house, and he had a wife. But his little brother was to him as it were a son; he it was who made for him his clothes; he it was who followed behind his oxen to the fields; he it was who did the ploughing; he it was who harvested the corn; he it was who did for him all the matters that were in the field. Behold, his younger brother grew to be an excellent worker, there was not his equal in the whole land; behold, the spirit of a god was in him.

Now after this the younger brother followed his oxen in his daily manner; and every evening he turned again to the house, laden with all the herbs of the field, with milk and with wood, and with all things of the field. And he put them down before his elder brother, who was sitting with his wife; and he drank and ate, and he lay down in his stable with the cattle. And at the dawn of day he took bread which he had baked, and laid it before his elder brother; and he took with him his bread to the field, and he drave his cattle to pasture in the fields. And as he walked behind his cattle, they said to him, "Good is the herbage which is in that place"; and he listened to all that they said, and he took them to the good place which they desired. And the cattle which were before him became exceeding excellent, and they multiplied greatly.

Now at the time of ploughing his elder brother said unto him: "Let us make ready for ourselves a goodly yoke of oxen for ploughing, for the land has come out from the water, it is fit for ploughing. Moreover, do thou come to the field with corn, for we will begin the ploughing in the morrow morning." Thus said he to him; and his younger brother did all things as his elder brother had spoken unto him to do them.

And when the morn was come, they went to the fields with their things; and their hearts were pleased exceedingly with their task in the beginning of their work. And it came to pass after this that as they were in the field they stopped for corn, and he sent his younger brother, saying, "Haste thou, bring to us corn from the farm." And the younger brother found the wife of his elder brother, as she was sitting tying her hair. He said to her: "Get up, and give to me corn, that I may run to the field, for my elder brother hastened me; do not delay." She said to him: "Go, open the bin, and thou shalt take to thyself according to thy will, that I may not drop my locks of hair while I dress them."

The youth went into the stable; he took a large measure, for he desired to take much corn; he loaded it with wheat and barley; and he went out carrying it. She said to him, "How much of the corn that is wanted, is that which is on thy shoulder?" He said to her: "Three bushels of barley, and two of wheat, in all five; these are what are upon my shoulder." Thus said he to her. And she conversed with him, saying, "There is great strength in thee, for I see thy might every day." And her heart knew him with the knowledge of youth. And she arose and came to him, and conversed with him, saying, "Come, stay with me, and it shall be well for thee, and I will make for thee beautiful garments." Then the youth became like a panther of the south with fury at the evil speech which she had made to him; and she feared greatly. And he spake unto her, saying: "Behold thou art to me as a mother, thy husband is to me as a father, for he who is elder than I has brought me up. What is this wickedness that thou hast said to me? Say it not to me again. For I will not tell it to any man, for I will not let it be uttered by the mouth of any man." He lifted up his burden, and he went to the field and came to his elder brother; and they took up their work, to labor at their task.

Now afterward, at eventime, his elder brother was returning to his house; and the younger brother was following after his oxen, and he loaded himself with all the things of the field; and he brought his oxen before him, to make them lie down in their stable which was in the farm. And behold the wife of the elder brother was afraid for the words which she had said. She took a parcel of fat, she became like one who is evilly beaten, desiring to say to her husband, "It is thy younger brother who has done this wrong." Her husband returned in the even, as was his wont of every day; he came unto his house; he found his wife ill of violence; she did not give him water upon his hands as he used to have, she did not make a light before him, his house was in darkness, and she was lying very sick. Her husband said to her, "Who has spoken, with thee?" Behold she said: "No one has spoken with me except thy younger brother. When he came to take for thee corn he found me sitting alone; he said to me, 'Come, let us stay together, tie up thy hair.' Thus spake he to me. I did not listen to him, but thus spake I to him: 'Behold, am I not thy mother, is not thy elder brother to thee as a father?' And he feared, and he beat me to stop me from making report to thee, and if thou lettest him live I shall die. Now behold he is coming in the evening; and I complain of these wicked words, for he would have done this even in daylight."

And the elder brother became as a panther of the south; he sharpened his knife; he took it in his hand; he stood behind the door of his stable to slay his younger brother as he came in the evening to bring his cattle into the stable.

Now the sun went down, and he loaded himself with herbs in his daily manner. He came, and his foremost cow entered the stable, and she said to her keeper, "Behold thou thy elder brother standing before thee with his knife to slay thee; flee from before him." He heard what his first cow had said; and the next entering, she also said likewise. He looked beneath the door of the stable; he saw the feet of his elder brother; he was standing behind the door, and his knife was in his hand. He cast down his load to the ground, and betook himself to flee swiftly; and his elder brother pursued after him with his knife. Then the younger brother cried out unto Ra Harakhti, saying, "My good Lord! Thou art he who divides the evil from the good." And Ra stood and heard all his cry; and Ra made a wide water between him and his elder brother, and it was full of crocodiles; and the one brother was on one bank, and the other on the other bank; and the elder brother smote twice on his hands at not slaying him. Thus did he. And the younger brother called to the elder on the bank, saying: "Stand still until the dawn of day; and when Ra ariseth, I shall judge with thee before him, and he discerneth between the good and the evil. For I shall not be with thee any more forever; I shall not be in the place in which thou art; I shall go to the valley of the acacia."

Now when the land was lightened, and the next day appeared, Ra Harakhti arose, and one looked unto the other. And the youth spake with his elder brother, saying: "Wherefore earnest thou after me to slay me in craftiness, when thou didst not hear the words of my mouth? For I am thy brother in truth, and thou art to me as a father, and thy wife even as a mother: is it not so? Verily, when I was sent to bring for us corn, thy wife said to me, 'Come, stay with me'; for behold this has been turned over unto thee into another wise." And he caused him to understand of all that happened with him and his wife. And he swore an oath by Ra Harakhti, saying, "Thy coming to slay me by deceit with thy knife was an abomination." Then the youth took a knife, and cut off of his flesh, and cast it into the water, and the fish swallowed it. He failed; he became faint; and his elder brother cursed his own heart greatly; he stood weeping for him afar off; he knew not how to pass over to where his younger brother was, because of the crocodiles. And the younger brother called unto him, saying: "Whereas thou hast devised an evil thing, wilt thou not also devise a good thing, even like that which I would do unto thee? When thou goest to thy house thou must look to thy cattle, for I shall not stay in the place where thou art; I am going to the valley of the acacia. And now as to what thou shalt do for me; it is even that thou shalt come to seek after me, if thou perceivest a matter, namely, that there are things happening unto me. And this is what shall come to pass, that I shall draw out my soul, and I shall put it upon the top of the flowers of the acacia, and when the acacia is cut down, and it falls to the ground, and thou comest to seek for it, if thou searchest for it seven years do not let thy heart be wearied. For thou wilt find it, and thou must put it in a cup of cold water, and expect that I shall live again, that I may make answer to what has been done wrong. And thou shalt know of this, that is to say, that things are happening to me, when one shall give to thee a cup of beer in thy hand, and it shall be troubled; stay not then, for verily it shall come to pass with thee."

And the youth went to the valley of the acacia; and his elder brother went unto his house; his hand was laid on his head, and he cast dust on his head; he came to his house, and he slew his wife, he cast her to the dogs, and he sat in mourning for his younger brother.

Now many days after these things, the younger brother was in the valley of the acacia; there was none with him; he spent his time in hunting the beasts of the desert, and he came back in the even to lie down under the acacia, which bore his soul upon the topmost flower. And after this he built himself a tower with his own hands, in the valley of the acacia; it was full of all good things, that he might provide for himself a home.

And he went out from his tower, and he met the Nine Gods, who were walking forth to look upon the whole land. The Nine Gods talked one with another, and they said unto him: "Ho! Bata, bull of the Nine Gods, art thou remaining alone? Thou hast left thy village for the wife of Anpu, thy elder brother. Behold his wife is slain. Thou hast given him an answer to all that was transgressed against thee." And their hearts were vexed for him exceedingly. And Ra Harakhti said to Khnumu, "Behold, frame thou a woman for Bata, that he may not remain alive alone." And Khnumu made for him a mate to dwell with him. She was more beautiful in her limbs than any woman who is in the whole land. The essence of every god was in her. The seven Hathors came to see her: they said with one mouth, "She will die a sharp death."

And Bata loved her very exceedingly, and she dwelt in his house; he passed his time in hunting the beasts of the desert, and brought and laid them before her. He said: "Go not outside, lest the sea seize thee; for I cannot rescue thee from it, for I am a woman like thee; my soul is placed on the head of the flower of the acacia; and if another find it, I must fight with him." And he opened unto her his heart in all its nature.

Now after these things Bata went to hunt in his daily manner. And the young girl went to walk under the acacia which was by the side of her house. Then the sea saw her, and cast its waves up after her. She betook herself to flee from before it. She entered her house. And the sea called unto the acacia, saying, "Oh, would that I could seize her!" And the acacia brought a lock from her hair, and the sea carried it to Egypt, and dropped it in the place of the fullers of Pharaoh's linen. The smell of the lock of hair entered into the clothes of Pharaoh; and they were wroth with the fullers of Pharaoh, saying, "The smell of ointment is in the clothes of Pharaoh." And the people were rebuked every day, they knew not what they should do. And the chief fuller of Pharaoh walked by the bank, and his heart was very evil within him after the daily quarrel with him. He stood still, he stood upon the sand opposite to the lock of hair, which was in the water, and he made one enter into the water and bring it to him; and there was found in it a smell, exceeding sweet. He took it to Pharaoh; and they brought the scribes and the wise men, and they said unto Pharaoh: "This lock of hair belongs to a daughter of Ra Harakhti: the essence of every god is in her, and it is a tribute to thee from another land. Let messengers go to every strange land to seek her: and as for the messenger who shall go to the valley of the acacia, let many men go with him to bring her." Then said his Majesty, "Excellent exceedingly is what has been said to us"; and they sent them. And many days after these things the people who were sent to strange lands came to give report unto the King: but there came not those who went to the valley of the acacia, for Bata had slain them, but let one of them return to give a report to the King. His Majesty sent many men and soldiers, as well as horsemen, to bring her back. And there was a woman among them, and to her had been given in her hand beautiful ornaments of a woman. And the girl came back with her, and they rejoiced over her in the whole land.

And his Majesty loved her exceedingly, and raised her to high estate; and he spake unto her that she should tell him concerning her husband. And she said, "Let the acacia be cut down, and let one chop it up." And they sent men and soldiers with their weapons to cut down the acacia; and they came to the acacia, and they cut the flower upon which was the soul of Bata, and he fell dead suddenly.

And when the next day came, and the earth was lightened, the acacia was cut down. And Anpu, the elder brother of Bata, entered his house, and washed his hands; and one gave him a cup of beer, and it became troubled; and one gave him another of wine, and the smell of it was evil. Then he took his staff, and his sandals, and likewise his clothes, with his weapons of war; and he betook himself forth to the valley of the acacia. He entered the tower of his younger brother, and he found him lying upon his mat; he was dead. And he wept when he saw his younger brother verily lying dead. And he went out to seek the soul of his younger brother under the acacia tree, under which his younger brother lay in the evening. He spent three years in seeking for it, but found it not. And when he began the fourth year, he desired in his heart to return into Egypt; he said, "I will go to-morrow morn." Thus spake he in his heart.

Now when the land lightened, and the next day appeared, he was walking under the acacia; he was spending his time in seeking it. And he returned in the evening, and labored at seeking it again. He found a seed. He returned with it. Behold this was the soul of his younger brother. He brought a cup of cold water, and he cast the seed into it: and he sat down, as he was wont. Now when the night came his soul sucked up the water; Bata shuddered in all his limbs, and he looked on his elder brother; his soul was in the cup. Then Anpu took the cup of cold water, in which the soul of his younger brother was; Bata drank it, his soul stood again in its place, and he became as he had been. They embraced each other, and they conversed together.

And Bata said to his elder brother: "Behold I am to become as a great bull, which bears, every good mark; no one knoweth its history, and thou must sit upon my back. When the sun arises I shall be in the place where my wife is, that I may return answer to her; and thou must take me to the place where the King is. For all good things shall be done for thee; for one shall lade thee with silver and gold, because thou bringest me to Pharaoh, for I become a great marvel, and they shall rejoice for me in all the land. And thou shalt go to thy village."

And when the land was lightened, and the next day appeared, Bata became in the form which he had told to his elder brother. And Anpu sat upon his back until the dawn. He came to the place where the King was, and they made his Majesty to know of him; he saw him, and he was exceeding joyful with him. He made for him great offerings, saying, "This is a great wonder which has come to pass." There were rejoicings over him in the whole land. They presented unto him silver and gold for his elder brother, who went and stayed in his village. They gave to the bull many men and many things, and Pharaoh loved him exceedingly above all that is in this land.

And after many days after these things, the bull entered the purified place; he stood in the place where the princess was; he began to speak with her, saying, "Behold, I am alive indeed." And she said to him, "And, pray, who art thou?" He said to her, "I am Bata. I perceived when thou causedst that they should destroy the acacia of Pharaoh, which was my abode, that I might not be suffered to live. Behold,

I am alive indeed, I am as an ox." Then the princess feared exceedingly for the words that her husband had spoken to her. And he went out from the purified place.

And his Majesty was sitting, making a good day with her: she was at the table of his Majesty, and the King was exceeding pleased with her. And she said to his Majesty, "Swear to me by God, saying, 'What thou shalt say, I will obey it for thy sake.' " He hearkened unto all that she said, even this. "Let me eat of the liver of the ox, because he is fit for naught." Thus spake she to him. And the King was exceeding sad at her words, the heart of Pharaoh grieved him greatly. And after the land was lightened, and the next day appeared, they proclaimed a great feast with offerings to the ox. And the King sent one of the chief butchers of his Majesty, to cause the ox to be sacrificed. And when he was sacrificed, as he was upon the shoulders of the people, he shook his neck, and he threw two drops of blood over against the two doors of his Majesty. The one fell upon the one side, on the great door of Pharaoh, and the other upon the other door. They grew as two great Persea trees, and each of them was excellent.

And one went to tell unto his Majesty, "Two great Persea trees have grown, as a great marvel of his Majesty, in the night by the side of the great gate of his Majesty." And there was rejoicing for them in all the land, and there were offerings made to them.

And when the days were multiplied after these things, his Majesty was adorned with the blue crown, with garlands of flowers on his neck, and he was upon the chariot of pale gold, and he went out from the palace to behold the Persea trees: the princess also was going out with horses behind his Majesty. And his Majesty sat beneath one of the Persea trees, and it spake thus with his wife: "Oh thou deceitful one, I am Bata, I am alive, though I have been evilly entreated. I knew who caused the acacia to be cut down by Pharaoh at my dwelling. I then became an ox, and thou causedst that I should be killed."

And many days after these things the princess stood at the table of Pharaoh, and the King was pleased with her. And she said to his Majesty, "Swear to me by God, saying, 'That which the princess shall say to me I will obey it for her.' " And he hearkened unto all she said. And he commanded, "Let these two Persea trees be cut down, and let them be made into goodly planks." And he hearkened unto all she said. And after this his Majesty sent skilful craftsmen, and they cut down the Persea trees of Pharaoh; and the princess, the royal wife, was standing looking on, and they did all that was in her heart unto the trees. But a chip flew up, and it entered into the mouth of the princess; she swallowed it, and after many days she bore a son. And one went to tell his Majesty, "There is born to thee a son." And they brought him, and gave to him a nurse and servants; and there were rejoicings in the whole land. And the King sat making a merry day, as they were about the naming of him, and his Majesty loved him exceedingly at that moment, and the King raised him to be the royal son of Kush.

Now after the days had multiplied after these things, his Majesty made him heir of all the land. And many days after that, when he had fulfilled many years as heir, his Majesty flew up to heaven. And the heir said, "Let my great nobles of his Majesty be brought before me, that I may make them to know all that has happened to me." And they brought also before him his wife, and he judged with her before him, and they agreed with him. They brought to him his elder brother; he made him hereditary prince in all his land. He was thirty years King of Egypt, and he died, and his elder brother stood in his place on the day of burial.

Excellently finished in peace, for the ka of the scribe of the treasury Kagabu, of the treasury of Pharaoh, and for the scribe Hora, and the scribe Meremapt. Written by the scribe Anena, the owner of this roll. He who speaks against this roll, may Tahuti smite him.

Setna And The Magic Book

The mighty King User.maat.ra (Rameses the Great) had a son named Setna Kha.em.uast who was a great scribe, and very learned in all the ancient writings. And he heard that the magic book of Thoth, by which a man may enchant heaven and earth, and know the language of all birds and beasts, was buried in the cemetery of Memphis. And he went to search for it with his brother An.he.hor.eru; and when they found the tomb of the King's son, Na.nefer.ka.ptah, son of the King of Upper and Lower Egypt, Mer.neb.ptah, Setna opened it and went in.

Now in the tomb was Na.nefer.ka.ptah, and with him was the ka of his wife Ahura; for though she was buried at Koptos, her ka dwelt at Memphis with her husband, whom she loved. And Setna saw them seated before their offerings, and the book lay between them. And Na.nefer.ka.ptah said to Setna, "Who are you that break into my tomb in this way?" He said, "I am Setna, son of the great King User.maat.ra, living forever, and I come for that book which I see between you." And Na.nefer.ka.ptah said, "It cannot be given to you." Then said Setna, "But I will carry it away by force."

Then Ahura said to Setna, "Do not take this book; for it will bring trouble on you, as it has upon us. Listen to what we have suffered for it."

Ahura's Tale

"We were the two children of the King Mer.neb.ptah, and he loved us very much, for he had no others; and Na.nefer.ka.ptah was in his palace as heir over all the land. And when we were grown, the King said to the Queen, 'I will marry Na.nefer.ka.ptah to the daughter of a general, and Ahura to the son of another general.' And the Queen said, 'No; he is the heir, let him marry his sister, like the heir of a king; none other is fit for him.' And the King said, 'That is not fair; they had better be married to the children of the general.'

"And the Queen said, 'It is you who are not dealing rightly with me.' And the King answered, 'If I have no more than these two children, is it right that they should marry one another? I will marry Na.nefer.ka.ptah to the daughter of an officer, and Ahura to the son of another officer. It has often been done so in our family.'

"And at a time when there was a great feast before the King, they came to fetch me to the feast. And I was very troubled, and did not behave as I used to do. And the King said to me, 'Ahura, have you sent someone to me about this sorry matter, saying, "Let me be married to my elder brother"?' I said to him, 'Well, let me marry the son of an officer, and he marry the daughter of another officer, as it often happens so in our family.' I laughed, and the King laughed. And the King told the steward of the palace, 'Let them take Ahura to the house of Na.nefer.ka.ptah to-night, and all kinds of good things with her.' So they brought me as a wife to the house of Na.nefer.ka.ptah; and the King ordered them to give me presents of silver and gold, and things from the palace.

"And Na.nefer.ka.ptah passed a happy time with me, and received all the presents from the palace; and we loved one another. And when I expected a child, they told the King, and he was most heartily glad; and he sent me many things, and a present of the best silver and gold and linen. And when the time came, I bore this little child that is before you. And they gave him the name of Mer-ab, and registered him in the book of the 'House of life.'

"And when my brother Na.nefer.ka.ptah went to the cemetery of Memphis, he did nothing on earth but read the writings that are in the catacombs of the kings, and the tablets of the 'House of life,' and the inscriptions that are seen on the monuments, and he worked hard on the writings. And there was a priest there called Nesi-ptah; and as Na.nefer.ka.ptah went into a temple to pray, it happened that he went behind this priest, and was reading the inscriptions that were on the chapels of the gods. And the priest mocked him and laughed. So Na.nefer.ka.ptah said to him, 'Why are you laughing at me?' And he replied, 'I was not laughing at you, or if I happened to do so, it was at your reading writings that are worthless. If you wish so much to read writings, come to me, and I will bring you to the place where the book is which Thoth himself wrote with his own hand, and which will bring you to the gods. When you read but two pages in this you will enchant the heaven, the earth, the abyss, the mountains, and the sea; you shall know what the birds of the sky and the crawling things are saying; you shall see the fishes of the deep, for a divine power is there to bring them up out of the depth. And when you read the second page, if you are in the world of ghosts, you will become again in the shape you were in on earth. You will see the sun shining in the sky, with all the gods, and the full moon.'

"And Na.nefer.ka.ptah said: 'By the life of the King! Tell me of anything you want done and I'll do it for you, if you will only send me where this book is.' And the priest answered Na.nefer.ka.ptah, 'If you want to go to the place where the book is, you must give me 100 pieces of silver for my funeral, and provide that they shall bury me as a rich priest.' So Na.nefer.ka.ptah called his lad and told him to give the priest 100 pieces of silver; and he made them do as he wished, even everything that he asked for. Then the priest said to Na.nefer.ka.ptah: 'This book is in the middle of the river at Koptos, in an iron box; in the iron box is a bronze box; in the bronze box is a sycamore box; in the sycamore box is an ivory and ebony box; in the ivory and ebony box is a silver box; in the silver box is a golden box, and in that is the book. It is twisted all round with snakes and scorpions and all the other crawling things around the box in which the book is; and there is a deathless snake by the box.' And when the priest told Na.nefer.ka.ptah, he did not know where on earth he was, he was so much delighted.

"And when he came from the temple he told me all that had happened to him. And he said: 'I shall go to Koptos, for I must fetch this book; I will not stay any longer in the north.' And I said, 'Let me dissuade you, for you prepare sorrow and you will bring me into trouble in the Thebaid.' And I laid my hand on Na.nefer.ka.ptah, to keep him from going to Koptos, but he would not listen to me; and he went to the King, and told the King all that the priest had said. The King asked him, 'What is it that you want?' and he replied, 'Let them give me the royal boat with its belongings, for I will go to the south with Ahura and her little boy Mer-ab, and fetch this book without delay.' So they gave him the royal boat with its belongings, and we went with him to the haven, and sailed from there up to Koptos.

"Then the priests of Isis of Koptos, and the high-priest of Isis, came down to us without waiting, to meet Na.nefer.ka.ptah, and their wives also came to me. We went into the temple of Isis and Harpokrates; and Na.nefer.ka.ptah brought an ox, a goose, and some wine, and made a burnt-offering and a drink-offering before Isis of Koptos and Harpokrates. They brought us to a very fine house, with all good things; and Na.nefer.ka.ptah spent four days there and feasted with the priests of Isis of Koptos, and the wives of the priests of Isis also made holiday with me.

"And the morning of the fifth day came; and Na.nefer.ka.ptah called a priest to him, and made a magic cabin that was full of men and tackle. He put the spell upon it, and put life in it, and gave them breath, and sank it in the water. He filled the royal boat with sand, and took leave of me, and sailed from the haven: and I sat by the river at Koptos that I might see what would become of him. And he said, 'Workmen, work for me, even at the place where the book is.' And they toiled by night and by day; and when they had reached it in three days, he threw the sand out, and made a shoal in the river. And then he found on it entwined serpents and scorpions and all kinds of crawling things around the box in which the book was; and by it he found a deathless snake around the box. And he laid the spell upon the entwined serpents and scorpions and all kinds of crawling things which were around the box, that they should not come out. And he went to the deathless snake, and fought with him, and killed him; but he came to life again, and took a new form. He then fought again with him a second time; but he came to life again, and took a third form. He then cut him in two parts, and put sand between the parts, that he should not appear again.

"Na.nefer.ka.ptah then went to the place where he found the box. He uncovered a box of iron, and opened it; he found then a box of bronze, and opened that; then he found a box of sycamore wood, and opened that; again, he found a box of ivory and ebony, and opened that; yet, he found a box of silver, and opened that; and then he found a box of gold; he opened that, and found the book in it. He took the book from the golden box, and read a page of spells from it. He enchanted the heaven and the earth, the abyss, the mountains, and the sea; he knew what the birds of the sky, the fish of the deep, and the beasts of the hills all said. He read another page of the spells, and saw the sun shining in the sky, with all the gods, the full moon, and the stars in their shapes; he saw the fishes of the deep, for a divine power was present that brought them up from the water. He then read the spell upon the workmen that he had made, and taken from the haven, and said to them, 'Work for me, back to the place from which I came.' And they toiled night and day, and so he came back to the place where I sat by the river of Koptos; I had not drunk nor eaten anything, and had done nothing on earth, but sat like one who is gone to the grave.

"I then told Na.nefer.ka.ptah that I wished to see this book, for which we had taken so much trouble. He gave the book into my hands; and when I read a page of the spells in it I also enchanted heaven and earth, the abyss, the mountains, and the sea. I also knew what the birds of the sky, the fishes of the deep, and the beasts of the hills all said. I read another page of the spells, and I saw the sun shining in the sky with all the gods, the full moon, and the stars in their shapes; I saw the fishes of the deep, for a divine power was present that brought them up from the water. As I could not write, I asked Na.nefer.ka.ptah, who was a good writer, and a very learned one; he called for a new piece of papyrus, and wrote on it all that was in the book before him. He dipped it in beer, and washed it off in the liquid; for he knew that if it were washed off, and he drank it, he would know all that there was in the writing.

"We returned back to Koptos the same day, and made a feast before Isis of Koptos and Harpokrates. We then went to the haven and sailed, and went northward of Koptos. And as we went on Thoth discovered all that Na.nefer.ka.ptah had done with the book; and Thoth hastened to tell Ra, and said, 'Now know that my book and my revelation are with Na.nefer.ka.ptah, son of the King Mer.neb.ptah. He has forced himself into my place, and robbed it, and seized my box with the writings, and killed my guards who protected it.' And Ra replied to him, 'He is before you, take him and all his kin.' He sent a power from heaven with the command, 'Do not let Na.nefer.ka.ptah return safe to Memphis with all his kin.' And after this hour, the little boy Mer-ab, going out from the awning of the royal boat, fell into the river: he called on Ra, and everybody who was on the bank raised a cry. Na.nefer.ka.ptah went out of the cabin, and read the spell over him; he brought his body up because a divine power brought him to the surface. He read another spell over him, and made him tell of all what happened to him, and of what Thoth had said before Ra.

"We turned back with him to Koptos. We brought him to the Good House, we fetched the people to him, and made one embalm him; and we buried him in his coffin in the cemetery of Koptos like a great and noble person.

"And Na.nefer.ka.ptah, my brother, said: 'Let us go down, let us not delay, for the King has not yet heard of what has happened to him, and his heart will be sad about it.' So we went to the haven, we sailed, and did not stay to the north of Koptos. When we were come to the place where the little boy Mer-ab had fallen into the water, I went out from the awning of the royal boat, and I fell into the river. They called Na.nefer.ka.ptah, and he came out from the cabin of the royal boat; he read a spell over me, and brought my body up, because a divine power brought me to the surface. He drew me out, and read the spell over me, and made me tell him of all that had happened to me, and of what Thoth had said before Ra. Then he turned back with me to Koptos, he brought me to the Good House, he fetched the people to me, and made one embalm me, as great and noble people are buried, and laid me in the tomb where Mer-ab my young child was.

"He turned to the haven, and sailed down, and delayed not in the north of Koptos. When he was come to the place where we fell into the river, he said to his heart: 'Shall I not better turn back again to Koptos, that I may lie by them? For, if not, when I go down to Memphis, and the King asks after his children, what shall I say to him? Can I tell him, "I have taken your children to the Thebaid, and killed them, while I remained alive, and I have come to Memphis still alive"?' Then he made them bring him a linen cloth of striped byssus; he made a band, and bound the book firmly, and tied it upon him. Na.nefer.ka.ptah then went out of the awning of the royal boat and fell into the river. He cried on Ra; and all those who were on the bank made an outcry, saying: 'Great woe! Sad woe! Is he lost, that good scribe and able man that has no equal?'

"The royal boat went on, without anyone on earth knowing where Na.nefer.ka.ptah was. It went on to Memphis, and they told all this to the King. Then the King went down to the royal boat in mourning, and all the soldiers and high-priests of Ptah were in mourning, and all the officials and courtiers. And when he saw Na.nefer.ka.ptah, who was in the inner cabin of the royal boat—from his rank of high scribe—he lifted him up. And they saw the book by him; and the King said, 'Let one hide this book that is with him.' And the officers of the King, the priests of Ptah, and the high-priest of Ptah, said to the King, 'Our Lord, may the King live as long as the sun! Na.nefer.ka.ptah was a good scribe, and a very skilful man.' And the King had him laid in his Good House to the sixteenth day, and then had him wrapped to the thirty-fifth day, and laid him out to the seventieth day, and then had him put in his grave in his resting-place.

"I have now told you the sorrow which has come upon us because of this book for which you ask, saying, 'Let it be given to me.' You have no claim to it; and, indeed, for the sake of it, we have given up our life on earth."

***

And Setna said to Ahura, "Give me the book which I see between you and Na.nefer.ka.ptah; for if you do not I will take it by force." Then Na.nefer.ka.ptah rose from his seat and said: "Are you Setna, to whom my wife has told of all these blows of fate, which you have not suffered? Can you take this book by your skill as a good scribe? If, indeed, you can play games with me, let us play a game, then, of 52 points." And Setna said, "I am ready," and the board and its pieces were put before him. And Na.nefer.ka.ptah won a game from Setna; and he put the spell upon him, and defended himself with the game board that was before him, and sunk him into the ground above his feet. He did the same at the second game, and won it from Setna, and sunk him into the ground to his waist. He did the same at the third game, and made him sink into the ground up to his ears. Then Setna struck Na.nefer.ka.ptah a great blow with his hand. And Setna called his brother An.he.hor.eru and said to him, "Make haste and go up upon earth, and tell the King all that has happened to me, and bring me the talisman of my father Ptah, and my magic books."

And he hurried up upon earth, and told the King all that had happened to Setna. The King said, "Bring him the talisman of his father Ptah, and his magic books." And An.he.hor.eru hurried down into the tomb; he laid the talisman on Setna, and he sprang up again immediately. And then Setna reached out his hand for the book, and took it. Then—as Setna went out from the tomb—there went a Light before him, and Darkness behind him. And Ahura wept at him, and she said: "Glory to the King of Darkness! Hail to the King of Light! all power is gone from the tomb." But Na.nefer.ka.ptah said to Ahura: "Do not let your heart be sad; I will make him bring back this book, with a forked stick in his hand, and a fire-pan on his head." And Setna went out from the tomb, and it closed behind him as it was before.

Then Setna went to the King, and told him everything that had happened to him with the book. And the King said to Setna, "Take back the book to the grave of Na.nefer.ka.ptah, like a prudent man, or else he will make you bring it with a forked stick in your hand, and a fire-pan on your head." But Setna would not listen to him; and when Setna had unrolled the book he did nothing on earth but read it to everybody.

[Here follows a story of how Setna, walking in the court of the temple of Ptah, met Tabubua, a fascinating girl, daughter of a priest of Bast, of Ankhtaui; how she repelled his advances, until she had beguiled him into giving up all his possessions, and slaying his children. At the last she gives a fearful cry and vanishes, leaving Setna bereft of even his clothes. This would seem to be merely a dream, by the disappearance of Tabubua, and by Setna finding his children alive after it all; but on the other hand he comes to his senses in an unknown place, and is so terrified as to be quite ready to make restitution to Na.nefer.ka.ptah. The episode, which is not creditable to Egyptian society, seems to be intended for one of the vivid dreams which the credulous readily accept as half realities.]

So Setna went to Memphis, and embraced his children for that they were alive. And the King said to him, "Were you not drunk to do so?" Then Setna told all things that had happened with Tabubua and Na.nefer.ka.ptah. And the King said, "Setna, I have already lifted up my hand against you before, and said, 'He will kill you if you do not take back the book to the place you took it from.' But you have never listened to me till this hour. Now, then, take the book to Na.nefer.ka.ptah, with a forked stick in your hand, and a fire-pan on your head."

So Setna went out from before the King, with a forked stick in his hand, and a fire-pan on his head. He went down to the tomb in which was Na.nefer.ka.ptah. And Ahura said to him, "It is Ptah, the great god, that has brought you back safe." Na.nefer.ka.ptah laughed, and he said, "This is the business that I told you before." And when Setna had praised Na.nefer.ka.ptah, he found it as the proverb says, "The sun was in the whole tomb." And Ahura and Na.nefer.ka.ptah besought Setna greatly. And Setna said, "Na.nefer.ka.ptah, is it aught disgraceful (that you lay on me to do)?" And Na.nefer.ka.ptah said, "Setna, you know this, that Ahura and Mer-ab, her child, behold! they are in Koptos; bring them here into this tomb, by the skill of a good scribe. Let it be impressed upon you to take pains, and to go to Koptos to bring them here." Setna then went out from the tomb to the King, and told the King all that Na.nefer.ka.ptah had told him.

The King said, "Setna, go to Koptos and bring back Ahura and Mer-ab." He answered the King, "Let one give me the royal boat and its belongings." And they gave him the royal boat and its belongings, and he left the haven, and sailed without stopping till he came to Koptos.

And they made this known to the priests of Isis at Koptos and to the high-priest of Isis; and behold they came down to him, and gave him their hand to the shore. He went up with them and entered into the temple of Isis of Koptos and of Harpokrates. He ordered one to offer for him an ox, a goose, and some wine, and he made a burnt-offering and a drink-offering before Isis of Koptos and Harpokrates. He went to the cemetery of Koptos with the priests of Isis and the high-priest of Isis. They dug about for three days and three nights, for they searched even in all the catacombs which were in the cemetery of Koptos; they turned over the steles of the scribes of the "double house of life," and read the inscriptions that they found on them. But they could not find the resting-place of Ahura and Mer-ab.

Now Na.nefer.ka.ptah perceived that they could not find the resting-place of Ahura and her child Mer-ab. So he raised himself up as a venerable, very old, ancient, and came before Setna. And Setna saw him, and Setna said to the ancient, "You look like a very old man; do you know where is the resting-place of Ahura and her child Mer-ab?" The ancient said to Setna: "It was told by the father of the father of my father to the father of my father, and the father of my father has told it to my father; the resting-place of Ahura and of her child Mer-ab is in a mound south of the town of Pehemato(?)." And Setna said to the ancient, "Perhaps we may do damage to Pehemato, and you are ready to lead one to the town for the sake of that." The ancient replied to Setna: "If one listens to me, shall he therefore destroy the town of Pehemato! If they do not find Ahura and her child Mer-ab under the south corner of their town may I be disgraced." They attended to the ancient, and found the resting-place of Ahura and her child Mer-ab under the south corner of the town of Pehemato. Setna laid them in the royal boat to bring them as honored persons, and restored the town of Pehemato as it originally was. And Na.nefer.ka.ptah made Setna to know that it was he who had come to Koptos, to enable them to find out where the resting-place was of Ahura and her child Mer-ab.

So Setna left the haven in the royal boat, and sailed without stopping, and reached Memphis with all the soldiers who were with him. And when they told the King he came down to the royal boat. He took them as honored persons escorted to the catacombs, in which Na.nefer.ka.ptah was, and smoothed down the ground over them.

This is the completed writing of the tale of Setna Kha.em.uast, and Na.nefer.ka.ptah, and his wife Ahura, and their child Mer-ab. It was written in the 35th year, the month Tybi.

Tales Of The Magicians

One day, when King Khufu reigned over all the land, he said to his chancellor, who stood before him, "Go call me my sons and my councillors, that I may ask of them a thing." And his sons and his councillors came and stood before him, and he said to them, "Know ye a man who can tell me tales of the deeds of the magicians?"

Then the royal son Khafra stood forth and said, "I will tell thy Majesty a tale of the days of thy forefather Nebka, the blessed; of what came to pass when he went into the temple of Ptah of Ankhtaui."

Khafra's Tale

"His Majesty was walking unto the temple of Ptah, and went unto the house of the chief reciter Uba-aner, with his train. Now when the wife of Uba-aner saw a page, among those who stood behind the King, her heart longed after him; and she sent her servant unto him, with a present of a box full of garments.

"And he came then with the servant. Now there was a lodge in the garden of Uba-aner; and one day the page said to the wife of Uba-aner, 'In the garden of Uba-aner there is now a lodge; behold, let us therein take our pleasure.' So the wife of Uba-aner sent to the steward who had charge over the garden, saying, 'Let the lodge which is in the garden be made ready.' And she remained there, and rested and drank with the page until the sun went down.

"And when the even was now come the page went forth to bathe. And the steward said, 'I must go and tell Uba-aner of this matter.' Now when this day was past, and another day came, then went the steward to Uba-aner, and told him of all these things.

"Then said Uba-aner, 'Bring me my casket of ebony and electrum.' And they brought it; and he fashioned a crocodile of wax, seven fingers long: and he enchanted it, and said, 'When the page comes and bathes in my lake, seize on him.' And he gave it to the steward, and said to him, 'When the page shall go down into the lake to bathe, as he is daily wont to do, then throw in this crocodile behind him.' And the steward went forth bearing the crocodile.

"And the wife of Uba-aner sent to the steward who had charge over the garden, saying, 'Let the lodge which is in the garden be made ready, for I come to tarry there.'

"And the lodge was prepared with all good things; and she came and made merry therein with the page. And when the even was now come, the page went forth to bathe as he was wont to do. And the steward cast in the wax crocodile after him into the water; and, behold! it became a great crocodile seven cubits in length, and it seized on the page.

"And Uba-aner abode yet seven days with the King of Upper and Lower Egypt, Nebka, the blessed, while the page was stifled in the crocodile. And after the seven days were passed, the King of Upper and Lower Egypt, Nebka, the blessed, went forth, and Uba-aner went before him.

"And Uba-aner said unto his Majesty, 'Will your Majesty come and see this wonder that has come to pass in your days unto a page?' And the King went with Uba-aner. And Uba-aner called unto the crocodile and said, 'Bring forth the page.' And the crocodile came forth from the lake with the page. Uba-aner said unto the King, 'Behold, whatever I command this crocodile he will do it.' And his Majesty said, 'I pray you send back this crocodile.' And Uba-aner stooped and took up the crocodile, and it became in his hand a crocodile of wax. And then Uba-aner told the King that which had passed in his house with the page and his wife. And his Majesty said unto the crocodile, 'Take to thee thy prey.' And the crocodile plunged into the lake with his prey, and no man knew whither he went.

"And his Majesty the King of Upper and Lower Egypt, Nebka, the blessed, commanded, and they brought forth the wife of Uba-aner to the north side of the harem, and burned her with fire, and cast her ashes in the river.

"This is a wonder that came to pass in the days of thy forefather the King of Upper and Lower Egypt, Nebka, of the acts of the chief reciter Uba-aner."

His Majesty the King of Upper and Lower Egypt, Khufu, then said, "Let there be presented to the King Nebka, the blessed, 1,000 loaves, 100 draughts of beer, an ox, two jars of incense; and let there be presented a loaf, a jar of beer, a jar of incense and a piece of meat to the chief reciter Uba-aner; for I have seen the token of his learning." And they did all things as his Majesty commanded.

Bau-F-Ra's Tale

The royal son Bau-f-ra then stood forth and spake. He said, "I will tell thy Majesty of a wonder which came to pass in the days of thy father Seneferu, the blessed, of the deeds of the chief reciter Zazamankh. One day King Seneferu, being weary, went throughout his palace seeking for a pleasure to lighten his heart, but he found none. And he said, 'Haste, and bring before me the chief reciter and scribe of the rolls Zazamankh;' and they straightway brought him. And the King said, 'I have sought in my palace for some delight, but I have found none.' Then said Zazamankh to him, 'Let thy Majesty go upon the lake of the palace, and let there be made ready a boat, with all the fair maidens of the harem of thy palace; and the heart of thy Majesty shall be refreshed with the sight, in seeing their rowing up and down the water, and seeing the goodly pools of the birds upon the lake, and beholding its sweet fields and grassy shores; thus will thy heart be lightened. And I also will go with thee. Bring me twenty oars of ebony inlaid with gold, with blades of light wood inlaid with electrum; and bring me twenty maidens, fair in their limbs, their bosoms, and their hair, all virgins; and bring me twenty nets, and give these nets unto the maidens for their garments.' And they did according to all the commands of his Majesty.

"And they rowed down the stream and up the stream, and the heart of his Majesty was glad with the sight of their rowing. But one of them at the steering struck her hair, and her jewel of new malachite fell into the water. And she ceased her song, and rowed not; and her companions ceased, and rowed not. And his Majesty said, 'Row you not further?' And they replied, 'Our little steerer here stays and rows not.' His Majesty then said to her, 'Wherefore rowest thou not?' She replied, 'It is for my jewel of new malachite which is fallen in the water.' And he said to her, 'Row on, for behold I will replace it.' And she answered, 'But I want my own piece back in its setting.' And his Majesty said, 'Haste, bring me the chief reciter Zazamankh,' and they brought him. And his Majesty said, 'Zazamankh, my brother, I have done as thou sayedst, and the heart of his Majesty is refreshed with the sight of their rowing. But now a jewel of new malachite of one of the little ones is fallen in the water, and she ceases and rows not, and she has spoiled the rowing of her side. And I said to her, "Wherefore rowest thou not?" and she answered to me, "It is for my jewel of new malachite which is fallen in the water." I replied to her, "Row on, for behold I will replace it;" and she answered to me, "But I want my own piece again back in its setting." ' Then the chief reciter Zazamankh spake his magic speech. And he placed one part of the waters of the lake upon the other, and discovered the jewel lying upon a shard; and he took it up and gave it unto its mistress. And the water, which was twelve cubits deep in the middle, reached now to twenty-four cubits after he turned it. And he spake, and used his magic speech; and he brought again the water of the lake to its place. And his Majesty spent a joyful day with the whole of the royal house. Then rewarded he the chief reciter Zazamankh with all good things. Behold, this is a wonder that came to pass in the days of thy father, the King of Upper and Lower Egypt, Seneferu, of the deeds of the chief reciter, the scribe of the rolls, Zazamankh."

Then said the majesty of the King of Upper and Lower Egypt, Khufu, the blessed, "Let there be presented an offering of 1,000 cakes, 100 draughts of beer, an ox, and two jars of incense to the King of Upper and Lower Egypt, Seneferu, the blessed; and let there be given a loaf, a jar of beer, and a jar of incense to the chief reciter, the scribe of the rolls, Zazamankh; for I have seen the token of his learning." And they did all things as his Majesty commanded.

Hordedef's Tale

The royal son Hordedef then stood forth and spake. He said: "Hitherto hast thou only heard tokens of those who have gone before, and of which no man knoweth their truth. But I will show thy Majesty a man of thine own days." And his Majesty said, "Who is he, Hordedef?" And the royal son Hordedef answered, "It is a certain man named Dedi, who dwells at Dedsneferu. He is a man of 110 years old; and he eats 500 loaves of bread and a side of beef, and drinks 100 draughts of beer, unto this day. He knows how to restore the head that is smitten off; he knows how to cause the lion to follow him trailing his halter on the ground; he knows the designs of the dwelling of Tahuti. The majesty of the King of Upper and Lower Egypt, Khufu, the blessed, has long sought for the designs of the dwelling of Tahuti, that he may make the like of them in his pyramid."

And his Majesty said, "Thou, thyself, Hordedef, my son, bring him to me." Then were the ships made ready for the King's son Hordedef, and he went up the stream to Dedsneferu. And when the ships had moored at the haven, he landed, and sat him in a litter of ebony, the poles of which were of cedar wood overlaid with gold. Now when he drew near to Dedi, they set down the litter. And he arose to greet Dedi, and found him lying on a palmstick couch at the door of his house; one servant held his head and rubbed him, and another rubbed his feet.

And the King's son Hordedef said, "Thy state is that of one who lives to good old age; for old age is the end of our voyage, the time of embalming, the time of burial. Lie, then, in the sun, free of infirmities, without the babble of dotage: this is the salutation to worthy age. I come from far to call thee, with a message from my father Khufu, the blessed, for thou shalt eat of the best which the King gives, and of the food which those have who follow after him; that he may bring thee in good estate to thy fathers who are in the tomb."

And Dedi replied to him: "Peace to thee! Peace to thee! Hordedef, son of the King, beloved of his father. May thy father Khufu, the blessed, praise thee, may he advance thee among the elders, may thy ka prevail against the enemy, may thy soul know the right road to the gate of him who clothes the afflicted; this is the salutation to the King's son." Then the King's son, Hordedef, stretched forth his hands to him, and raised him up, and went with him to the haven, giving unto him his arm. Then said Dedi, "Let there be given me a boat, to bring me my youths and my books." And they made ready for him two boats with their rowers. And Dedi went down the river in the barge in which was the King's son, Hordedef. And when he had reached the palace, the King's son, Hordedef, entered in to give account unto his Majesty the King of Upper and Lower Egypt, Khufu, the blessed. Then said the King's son Hordedef, "O King, life, wealth, and health! My lord, I have brought Dedi." His Majesty replied, "Bring him to me speedily." And his Majesty went into the hall of columns of Pharaoh (life, wealth, and health), and Dedi was led before him. And his Majesty said, "Wherefore is it, Dedi, that I have not yet seen thee?" And Dedi answered: "He who is called it is that comes; the King (life, wealth, and health) calls me, and behold I come." And his Majesty said, "Is it true, that which men say, that thou canst restore the head which is smitten off?" And Dedi replied, "Truly, I know that, O King (life, wealth, and health), my lord." And his Majesty said, "Let one bring me a prisoner who is in prison, that his punishment may be fulfilled." And Dedi said: "Let it not be a man, O King, my lord; behold we do not even thus to our cattle." And a duck was brought unto him, and its head was cut off. And the duck was laid on the west side of the hall, and its head on the east side of the hall. And Dedi spake his magic speech. And the duck fluttered along the ground, and its head came likewise; and when it had come part to part the duck stood and quacked. And they brought likewise a goose before him, and he did even so unto it. His Majesty caused an ox to be brought, and its head cast on the ground. And Dedi spake his magic speech. And the ox stood upright behind him, and followed him with his halter trailing on the ground.

And King Khufu said, "And is it true what is said, that thou knowest the number of the designs of the dwelling of Tahuti?" And Dedi replied, "Pardon me, I know not their number, O King (life, wealth, and health), but I know where they are." And his Majesty said, "Where is that?" And Dedi replied: "There is a chest of whetstone in a chamber named the plan-room, in Heliopolis; they are in this chest." And Dedi said further unto him, "O King (life, wealth, and health), my lord, it is not I that is to bring them to thee." And his Majesty said, "Who, then, is it that shall bring them to me?" And Dedi answered to him, "It is the eldest of the three children who are in the body of Rud-didet who shall bring them to thee." And his Majesty said: "Would that it may be as thou sayest! And who is this Rud-didet?" And Dedi replied: "She is the wife of a priest of Ra, lord of Sakhebu. And she has conceived these three sons by Ra, lord of Sakhebu, and the god has promised her that they shall fulfil this noble office (of reigning) over all this land, and that the eldest of them shall be high-priest in Heliopolis." And his Majesty's heart became troubled for this; but Dedi spake unto him: "What is this that thou thinkest, O King (life, wealth, health), my lord? Is it because of these three children? I tell thee thy son shall reign, and thy son's son, and then one of them." His Majesty said, "And when shall Rud-didet bear these?" And he replied, "She shall bear them on the twenty-fifth of the month Tybi." And his Majesty said, "When the banks of the canal of Letopolis are cut, I will walk there that I may see the temple of Ra, lord of Sakhebu." And Dedi replied, "Then I will cause that there be four cubits of water by the banks of the canal of Letopolis." When his Majesty returned to his palace, his Majesty said: "Let them place Dedi in the house of the royal son Hordedef, that he may dwell with him, and let them give him a daily portion of 1,000 loaves, 100 draughts of beer, an ox, and 100 bunches of onions." And they did everything as his Majesty commanded.

And one day it came to pass that Rud-didet felt the pains of birth. And the majesty of Ra, Lord of Sakhebu, said unto Isis, to Nebhat, to Meskhent, to Hakt, and to Khnumu: "Go ye, and deliver Rud-didet of these three children that she shall bear, who are to fulfil this noble office over all this land; that they may build up your temples, furnish your altars with offerings, supply your tables of libation, and increase your endowments." Then went these deities; their fashion they made as that of dancing-girls, and Khnumu was with them as a porter. They drew near unto the house of Ra-user, and found him standing, with his girdle fallen. And they played before him with their instruments of music. But he said unto them, "My ladies, behold, here is a woman who feels the pains of birth." They said to him, "Let us see her, for we know how to help her." And he replied, "Come, then." And they entered in straightway to Rud-didet, and they closed the door on her and on themselves. Then Isis stood before her, and Nebhat stood behind her, and Hakt helped her. And Isis said, "O child, by thy name of User-ref, do not do violence." And the child came upon her hands, as a child of a cubit; its bones were strong, the beauty of its limbs was like gold, and its hair was like true lapis-lazuli. They washed him, and prepared him, and placed him on a carpet on the brickwork. Then Meskhent approached him and said, "This is a king who shall reign over all the land." And Khnumu gave strength to his limbs. Then Isis stood before her, and Nebhat stood behind her, and Hakt helped her. And Isis said, "O child, by thy name of Sah-ra, stay not in her." Then the child came upon her hands, a child of a cubit; its bones were strong, the beauty of its limbs was like gold, and its hair was like true lapis-lazuli. They washed him, and prepared him, and laid him on a carpet on the brickwork. Then Meskhent approached him and said, "This is a king who shall reign over all the land." And Khnumu gave strength to his limbs. Then Isis stood before her, and Nebhat stood behind her, and Hakt helped her. And Isis said, "O child, by thy name of Kaku, remain not in darkness in her." And the child came upon her hands, a child of a cubit; its bones were strong, the beauty of its limbs was like gold, and its hair was like true lapis-lazuli. And Meskhent approached him and said, "This is a king who shall reign over all the land." And Khnumu gave strength to his limbs. And they washed him, and prepared him, and laid him on a carpet on the brickwork.

And the deities went out, having delivered Rud-didet of the three children. And they said, "Rejoice! O Ra-user, for behold three children are born unto thee." And he said unto them, "My ladies, and what shall I give unto ye? Behold, give this bushel of barley here unto your porter, that ye may take it as your reward to the brew-house." And Khnumu loaded himself with the bushel of barley. And they went away toward the place from which they came. And Isis spake unto these goddesses, and said, "Wherefore have we come without doing a marvel for these children, that we may tell it to their father who has sent us?" Then made they the divine diadems of the King (life, wealth, and health), and laid them in the bushel of barley. And they caused the clouds to come with wind and rain; and they turned back again unto the house. And they said, "Let us put this barley in a closed chamber, sealed up, until we return northward, dancing." And they placed the barley in a close chamber.

And Rud-didet purified herself, with a purification of fourteen days. And she said to her handmaid, "Is the house made ready?" And she replied, "All things are made ready, but the brewing barley is not yet brought." And Rud-didet said, "Wherefore is the brewing barley not yet brought?" And the servant answered, "It would all of it long since be ready if the barley had not been given to the dancing-girls, and lay in the chamber under their seal." Rud-didet said, "Go down, and bring of it, and Ra-user shall give them in its stead when he shall come." And the handmaid went, and opened the chamber. And she heard talking and singing, music and dancing, quavering, and all things which are performed for a king in his chamber. And she returned and told to Rud-didet all that she had heard. And she went through the chamber, but she found not the place where the sound was. And she laid her temple to the sack, and found that the sounds were in it. She placed it in a chest, and put that in another locker, and tied it fast with leather, and laid it in the storeroom, where the things were, and sealed it. And Ra-user came returning from the field; and Rud-didet repeated unto him these things; and his heart was glad above all things; and they sat down and made a joyful day.

And after these days it came to pass that Rud-didet was wroth with her servant, and beat her with stripes. And the servant said unto those that were in the house: "Shall it be done thus unto me? She has borne three kings, and I will go and tell this to his Majesty King Khufu the blessed." And she went, and found the eldest brother of her mother, who was binding his flax on the floor. And he said to her, "Whither goest thou, my little maid?" And she told him of all these things. And her brother said to her: "Wherefore comest thou thus to me? Shall I agree to treachery?" And he took a bunch of the flax to her, and laid on her a violent blow. And the servant went to fetch a handful of water, and a crocodile carried her away.

Her uncle went therefore to tell of this to Rud-didet; and he found Rud-didet sitting, her head on her knees, and her heart beyond measure sad. And he said to her, "My lady, why makest thou thy heart thus?" And she answered, "It is because of this little wretch that was in the house; behold she went out saying, 'I will go and tell it.' " And he bowed his head unto the ground, and said, "My lady, she came and told me of these things, and made her complaint unto me; and I laid on her a violent blow. And she went forth to draw water, and a crocodile carried her away."

(The rest of the tale is lost.)

The Peasant And The Workman

There dwelt in the Sekhet Hemat—or Salt Country—a peasant called the Sekhti, with his wife and children, his asses and his dogs; and he trafficked in all good things of the Sekhet Hemat to Henenseten. Behold now he went with rushes, natron, and salt, with wood and pods, with stones and seeds, and all good products of the Sekhet Hemat. And this Sekhti journeyed to the south unto Henenseten; and when he came to the lands of the house of Fefa, north of Denat, he found a man there standing on the bank, a man called Hemti—the workman—son of a man called Asri, who was a serf of the high-steward Meruitensa. Now said this Hemti, when he saw the asses of Sekhti, that were pleasing in his eyes, "Oh that some good god would grant me to steal away the goods of Sekhti from him!"

Now the Hemti's house was by the dike of the tow-path, which was straightened, and not wide, as much as the width of a waistcloth: on the one side of it was the water, and on the other side of it grew his corn. Hemti said then to his servant, "Hasten! bring me a shawl from the house," and it was brought instantly. Then spread he out this shawl on the face of the dike, and it lay with its fastening on the water and its fringe on the corn.

Now Sekhti approached along the path used by all men. Said Hemti: "Have a care, Sekhti! you are not going to trample on my clothes!" Said Sekhti, "I will do as you like, I will pass carefully." Then went he up on the higher side. But Hemti said, "Go you over my corn, instead of the path?" Said Sekhti: "I am going carefully; this high field of corn is not my choice, but you have stopped your path with your clothes, and will you then not let us pass by the side of the path?" And one of the asses filled its mouth with a cluster of corn. Said Hemti: "Look you, I shall take away your ass, Sekhti, for eating my corn; behold it will have to pay according to the amount of the injury." Said Sekhti: "I am going carefully; the one way is stopped, therefore took I my ass by the inclosed ground; and do you seize it for filling its mouth with a cluster of corn? Moreover, I know unto whom this domain belongs, even unto the lord steward Meruitensa. He it is who smites every robber in this whole land; and shall I then be robbed in his domain?"

Said Hemti, "This is the proverb which men speak: 'A poor man's name is only his own matter.' I am he of whom you spake, even the lord steward of whom you think." Thereon he took to him branches of green tamarisk and scourged all his limbs, took his asses, and drave them into the pasture. And Sekhti wept very greatly, by reason of the pain of what he had suffered. Said Hemti, "Lift not up your voice, Sekhti, or you shall go to the demon of silence." Sekhti answered: "You beat me, you steal my goods, and now would take away even my voice, O demon of silence! If you will restore my goods, then will I cease to cry out at your violence."

Sekhti stayed the whole day petitioning Hemti, but he would not give ear unto him. And Sekhti went his way to Khenensuten to complain to the lord steward Meruitensa. He found him coming out from the door of his house to embark on his boat, that he might go to the judgment-hall. Sekhti said: "Ho! turn, that I may please thy heart with this discourse. Now at this time let one of thy followers, whom thou wilt, come to me that I may send him to thee concerning it." The lord steward Meruitensa made his follower, whom he chose, go straight unto him, and Sekhti sent him back with an account of all these matters. Then the lord steward Meruitensa accused Hemti unto the nobles who sat with him; and they said unto him: "By your leave: As to this Sekhti of yours, let him bring a witness. Behold thou it is our custom with our Sekhtis; witnesses come with them; behold, that is our custom. Then it will be fitting to beat this Hemti for a trifle of natron and a trifle of salt; if he is commanded to pay for it, he will pay for it." But the high steward Meruitensa held his peace; for he would not reply unto these nobles, but would reply unto the Sekhti.

Now Sekhti came to appeal to the lord steward Meruitensa, and said, "O my lord steward, greatest of the great, guide of the needy:

> When thou embarkest on the lake of truth—
> Mayest thou sail upon it with a fair wind;
> May thy mainsail not fly loose.
> May there not be lamentation in thy cabin;
> May not misfortune come after thee.
> May not thy mainstays be snapped;
> Mayest thou not run aground.

May not the wave seize thee;
Mayest thou not taste the impurities of the river;
Mayest thou not see the face of fear.

May the fish come to thee without escape;
Mayest thou reach unto plump water-fowl.
For thou art the orphan's father, the widow's husband,
The desolate woman's brother, the garment of the motherless.
Let me celebrate thy name in this land for every virtue,
A guide without greediness of heart;
A great one without any meanness.

Destroying deceit, encouraging justice;
Coming to the cry, and allowing utterance.

Let me speak, do thou hear and do justice;
O praised! whom the praised ones praise.

Abolish oppression, behold me, I am overladen,
Reckon with me, behold me defrauded."

Now the Sekhti made this speech in the time of the majesty of the King Neb-ka-n-ra, blessed. The lord steward Meruitensa went away straight to the King and said: "My lord, I have found one of these Sekhti, excellent of speech, in very truth; stolen are his goods, and he has come to complain to me of the matter."

His Majesty said: "As thou wishest that I may see health! lengthen out his complaint, without replying to any of his speeches. He who desireth him to continue speaking should be silent; behold, bring us his words in writing, that we may listen to them. But provide for his wife and his children, and let the Sekhti himself also have a living. Thou must cause one to give him his portion without letting him know that thou art he who is giving it to him."

There were given to him four loaves and two draughts of beer each day; which the lord steward Meruitensa provided for him, giving it to a friend of his, who furnished it unto him. Then the lord steward Meruitensa sent the governor of the Sekhet Hemat to make provision for the wife of the Sekhti, three rations of corn each day.

Then came the Sekhti a second time, and even a third time, unto the lord steward Meruitensa; but he told two of his followers to go unto the Sekhti, and seize on him, and beat him with staves. But he came again unto him, even unto six times, and said:

"My Lord Steward—
Destroying deceit, and encouraging justice;
Raising up every good thing, and crushing every evil;
As plenty comes removing famine,
As clothing covers nakedness,
As clear sky after storm warms the shivering;
As fire cooks that which is raw,
As water quenches the thirst;
Look with thy face upon my lot; do not covet, but content me without fail; do the right and do not evil,"

But yet Meruitensa would not hearken unto his complaint; and the Sekhti came yet, and yet again, even unto the ninth time. Then the lord steward told two of his followers to go unto the Sekhti; and the Sekhti feared that he should be beaten as at the third request. But the lord steward Meruitensa then said unto him: "Fear not, Sekhti, for what thou hast done. The Sekhti has made many speeches, delightful to the heart of his Majesty, and I take an oath—as I eat bread, and as I drink water—that thou shalt be remembered to eternity." Said the lord steward, "Moreover, thou shalt be satisfied when thou shalt hear of thy complaints." He caused to be written on a clean roll of papyrus each petition to the end, and the lord steward Meruitensa sent it to the majesty of the King Neb-ka-n-ra, blessed, and it was good to him more than anything that is in the whole land: but his Majesty said to Meruitensa: "Judge it thyself; I do not desire it."

The lord steward Meruitensa made two of his followers to go to the Sekhet Hemat, and bring a list of the household of the Sekhti; and its amount was six persons, beside his oxen and his goats, his wheat and his barley, his asses and his dogs; and moreover he gave all that which belonged unto the Hemti to the Sekhti, even all his property and his officers, and the Sekhti was beloved of the King more than all his overseers, and ate of all the good things of the King, with all his household.

The Shipwrecked Sailor

The wise servant said: "Let thy heart be satisfied, O my lord, for that we have come back to the country; after we have long been on board, and rowed much, the prow has at last touched land. All the people rejoice, and embrace us one after another. Moreover, we have come back in good health, and not a man is lacking; although we have been to the ends of Wawat, and gone through the land of Senmut, we have returned in peace, and our land—behold, we have come back to it. Hear me, my lord; I have no other refuge. Wash thee, and turn the water over thy fingers; then go and tell the tale to the Majesty."

His lord replied: "Thy heart continues still its wandering words! but although the mouth of a man may save him, his words may also cover his face with confusion. Wilt thou do then as thy heart moves thee? This that thou wilt say, tell quietly."

The sailor then answered: "Now I shall tell that which has happened to me, to my very self. I was going to the mines of Pharaoh, and I went down on the sea on a ship of 150 cubits long and forty cubits wide, with 150 sailors of the best of Egypt, who had seen heaven and earth, and whose hearts were stronger than lions. They had said that the wind would not be contrary, or that there would be none. But as we approached the land the wind arose, and threw up waves eight cubits high. As for me, I seized a piece of wood; but those who were in the vessel perished, without one remaining. A wave threw me on an island, after that I had been three days alone, without a companion beside my own heart. I laid me in a thicket, and the shadow covered me. Then stretched I my limbs to try to find something for my mouth. I found there figs and grapes, all manner of good herbs, berries and grain, melons of all kinds, fishes and birds. Nothing was lacking. And I satisfied myself; and left on the ground that which was over, of what my arms had been filled withal. I dug a pit, I lighted a fire, and I made a burnt-offering unto the gods.

"Suddenly I heard a noise as of thunder, which I thought to be that of a wave of the sea. The trees shook, and the earth was moved. I uncovered my face, and I saw that a serpent drew near. He was thirty cubits long, and his beard greater than two cubits; his body was as overlaid with gold, and his color as that of true lazuli. He coiled himself before me.

"Then he opened his mouth, while that I lay on my face before him, and he said to me: 'What has brought thee, what has brought thee, little one, what has brought thee? If thou sayest not speedily what has brought thee to this isle, I will make thee know thyself; as a flame thou shalt vanish, if thou tellest me not something I had not heard, or which I knew not, before thee.'

"Then he took me in his mouth and carried me to his resting-place, and laid me down without any hurt. I was whole and sound, and nothing was gone from me. Then he opened his mouth against me, while that I lay on my face before him, and he said, 'What has brought thee, what has brought thee, little one, what has brought thee to this isle which is in the sea, and of which the shores are in the midst of the waves?'

"Then I replied to him, and holding my arms low before him, I said to him: 'I was embarked for the mines by the order of the majesty, in a ship; 150 cubits was its length, and the width of it forty cubits. It had 150 sailors of the best of Egypt, who had seen heaven and earth, and the hearts of whom were stronger than lions. They said that the wind would not be contrary, or that there would be none. Each of them exceeded his companion in the prudence of his heart and the strength of his arm, and I was not beneath any of them. A storm came upon us while we were on the sea. Hardly could we reach to the shore when the wind waxed yet greater, and the waves rose even eight cubits. As for me, I seized a piece of wood, while those who were in the boat perished without one being left with me for three days. Behold me now before thee, for I was brought to this isle by a wave of the sea.'

"Then said he to me: 'Fear not, fear not, little one, and make not thy face sad. If thou hast come to me, it is God who has let thee live. For it is he who has brought thee to this isle of the blest, where nothing is lacking, and which is filled with all good things. See now, thou shalt pass one month after another, until thou shalt be four months in this isle. Then a ship shall come from thy land with sailors, and thou shalt leave with them and go to thy country, and thou shalt die in thy town.'

" 'Converse is pleasing, and he who tastes of it passes over his misery. I will therefore tell thee of that which is in this isle. I am here with my brethren and my children around me; we are seventy-five serpents, children and kindred; without naming a young girl who was brought unto me by chance, and on whom the fire of heaven fell, and burnt her to ashes.

"'As for thee if thou art strong, and if thy heart waits patiently, thou shalt press thy infants to thy bosom and embrace thy wife. Thou shalt return to thy house, which is full of all good things; thou shalt see thy land, where thou shalt dwell in the midst of thy kindred.'

"Then I bowed, in my obeisance, and I touched the ground before him. 'Behold now that which I have told thee before. I shall tell of thy presence unto Pharaoh, I shall make him to know of thy greatness, and I will bring to thee of the sacred oils and perfumes, and of incense of the temples with which all gods are honored. I shall tell, moreover, of that which I do now see (thanks to him), and there shall be rendered to thee praises before the fulness of all the land. I shall slay asses for thee in sacrifice, I shall pluck for thee the birds, and I shall bring for thee ships full of all kinds of the treasures of Egypt, as is comely to do unto a god, a friend of men in a far country, of which men know not.'

"Then he smiled at my speech, because of that which was in his heart, for he said to me: 'Thou art not rich in perfumes, for all that thou hast is but common incense. As for me I am Prince of the land of Punt, and I have perfumes. Only the oil which thou sayest thou wouldst bring is not common in this isle. But, when thou shalt depart from this place, thou shalt never more see this isle; it shall be changed into waves.'

"And, behold, when the ship drew near, according to all that he had told me before, I got me up into an high tree, to strive to see those who were within it. Then I came and told to him this matter; but it was already known unto him before. Then he said to me: 'Farewell, farewell; go to thy house, little one, see again thy children, and let thy name be good in thy town; these are my wishes for thee.'

"Then I bowed myself before him, and held my arms low before him, and he, he gave me gifts of precious perfumes, of cassia, of sweet woods, of kohl, of cypress, an abundance of incense, of ivory tusks, of baboons, of apes, and all kinds of precious things. I embarked all in the ship which was come, and, bowing myself, I prayed God for him.

"Then he said to me, 'Behold thou shalt come to thy country in two months, thou shalt press to thy bosom thy children, and thou shalt rest in thy tomb.' After this I went down to the shore unto the ship, and I called to the sailors who were there. Then on the shore I rendered adoration to the master of this isle and to those who dwelt therein.

"When we shall come, in our return, to the house of Pharaoh, in the second month, according to all that the serpent has said, we shall approach unto the palace. And I shall go in before Pharaoh, I shall bring the gifts which I have brought from this isle into the country. Then he shall thank me before the fulness of all the land. Grant them unto me a follower, and lead me to the courtiers of the King. Cast thy eye upon me, after that I am come to land again, after that I have both seen and proved this. Hear my prayer, for it is good to listen to people. It was said unto me, 'Become a wise man, and thou shalt come to honor,' and behold I have become such."

This is finished from its beginning unto its end, even as it was found in a writing. It is written by the scribe of cunning fingers Ameni-amen-aa; may he live in life, wealth, and health!

The Adventures Of Sanehat

The hereditary prince, royal seal-bearer, confidential friend, judge, keeper of the gate of the foreigners, true and beloved royal acquaintance, the royal follower Sanehat says:

I attended my lord as a follower of the King, of the house of the hereditary princess, the greatly favored, the royal wife, Ankhet-Usertesen, who shares the dwelling of the royal son Amenemhat in Kanefer.

In the thirtieth year, the month Paophi, the seventh day the god entered his horizon, the King Sehotepabra flew up to heaven and joined the sun's disk, the follower of the god met his maker. The palace was silenced, and in mourning, the great gates were closed, the courtiers crouching on the ground, the people in hushed mourning.

His Majesty had sent a great army with the nobles to the land of the Temehu (Lybia), his son and heir, the good god King Usertesen as their leader. Now he was returning, and had brought away living captives and all kinds of cattle without end. The councillors of the palace had sent to the West to let the King know the matter that had come to pass in the inner hall. The messenger was to meet him on the road, and reach him at the time of evening: the matter was urgent. "A hawk had soared with his followers." Thus said he, not to let the army know of it. Even if the royal sons who commanded in that army send a message, he was not to speak to a single one of them. But I was standing near, and heard his voice while he was speaking. I fled far away, my heart beating, my arms failing, trembling had fallen on all my limbs. I turned about in running to seek a place to hide me, and I threw myself between two bushes, to wait while they should pass by. Then I turned me toward the south, not from wishing to come into this place—for I knew not if war was declared—nor even thinking a wish to live after this sovereign, I turned my back to the sycamore, I reached Shi-Seneferu, and rested on the open field. In the morning I went on and overtook a man, who passed by the edge of the road. He asked of me mercy, for he feared me. By the evening I drew near to Kher-ahau (? old Cairo), and I crossed the river on a raft without a rudder. Carried over by the west wind, I passed over to the east to the quarries of Aku and the land of the goddess Herit, mistress of the red mountain (Gebel Ahmar). Then I fled on foot, northward, and reached the walls of the prince, built to repel the Sati. I crouched in a bush for fear of being seen by the guards, changed each day, who watch on the top of the fortress. I took my way by night, and at the lighting of the day I reached Peten, and turned me toward the valley of Kemur. Then thirst hasted me on; I dried up, and my throat narrowed, and I said, "This is the taste of death." When I lifted up my heart and gathered strength, I heard a voice and the lowing of cattle. I saw men of the Sati, and one of them—a friend unto Egypt—knew me. Behold he gave me water and boiled me milk, and I went with him to his camp; they did me good, and one tribe passed me on to another. I passed on to Sun, and reached the land of Adim (Edom).

When I had dwelt there half a year Amu-an-shi—who is the Prince of the Upper Tenu—sent for me and said: "Dwell thou with me that thou mayest hear the speech of Egypt." He said thus for that he knew of my excellence, and had heard tell of my worth, for men of Egypt who were there with him bore witness of me. Behold he said to me: "For what cause hast thou come hither? Has a matter come to pass in the palace? Has the King of the two lands, Sehetepabra, gone to heaven? That which has happened about this is not known." But I answered with concealment, and said: "When I came from the land of the Tamahu, and my desires were there changed in me, if I fled away it was not by reason of remorse that I took the way of a fugitive; I have not failed in my duty, my mouth has not said any bitter words, I have not heard any evil counsel, my name has not come into the mouth of a magistrate. I know not by what I have been led into this land." And Amu-an-shi said: "This is by the will of the god (King of Egypt); for what is a land like if it know not that excellent god, of whom the dread is upon the lands of strangers, as they dread Sekhet in a year of pestilence?" I spake to him, and replied: "Forgive me; his son now enters the palace, and has received the heritage of his father. He is a god who has none like him, and there is none before him. He is a master of wisdom, prudent in his designs, excellent in his decrees, with good-will to him who goes or who comes; he subdued the land of strangers while his father yet lived in his palace, and he rendered account of that which his father destined him to perform. He is a brave man, who verily strikes with his sword; a valiant one, who has not his equal; he springs upon the barbarians, and throws himself on the spoilers; he breaks the horns and weakens the hands, and those whom he smites cannot raise the buckler. He is fearless, and dashes the heads, and none can stand before him. He is swift of foot, to destroy him who flies; and none who flees from him reaches his home. His heart is strong in his time; he is a lion who strikes with the claw, and never has he turned his back. His heart is closed to pity; and when he sees multitudes, he leaves none to live behind him. He is a valiant one who springs in front when he sees resistance; he is a warrior who rejoices when he flies on the barbarians. He seizes the buckler, he rushes forward, he never needs to strike again, he slays and none can turn his lance; and when he takes the bow the barbarians flee from his arms like dogs; for the great goddess has given to him to strike those who know her not; and if he reaches forth he spares none, and leaves naught behind. He is a friend of great sweetness, who knows how to gain love; his land loves him more than itself, and rejoices in him more than in its own god; men and women run to his call. A king, he has ruled from his birth; he, from his birth, has increased births, a sole being, a divine essence, by whom this land rejoices to be governed. He enlarges the borders of the South; but he covets not the lands of the North: he does not smite the Sati, nor crush the Nemau-shau. If he descends here, let him know thy name, by the homage which thou wilt pay to his majesty. For he refuses not to bless the land which obeys him."

And he replied to me: "Egypt is indeed happy and well settled; behold thou art far from it, but whilst thou art with me I will do good unto thee." And he placed me before his children, he married his eldest daughter to me, and gave me the choice of all his land, even among the best of that which he had on the border of the next land. It is a goodly land, Iaa is its name. There are figs and grapes; there is wine commoner than water; abundant is the honey, many are its olives; and all fruits are upon its trees: there are barley and wheat, and cattle of kinds without end. This was truly a great thing that he granted me, when the prince came to invest me, and establish me as prince of a tribe in the best of his land. I had my continual portion of bread and of wine each day, of cooked meat, of roasted fowl, as well as the wild game which I took, or which was brought to me, beside what my dogs captured. They made me much butter, and prepared milk of all kinds. I passed many years, the children that I had became great, each ruling his tribe. When a messenger went or came to the palace, he turned aside from the way to come to me; for I helped every man. I gave water to the thirsty, I set on his way him who went astray, and I rescued the robbed. The Sati who went far, to strike and turn back the princes of other lands, I ordained their goings; for the Prince of the Tenu for many years appointed me to be general of his soldiers. In every land which I attacked I played the champion, I took the cattle, I led away the vassals, I carried off the slaves, I slew the people, by my sword, my bow, my marches and my good devices. I was excellent to the heart of my prince; he loved me when he knew my power, and set me over his children when he saw the strength of my arms.

A champion of the Tenu came to defy me in my tent: a bold man without equal, for he had vanquished the whole country. He said, "Let Sanehat fight with me"; for he desired to overthrow me; he thought to take my cattle for his tribe. The prince counselled with me. I said: "I know him not. I certainly am not of his degree, I hold me far from his place. Have I ever opened his door, or leaped over his fence? It is some envious jealousy from seeing me; does he think that I am like some steer among the cows, whom the bull overthrows? If this is a wretch who thinks to enrich himself at my cost, not a Bedawi and a Bedawi fit for fight, then let us put the matter to judgment. Verily a true bull loves battle, but a vainglorious bull turns his back for fear of contest; if he has a heart for combat, let him speak what he pleases. Will God forget what he has ordained, and how shall that be known?" I lay down; and when I had rested I strung my bow, I made ready my arrows, I loosened my poniard, I furbished my arms. At dawn the land of the Tenu came together; it had gathered its tribes and called all the neighboring people, it spake of nothing but the fight. Each heart burnt for me, men and women crying out; for each heart was troubled for me, and they said: "Is there another strong one who would fight with him? Behold the adversary has a buckler, a battle-axe, and an armful of javelins." Then I drew him to the attack; I turned aside his arrows, and they struck the ground in vain. One drew near to the other, and he fell on me, and then I shot him. My arrow fastened in his neck, he cried out, and fell on his face: I drove his lance into him, and raised my shout of victory on his back. While all the men of the land rejoiced, I, and his vassals whom he had oppressed, gave thanks unto Mentu. This prince, Amu-an-shi, embraced me. Then I carried off his goods and took his cattle, that which he had wished to do to me, I did even so unto him; I seized that which was in his tent, I spoiled his dwelling. As time went on I increased the richness of my treasures and the number of my cattle.

Petition To The King Of Egypt

"Now behold what the god has done for me who trusted in him. Having once fled away, yet now there is a witness of me in the palace. Once having fled away, as a fugitive—now all in the palace give unto me a good name. After that I had been dying of hunger, now I give bread to those around. I had left my land naked, and now I am clothed in fine linen. After having been a wanderer without followers, now I possess many serfs. My house is fine, my land wide, my memory is established in the temple of all the gods. And let this flight obtain thy forgiveness; that I may be appointed in the palace; that I may see the place where my heart dwells. How great a thing is it that my body should be embalmed in the land where I was born! To return there is happiness. I have made offering to God to grant me this thing. His heart suffers who has run away unto a strange land. Let him hear the prayer of him who is afar off, that he may revisit the place of his birth, and the place from which he removed.

"May the King of Egypt be gracious to me that I may live of his favor. And I render my homage to the mistress of the land, who is in his palace; may I hear the news of her children. Thus will my limbs grow young again. Now old age comes, feebleness seizes me, my eyes are heavy, my arms are feeble, my legs will not move, my heart is slow. Death draws nigh to me, soon shall they lead me to the city of eternity. Let me follow the mistress of all (the queen, his former mistress); lo! let her tell me the excellencies of her children; may she bring eternity to me."

Then the majesty of King Kheper-ka-ra, the blessed, spake upon this my desire that I had made to him. His Majesty sent unto me with presents from the King, that he might enlarge the heart of his servant, like unto the province of any strange land; and the royal sons who are in the palace addressed themselves unto me.

Copy of the Decree Which Was Brought, To Me Who Speak To You, To Lead Me Back Into Egypt

"The Horus, life of births, lord of the crowns, life of births, King of Upper and Lower Egypt, Kheper-ka-ra, son of the Sun, Amen-em-hat, ever living unto eternity. Order for the follower Sanehat. Behold this order of the King is sent to thee to instruct thee of his will.

"Now, although thou hast gone through strange lands from Adim to Tenu, and passed from one country to another at the wish of thy heart—behold, what hast thou done, or what has been done against thee, that is amiss? Moreover, thou reviledst not; but if thy word was denied, thou didst not speak again in the assembly of the nobles, even if thou wast desired. Now, therefore, that thou hast thought on this matter which has come to thy mind, let thy heart not change again; for this thy Heaven (queen), who is in the palace is fixed, she is flourishing, she is enjoying the best in the kingdom of the land, and her children are in the chambers of the palace.

"Leave all the riches that thou hast, and that are with thee, altogether. When thou shalt come into Egypt behold the palace, and when thou shalt enter the palace, bow thy face to the ground before the Great House; thou shalt be chief among the companions. And day by day behold thou growest old; thy vigor is lost, and thou thinkest on the day of burial. Thou shalt see thyself come to the blessed state, they shall give thee the bandages from the hand of Tait, the night of applying the oil of embalming. They shall follow thy funeral, and visit the tomb on the day of burial, which shall be in a gilded case, the head painted with blue, a canopy of cypress wood above thee, and oxen shall draw thee, the singers going before thee, and they shall dance the funeral dance. The weepers crouching at the door of thy tomb shall cry aloud the prayers for offerings: they shall slay victims for thee at the door of thy pit; and thy pyramid shall be carved in white stone, in the company of the royal children. Thus thou shalt not die in a strange land, nor be buried by the Amu; thou shalt not be laid in a sheepskin when thou art buried; all people shall beat the earth, and lament on thy body when thou goest to the tomb."

When this order came to me, I was in the midst of my tribe. When it was read unto me, I threw me on the dust, I threw dust in my hair; I went around my tent rejoicing and saying: "How may it be that such a thing is done to the servant, who with a rebellious heart has fled to strange lands? Now with an excellent deliverance, and mercy delivering me from death, thou shalt cause me to end my days in the palace."

Copy Of The Answer To This Order

"The follower Sanehat says: In excellent peace above everything consider of this flight that he made here in his ignorance; Thou, the Good God, Lord of both Lands, Loved of Rā, Favorite of Mentu, the Lord of Thebes, and of Amen, lord of thrones of the lands, of Sebek, Rā, Horus, Hathor, Atmu, and of his fellow-gods, of Sopdu, Neferbiu, Samsetu, Horus, lord of the east, and of the royal uræus which rules on thy head, of the chief gods of the waters, of Min, Horus of the desert, Urrit, mistress of Punt, Nut, Harnekht, Rā, all the gods of the land of Egypt, and of the isles of the sea. May they give life and peace to thy nostril, may they load thee with their gifts, may they give to thee eternity without end, everlastingness without bound. May the fear of thee be doubled in the lands of the deserts. Mayest thou subdue the circuit of the sun's disk. This is the prayer to his master of the humble servant who is saved from a foreign land.

"O wise King, the wise words which are pronounced in the wisdom of the majesty of the sovereign, thy humble servant fears to tell. It is a great thing to repeat. O great God, like unto Rā in fulfilling that to which he has set his hand, what am I that he should take thought for me? Am I among those whom he regards, and for whom he arranges? Thy majesty is as Horus, and the strength of thy arms extends to all lands.

"Then let his Majesty bring Maki of Adma, Kenti-au-ush of Khenti-keshu, and Tenus from the two lands of the Fen-khu; these are the princes who bear witness of me as to all that has passed, out of love for thyself. Does not Tenu believe that it belongs to thee like thy dogs? Behold this flight that I have made: I did not have it in my heart; it was like the leading of a dream, as a man of Adehi (Delta) sees himself in Abu (Elephantine), as a man of the plain of Egypt who sees himself in the deserts. There was no fear, there was no hastening after me, I did not listen to an evil plot, my name was not heard in the mouth of the magistrate; but my limbs went, my feet wandered, my heart drew me; my god commanded this flight, and drew me on; but I am not stiff-necked. Does a man fear when he sees his own land? Rā spread thy fear over the land, thy terrors in every strange land. Behold me now in the palace, behold me in this place; and lo! thou art he who is over all the horizon; the sun rises at thy pleasure, the water in the rivers is drunk at thy will, the wind in heaven is breathed at thy saying.

"I who speak to thee shall leave my goods to the generations to follow in this land. And as to this messenger who is come even let thy majesty do as pleaseth him, for one lives by the breath that thou givest. O thou who art beloved of Rā, of Horus, and of Hathor; Mentu, lord of Thebes, desires that thy august nostril should live forever."

I made a feast in Iaa, to pass over my goods to my children. My eldest son was leading my tribe, all my goods passed to him, and I gave him my corn and all my cattle, my fruit, and all my pleasant trees. When I had taken my road to the south, and arrived at the roads of Horus, the officer who was over the garrison sent a messenger to the palace to give notice. His Majesty sent the good overseer of the peasants of the King's domains, and boats laden with presents from the King for the Sati who had come to conduct me to the roads of Horus. I spoke to each one by his name, and I gave the presents to each as was intended. I received and I returned the salutation, and I continued thus until I reached the city of Thetu.

When the land was brightened, and the new day began, four men came with a summons for me; and the four men went to lead me to the palace. I saluted with both my hands on the ground; the royal children stood at the courtyard to conduct me: the courtiers who were to lead me to the hall brought me on the way to the royal chamber.

I found his Majesty on the great throne in the hall of pale gold. Then I threw myself on my belly; this god, in whose presence I was, knew me not. He questioned me graciously, but I was as one seized with blindness, my spirit fainted, my limbs failed, my heart was no longer in my bosom, and I knew the difference between life and death. His Majesty said to one of the companions, "Lift him up, let him speak to me." And his Majesty said, "Behold thou hast come, thou hast trodden the deserts, thou hast played the wanderer. Decay falls on thee, old age has reached thee; it is no small thing that thy body should be embalmed, that the Pedtiu shall not bury thee. Do not, do not, be silent and speechless; tell thy name; is it fear that prevents thee?" I answered in reply, "I fear, what is it that my lord has said that I should answer it? I have not called on me the hand of God, but it is terror in my body, like that which brings sudden death. Now behold I am before thee; thou art life; let thy Majesty do what pleaseth him."

The royal children were brought in, and his Majesty said to the Queen, "Behold thou Sanehat has come as an Amu, whom the Sati have produced."

She cried aloud, and the royal children spake with one voice, saying, before his Majesty, "Verily it is not so, O King, my lord." Said his Majesty, "It is verily he." Then they brought their collars, and their wands, and their sistra in their hands, and displayed them before his Majesty; and they sang—

"May thy hands prosper, O King;
May the ornaments of the Lady of Heaven continue.
May the Goddess Nub give life to thy nostril;
May the mistress of the stars favor thee, when thou sailest south and north.
All wisdom is in the mouth of thy Majesty;
Thy uræus is on thy forehead, thou drivest away the miserable.
Thou art pacified, O Ra, lord of the lands;
They call on thee as on the mistress of all.
 Strong is thy horn,
 Thou lettest fly thine arrow.
Grant the breath to him who is without it;
Grant good things to this traveller, Samehit the Pedti, born in the land of Egypt,
Who fled away from fear of thee,
And fled this land from thy terrors.
Does not the face grow pale, of him who beholds thy countenance;
Does not the eye fear, which looks upon thee."

 Said his Majesty, "Let him not fear, let him be freed from terror. He shall be a Royal Friend amongst the nobles; he shall be put within the circle of the courtiers. Go ye to the chamber of praise to seek wealth for him."

 When I went out from the palace, the royal children offered their hands to me; we walked afterward to the Great Gates. I was placed in a house of a king's son, in which were delicate things, a place of coolness, fruits of the granary, treasures of the White House, clothes of the King's guardrobe, frankincense, the finest perfumes of the King and the nobles whom he loves, in every chamber. All the servitors were in their several offices.

 Years were removed from my limbs: I was shaved, and polled my locks of hair; the foulness was cast to the desert with the garments of the Nemau-sha. I clothed me in fine linen, and anointed myself with the fine oil of Egypt; I laid me on a bed. I gave up the sand to those who lie on it; the oil of wood to him who would anoint himself therewith. There was given to me the mansion of a lord of serfs, which had belonged to a royal friend. There many excellent things were in its buildings; all its wood was renewed. There were brought to me portions from the palace, thrice and four times each day; beside the gifts of the royal children, always without ceasing. There was built for me a pyramid of stone among the pyramids. The overseer of the architects measured its ground; the chief treasurer wrote it; the sacred masons cut the well; the chief of the laborers on the tombs brought the bricks; all things used to make a strong building were there used. There were given to me peasants; there were made for me a garden, and fields in it before my mansion, as is done for the chief royal friend. My statue was inlaid with gold, its girdle of pale gold; his majesty caused it to be made. Such is not done to a man of low degree.

 May I be in the favor of the King until the day shall come of my death!

(This is finished from beginning to end, as was found in the writing.)

THE TELL AMARNA TABLETS

Translated by C. R. Conder, D.C.L., LL.D., M.R.A.S.

The Hittite Invasion Of Damascus

No. 36 B. M.—"To King Annumuria (127) (Amenophis III) Son of the Sun, my Lord thus (says) this thy servant Akizzi.(128) Seven times at the feet of my Lord I bow. My Lord in these my lands I am afraid. Mayst thou protect one who is thy servant under the yoke of my Lord. From the yoke of my Lord I do not rebel. Lo! there is fear of my foes. The people of this thy servant are under thy yoke: this country is among thy lands: the city Katna (129) is thy city: I am on the side of my Lord's rule (yoke). Lo! the soldiers and the chariots of my Lord's government have received corn and drink, oxen and beasts (oil and honey?), meeting the soldiers and the chariots of my Lord's dominion (coming?) to me. And now let my Lord ask the great men of his dominion. My Lord, all lands tremble before thy soldiers and thy chariots. If these lands are under the dominion of my Lord's land, and they are seizing them, let him order his soldiers and his chariots this year, and let him take the land of Marhasse,(130) the whole of it, to the yoke of my Lord, when—my Lord—the soldiers of the slaves(131) are(132) ... For six days ago he went out into the land of Hu(ba), and truly Aziru is sending them, and if in this year my Lord does not send out the soldiers and the chariots of his government ... to meet Aziru (and) make him flee ... all will rebel ... My Lord, know him. My Lord (know) the men who are his foes ... And lo! now the King of the land of the Hittites ... with pride rebels against his gods. And men who are destroyers serve the King of the land of the Hittites: he sends them forth. My Lord, my servants, the men of the city of Katna, Aziru expels, and all that is theirs, out of the land of the dominion of my Lord; and behold (he takes?) the northern lands of the dominion of my Lord. Let (my Lord) save the ... of the men of the city Katna. My Lord truly they made ... he steals their gold my Lord; as has been said there is fear, and truly they give gold. My Lord—Sun God, my fathers' god(133)—the men have made themselves your foes, and they have wasted from over against the abode of their camp (or fortress); and now behold—O Sun God of my fathers—the King of the Hittites makes them march. And know of them, my Lord—may the gods make slack their hand. As has been said there is fear. And lo! perchance the Sun God of my fathers will turn his heart toward me. My Lord's word is sure, and let the (increase or tithe of gold?) be given him, as we have purposed for the Sun God of my fathers. As has been said they have done to me; and they have destroyed the ... of my Lord. For this corner—the dwelling of their fortress (or camp)—is out of sight of the Sun God."

37 B. M.—"To King Annumuria, Son of the Sun, my Lord, thus (says) Akizzi thy servant: seven times ... at the feet of my Lord I bow. My Lord, now there is flight and no breathing of the ... of the King my Lord. And behold now the ... of this dominion of my Lord, in these lands ... and behold now ... the King of the land of the Hittites ... sends forth ... and the heart of ... smites him. And now behold the King my Lord sends to me, and is complaining ... with me as to the rule of the King of the land of the Hittites. And as for me ... the King of the land of the Hittites. As for me I am with the King my Lord, and with the land of Egypt. I sent and ... as to the rule of the King of the land of the Hittites."

This text is much damaged; it goes on to speak of Aidugama,(134)the Hittite King, in the country of the King of Egypt, who has taken various things—enumerated, but not intelligible—including, perhaps, ships or boats, and dwellings; and it mentions Neboyapiza. It then continues:

"My Lord: Teuiatti of the city of Lapana,(135) and Arzuia of the city Ruhizzi,(136) minister before Aidugama; but this land is the land of the dominion of my Lord. He is burning it with fire. My Lord, as said, I am on the side of the King my Lord. I am afraid also because of the King of the land of Marhasse, and the King of the land of Ni, and the King of the land of Zinzaar,(137) and the King of the land of Canaan. And all of these are kings under the dominion (or, of the rule) of my Lord—chiefs who are servants. As said let the King my Lord live and become mighty, and so O King my Lord wilt not thou go forth? and let the King my Lord despatch the bitati (138) soldiers, let them expel (them) from this land. As said, my Lord, these kings have ... the chief of my Lord's government, and let him say what they are to do, and let them be confirmed. Because my Lord this land ministers heartily to the King my Lord. And let him speed soldiers, and let them march; and let the messengers of the dominion of the King my Lord arrive. For my Lord Arzuia of the city Ruhizzi, and Teuiatti of the city Lapana, dwelt in the land of Huba,(139) and Dasru dwelt in the land Amma,(140) and truly my Lord has known them. Behold the land of Hobah was at peace my Lord in the days of this government. They will be subject to Aidugama. Because we ask, march thou here and mayest ... all the land of Hobah. My Lord, as said, the city Timasgi,(141) in the land of Hobah, is without sin at thy feet; and aid thou the city Katna which is without sin at thyfeet. It has been feeble. And my Lord in presence of my messenger the master shall ordain (our) fate. As has been said, have not I served in the presence of the bitati soldiers of my Lord? Behold, as said, my Lord has promised soldiers to this my land, and they shall ... in the city Katna."

96 B., a letter mainly complimentary, from Neboyapiza (142) to the King of Egypt, ends as follows:

"Behold I myself, with my soldiers and my chariots, with my brethren and with (men of blood?) and with my people the men of my kindred go to meet the Egyptian soldiers, as far as the ground which the King my Lord will name."

142 B.—"To the King my Lord thus saith this thy servant. At the feet of my Lord my Sun seven times on my face, seven times I bow. My Lord I am thy servant, and they will devour me—Neboyapiza: we abide before thy face, my Lord, and lo! they will devour me in your sight. Behold every fortress of my fathers is taken, by the people out of the city Gidisi.(143) And my fortresses (say) 'Speed us avengers.' I make ready, and (because that?) the Pakas (144) of the King my Lord, and the chiefs of his land have known my faithfulness, behold I complain to the ruler being one approved; let the ruler consider that (Neboyapiza) has given proof ... for now they have cast thee out. As for me, I have (gathered?) all my brethren, and we have made the place strong for the King my Lord. I have caused them to march with my soldiers and with my chariots, and with all my people. And behold Neboyapiza has sped to all the fortresses of the King my Lord. Part of the men of blood are from the land Ammusi,(145) and (part) from the land of Hubi, and it is won (or reached). But march fast, thou who art a God(146) and a Sun in my sight, and restore the strongholds holds to the King my Lord from the men of blood. For they have cast him out; and the men of blood have rebelled, and are invaders of the King my Lord. We were obedient to thy yoke, and they have cast out the King my Lord, and all my brethren."

It appears, from other letters, that the city of this chief was the important town Cumidi, now Kamid, in the southern Lebanon, at the south end of the Baalbek plain, west of Baal Gad. In Abu el Feda's time this town was the capital of the surrounding district.

189 B. is much broken. It is from Arzana, chief of the city Khazi.(147) He speaks of an attack on Tusulti, by bloody soldiers fighting against the place, and perhaps of the city Bel Gidda (Baal Gad),(148) and mentions a Paka, or Egyptian official, called Aman Khatbi, named after the Egyptian god Amen. The foes are spoiling the valley (of Baalbek) in sight of the Egyptian general, and are attacking Khazi, his city. They had already taken Maguzi,(149) and are spoiling Baal Gad. It seems that he asks the King not to blame his general, and speaks finally of friendly and faithful men.

43 B. M., broken at the top, reads thus:

"... his horses and his chariots ... to men of blood and not ... As for me, I declare myself for the King my Lord, and a servant to preserve these to the King entirely. Biridasia perceives this, and has betrayed it, and he has secretly passed beyond my city Maramma;(150) and the great pass is open behind me. And he is marching chariots from the city Astarti,(151) and commands them for the men of blood, and does not command them for the King my Lord. Friendly to him is the King of the city Buzruna;(152) and the King of the city Khalavunni (153) has made promises to him: both have fought with Biridasia against me. Wickedly they vex us. I have marched our kinsmen—the people of Neboyapiza—but his success never fails ... and he rebels. As for me from ... and he sends out from ... the city Dimasca (Damascus) behold ... they complain ... they afflict. I am complaining to the King of Egypt as a servant; and Arzaiaia is marching to the city Gizza,(154) and Azi (ru) takes soldiers ... The Lord of the city Saddu (155) declares for the men of blood, and her chief does not declare for the King my Lord; and as far as this tribe marches it has afflicted the land of Gizza. Arzaiaia with Biridasia afflicts the land (which is wretched? or Abitu), and the King witnesses the division of his land. Let not men who have been hired disturb her. Lo! my brethren have fought for me. As for me, I will guard the town of Cumidi (Kamid), the city of the King my Lord. But truly the King forgets his servant ... his servant, O King ... have arrayed kings ... the men of the wretched land" (or of the land Abitu).

152 B.—"... thus Ara (ga?) chief of the city Cumidi (156) (Kamid) ... at the feet of the King my Lord seven times seven times I bow. Behold as to me I am thy faithful servant: let the King my Lord ask of his Pakas (chiefs) as to me, a faithful servant of the King my Lord, one whom they have ruined. Truly I am a faithful servant of the King my Lord, and let the King my Lord excuse this dog, and let him (bear me in remembrance?). But never a horse and never a chariot is mine, and let this be considered in sight of the King my Lord; and closely allied(157) is his servant; and to explain this I am despatching my son to the land of the King my Lord, and let the King my Lord deign to hear me."

46 B. M.—"At the feet of the King my Lord seven and seven (times) I bow. Behold what this our saying tells, as to the land Am (Ham) the fortresses of the King my Lord. A man named Eda ... has arisen, a chief of the land Cinza east of the land of the Hittites, to take the fortresses of the King my Lord ... and we made the fortresses for the King my Lord my God my Sun, and we have lived in the fortresses of the King myLord."

125 B.—"To the King my Lord thus Arzaiaia, chief of the city Mikhiza.(158) At the feet of my Lord I bow. King my Lord, I have heard as to going to meet the Egyptian (bitati) soldiers of the King my Lord who are with us, to meet the general (Paka) with (all the infantry?) ... all who have marched to overthrow the King my Lord. Truly a (great strength to the people?) are the Egyptian (bitati) soldiers of the King my Lord, and his commander (Paka). As for me, do I not order all to ... after them? Behold they have been speedy, O King my Lord, and his foes are delayed by them by the hand of the King my Lord."

126 B.—The same writer, in a broken letter, calls himself a faithful servant of the King. This was perhaps at an earlier period of the war, before the events recorded by Neboyapiza (189 B., 43 B. M.).

75 B. M.—A short letter from Dasru to say he has heard the King's message. He lived in the land of Ham (37 B. M.).

127 B. M.—The same writer says that all that the King does for his land is of good omen.

171 B.—"A message and information from the servant of the King my Lord my God.... And behold what the chief of Simyra has done to my brethren of the city of Tubakhi;(159) and he marches to waste the fortresses of the King my Lord my God my Sun ... the land of the Amorites. He has wearied out our chiefs. The fortresses of the King my Lord my God ... are for men of blood. And now strong is the god of the King my Lord my God my Sun; and the city of Tubakhi goes forth to war, and I have stirred up my brethren, and I guard the city of Tubakhi for the King my Lord my God my Sun. And behold this city of Tubakhi is the city of the plains of my fathers."

132 B.—"To the King my Lord by letter thus (says) Artabania, chief of the city Ziribasani (160) thy servant. At the feet of the King my Lord seven times, on my face, seven times I bow. Behold a message to me to speed to meet the Egyptian (bitati) soldiers. And who am I but a dog only, and shall I not march? Behold me, with my soldiers and my chariots meeting the Egyptian soldiers at the place of which the King my Lord speaks."

78 B. M.—"To the King my Lord thus the chief of the city Gubbu (161) thy servant. At the feet of the King my Lord my Sun (permit?) that seven times, on my face, seven times I bow. Thou hast sent as to going to meet the Egyptian soldiers, and now I with my soldiers and my chariots meet the soldiers of the King my Lord, at the place you march to."

64 B. M.—"To Yankhamu (162) my Lord by letter thus Muu-taddu thy servant. I bow at my Lord's feet as this says, announcing that the enemy is hastening speedily as—my Lord—was announced to the King of the city Bikhisi (163) from friends(164) of his Lord. Let the King my Lord speed: let the King my Lord fly: for the foe is wasting in the city Bikhisi this two months, there is none ... On account of (Bibelu?) having told me this one has asked then ... until by the arrival of Anamarut (Amenophis IV)(165) the city of Ashtoreth is occupied.(166) Behold they have destroyed all the fortresses of neighboring lands: the city Udumu,(167) the city Aduri,(168) the city Araru,(169) the city Meis (pa?),(170) the city Macdalim,(171) the city Khini.(172) I announced that they had taken the city Zaar.(173) They are fighting this city, the city Yabisi.(174) Moreover, fearing the force against me, I am

watching it till you arrive. One has come from your way to the city Bikhisi,(175) and he has made us hear the news."

134 B.—"To the King my Lord by letter thus Abdmelec the chief of this city Saskhi (176) thy servant. At the feet of the King my Lord ... on my face seven times I bow. Thou hast sent as to going to meet the Egyptian soldiers, accordingly I with my soldiers and my chariots (am) meeting the soldiers of the King my Lord, at the place to which you will march."

143 B.—"To the King our Lord thus (says) Addubaya and thus also Betili. At the feet of our Lord we bow. Peace indeed to the face of our Lord. And (as is fit?) from the lands of our Lord, much they salute. O our Lord, will not you settle everything in your heart? Will not you harden your heart as to this combat O our Lord? But their intention is clear—to make war on the stations, as in our country they do not follow after thee. Lupackhallu (177) has removed the soldiers of the Hittites; they will go against the cities of the land of Ham (Am) and from Atadumi they will (take?) them. And let our Lord know, since we hear that Zitana (178) the Phœnician (Kharu) has deserted, who will march. And nine chiefs of the soldiers of the government are with us, who march, and the message is unfavorable: a gathering in the land they have made; and they will arrive from the land of Marhasse (Mer'ash). But I cause Betili to send against this (foe). Thus we wage war against them. And my trusty messenger I cause to be sent to your presence, as said; for you to return an order whether we shall do so or whether not. To Raban and Abdbaal, to Rabana and Rabziddu thus: behold to all of you be peace indeed, and will not you harden your hearts, and will not you settle all in your hearts, and do what is fitting from your places? Much peace; and to (the people?) peace be increased."

91 B.—"To the King my Lord thus (says) the city Gebal (179) (and) thus Rabikhar ('the Lord of Phœnicia') thy servant. At the feet of my Lord the Sun seven times I bow. Do not be angry, O King my Lord, with the city of Gebal (Gubla) thy handmaid—a city of the King from of old, obeying what the King commands as to Aziru, and it did as he wished. Behold Aziru slew Adunu, Lord of the land of Ammia,(180) and the King of the land of Ardata,(181) and has slain the great men, and has taken their cities for himself. The city Simyra is his. Of the cities of the King only the city Gebal escapes for the King. Behold the city Simyra is subjected. He has smitten the city Ullaza.(182) The captains of both have gone into exile. Behold this sin Aziru wrought. Sinful are his strivings against her ... he has smitten all the lands of Ham (Am), lands of the King; and now he has despatched his men to destroy all the lands of Ham; and the King of the land of the Hittites, and the king of the land of Nereb (Nariba)(183) (have made?) the land conquered land."

From these letters we learn clearly that the Mongol kings near the Euphrates (and, as appears later, in Armenia) were leagued with the Hittites of Mer'ash in the extreme north of Syria, and of Kadesh on the Orontes, and were supported by the Amorites of the northern Lebanon and by some of the Phœnicians; that the enemy marched south, a distance of 300 miles, taking all the towns in the Baalbek Valley, reaching Damascus by the gorge of the Barada River, and advancing into the land of Ham—in Bashan—where all the chief towns fell. This serves to make clear the treachery of Aziru's letters which follow. The Amorite advance on the Phœnician coast was contemporary, and extended to Tyre. It appears, however, that the Amorites were a Semitic people, while the names of the Hittites are Mongolic.

The Amorite Treachery

No. 35 B.—"To the King my Lord my God my Sun Aziru thy servant; and seven times at the feet of my Lord my God my Sun I bow." The letter is much broken, but promises he will never rebel, and says he is sincere. He desires land of the King (at Simyra), and says the men of the government are friendly, but that the city of Simyra is to be made promptly to fulfil its engagements.

35 B. M.—"To the Great King my Lord my God my Sun thus (says) this thy servant Aziru. Seven times and seven times at the feet of my Lord my God my Sun I bow. My Lord I am thy servant, and (from my youth?) in the presence of the King my Lord, and I fulfil all my orders to the sight of my Lord. And what they who are my (agents?) shall say to my Lord as to the chiefs who are faithful, in the sight of the King my Lord, will not you hear me speak, I who am thy servant sincere as long as I live? But when the King my Lord sent Khani,(184) I was resting in the city of Tunip (Tennib) and there was no knowledge behold of his arriving. Whereupon he gave notice, and coming after him also, have I not reached him? And let Khani speak to testify with what humility, and let the King my Lord ask him how my brethren have prepared to tend (him), and Betilu will send to his presence oxen and beasts and fowls: his food and his drink will be provided. I shall give horses and beasts for his journey; and may the King my Lord hear my messages, with my assurances in the presence of the King my Lord. Khani will march much cared for in my sight, he accompanies me as my comrade, like my father; and lo! my Lord says, 'You turn away from the appearance of Khani.' Thus thy Gods and the Sun-God truly had known if I did not stay in the city of Tunip. Moreover because of the intention to set in order the city of Simyra, the King my Lord has sent word (and) the Kings of the land of Marshasse (Mer'ash) have been foes to me. They have marched on my cities: they have observed the desire of Khatib,(185) and has not he promised them? lo! hastily he has promised them. And truly my Lord has known that half of the possessions that the King my Lord has given Khatib takes: the tribute, and the gold and the silver that the King my Lord has given me; and Khatib takes all the tribute; and truly my Lord has known. Moreover as against my Lord the King's having said, 'Why dost thou yield service to the messenger of the King of the land of the Hittites, and dost not yield service to my messenger?' this region is the land of my Lord, he establishes me in it, with men of government. Let a messenger of my Lord come, and all that I speak of in the sight of my Lord let me give. Tin and ships, men(186) and weapons, and trees let me give."

40 B.—"To Dudu (187) my Lord my father thus (says) Aziru your son your servant: at the feet of my father I bow. Lo! let Dudu send the wishes of my Lord ... and I ... Moreover behold thou shalt not reject (me) my father, and whatever are the wishes of Dudu my father, send, and will not I ... Behold thou art my father and my Lord: I am thy son: the land of the Amorites is your land; and my house is your house.(188) Say what you wish and I will truly perform your wishes." The latter part is broken, but states that he will not rebel against the wishes of the King or those of Dudu.

38 B.—"To Dudu my Lord my father thus Aziru thy servant. At my lord's feet I bow. Khatib will march, and has carefully followed the messages (or orders) of the King my Lord before (he goes); and what is good increases; and I have been gladdened very much; and my brethren, men serving the King my Lord, and men who are servants of Dudu my Lord. They had feared exceedingly. Behold he will march, to command for the King my Lord with me. From the orders of my Lord my God and my Sun, and from the orders of Dudu my Lord, I will never depart. My Lord now Khatib goes forth with me, and also he will march to strengthen me. My Lord, the King of the land of the Hittites will march from the land of Marhasse (Mer'ash), and has he not boasted to meet me? and the King of the Hittites will rebel, and behold I and Khatib will march. Let the King my Lord hear my messages. I have feared without the countenance of the King my Lord, and without the countenance of Dudu; and now (my Gods and my messenger(189)). And truly these are my brethren—Dudu and the great men of the King my Lord; and truly I will march; and since O Dudu both the King my Lord and the chiefs thus are ready, everything against Aziru is forgiven which has been unfavorable for my God,(190) and for us. And now I and Khatib have appeared servants of the King. Truly thou knowest Dudu, behold I go forth mightily."

31 B.—"To Khai (191) my brother thus (says) this thy brother Aziru. With thee (be) peace indeed, and from the Egyptian soldiers of the King my Lord there is much safety. Whoever (is) against it the promise remains, in sight of the King my Lord; being formerly promised it remains. I and my sons and my brethren are all servants of the King: it is good for me. Now I and Khatib will both march, behold, with speed. O Khai, as among you truly it is known, lo! I have been troubled. From the orders of my Lord there is no rebellion, nor from your orders. I am a servant of my Lord. The King of the land of the Hittites dwells in the land of Marhasse (Mer'ash) and I have feared his appearance. They who are in the West lands(192) have armed. He gathers; and while the city of Tunip is unoccupied, he dwells two swift marches from the city. And I have been afraid of his appearance; and contrary to messages of promise he goes forth to his rebellions. But now we shall both march, I and Khatib, with speed."

32 B. repeats the preceding—perhaps to another correspondent: it mentions Dudu, and says: "I have been afraid of this rebel son of a dog, and I have been troubled. Now he has sent a message from the Western land—the land of my Lord: they will both march together, and I have been afraid for my Lord's land."

33 B., much broken at the top, refers to the existing promise or treaty, and continues: "I cause the land of my Lord to be guarded, and my countenance is toward the men who are servants of the King my Lord in peace. My Lord now I and Khatib are made friends,(193) and let my Lord know behold I have ... in haste. The King of the land of the Hittites dwells ... and I have been afraid ... have armed ... of the land ... my Lord I remain quietly ... in the West land ... King my Lord to defend his land ... and now behold in the land of Marhasse he dwells—two swift marches from the city of Tunip; and I fear his wastings. Let the city of Tunip be defended: my Lord is a shield to men who serve him; mayst thou hear what is said and my sons will ... forever."

39 B., broken at the top. "I have strengthened this ... I have strengthened this wall in front of the mouth of the great pass,(194) and my Lord's fortress. And let my Lord hear as to the servants of his servant—thy servant Aziru: they will keep watch: strife surrounds us: I trust there will be an expedition; and let us watch the lands of the King our Lord. Moreover to Dudu my Lord. Hear the message of the King of the land of Marhasse to me. They said: 'Your father(195) what gold has this King of Egypt given him, and what has his Lord promised him out of the Land of Egypt; and all the lands, and all the soldier slaves they have fought against?' (thus) they said ... to Aziru ... out of the Land of Egypt, and behold the slaves come round from the Land of ... Ni (196): they have rebelled; and I repeat that thirty chiefs push on against me ... land of Egypt he remains ... my Lord to Aziru ... soldiers ... Marhasse."

34 B.—"To the King my Lord my God my Sun thus (says) this Aziru thy servant: seven times and seven times at the feet of my Lord I bow. Now what you wish is desirable. Sun God my Lord I am thy servant forever; and my sons serve thee.... Now two men ... I have commanded as envoys ... what he says ... and let him rule ... in the land of the Amorites."

34a B.—The salutation of the usual type is here injured. The letter continues: "My Lord my God my Sun, I am thy servant and my sons and my brethren, to serve the King my Lord forever. Now all my Lord's wishes, and what he causes to be despatched, duly ... the King my Lord having despatched. Now eight chiefs who are great, and many (decrees?) we ... all of which ... from ... the King my Lord ... And the Kings of the Land of Marhasse will follow with ... and are these not promised (or leagued) to the city Simyra these thirty years? I turn me to the city Simyra. My Lord I am thy servant forever, and a King of men who are friends; will not my (agents?) ... my Lord (wilt not thou hear?). And the King is my Lord my God and my Sun: let him send his messenger with my messenger, and let them go up who serve the King ..."

36 B.—"To the King ... thus Aziru: seven times and seven times at ... of my God and Sun. Behold truly thou hast known this, O King my Lord; behold I am thy servant forever; from my Lord's commands I never rebel: my Lord from of old (it has been) thus. I am kind to the men who are servants of my King; but the chiefs of the city Simyra have not kept faith righteously with us; and behold neither one nor all are with us: my Lord the King did not you cause to be asked? The King my Lord has known that the chiefs are sinful; and why ask, 'What does he contend for?' I say nay ..."

From these letters by Aziru, we must conclude either that he was a great liar or that he was induced to change sides later. The other correspondents seem to have believed that he had long deceived the King of Egypt; but, in the end, his invasion of Phœnicia—perhaps cloaked by pretences of hostility to the Hittite league—caused him, as we shall see, to be proclaimed a rebel. The quarrel with Simyra may have been due to his being pushed south, out of his dominions, but is here said to be due to a Phœnician league with his foes. It does not appear who Khatib was. Perhaps the name was Hittite,(197) and he may have been the Prince of Hamath or of Emesa. The following letter from Aziru's father, Abdasherah, belongs to a later period of the war, when Ullaza and all the cities north of Gebal had been conquered by the Amorites. It is couched in the same insidious language; and the letters of Ribadda, which follow, show that Amenophis was not open to conviction for a long time, though warned by his true friends. The proclamation is still later, after the attack on Sidon, and may fitly conclude the Amorite correspondence.

97 B.—"To the King my Son my Lord thus Abdasratu (198) thy servant, the dust of thy feet. At the feet of the King my Lord seven times and seven times I bow. Behold I am the King's servant, and a dog who is his neighbor (or his 'friend'?); and all the land of the Amorites is his. I often said to Pakhanati (199) my Paka (Egyptian resident), 'Let him gather soldiers to defend the people of this King.' Now all (cursed?) as King, the King of the Phœnician (Kharri) soldiers ... Kharri: the King shall ask if I do not guard the city of Simyra (and) the city Ullaza. Lo my Paka is in her: I proclaim the Sun-King; and I have (given orders?) to obey. The city Simyra is a neighbor,(200) and all the lands are the King's—my Sun, my Lord; I watch for him: and I know that the King my Lord is very glorious; and Pakhanati my Paka is established to judge therein."

COPY OF A PROCLAMATION AGAINST AZIRU, SENT TO EGYPT BY KHANNI, WHEN SENT AGAIN TO SYRIA

92 B.—"To the Chief of the Amorite city by letter thus (says) your Lord. A chief of the city of Gebal has said thus in his petition: 'Send him away from my gate (he says); he is robbing me and disputes with me in my chief city.'(201) And I have heard this and much beside which they have said to me as I now speak to say.

"Thou hast sent to the King thy Lord (saying thus), 'I am thy servant as all former guardians(202) who have been in this city.' And you do well to say thus. (But) I hear so to say a ruler of ours whose petition (is), 'Send him away from my gate, (he is) out of his city.' And in the city Zituna (Sidon) he abides, and has subjected himself among chiefs who are governors; and, though certainly knowing what is said, thou dost not confess the persecution of these chiefs. If thou art, as is assured, a servant of the King, how is his cutting off lawful in the sight of the King your Lord? Thus this ruler beseeches me, 'Let a supplicant be protected, for he is disputing my chief city with me.' And if you do as is asserted, and not according to all the messages that I send against these things, you are hindering the King traitorously. So will be understood all that has been said.

"And now a certain Chief hears of a gathering with the Chief of the city of Ciidsa (Kadesh on Orontes, the capital of the southern Hittites); devising hostilities, ready to fight, you have made alliance. And if so, why dost thou so? Why should a chief foregather with a chief save that he is on his side? But if you cause what is assured to be done, and you respect the orders to yourself and to him, I say nothing more as to the messages you formerly made (and) as to what was pretended by you in them. But thou art not on the side of the King thy Lord.

"Lo! this is the message, that their fortress burns in flames through (your burning?) and thou ragest against everything grievously. But if thou dost service to the King thy Lord, what is it that I will not do to interceding with the King? If then thou ragest against everything, I make God my witness; and if you persist, God is my witness, that messages of war (will be) in your midst, and by the might of the King thou diest, and as many as are with thee.

"But do service to the King thy Lord and live. And thou thyself knowest that the King does not deem needful a subjection of the land of Canaan.(203) So he is wroth. And as I sent, truly was commanded me of the King my Lord this year and not ... in another year. My son (this) contumacy in the sight of the King thy Lord is vain.

"And now the King thy Lord is anxious as to thee this year. If it is difficult for thee to come, then send thy son. And thou beholdest a King at whose commands many lands tremble: and dost not thou (fear?): thus truly is ordered this year concerning us; failing to go to the presence of the King thy Lord, send thy son to the King thy Lord as a hostage, and let him not delay at all.

"And now the King thy Lord hears, for I send to the King. Thus truly has the King commanded me—Khanni—a second time a messenger of the King. Truly it is to fetch to his hands men who are the foes of his house. Behold now I have been sent, as they are troublous; and moreover thou shalt bind them, and shalt not leave one among them. Now I am desired by the King thy Lord to name the men who are foes of the King in the letter from Khanni the King's messenger; and once more I am obeying the King thy Lord; and thou shalt not leave one among them. A chain of bronze exceeding heavy shall shackle their feet. Behold the men thou shalt fetch to the King thy Lord. Sarru with all his sons; Tuia; Lieia with all his sons: Pisyari (204) with all his sons: the son-in-law of Mania with all his sons, with his wives, the women of his household: the chief of Pabaha,(205) whose wickedness is abhorred, who made the trumpet to be blown: Dasarti: Paluma: Numahe—a fugitive in the land of the Amorites.

"And knowest thou not that the glory of the King is as the Sun in heaven; his soldiers and his chariots are many. From the shore lands to the land of Gutium,(206) from the rising of the Sun to the going down of the same, there is much salutation."

The attack on Sidon was thus apparently the fact which opened the eyes of Amenophis. It appears to have preceded the final success, when the wealthy city of Gebal was taken by Aziru.

The War In Phœnicia

LETTERS FROM CITIES NEAR GEBAL

No. 42 B. M.—"This letter is the letter of the city Irkata (207) to the King. O our Lord, thus (says) the city of Irkata, and her men, her (flock? or lords?). At the feet of the King our Lord seven times seven times they bow. To the King our Lord thus (saith) the city of Irkata. Knowing the heart of the King our Lord we have guarded the city of Irkata for him ... Behold the King our Lord orders Abbikha ... he speaks to us thus, O King ... to guard it. The city of Irkata answers ... the man ruling for the King.... 'It is well. Let us save ... the city of Irkata. It is well to save (a city?) faithful to the King.' ... Behold many fight ... the people ... are frightened ... Thirty horses and chariots enter the city of Irkata. Lo! has arrived ... a letter of the King as to arriving ... thy land they reach. The men of the city ... (belonging) to the King have made ... to fight with us for the King our Lord. You send your chief to us that he may be our protector. Let the King our Lord hear the message of these his servants, and appoint us provision for his servant, and thou shalt exult over our foes and thou shalt prevail. The message of command of the King thou shalt not deny us. Our destroyer was troubled at the coming of the King's order to us. Mightily he has fought against us, exceeding much."

128 B.—"To Yankhamu by letter thus (says) Yapaaddu.(208) Why is it spoken? Lo! from the city of Simyra a destruction by Aziru of all the lands, in length from the city of Gebal to the city of Ugariti;(209) and the destruction of this the city Sigata,(210) and of the city Ambi.(211) Behold ... the slave has (broken?) the ships ... in the city Ambi and in the city Sigata, and in all which dispute for the lands with the city of Simyra: and shall we not arise to enter the city Simyra.(212) or what shall we ourselves do? But send this news to your great city (or palace).(213) It is regretted that the ... is unfortunate."

44 B. M.—This letter seems to be an appeal by the cities of Phœnicia on behalf of Ribadda, the brave King of Gebal, during the time of his resistance to Aziru, which failed because no help was given to him from Egypt, where Aziru was still thought faithful. The spokesman Khaia is perhaps the same Egyptian mentioned in Aziru's letters.
"Thus (saith) our confederacy to the King and the men of Sidon and the men of Beruta (Beirût). Whose are these cities—are not they the King's? Place a chief one chief in the midst of the city, and shall not he judge the ships of the land of the Amorites? and to slay Abdasherah the King shall set him up against them. Does not the King mourn for three cities and the ships of the men of Misi?(214) and you march not to the land of the Amorites, and Abdasherah has gone forth to war; and judge for thine own self, and hear the message of thy faithful servant. Moreover, who has fought as a son for the King—is it not Khaia? Will you gather us ships of men of Misi for the land of the Amorites and to slay Abdasherah? Lo! there is no message as to them and no memorial: they have shut the road—they have closed the way. In order to give passage to the land of Mitana (215) he has left the fleet which he has built. Was not this a plot against me of the men of Arāda?(216) But if behold they are with you, seize the ships of the men of the city of Arāda which they have made in the land of Egypt. Again behold Khaiya laments ... for you do not ... and as for us we ... by the land of the Amorites."

45 B. M., a broken letter with passages of interest as follows:
"Moreover, now this city of Gula (217) is afflicted. The region behold of the city of Gula is for the King my Lord. Cannot you do what we desire? But he has done as his heart (desired) with all the lands of the King. Behold this sin which Aziru ... with the King; (he has slain) the King of the land of Ammiya (218) and (the King of Ar) data: and the King of the Land of Ni ... (has slain?) a Paka ('chief') of the King my Lord ... and the King knows his faithful servant, and he has despatched a garrison from his city, thirty men and fifty chariots, to the city of Gebal. I have been right. He had turned, O King, his heart from everything that Aziru orders him. For everything that he orders, the messages are unanswered. But every governor of the King he has ordered to be slain. I am forgotten. Behold Aziru has cursed the King my Lord."

158 B.—The greater part of this letter is too broken to read, but refers to Abdasherah, and appears to be written to Yankhamu. The city of Simyra is mentioned, and the city Arpad,(219) and the palace or fortress of the former, with certain men therein. The soldiers of a city Sekhlali are also noticed, but it is not clear where this place is to be sought.

RIBADDA'S LETTERS FROM GEBAL

47 B.—" Ribadda (220) of the city of Gebal (221) (Gubla) to his Lord the King of many lands, the prosperous King. Baalath of Gebal she hath given power to the King my Lord. At the feet of the King my Lord my Sun seven times seven times I bow. Behold this ... it will grieve me ... our city ... my foes ... the chief ... watches O King ... no men of garrison ... were given to the King's chiefs, or preservation by the King against him, and this I (say) is not defended, and the King has not preserved me; and being angry Pakhura has gathered and has despatched men of the land Umuti (Hamath).(222) They have slain a chief servant; and three chiefs (he has bound?) without appeal to the land of Egypt; and he has made gifts seducing the city against me; and woe to the place, she has become ungrateful: the city which was not base in old times is base to us. But the King shall hear the message of his servant and you shall give orders to the chiefs. Do not you ... this sin they do? ... my destruction is before me, and is it not my order that chiefs in the sight of the King should ... my destruction. Behold now since I shall gather to ... and (perchance I shall repel this?)."

46 B.—The salutation, as in the preceding letter, is peculiar to Ribadda. "Lo! the King is sending to me Irimaia (223): maybe, he will arrive to gladden us from before thee: he has not come before me. The King sends to me the most distinguished of thy great men, the chiefest of the city of the King that thou hast, who shall defend me ... mighty before my foes ... Now they will make a government: the city they rule shall be smitten like as (is smitten?) a dog, and none that breathes shall be left behind him, for what they have done to us. I am laid waste (by foes?) by men of blood: thus on account of this slave there was no help from the King for me. (But?) my free men of the lands have fought for me. If the heart of the King is toward the guarding of his city, and of his servant, thou wilt order men to guard, and thou shalt defend the city, thou shalt guard my ... made prosperous ..."

18 B. M.—The salutation as in the first letter (47 B.). "Again behold thy faithful city of Gebal. Abdasherah was coming out against me aforetime and I sent to thy father who ordered soldiers of the King (bitati) to speed, and I went up over all his land. No allies marched to Abdasherah. But behold this: Aziru has chosen all the men of blood and has said to them: 'If the city of Gebal is not ... he has come ..., then Yankhamu is with thee, and ... if I am not obedient to his wishes. Thou art deceived ... Abdasherah has marched without stopping to ... but he has watched the city of the King his Lord obediently. So now as to Paia ... and is it not heard from the messages of Kha ... their father, as he desires ... This Khaib gave to the city Simyra. Lo! I lament that the King is not able to do this (for) the Paka (general) when behold it has been asked. And Bikhura has not marched from the city Cumidi (Kamid). I have been friends with all the men of thy Government ... Lo whereas I was upright to the King ... and he makes no sign (to me?) Despatch soldiers: thou shalt march with every ... Five thousand men and 3,000 ... fifty chariots, 1,000 ... the bitati soldiers, and cause (them) to take captive ... the land.'"

13 B. M.—The usual salutation, as given in the first letter. "Does the King know? Behold Aziru has fought my chiefs, and has taken twelve of my chiefs, and has insisted on receiving at our expense fifty talents; and the chiefs whom I despatched to the city Simyra he has caused to be seized in the city. Both the city Beruta (Beirût) and the city Ziduna (Sidon) are sending ships to the city Simyra. All who are in the land of the Amorites have gathered themselves. I am to be attacked; and behold this: Yapaaddu has fought for me with Aziru, but afterward behold he was entangled in the midst of the enemy when my ships were taken. And the King sees as to his city and his servant, and I need men to save the rebellion of this land if you will not come up to save from the hands of my enemies (or destroyers). Send me back a message, and know the deed that they have done. Now as they send to thee concerning the city Simyra he now marches. But (give?) me soldiers for ... and these shall deliver her ... they have tried but ... now."

61 B.—The usual salutation precedes, here much broken. "Does the King my Lord know? Lo! we know that he has fought mightily. Lo! they tell of us in thy presence what the city Simyra has done to the King. Know O King boldly marching they have contrived to seize her—the sons of Abdasherah, and (there is) none who lives to carry the message to the King. But counsel now thy faithful servant. I say

also the whole of the fortress they have destroyed ... I sent to the King ... of advice as to the city Simyra. As a bird in the midst of the net she has remained. The siege of the usurpers is exceeding strong, and the messenger who from..."

The letter is much broken. It refers to Yapaaddu and to his own faithfulness to the Pakas ("chiefs") of the King. He also appears to refer to the King destroying the Amorites, and goes on:

"The ruins perchance he will assign to his servant; and he has been constant and is upright against this thing—to subdue all the King's ... (provinces?). He has lost all the cities which ... this has befallen to ... and from the destruction ... against me none who ... them. The two or three that have held fast are turning round. But he hears his faithful servant's message, and a servant who has been constant in all labor, and his handmaid the city of Gebal (is) the only one that holds fast for me. The evils of this deed are equally thine, but I am broken in pieces. Henceforth Aziru is the foe of Yapaaddu. They have marched; and (there is) news that they have been cruel in their ravages against me. They rest not: they desire the evil of all that are with me. So they have waxed strong, powerful against me (a servant) faithful to the King from of old ... Moreover, behold I am a faithful servant: this evil is wrought me: behold this message: lo! I am the dust of the King's feet. Behold thy father did not wring, did not smite the lands of his rulers (Khazani) and the Gods established him—the Sun God, the God ... and Baalath of Gebal. But the sons of Abdasherah have destroyed from ... us the throne of thy father's house, and ... to take the King's lands for themselves. They have joined the King of the land of Mitana,(224) and the King of the land of Casi (225) and the King of the land of the Hittites ... the King will order soldiers (bitati). Yankhamu with the ... of my poor land ... The Paka of the city Cumidi ... and they have marched ... Gebal ... to a faithful servant."

83 B.—A much broken fragment, referring to the taking of Simyra, appears to belong to this period.

43 B.—" Ribadda speaks to the King of many lands. At the feet (of my Lord) seven times and seven times I bow (a servant) forever. Lo! the city of Gebal is his place—the Sun-God revered by many lands. Lo! I am the footstool at the feet of the King my Lord; I am also his faithful servant. Now as to the city Simyra the sword of these fellows(226) has risen very strong against her and against me. And so now the destruction of the city of Simyra is at her gates. She has bowed down before them and they have conquered her power.

"To what purpose have they sent here to Ribadda a letter (saying) thus: 'Peace to the palace from its brethren before Simyra.' Me! they have fought against me for five years, and thus they have sent to my Lord. As for me not (to be forgotten is?) Yapahaddu not to be forgotten is Zimridi.(227) All the fortresses they have ruined ... there was no cause of strife with the city of Simyra..." The next passage is much damaged. "And as said to what purpose have they sent a letter to Ribadda? In the sight of the King my Lord they have feigned to please me, they have pretended to please me, and now they proclaim peace. Truly thus behold it is with me. Let me learn the intention of my Lord, and will not he order Yankhamu with the Paka, Yankhamu joined beside the King my Lord, to lay waste? From before the chiefs of the Hittite chief men have fled and all the chiefs are afraid thereat. May it please my Lord also shall not he be (degraded?) who was thy commander of the horse with thy servant, to move the chiefs when we two went forth to the wars of the King my Lord, to occupy my cities which I name before my Lord. Know my Lord when they went forth with the ally he has left your soldiers fighting hard, and all have been slain."

52 B.—The ordinary salutation. The letter is much damaged. It states that the land of Mitana had formerly fought against the King's enemies; that the sons of the dog Abdasherah destroy the cities and the corn, and attack the governors, and had demanded fifty talents. It appears that Yankhamu has arrived, and has known the chief whom the King had established. Apparently a written letter has been sent "to the Amorite land for them to swallow." He continues: "Behold I am a faithful servant of the King, and there was none was like me a servant, before this man lied to the King of the Land of Egypt. But they have mastered the lands of our home." They have slain Egyptians, he continues, and have done something (the verb is lost) to the temples of the Gods of Gebal; they have carried off a chief and shed his blood. He finally mentions his son Khamu.

25 B. M., a short letter with the usual salutation. He requests soldiers to guard the lands for the rulers, which have been torn in pieces. The King sends no messages about himself to the writer or to Yankhamu. The governor's men have gathered to fight (for the Khar or Phœnicians?).

42 B. begins with the usual salutation given in the first letter. "Having just heard the chiefs from the presence of the King it is fit that I send back a messenger (or message). Behold O Sun descending from heaven, the Sons of Abdasherah are wasting (shamefully?), as among them there is not one of the horses of the King or chariots, and the chiefs have devised evil—a rebellious race. And a chief is here with us of the Amorite country, with a written message from the allies which is with me. They have demanded what is shameful. Hereby is spoken a friendly message in the presence of the King—the Sun God. As for me I am thy faithful servant, and the news which is known, and which I hear, I send to the King my Lord. (What are they but dogs trembling?) in the presence of the Egyptian soldiers (bitati) of the King—the Sun God. I sent to your father and he ... 'to my servant ... soldiers' ... they have not marched ... Abdasherah ... the chiefs of this government ... their faces against him. So now they have joined ... But the Misi men (Egyptians) ... have brought us, with speed, corn ... So now not without favor ... I have become a great man, behold: strong and powerful in their sight we have been made. But mighty and rebellious to the King is this power. (His land does not intend to help the land?) Behold I am despatching two men to the city of Simyra, and all the men of its chief have gathered in order to consult as to messages to the King, who will know why you hear from us your chiefs. Good is the letter they have brought us, and the letter which the messengers of the King have uttered to us.(228) Through the pretensions of this dog the King's heart has been grieved with men, and ... has been unrighteously set up, devising in their hearts ... and ... (your chief?). I go against the men of blood from the city Simyra ... to keep ... and whatsoever I have been commanded. And let the King ... the news of his servant. I have despatched ten chiefs of the Land of Nubia,(229) twenty chiefs of the Land of Egypt, as a guard to the King. Sun-God and Lord thy servant is faithful to thee."

73 B.—"To the King ... thus says Ribadda thy servant, the footstool of the feet of the Sun-God my Lord. Seven times and seven times at his feet I bow. Grievous it is to say what, in the sight of the King, he has done—the dog Abdasherah. Behold what has befallen the lands of the King on account of him; and he cried peace to the land, and now behold what has befallen the city of Simyra—a station of my Lord, a fortress ... and they spoil our fortress ... and the cries of the place ... a violent man and a dog."

The next message is too broken to read, but refers to the city of Gebal. The letter continues:

"Will not the King order his Paka to pronounce judgment? and let him guard the chief city of my Lord, and order me as I (say), and let my Lord the Sun set free the lands, and truly my lord shall order the wicked men all of them to go out. I present my memorial in the sight of my Lord, but this dog has not taken any of thy Gods. Prosperity has fled which abode in Gebal, which city of Gebal was as a city very friendly to the King. It is grievous. Behold I have associated Abdbaal the prefect with Ben Khia (or Ben Tobia) a man of (war?); but despatch thou him to thy servant..."

57 B.—The salutation as usual mentions Baalath of Gebal. "Why shall the King my Lord send to me? The best indeed trembles, of those who watch for him against my foes, and of my freemen. What shall defend me if the King will not defend his servant?... if the King will order for us chiefs of the Land of Egypt, and of the Land of Nubia, and horses, by the hand of this my chief as I hope, and preservation for the servants of the King my Lord. If none at all ... to me ... to march horses ... my land is miserable. By my soul's life! if the King cared at heart for the life of his servant, and of his chief city, he would have sent a garrison, and they had guarded thy city and thy servant. That the King shall know ... of our lands; and Egyptian soldiers (bitati) shall be ordered; and to save all that live in his land, therefore it is spoken as a message to the King (with thy messengers?) As to the ... of this dispute of Khaia with the city of Simyra, that they should send us without delay thirteen talents (or pieces of gold): I gave the proclamation. The men of blood are named in the letter to the city of Simyra.(230) It avails not. Ask Khaia as to the letter of our previous dispute with the city of Simyra—to satisfy the King, and to give security to the King, they are sending again, and..."

24 B. M.—This is broken at the top.
"And King my Lord, soldiers are moving to the city of Gebal, and behold the city Durubli (231) has sent forth soldiers to war to the city Simyra. If the heart of the King my Lord is toward the city of Durubli my Lord will also order many soldiers, thirty chariots and an hundred chief men of your land; and you will halt at the city Durubli, my Lord's city. If the lands are to be defended, the King will order the departure of Egyptian soldiers (bitati) to the city of Gebal, and (I doubt not?) you will march to us. And I ... to slay him, and ... behold the King my Lord ... faithful; and they have warred with the men Kau Paur (232) (Egyptian magnates) of the King. Lo! they have slain Biari the Paur (magnate) of the King, and he has given gifts to my ... and they are helping. And none are servants of the King. And evil in our eyes behold is this. I am spoiled, and I fear lest ... no wish of the faithful chief be granted to him. Lo! you will make my kindred to be afflicted. The King shall arm the land ... thy soldiers great and

small, all of them; and Pakhamnata (233) did not listen to me and they do a deed that ... and thou shalt tell him this, that he shall set free the city of Simyra; and (the King) will listen to the message of his servant, and shall (send) Egyptian soldiers. Behold he will say to the King that the Egyptian soldiers have no corn or food to eat, all the enemies have cut off from the midst of the cities of the King my Lord the food and the corn ... and (I) have raised soldiers gathering (in) the city of Gebal ... there is not ... you shall send to us ... and to march to it, and I have stopped ... and not one of the lands of the Canaanites helps Yankhamu though he is for the King."

58 B.—This is a large and important tablet, but much broken; it begins with a short salutation, and then says at once, "I am laid low." It refers to the loss of the city Abur,(234) and mentions the names of Aziru and Abdasherah, and says there is no garrison. The enemy are marching on to the capital. He says: "I sent to the palace (or capital of Egypt) for soldiers and you gave me no soldiers." "They have burned the city Abur, and have made an end in the sight of Khamu my son." "The man of sin Aziru has marched ... he has remained in the midst ... I have despatched my son to the palace more than three months (ago) who has not appeared before the King. Thus (says) my chief of the city of Takhida (235)—they are reaching him: of what use are the fortifications to the men left therein?" "The chief who came out of the lands of Egypt to inform, whom you announced us on account of Aziru formerly, I shall send to the King. You will not have heard this message as to the city Abur. The dogs are wasting, as is said, do you not mark the news? If the King had thought of his servant, and had given me soldiers. .." The next passages are much damaged, but refer to the same general subject of complaint. The next intelligible sentence is: "The people have been enraged expecting that the King my Lord would give me for my chief city corn for the food of the people of the strongholds." He then protests his good faith, and says finally: "And my sons are servants of the King, and our expectation is from the King ... The city is perishing, my Lord has pronounced our death ..."

77 B.—After a short salutation: "Let the King hear the news of his faithful servant. It is ill with me: mightily fighting, the sons of Abdasherah have striven in the land of the Amorites. They had subdued all the land of the city of Simyra, and they have wrecked the city Irkata (Arkah) for its ruler. And now they are coming out of the city of Simyra, and it is ill for the ruler (who is) in face of the foes who come out." The tablet is here broken, but refers to Gebal and to the rulers Zimridi and Yapaaddu. The writer hopes for the arrival of troops. "Egyptian soldiers; and the Sun-King will protect me. Friendly men have been (shut up?) in the midst of his land. Moreover, the King my Lord shall hear the message of his servant, and deliver the garrison of Simyra and of Irkata: for all the garrison have ... out of the city Simyra and ... Sun-God Lord of the lands will order for me also twenty (companies?— tapal) of horse, and, as I trust, to the city of Simyra (to defend her) you will speed (a division?) instructing the garrisons to be strong and zealous, and to encourage the chiefs in the midst of the city. If also you grant us no Egyptian soldiers no city in the plains will be zealous for thee. But the chain of the Egyptian soldiers has quitted all the lands—they have disappeared to the King."(236)

14 B. M.—" Ribadda speaks to his Lord the King of many lands the Great King. Baalath of Gebal has given power to the King my Lord: at the feet of my Lord, my Sun, seven times seven times I bow. Why wilt not thou utter for us a message to me? And (now) know the demand which my chief is despatched to make in presence of the King my Lord; and his division of horse has marched, but the man has delayed marching—its chief—as the letters to the King were not given to the hand of my chief ... as to what has been said ... of your land, is it not needful that the allies of the Paka should march to the men of blood; have not all the lands been grieved? It will be necessary for the allies, but they come not being slow. Moreover I sent for men of garrison and for horses, but you care not for us (even) to return us a message for me. And I am destroyed by Abdasherah like Yapaaddu and Zimridi—and they are fugitives. Moreover, the revolt of the city of Simyra and of the city Saarti (237) continues against him. We remain under the hand of Yankhamu; and he gives us corn for my eating. We two guard the King's city for him, and he collects for the King, and orders my chief, appointing chiefs to assist for me, fulfilling the decree which thou hast thyself appointed. We have trusted in the King. And two chiefs of the city have been despatched to be sent, having come down bound from the camp of Yankhamu. Moreover, as to this assistance to Yankhamu, Ribadda is in your hands, and all that is done for him (is) before you; it is not for me to punish thy soldiers. My superior is over me. And I will send to him if you do not speak about this, or he gives up the city, or I depart. Moreover, if you do not utter for us a message for me, both the city will be surrendered, and I shall go away with the men who support me. And learn that our corn also is failing, and Milcuru has measured the corn—measure of Baalath (238) ... very much ..."

89 B.—This is much broken. After the usual salutation he says that Abdasherah has fought strongly, and has seized cities belonging to Gebal; that news has reached the city as to what has befallen

the city Ammia (Amyun) from the men of blood. A certain Berber (239) chief is mentioned. He speaks of "two months," apparently as the limit of time in which he expects to be aided by the bitati, or Egyptian soldiers. Abdasherah is marching on Gebal.

79 B.—Also broken. With the usual salutation, speaks of a great fight with the men of blood, who made an end of men, women, and soldiers of his poor country. He sent men, and they were beaten. The city of Irkata (Arkah) is mentioned, and the King of the Hittites, who is making war on all the lands. The King of Mitani will be king of the weak (or false) land of the writer's people. He concludes by calling Abdasherah a dog.

44 B.—After the usual salutation, this letter appears perhaps to refer to the coming of Irimaia. "Lo the King shall send the choicest of thy chiefs—a son of Memphis (Nupi) to guard the city." The text is then much broken, referring to the palace and to cavalry, and to guarding the city for the King. He will fulfil the wishes of the Pakas, and is a faithful servant, as they would testify. The lands are to be made quiet again. "I say as to myself, lo! my heart is not at all changed as to my intention to serve the King my Lord. Now pronounce this judgment O Lord of justice. Cause all to be told that whoever crosses over from his own place the King my Lord will ... My Lord shall decide that this evil shall not go on. Who shall say anything against it? Now return a letter, and all my possessions that are with Yapaaddu (he will make equally safe?) in the sight of the King."

72 B.—"To Khaia (240) the Pa ... (an Egyptian title) thus says Ribadda. I bow at thy feet. The God Amen and the God Sa ...(241) have given you power in the presence of the King. Behold thou art a man of good ... the King knows, and through your zeal the King sends you for a Paka. Why is it asked and you will not speak to the King? that he should order for us Egyptian soldiers to go up to the place—the city Simyra. Who is Abdasherah?—a slave, a dog, and shall the King's land be smitten by him? Who set him up? And mighty with men of blood is the strength of his power. But send reinforcements: fifty tapal (companies?) of horse and 200 foot soldiers; and both shall go forth from the city Sigata (242) (Shakkah). Know his intentions. Until the (bitati) Egyptian soldiers are sent he will not be mastered, (nor) any of the men of blood, and the city of Sigata and the city of Ambi (243) are both taken, and thus ..."

17 B. M.—" Ribadda speaks to ... (Amenophis IV?(244)) the King of many Lands: at the feet of ... my Sun-God. And I repeat as to ... (the expedition?) against the city of Kappa (245) ... and against the city Amma ... cities faithful to the King my Lord. Who is this Abdasherah?—a slave, a dog, and shall he ... in the midst in the lands of my Lord? ... the King my Lord has asked as to his servant, and ... I send my messenger. Lo ... my cities, and with the letter ... my messages. And now behold he is marching to the city Batruna (246) and he will cut it off from my rule. They have seized the city of Kalbi (247)—the great pass of the city of Gebal. Truly the confederates are pushing on secretly from the great pass, and they have not made an end—mightily contumacious. For they have promised to take the city of Gebal ... And let the King my Lord hear ... this day ... they have hastened chariots and ... I trust and ... and the fate of the city of Gebal ... by them, and all the lands ... as far as the land of Egypt have been filled with men of blood. My Lord has sent no news as to this decree as I hoped by letter. And we desire that the city be saved, and the villages of the city, from him, for my inhabiting. I have been hard pushed. Help speedily O King my Lord ... soldiers and chariots, and you will strengthen the chief city of the King my Lord. Behold the city of Gebal: there is not, as is said, of chief cities (like) the city Gebal a chief city with the King my Lord from of old. The messenger of the King of the city of Acca (248) (Accho) honor thou with (my) messenger. And we have given cavalry at his pleasure ... and a division of horse ... because of pleasuring him(249) ..."

60 B.—After salutation: "The King my Lord shall know: behold Benmabenat (250) son of Abdasherah strives for the city Gatza.(251) They have subdued the city of Ardata, the city Yahlia, the city Ambi, the city Sigata,(252) all the cities are theirs; and the King shall order the cutting off of the city Simyra, so that the King may rule his land. Who is this Abdasherah?—a slave, a dog. O King it is thy land, and they have joined the King of the land of Mitani. But come to us to the King's land to ... before the cities of your rulers are destroyed; and lo! this has been said ... thy Paka, and not ... his cities to them. Now they have taken the city of Ullaza (253) for it is as has been said, until you shall march to this city of Simyra. And they have slain for us the Paka and the Egyptian (bitati) soldiers who (were) in the city of Simyra ... they have done to us, and shall not I go up ... to the city of Simyra? The cities Ambi, Sigata, Ullaza, (Caphar?) Yazu (254) have fought for me. Their destruction for us by them, will be pleaded against the city of Simyra, these cities ... and the sons of Abdasherah ... Alas! and the city of Gebal demands of the men of blood as to the city Tikhedi.(255) I marched; but there befell an entering-in to spoil by the men of blood."

23 B. M.—The usual salutation is absent, and it seems to be written to an official: "To ... as a letter thus Ribadda. I bow at thy feet. Baalath of Gebal the God of the King my Lord may (she?) strengthen thy power in the presence of the King thy Lord—the Sun of the lands. You know behold that a (covenant?) has been engraved. But why was it sent? And lo! this thou shalt announce: I am left in fear that an end will be made of all. Thou shalt make the whole known. Behold it was sent to me. 'Do not wait to go forth to the city Simyra till I come.' Behold you know, the wars are exceeding mighty against me, but he comes not. I did march, and lo! the city of Ambi ('Aba) has been burned by me. You know that the chief and the principal men of this city have gathered with Abdasherah, and behold I did not march farther. Behold you know all that has been; and on this account ... having asked my question of my prophet(256) behold I feared accordingly. Hear me speak—favorably as I trust (as to) coming; and you know that they strive with our country, who behold are men of good will. Because ... your favor is strong ... do not you urge ... a message to this city, and out of its midst she sends to ..."

86 B., a much-broken letter, supposed to be from Ribadda, mentions Batruna and Ambi.(257) Toward the end it reads continuously: "The King of the land of the Hittites behold is ... to the sons of Abdasherah, for he hastens to despatch soldiers of the royal ... and the neighboring places have joined: the lands of the King my Lord are made a desert, which the dogs bring to naught: they have mourned. If Neboyapiza fears the King my Lord will he not march on them, if the King my Lord will speak to the great man of the chief city—to the great man of the chief city of Cumidi (258) (Kamid ... to march to join ... to me..."

41 B. begins with the usual salutation from Ribadda. "Behold I am a faithful servant of the Sun-King, and I confess that my messages have been sad for the King, as you own. The King my Lord shall hear the messages of his faithful servant, and Buri is sending out in the direction of the city Simyra and Hadar ... has marched against you, and they have beaten us, and they have brought us low. (These foes?) are destroying in my sight, and I was ready (to go out?) with the Paka to keep watch in the presence of the chiefs of the governments. And my Lord shall hear the news. Now Aziru the son of Abdasherah is marching with his brethren from(259) the city Gebal: and despatch Egyptian soldiers (bitati), and thou shalt march against him and smite him—the land is the King's land; and since one has talked thus and you have not moved, the city of Simyra has been lost. The King my Lord shall hear the news of his faithful servant. There is no money to buy me horses, all is finished, we have been spoiled. Give me thirty (companies—tapal?) of horse with chariots ... men ... there is none of this with me ... not a horse ..."

22 B. M.—"To Amanabba (260) ... as a letter, thus says this Ribadda thy servant. I bow at my Lord's feet. The God Amen and Baalath of Gebal have established your power in the presence of the King my Lord. To what purpose is thy messenger with me to go to the King your Lord? And may I indeed expect horses and chariots to be ordered of thee? Will not you fortify the city? And this is heard by your message, and I am sincere, but the covenant is mocked and no soldiers are heard of with it. And they have routed the ... The city of Batruna (Batrûn) is his; and bloody soldiers and chariots have established themselves in the midst of the city, and I had lain in wait for them outside the great pass of the city of Gebal (261) ... to the King my Lord ... with thee the soldiers of the prefect ... chariots and ... here with ..."

45 B. begins with the usual salutation, and continues: "The King my Lord will be sad. Why will you not send him to me? Behold I have no ruler over my fugitives. The city of Simyra they have (shut up?); all have turned on me: and two chiefs of the land of Egypt, who travelled from the palace, went not forth. No man has travelled to the King who might carry my letter to the palace. Now these two chiefs brought us letters for the King, and the two have not gone forth, as being now afraid, and (refusing?) to my face ... I send to the palace (or capital), and Azru (Aziru?) is laying snares, gathering soldiers: has not Abdasherah marched with whatever he had? As I am told they will send friendly messages to my Lord, but thou wilt say 'Why do ye send friendly messages to me when you refuse my message?'(262)

"I have been afraid of the snare. Azaru (is) like ... Lo! I am strong through the King ... The sons of Abdasherah—the slave dog—have pretended that the cities of the governments of the King are given to them—our cities. The fortress has not opened to Aziru ... O King as to their cities are they not subject to them? From the city Simyra, to the city Ullaza, the city Sapi (263) ... chariots ... land of Egypt ... from their hands for me. So now I am despatching this chief: he has left: do I not send to the King? Now the two chiefs of the land of Egypt, they whom you sent us remain with me, and have not gone out, since no soldiers are (intended for?) me, and ... the lands for the men of blood. And since the King's heart altogether has forgotten my Egyptian soldiers (bitati) I send to Yankhamu and to Biri. They have taken those that were with the governors. Lo! may the land of the Amorites become (their) conquest. The corn which they have threshed for me has been stored up, a part of the whole with my ... and one part with me; and ... the King will order ... we ... all whatever breathes; (it is not right to shut them up?) for the King; he is not coming to him: the chief must help himself to what was ordered to be stored up for the King. The King shall order a memorial as to the innocence of his servant. And as to the produce of the city O King there is none at all with me; all is finished from being distributed for (my own subsistence?). But as to this chief, the King will order him as I trust, and will give us men of garrison for ... to guard his faithful servant and his chief city, and the men of Nubia who are with us, as those who are your foes (exult?). Moreover behold (much to say?) ... Thinking this, I shall send to the palace for a garrison—men of Nubia ... The King will ... men of garrison ... of the land of Nubia for its guarding, you will not ... this city to the men of blood."

51 B.—The ordinary salutation: the letter goes on in an eloquent strain: "The storm (or a tumult) has burst forth. Let the King behold the city of Simyra. Lo! the city of Simyra has remained as a bird caught in the snare: so her ... is left to the city of Simyra. The sons of Abdasherah by their devices, and the men of the city of Arāda (Arvad) by their hostility have made her wroth, and a fleet has sped ... in the sight of Yankhamu ... men of the city ... they have seized, and ... Lo! the men of the city Arvad searched for the coming forth of the Egyptian soldiers (bitati); Abdasherah is with them, has he not marched? and their ships are set against the reinforcements from the Land of Egypt. So now there is no navigation. Let them make haste. Now they have seized the city Ullaza (Kefr Khullis) and all whatsoever Abdasherah has ... to the chiefs. And lo! we ... and the ships of the men of Misi (the Delta?)(264) have been broken, with whatsoever was theirs. And as for me they went not up to fight for the mastery of the city of Simyra. Yapaaddu has fought on my side, against whosoever was not faithful (or constant). They have trodden me down ... So now in sight of Zabandi (265) and of Ibikhaza also, I have (joined?) myself to Yankhamu; and you will know their (good opinion?) of my faithfulness: as to what he thinks of my zeal make him confess, so he will (make it known?). He has fought for me and lo! they are wasting the city Ullaza (to make an end thereof?)."

The back of this long letter is unfortunately quite destroyed. The final sentences are on the edge, the tablet being of considerable thickness:

"I have desired peace (like?) a faithful servant of the King. The men of Egypt, expelled from this city of our neighbor, are with me; and there is no ... for them to eat. Yapaaddu has not granted my servants this ... this poor country; but we have been swift to help the city Simyra ... they have gone up to fight the ships (of the city) of Arāda (Arvad) ... (it was grievous?) ... Riib ..."

55 B.—A much-broken letter appears to refer to a message from the King being seized, and that 300 men poured out and burned a city. It speaks of a Paka and of Egyptian soldiers, and of the city Beruti (Beirût) and of Abdasherah's forces.

16 B. M.—"To the King my Lord thus says Ribadda thy servant, the dust of thy feet. I bow seven times and seven times at the feet of my Lord. And will not my Lord hear the message of thy servant? Men of the city of Gebal, and my family; and a wife whom I loved, they have taken away after the son of Abdasherah; and we have made a gathering; we have searched; and I cannot hear a word spoken about them. I am sending to the King my Lord, and once more, despatch thou men of garrison, men of war, for thy servant; and will you not defend the city of the King my Lord? But news has not arrived from the King my Lord for his servant. But he will be generous; he will remember me; and the advice (I speak) comes from my heart. The region near (us) Ammunira (266) has traversed throughout, and I went to him, for he gave assistance. And I myself searched for my family, but it has been made to vanish from my sight; and the King my Lord shall counsel his servant. Lo! the ally is zealous; and he has decreed a gathering of the Egyptian soldiers (bitati) of the King my Lord; and the King my Lord will counsel his servant. If there is no wish to be kind on the part of the King my Lord, I myself am helpless; and the King has no servants. Moreover, my son and my wife have been subjected to a man who sins against the King."(267)

15 B. M.—"To Amanabba my father, thus Ribadda thy son. I bow at my father's feet. Baalath of the city Gebal strengthens your favor in the sight of the King your Lord. Why has it been asked, and no complaint (is made) to the King? and you hesitate about the Egyptian soldiers (bitati), and you are brought low before the land of the Amorites. If you had heard of us (that) the Egyptian soldiers (are) strong, and that they have deserted their towns, and gone away, you know not the land of the Amorites. Behold they have taken these places from us, and I am ill at ease. Behold now do not they support

Abdasherah? behold they have deceived us about them, and you promise us, day and night to send the Egyptian soldiers, and we are made sad about it, and all the chiefs of the Government. Thou shalt promise us to do this thing to Abdasherah: lo! he sends to the chiefs of the city of Ammiya (Amyûn) to slay him who was established as Lord, and they submitted to the men of blood. So now thou shalt say for us—the Chiefs of the Government; so now they are doing to us, and thou shalt announce to him (that) all the lands are for men of blood, and speak thou this message in the presence of the King my Lord. Lo! a father and a lord this thou art to me; and as for thee my face I bend, you know, to my master: behold what is done in the city of Simyra, lo! I am ... with thee. But complain to the King thy Lord, and you will send ... to me as I trust."

20 B. M.—" Ribadda sends to his Lord the Great King, the King of many lands to the prosperous King. Baalath of Gebal has confirmed the power of the King my Lord. At the feet of my Lord the Sun seven times seven times he bows him. A petition has been made long ago, made for the city of Gebal, to despatch Bikuru (to the) chiefs of the Land of Egada (268) ... served me, which ... I ... three of the chiefs ... they strove ... the Land of Egypt ... and ... then the King my Lord ... a sin against....

"If the King my Lord supports his faithful servant; and despatch thou ... this her chief (speedily?); and we two watch the city for the King. The King shall send the choicest of thy great men, from among those who guard him. The three chiefs whom Bikhuru strove to despatch, but who have fled, (are) Abdirama, Iddinaddu, Abdmelec, these are sons of Abdasherah;(269) and they have taken the King's land for themselves. He shall send the bitati..."

21 B. M.—"To Amanabba ... (by letter) thus (says) this Ribadda thy servant. I bow (at my Lord's feet). The god Amen ... of thy Lord, builds up thy favor (with) the King thy Lord. Hear ... (they have fought) mightily, and over the Egyptian soldiers are victorious, and ... to the Land of the Amorites." The letter becomes too broken to read consecutively, but refers to the Land of Mitana, and apparently to a defeat of Yankhamu. He asks for corn, and speaks of having nothing to eat, in connection with the city of Gebal; and refers to three years of (dearth?), and to the corn failing.

19 B. M.—After the usual salutation to the King, this letter reads: "The King my Lord will say that the choicest of thy great men, and the choicest of thy city that thou hast are among those who guard us. My great men and (those of?) the city, were formerly men of garrison with me; and the King asked of us corn for them to eat, from my poor country. But now behold Aziru is destroying me, and I repeat there (are) no oxen, nor ... for me; Aziru has taken all. And there is no corn for my eating. And the chiefs—the Pakas—also have been nourished by the cities, exhausting the corn for their eating. Again: (being faithful), the King shall establish for me, as men of government, the men of government of their own cities, the men who at first were with their subjects. But as for me my cities are Aziru's, and they long for me, to whom destruction is made by him, who is a dog of the sons of Abdasherah, and either you shall do for us as they wish, or you shall give orders for us to the King's cities in these matters."

48 B.—This begins with the usual salutation, and then continues: "If perchance I send a message to the King my Lord, do not thou refuse the request of my memorial. Lo! thrice has come upon me a year of storms (or tumults), and again a year of storms begins. My wheat is naught; the wheat for us to eat: that which was for sowing for my freemen is finished; their beasts, their herbs, the trees of their gardens, are wretched, in my unhappy land. Our corn has failed. Once more the King will hear the message of his faithful servant, and will order wheat in ships, and his servant shall live; and be thou moved and send us com. The chiefs (will send?) horses, as commanded, to Zu ... And thou shalt defend the city (by so doing?) ... behold Yankhamu says (or asks) ... that wheat be given to Ribadda ... to him ... corn (the bread of men?) ... and now with Yapaaddu ... their money henceforth ... ask him, he will tell all in your presence. Mayest thou know when it is spoken in the presence of the King my Lord. And this year of storms makes the wheat scarce (in) my unhappy land ... there was scarcity before in the city Simyra, and now behold in the city Gebal."

The text is here too broken to be read. It seems, perhaps, to refer to the enemy having possession of the sea, and to the entreaties of Yankhamu, and to certain waters, and the general wretchedness. A paragraph then begins:(270)

"The King of the Land Taratzi (271) has coveted the city of Simyra; and they desired to march to the city of Gebal; and none now has urged him, and he has stayed in his land. Now as he is strong he will send to the great ... by my wish ... they have returned to us." The letter is again much broken; it refers to a ruler, saying: "His heart is with my heart; but Abdasherah has conquered beyond the land of the Amorites, also since the time of your father the city of Sidon has submitted to the occupation by his allies: the lands are for the men of blood, so now there is none who is a friend (or kin) to me. Let the

King regard the message of his servant. Let him give men to guard his city. Is not she insulted by all the men of blood?"

The latter part, referring to allies, is much broken.

  54 B.—This is broken at the top, and considerably injured. It demands soldiers, and the restoration of the rulers. "The city of (Sidon?), and the city of Beirût, the sons of Abdasherah have silenced: they fought for the King, but the city of Sidon and the city of Beirût are not the King's. We sent a Paka: he did not desert his duty to you, but she has rebelled to your face: for it was permitted by the freemen. The men of blood have seized the city.(272) Behold as for me this is my repetition ... city Atsar ... restraint ..."

  49 B.—This letter is much damaged; it begins with the usual salutation, and continues: "Lo! he makes the chiefs of (Ukri?) to dwell in fear of making an end. Lo! the King asked from his rulers as to my brethren. O King, is it not right to approach them, when the King shall ask? and we have set our faces fast toward thy servants. I desire this to strengthen my neighbor ... the city of (Ukri?).(273) Their ruler will go out then from my presence. They have interfered with my sister (town), and the waters of my brother's growing corn. I am despatching to the city Ukri ... from the presence of Abdasherah ... The King ... all the lands ... if as to my brethren ... the King will ask ... a neighbor ... I shall send to the King this ... Blame us not for his weakness (or affliction), and in time past we have ruled over him, and if you will ask as to my brethren, and shall be grieved, this city (has) no (government that the King should ask after it?). Do not we know this day (what) he did to all? and trust me, if the King will not ask of the rulers. Lo! if he ceases oppression as an enemy I am well pleased. Behold the land of the city of Ukri: there are no lands (or towns) of rulers ... his ... spoiled the land for us." The next passage about servants, governors, and the Paka is too broken to read. The letter concludes by asking support, and asks excuse on account of the enemy's success.

  75 B.—The usual salutation is here damaged, and the middle of the text. "Behold since the arrival of Amanappa in my presence all the men of blood have set their faces to me; they have fulfilled the wishes of Abdasherah; and my Lord shall hear the messages of his servant; and ... men of garrison, for the defence of the royal city. Send the Egyptian soldiers (bitati) ... as there are no Egyptian soldiers it befalls thee, that the lands ... to the men of blood; since the seizing of the city Maar ... (274) at the command of Abdasherah; and so our limits are the city of Gebal and the city of Batruna;(275) but so not all the lands are to the men of blood—two chief cities which are (still) to be wrecked for (us). And they have turned back(276) to take from us ... She has remained peaceful to the King, and my Lord shall order men of garrison for his two cities, till the Egyptian soldiers march forth. But everything fails me, of the food of the land (our teeth have gnawed nothing at all?). As the heart of a bird fails, seeing the snare, this city has remained. She is helpless before them ... lamenting. Once more ... they have shut up my ... it has come to pass ... the lands ... Abdasherah, the slave dog ... the lands of the King to himself."

  84 B. is much broken; all the cities are taken except Gebal and Batruna, which remain like birds in the snare. But he still "trusts."

  12 B. M.—" Ribadda speaks to the King of Lands, of many lands, the great King the prosperous King. The Lady (Ballath) of Gebal gives power to the King my Lord. I bow at my Lord's feet—the Sun-God—seven times seven times. Let the King know! behold! the city Gebal his handmaid, faithful to the King, has gathered because of the allies who are his foes. And I am ill at ease: behold the King lets slip from his hand the chief city that is faithful to him. Let the King smite the lands of those who rob him. Lo! is not he a faithful servant, her chief who abides in the city of Gebal? Do not you say so to your servant, when there is a mighty fighting against him of men of blood, and the Gods of the land are (evilly disposed?), and our sons have been worn out, and our daughters have fled, and there is weakness in my unhappy land. For our living, my fields gave sustenance, which no ... secured. For as many as I possess, all my cities which are in flames, also the foe has overthrown: they submitted to the bloody soldiers. The city of Gebal with two cities, remains to me; and I am ill at ease because Abdasherah is marching. The city of Sigata (is) his; and he is saying to the chiefs of the city of Ammia (Amyun), 'They have slain your chief and you have done like us, and you have rebelled, and you obeyed his order, and they will punish you as men of blood.' And I am ill at ease. Lo! now Abdasherah sends for soldiers. I have remained alone—they will be rejoiced at it, and there is ruin before the city of Gebal, if there is no great man to gain me safety from his hands. And the chiefs of the government are expelled from the midst of the lands; and you relinquish all the lands to the men of blood, squandering the wealth of all the lands; and they have torn away sons and daughters nobly born; and (this) while the King is pondering about it, and all the lands have fought for him. And from what they have done to us, behold

now thou wilt become naked to their destructions. And so now I am exceedingly afraid. Behold now there is no great man who wins me salvation from their hands. As birds that are in the midst of the snares this place has remained. I myself am in the city of Gebal. Why is there this overthrow of thy land? Now I send (complaint?) to the palace (or great city) and you will not hear us. Now this (is) my message. Amanabba is with thee, ask him: he has fled,(277) and he will show the evils that are against me. Let the King hear his servant's message; and he shall establish his servant's life, and his servant shall live, and shall defend the ... with him."

The remainder of the letter is broken. It asks for advice and information, and for consideration of the memorial. Ribadda's letters increase in pathetic eloquence as the great catastrophe approaches.

56 B., a much-broken letter. They are advancing to take Gebal. Money has been given to a certain chief who has turned against Ribadda.

62 B., a mere fragment. The enemy are advancing on Gebal with the intention of taking it.

63 B.—This also is much broken. It refers to Yapaaddu, to the King's Paka receiving orders, and to the rulers, and contains the statement, "They have cut off two of my ships, with my sons (or men) and all that was mine."

80 B. begins with the usual salutation, and continues: "Does the King my Lord know? Behold the city of Gebal has gathered, she has gathered those faithful to the King, and very mighty was the battle of the men of blood against me, and there is no rest through the city of Simyra. (Defeat has not befallen?) the men of blood, through the King's Paka (chief), whom they cast out from the city of Simyra. The chief city is troubled. Now Pakha (mnata), the King's Paka, who (was) in the city of Simyra, has sent a message—he has failed. Sixty minas (mana)(278) it is that they are asking the city of Gebal, from my unhappy land. The battle was waged very mightily against us, and the King is not defended by his fortress."

81 B.—"To Rabzabi (279) ... thus Ribadda thy son." The letter is much broken. He refers to money, and asks him to complain to the King. He says he is afraid that the freemen are not (faithful?) to the King's governor, if the broken portion may be so understood.

82 B.—"To Ribadda my son thus by letter (says) King Rabzabi thy father. May our Gods prosper thee, prosper thy fortress. Let him ask to know. The sons of our Lord have spoken accordingly. They have spoken of the strife of the chiefs of the city of Simyra. (He has vanquished my fears?) of being made to perish by the city of Simyra, of our perishing by these chiefs; and lo! they have allotted decrees, they are creating a memorial. Have I not been bent upon the decrees? and decrees of the King have followed. And unless they have destroyed everything, the King makes sure to show them their master. For the King is imposing decrees. The decrees of the King are saying: 'Why do ye make a waste land to those who are servants of the King? I shall despatch men. I shall send a garrison for the chief city.' I am sending the King's ... to you ... soldiers ... in ... A gathering they are making of all."

In spite of his father's zealous assistance in Egypt, this favorable intention came too late.

76 B.—"From Riibiddi as a letter to the King my Lord: beneath the feet of my Lord seven times and seven times I bow. Behold my Lord's message from this (remnant?): from the lands of the despised, and from the chief city of fugitives, they have wandered. To go for us, accordingly I have ordered my ships to go out from shore (or wall). Lo! Aziru has fought with me. And all the chiefs of the government gathered, hardening their hearts. I have gathered to us their ships; and as they go to us in haste their abodes are deserted, which are subject (to) this Amorite race; and they have been suddenly destroyed. I am chosen chief of the chiefs of the government. To me accordingly they have subjected everything; and they have removed—on account of the success of the chiefs of my enemies—the silver from the palaces, and all else, on account of his destructions. But the King shall order soldiers for them, and now I shall send to my Lord for soldiers; and soldiers of garrison do not thou ..."

The letter is much broken here. It refers to the son of Abdasherah, and to the chief city of the Giblites, to his messenger, and to there being no news of soldiers coming. "You will not (even) glance at us ... and despatch him. The lean soldiers are growling. 'When (is) the King to feed this city? and he thinks evil of her.' Speed your chief to ... her. Why is he not ordered from the palace, being said that soldiers (are to be) sent? They have destroyed us, and they ravage the lands ... I cause to be sent repeatedly; a message is not returned us for me. They have seized all the lands of the King my Lord; and my Lord has said that they are to repent. But now behold the soldiers of the land of the Hittites have trampled down our papyrus.(280) The chief city of Gebal (has) no food. But counsel the city ... and accordingly I will listen. O King! for the Misi (Delta) men—all of them, you ordered of me presents of the royal gold, because of the sons of Abdasherah; and when you ordered me they were subjecting the sons of Abdasherah to the King; and so now it is lawful."

85 B.—This is a list of various articles, with a broken name, apparently (Rib) adda's, at the top, including perhaps either presents or his own property sent to Egypt. The tablet is much injured. It appears to mention precious stones and articles of gold, and includes male and female slaves. Yazimi, "the servant of God," with Abdaddu, is mentioned near the end.

71 B.—" Ribadda ... to the King my Lord ... at the feet ... seven times and seven times(281) ... I send and I repeat (the message), and you listen not thereto ... The King my Lord shall hear the message, and it explains to the Paur (magnate) ... to the Lords of the Palace, because in vain the soldiers of garrison have hasted to him. And you will remember my ... Lo! it is not granted to my sons to take root for me, as the prophets have perceived of old; and the race of the foes (will) remain. I being asked am going to those who are free, to Khamu my son, and to my younger brother, who have both left the city of Gebal. There was good-fortune for the sons of Abdasherah, as to the subjugation of the capital city; behold my brother has commanded, he went out as my envoy. It is no use: the soldiers of the garrison failed with him; and they have defeated me; and so the evil is done; and they make me flee from the city: it is not defended from the power of the enemy. Now I say do not prevent a descent to the Lands of Egypt, and a settlement. And you will help me very much. My great men consent; and the King my Lord will consider. Lo! the Gods of Gebal (be with him) and you will help me very much; and 'It is well' they have said: good are my wishes to the Gods. So now I shall not come down to the presence of the King my Lord. But now my son, a servant of the King my Lord, I am sending to the presence of the King my Lord, and the King shall hear the desire of his faithful servant, and appoint us Egyptian soldiers (bitati). And request (has been made) to the King of Babeli (Babylon,(282) an ally of Egypt); but he ... no soldiers of his host ... in her midst.... Egyptian soldiers of the King my Lord ... to come to her. Behold the entanglement of the chiefs friendly to my (throne?) in the midst of the city. A son of one of the chiefs is a friend in her midst. The Egyptian soldiers are strong; and they have heard of those who are reaching her; and the city has remained to the King my Lord; and the King my Lord knows that it is against him that they have (cried war?). Now I am going to a town (that) I defend for my Lord, determined in heart, before the King my Lord, that the chief city shall not be given to the sons of Abdasherah. So my brother has fought him: the city is stubborn against the sons of Abdasherah. He is not able to leave the town,(283) when there is plenty of silver and gold in her midst in the Temple of Gods, plenty of everything if they take her. O King my Lord what is done to his servant by them is done. But appoint the town of Buruzizi (284) for my dwelling. Lo! Khamu my son (sets forth?) the request in the presence. Behold! this dwelling of the chief city—the town of Buruzizi—the sons of Abdasherah have been afraid to smite. Lo! Khamu my son is going to the presence: for the sons of Abdasherah have pricked against me, and none remains to mourn, O King, for me. And I mourn to the King my Lord. Behold the city of Gebal is a city truly like our eye: there is plenty of all that is royal in her midst: the servants of the chief city were at peace, the chiefs were our well-wishers before time when the King's voice was for all. It is the chief city of the land they have wasted for me—and is none of his. Will not this desire prevail with the King? Behold thy servant, my son, I am despatching to the presence of the King my Lord; and there shall be ordered him protection of the King by soldiers ... you will come marching to us. For the King my Lord will protect me. And restore thou me to the chief city, and to my house as of old. O King my Lord ... of the King my Lord in her midst; and ... the city from (shame?) ... as ... Khamu ... till ... shall hear ... their servant ... to her midst ... the soldiers (bitati) of the King my Lord; and you will strengthen the soldiers of this place speedily ... the chief city, as I trust; and you will march to the city ... Lo! what he is saying in the presence of the King cannot it be done? O King my Lord ... the chief city of a neighbor (Gur); and which has been laid low to the demands ... of those that hate the same ... it is not just to see what is done to the lands ... the soldiers of the King my Lord; and she trusts the King my Lord."

This seems to be the last of Ribadda's fifty letters. There is no mention of any return to Gebal, or of victory over the Amorites. We do not know that he got safe to Buruzizi, but can only hope he did. It was too late when his father obtained promise of aid. So energetic a writer would probably have written again if he had been alive to do so. The Amorite letters had blinded the eyes of Amenophis so long that their position was secured. As we shall see also, there were other appeals from every part of the country.

SUBANDI'S LETTERS

If Subandi be the Zabandi of Ribadda's letter (51 B.), the following also belong to the Phœnician-Amorite war:

38 B. M.—"To the King my Lord my God my Sun, the Sun from heaven, thus says Subandi thy servant, the captain of thy horse: at the feet of the King my Lord, the Sun from heaven, seven times and seven times is made to bow both the heart and also the body. I hear all the messages of the King my Lord, the Sun from heaven, and now I shall guard the land of the King that is with me, and ... I hear ... exceeding much."

39 B. M. is an almost identical letter from the same writer.

40 B. M.—The salutation by Subandi is the same. The letter is broken. He speaks of a message from the King, and of fighting. He speaks of assisting the King's servant and the fortresses, and mentions the arrival of the King as expected, and the Kau Mas. These latter words are evidently Egyptian, Kau meaning "men" and Masa "infantry."

116 B.—The same salutation. It is a short letter acknowledging the receipt of a letter, and ends by speaking of men of blood, and that the "King knows about his cities."

117 B.—The same salutation: "The King my Lord, the Sun from heaven, has sent Khanni to me." It is injured, but seems to refer to "an hundred oxen and thirty women. For the King my Lord, the Sun from heaven, has instructed."

118 B.—A similar salutation. He will defend the King's land. "(Ask?) the great man if we have not listened to the King's Paka: now he has been listened to exceeding much—the Paka of the King my Lord, Son of the Sun from heaven."

120 B., a short letter from Subandi, merely saying that he has received the King's message.(285)

Northern Palestine

LETTERS FROM BEIRUT

No. 26 B. M.—"To the King my Lord my Sun my God, to the King my Lord by letter thus Ammunira, chief of the city of Burutu, thy servant, the dust of thy feet: at the feet of the King my Lord my Sun my God—the King my Lord—seven and seven times I bow. I hear the messages of ... of the King my Lord my Sun my God—the ruler of my life, and they have drawn the heart of thy servant, and the dust of the feet of the King my Lord my Sun and my God—the King my Lord—exceeding much. Sufficient is the order of the King my Lord my Sun my God, for his servant and the dust of his feet. Behold the King my Lord my Sun has sent to his servant, and the dust of his feet, 'Speed to the presence of the Egyptian soldiers (bitati) of the King thy Lord.' I listen exceeding much, and now I have sped, with my horses, and with my chariots, and with all who march with the servant of the King my Lord, to meet the Egyptian soldiers of the King my Lord. And art not thou confident of the event? The breast of the enemies of the King my Lord my Sun my God shall be troubled. And shall not the eyes of thy servant behold this, through the mastery of the King my Lord; and the King my Lord my Sun my God, the King my Lord, shall see. Thou increasest the favors of thy servant. Now as to the servant of the King my Lord, and the footstool of his feet, now let him fortify the city of the King my Lord my Sun—the ruler of my life, and her gardens (that is to say the mulberries),(286) till the eyes behold the Egyptian soldiers of the King my Lord, and ... the servant of the King I proclaim" (or predict).

27 B. M.—"To the King ... my Lord thus says Ammunira thy servant, the dust of thy feet. At the feet of the King my Lord seven and seven times I bow. I hear the message of the letter, and what is thereby commanded to me O King my Lord. And I hear (the precept?) of the message of the scribe of my Lord, and my heart is eager, and my eyes are enlightened exceedingly. Now I have watched much, and have caused the city of Burutu to be fortified for the King my Lord, until the coming of the Egyptian soldiers (bitati) of the King my Lord. As to the chief of the city of Gebal who is in trouble together with me, now they defend him till there shall be counsel of the King to his servant. The King my Lord is shown the grief of one's brother, which troubles us both. From the city of Gebal, lo! the sons of Ribaadda who is in trouble with me, are subjected to chiefs who are sinners to the King, who (are) from the land of the Amorites. Now I have caused them to haste with my horses and with my chariots and with all who are with me, to meet the soldiers (bitati) of the King my Lord. At the feet of the King my Lord seven and seven times I bow."

Ammunira was Ribadda's friend (see 16 B. M.), and his letter agrees with Ribadda's: clearly, therefore, the seizure of Ribadda's sons comes historically before the loss of Beirût, Mearah, and Sidon (54 B., 75 B.).

LETTER FROM SIDON

90 B.—"To the King my Lord my God my Sun—the King my Lord(287)—by letter thus Zimridi, the Governor of the city of Sidon (Ziduna): at the feet of the King my Lord my God my Sun—the King my Lord—seven times and seven times I bow. Does not the King my Lord know? Lo! the city of Sidon has gathered. I am gathering, O King my Lord, all who are faithful to my hands (power). And lo! I hear the message of the King my Lord. Behold, he causes it to be sent to his servant, and my heart rejoices, and my head is raised, and my eyes are enlightened; my ears hear the message of the King my Lord; and know O King I have proclaimed in presence of the Egyptian soldiers (bitati) of the King my Lord, I have proclaimed all, as the King my Lord has spoken; and know O King my Lord lo! mighty has been the battle against me: all ... who are faithful to the King in ... it has come to pass, and the chiefs ... sons, and are faithful to the King ... and her chief who goes out in the presence of the King's Egyptian soldiers (bitati). The greatest of the fortresses deserts to the enemies: which has gone well for the men of blood, and they are gaining them from my hands, and my destruction is before me. O King my Lord as said the chiefs who are my foes have done."

From the letters of the King of Tyre which follow (99 B. and 28-31 B. M.) we see that Zimridi was a weak ruler. His own letter agrees with one from Ribadda (54 B.) as showing that Sidon fell by treachery, not by war.

LETTERS FROM TYRE

These appear to begin early, before the appearance of Aziru, and show that the rivalry of Tyre and Sidon was of early origin. None of the letters mention Tyre except those written by her King.

99 B.—"To the King my Lord my God my Sun thus (says) Abimelec (288) thy servant: seven and seven (times) at the feet of the King my Lord (I bow). The King my Lord sends (to ask) if I have finished what is doing with me. I present to the King my Lord 100 ornaments (or 'crowns,' perhaps 'shekels'—tacilal); and let the King my Lord give his countenance to his servant, and let him give the city Huzu (289) to his servant—a fountain to supply water for his drinking: let the King my Lord grant (a chief a subject?)(290) to guard his town; and let me plead, and let the face of the King my Lord regard my explanation before the King my Lord. As said behold let the King my Lord confide in me to defend his city. Lo! the King of the city of Sidon is taking the people who are my subjects—a chief who is my inferior (or foe). Let the King give his countenance to his servant, and let him order his Paka (chief), and let him give the city of Huzu for waters to his servant, to take trees for our use for the dwellings. Lo! he has made war: nothing is left. In vain have they threshed corn if the King of Sidon despoils the King's land. The King of the city of Khazura (Hazor)(291) is leaving his city, and goes out with men of blood. Let the King show their borders to the hostile (or inferior) chiefs. The King's land is vexed by men of blood. Let the King send his Paka (chief) who is in our land."

29 B. M.—"To the King my Lord, my God, my Sun thus (says) Abimelec thy servant: seven and seven (times) at the feet of the King my Lord I bow. I (am) the dust beneath the shoes of the King my Lord my master—the Sun-God who comes forth in presence of the world from day to day, as the manifestation of the Sun-God his gracious father: who gives life by his good word, and gives light to what is obscure: who frees all lands from dissensions by just rule of a free country; who gives this his compassion from heaven, like the God Adonis, and causes all lands to rest through his mercy. This is the message of a servant to his Lord. Lo! I hear the gracious messenger of the King who reaches his servant, and the good utterance which comes from the hands of the King my Lord for his servant; and the utterance it makes clear, since the arrival of the messenger of the King my Lord. Does not he make it clear?—the utterance is clear. The lands of my fathers behold it records. Lo! the utterance of the King comes to me, and I rejoice exceedingly and (my heart has risen?) from day to day because the land is not ... Behold I heard the gracious messenger from my Lord, and all my land has been afraid as to my Lord's countenance. Lo! I heard the good utterance; and the gracious messenger who reaches me, behold he said, O King my Lord, that the region (is) to be established by the presence of many soldiers; and the servant says for his Lord that my plain is my land over against my highlands, over against the plain of my cities. He has borne the order of the King my Lord listening to the King his Lord, and has served him (in his integrity?), and the Sun-God he has proclaimed before him; and he makes clear the good utterance from the hands of his Lord, and does he not listen to the order of his Lord? The portion of his town his Lord has divided. His word none shall overthrow in all the lands forever. Behold (this is) the duty that he heard from his Lord. His city will rest, will rest from overthrowing his utterance for all time. Thou art the Sun-God whom he has proclaimed before him; and the decision which shall set at rest is lasting for one. And because she judges that the King my Lord is just our land obeys—the land that I am given. This Abimelec says to the Sun-God. My Lord I am given what appears before the King my Lord. And now the city Zarbitu (292)is to be guarded by the city of Tyre (Tsuru) for the King my Lord."

31 B. M.—"To the King the Sun ... thus says Abimel (ec) ... seven times and seven times at the feet ... I am the dust from ... below ... and the King the Sun forever ... The King spoke to his servant (and) to his servant my comrade: he has granted that extension be given, and as to waters for (his servant's) drinking And they did not as the King my Lord has said; and we arrive at no fulfilment. And let the King counsel his servant my comrade. He has granted that the waters be given, because of the abundance there to drink. My Lord the King, behold, there is no one to tend my trees, no one (to tend) my waters, no one to make ... Let the King my Lord know." The next lines are much broken, and the letter then continues: "... As the King has said. And let the King assign to his servant and to the city of Tyre (Tsuru) the city that my comrade has given, and what the order lays down on the side of the King for his servant, which the King made an order (less than a year ago?). The King is the eternal Sun-God,

and to his faithful servant the King my Lord shall ... for guardians of the town that my comrade has granted. My requests as to this town ... Moreover, my Lord ... soldiers against me ... to my desire ... King ... Lo! his heart is evil ... King my Lord; and he turns away from my wish; and O King my Lord (thou knowest the hearts of all those in the land?), and let the King give his countenance to his servant; and to the city of Tyre the town that my comrade has granted (is) to be given ... waters for (irrigation?). Moreover, my Lord ... Let the King ask his Paka. Lo! the chief of the city of Zar (epta) has followed the city of Simyra (with) a ship. I am marching, and the chief of the city of Sidon marches out; and as for me he has marched with all ... and let the King counsel his servant ..."

30 B. M.— Abimelec begins with his ordinary salutation. "Thus far I defend the King's city which he confides to my hands very much. My intention (has been) to walk in sight of the face of the King my Lord, and not to take by force from the hands of Zimridi of the city of Sidon. Lo! I hear me that he will strive, and has made war with me. Let the King my Lord send down to me ... chiefs for guards of the city of the King my Lord; and let me strive (or plead) for the dwellings of the King my Lord, with those who deceive his gracious countenance. I set my face to (encourage?) the region of those who are peaceful with the King my Lord; and let the King my Lord ask his Paka (chief). Lo! I set my face (or, confirm my intention) forever, O King my Lord. Now a messenger I am despatching to ... of the King my Lord, and ... the King my Lord the messenger ... ... his letter ... and may it be the means of ... the King my Lord ... (that) he sets his face ... forever to ... the face of the King my Lord. His servant will not let slip ... from (his) hands ... Let the King my Lord give his countenance ... and (he) shall ... waters for the drawing ... and woods for his servant.... Know O King my Lord behold they are plucking the fruit that we left. There are no waters and no woods for us. Now Elisaru the messenger to the presence of the King my Lord has hasted, and I have made bold to present five precious things of copper, this agate, one throne of gold. The King my Lord sends to me (saying) 'Send to me all you hear from the land of Canaan' (Cina'ana). The King of Danuna (293) has been destroyed, and his brother is ruling after him, and his land has broken out, and they have seized the King of the town of Hugarit,(294) and mighty is the slaughter that follows him. He is strong, and none are saved from him, nor any from the chiefs of the army of the land of the Hittites. The proud Edagama (295) of the city Ciidzi (Kadesh on Orontes, the capital of the Southern Hittites, now Kades) and Aziru have fought—they have fought with Neboyapiza; they have come to the regions of Zimridi. Lo! he gathers ships of soldiers against me from the fortresses of Aziru. And lo! they have grievously opposed my Lord's subjects, and all will break out. Let the King give countenance to his servant, and let him leap forth to go out a conqueror" (or "to the region").

28 B. M.—"To the King my Lord my Sun my God thus (says) Abimelec thy servant; seven and seven (times) at the feet of the King my Lord I bow. I am the dust beneath the feet. Consider me O King my Lord. The King my Lord (is) like the Sun; like the air god (or Adonis) in heaven art thou. Let the King advise his servant: the King my Lord confides in me. I watch the city of Tyre the handmaid of the King. And I send a hasty letter to the King my Lord, and no order does he return to me. I am the Paka (296) (chief) of the King my Lord, and I have diligently followed what was ordered. But as to our silence to the King my Lord let the King be assured. As a subject I guard his city. And let me plead (or strive) before the King my Lord, and let him see his face. Who shall preserve one born a subject? Lo there has gone forth no command from the hands of the King his Lord; and he may not know when the King sends to his servant. He may never know. As for me ..."

The letter is here too broken to read consecutively. It refers to the "west," and apparently to "burning," to Aziru, and to someone, perhaps a king's messenger, called Khabi. The letter becomes readable on the back of the tablet.

"... by Elisaru the messenger it is confirmed that the city of Simyra is Aziru's. And is not the King nourished by his city of Tyre, by his country? Lo! if I shall be destroyed the King is destroyed. But thus his fortress has been wasted, and there has been great fear, and all the lands have feared; for he has not walked after (i.e., obeyed) the King my Lord. O King know: desolation has remained with me—with the Paka in the city of Tyre. Zimridi is gone to the city Irib.(297) He has escaped from slavery; and there is no water or wood for us; and alas! there is none remaining to stand up for me. The chief is helpless. And let the King my Lord advise his servant by a letter he sends to me, whom you thus hear. And Zimrida of the city of Sidon has sent to the King, and Aziru is a man sinful against the King, and the chiefs of the city Arāda (Arvad) destroy me,(298) and (everything is altered?) through their ravages; and they will gather their ships, their chariots, their foot soldiers, to seize the city of Tyre the King's handmaid. She has been very constant to the King's hand, and the city of Tyre has been crushed by them. Were they not violent in taking the city of imyra? They took from the hands of Zimrida him who bore the King's order to Aziru; and I sent a letter to the King my Lord, and he returns me not an order for his servant.

They have fought (for a long time?) against me. There are no waters(299) and no trees. Let there be ordered a letter for his servant, and let me plead, and let me see his face, and the King ... to his servant, and to his city, and not ... his city and his land. Why do they ... the King our Lord from the land, and ... and he has known that I honor the King's power, who ... no ... to my letter—a subject before the King my Sun, my Lord; and let the King answer his servant."

LETTERS FROM ACCHO

93 B.— Surata, chief of Acca, sends the usual formula of compliment, and continues: "What chief is there who when the King his Lord sends to him will not hear? As this is sent out by desire of the Sun-God from heaven, so now it is promised him."

32 B. M., a short letter from Zitatna, of Accho, merely says that he bows seven times and seven times at the King's feet.

94 B., another short letter by the same, states that he listens to the King's wishes.

95 B.—"To the King my Lord my ... the Sun from heaven thus says Zatatna chief of the city of Acca, thy servant, the King's servant, and the dust at the feet trampled under the feet of the King my Lord—the Sun-God from heaven: seven times and seven times he bows both heart and body. The King my Lord shall hear the message of his servant; the woman my wife ... He has left from ... Neboyapiza ... with Suta ... of the King, in the city of Acca ... to say anything ... him. She has urged (that) soldiers of the King my Lord shall go out with her from the city Magid ... No word is mentioned as to him or explanation before me; and now we two are sending. My reason (is) to assure her—Ziza the woman my wife—as to Neboyapiza, and she has not slept because of him. Behold the city of Acca like the city of Makdani (300) (is) with the Land of Egypt, and the King will not refuse ... and will send ... before me, and is it not that the King my Lord ... his Paka, and let him empower him."

LETTERS FROM HAZOR

48 B. M.—"To the King my Lord by letter thus says Iebaenu (Jabin) chief of the city Khazura (Hazor) thy servant. At the feet of the King my Lord I bow, who behold am one of the faithful servants of the King my Lord; and all those who guard the city of Hazor (301) with her fortresses belonging to the King my Lord; and let him expect this. Let him recall to the King my Lord all that the city Hazor—thy city, and thy servant is made to suffer."

47 B. M.—"To the King my Lord thus (says) the King of the city of Hazor: I bow at the feet of my Lord. Lo! I am guarding the fortresses belonging to the King my Lord, until the arrival of my Lord my God; and lo! I hear all these messages, and I am departing O Sun-God my God ... and I am being brought low: the ... that they have taken is increased, and the Gods have nodded to his revolt over me, and now I am causing all to be despatched till the coming of the King my Lord. Behold this, lo! they come ... your envoy ... very much ... my Lord ... safety ... the city of Hazor ... when the land ... and all ... Lo ... Moreover behold ... and my place ... with soldiers."

Unfortunately King Jabin does not mention the nationality of the enemy. From the Tyre letters he seems to have been an enemy of the Phœnicians, being perhaps on the side of Aziru; but the date of the present letters is not fixed by any reference to persons mentioned in the other letters. It is quite possible that the Hebrews, and not the Hittites, were his foes, since the Hebrew conquest took place in the lifetime of Yankhamu and Suta, who are noticed in the northern letters also. If he was a friend of Aziru's, the enemy, though enemies of Egypt, could not well have been Hittites or Amorites; and the name of the King is that of Joshua's enemy, Jabin of Hazor. It is clear that the Egyptians, though expected, were not in Hazor at the time. The kings of Hazor ruled lower Galilee, where they had a force of chariots a century later. In Joshua's time (Josh. xi.) there were also many chariots in and near Hazor.

It is remarkable that none of the letters from Tell Amarna refer to central Palestine. There is no mention of any town in lower Galilee or in Samaria, except Zabuba and Megiddo. Taanach, Shechem, Jezreel, Dothan, Bethel, and other such places are unnoticed, as well as Heshbon, Medeba, Rabbath-Ammon, Ramoth Gilead, and other places in Moab and Gilead. The Egyptians probably had no stations in these wild mountains, where their chariots could not pass. The Egyptian traveller mentions no town between Megiddo and Joppa in the time of Rameses II, and no towns in the regions of Samaria or Gilead or Moab occur in the list of places taken by Thothmes III; nor were there any stations in the Hebron mountains.(302) On the other hand, many places in Sharon and Philistia, and in the lower hills to the east, and in the Negeb hills south of Hebron, were conquered by the last-mentioned king, and are again mentioned by the traveller of the time of Rameses II, and these occur in the present letters. We are thus at once transported to the south of the country.

Southern Palestine

LETTERS FROM JOPPA

No. 57 B. M.—"To the King my Lord my God my Lord of Hosts, by letter thus (says) Yabitiri (Abiathar?) thy servant, the dust of the feet of the King my Lord my God my Lord of Hosts. Seven times and seven times I bow. As thou seest I am among the faithful servants of the King my Lord. I am arraying. But if I am arraying has not he been furious? and I am arraying before the King; and he has been furious. Shall the brick (letter) hide it under deceptions? But I will not conceal under deep sayings (emiki) to the King my Lord. And the King my Lord shall ask Yankhamu his Paka. Lo! I am a warrior, and I am casting down the rebellion, O King my Lord, and I am sending out from the pass belonging to the King my Lord. And let the King my Lord ask his Paka ('head man'). Lo! I am defending the pass (or great gate) of the city of Azati (Gaza) and the passage of the city of Yapu (Joppa), and I myself and the soldiers (bitati) of the King my Lord have marched to the lands. I myself (am) with them, and now, and lo! now, I myself (am) with them. The yoke of the King my Lord (is) on my neck and I will bear it."

71 B. M.—The usual salutation from a servant of the King, whose name is broken, but reads Mus ... ni. "I hear the messages of the King my Lord which he sends to his servant, hearing what is spoken by thy chief (Ka), and (it is) 'Strengthen thou the fortresses of the King thy Lord which are with thee.' Now they have minded the message of the King my Lord to me, and the King my Lord learns of his servant. Now Biia the son of the woman Gulata (303) was my ... of my brethren whom I am despatching to go down from the city Yapu (Joppa), and to be the defenders of the messengers returning to the King my Lord; and now Biia is the son of Gulata, he took them; and the King my Lord shall learn this message of his servant. Thus since the King my Lord said to me, 'Make him leave thy city, on the appearance of Biia.' He also indeed is made to leave; and both go, and indeed both are sent down O King my Lord day and night till they reach the place."

Joppa is not mentioned in the history of Joshua's wars in the south, but the "border before (east of) Japho" is noticed in the later topographical charter (Josh. xix. 46).

LETTERS FROM ASCALON

129 B.—"To the Great King my Lord Dagantacala (304) thy servant speaks. Seven times and seven times at the feet of the Great King my Lord I bow. And now behold Dagantacala is thy servant O Great King my Lord. He hears carefully the message of the Great King his Lord ... like my fathers, (and) what my fathers have not done for the Great King I have done for the Great King my Lord. And the Great King my Lord says to me, 'Listen thou for us to the head man (Ka) thy governor.'(305) I hear this carefully as to the chief governor, and the ruler knows it."

74 B. M.—This begins with the same salutation from Dagantacala, and continues: "Redeem me from the strong foes, from the hands of men of blood. The chiefs are hiding and the chiefs are flying, and redeem thou me O Great King my Lord. And the son of a dog has ... But thou (art) the Great King my Lord. Come down redeem me, and I shall rejoice because of the Great King my Lord."

118 B.—From Yadaya of Ascalon, a captain of the horse of the "King—the Sun from Heaven." The usual salutation is much broken. The letter continues: "Now I shall defend the places of the King that are with me. The strong chiefs who are not foes of the Law (or throne) have cherished greatly the King's Paka. Now both they and I listen to him very exceedingly—to the Paka of the King my Lord the Son of the Sun from the heavens."

119 B.—From the same Yadaya, chief of the city of Ascalon, with the usual salutation. He is a captain of the horse and the dust of the King's feet. He continues: "The trusty adherent—the chief of the King my Lord, who is sent by the King my Lord—the Sun from heaven—to me, I listen exceeding much to his messages; now I will defend the King's land which is with me."

121 B.—From the same writer, with the same salutations. "Now the King's land which is with me is defended, and all that the King has sent to me they hear. The decree is very powerful. Who am I but a dog, and shall such a one not listen to the message of the King his Lord, the Son of the Sun?"

122 B.—From Yadia, the captain of the horse, with the usual salutation; it continues: "Now they guard ... my. May the Gods of the King my Lord grant to all his lands not to be confounded. I hear the message of the King my Lord to his Paka. Lo! without resting he has caused the land of the King my Lord to be defended; and now establish O King my Lord one who is in favor in the sight of the Paka of the King my Lord, who is mighty in the sight of the King my Lord. He will work with joy to ... whatever is (proclaimed?) by desire of the King my Lord. Now he will watch the land carefully."

54 B. M.—From the same Yadaya, captain of the horse, with the usual salutation; it continues: "Now (they watch for a message?) of the King my Lord the Son of the Sun. And now I am sending drink, oil, sheep, oxen, beasts, to meet the soldiers of the King my Lord ... with all for the soldiers of the King my Lord. Who am I—a dog, and shall such a one not hear the messages of the King my Lord the Son of the Sun?"

53 B. M.—The same salutation from Yadaya, captain of horse and "dust of the King's feet." "Now they guard the land of the King my Lord, and the King's chief city, as has asked the King my Lord—the Sun from Heaven. Behold what the King my Lord has said to his servant—to take arms: I am now sending to the King my Lord thirty bands to carry weapons. Moreover, who am I but a dog, and shall such a one not hear the message of the King my Lord the Sun from Heaven? the Sun—Son of the Sun whom you adore."

52 B. M. is very similar to 54 B. M. Yadia watches the land and the city, and is a dog unworthy to hear the King's message; he sends drink (beer, according to one value of the sign—and the Egyptians drank beer)(306) and oxen, and beasts, and (beans?), and all that the King requires for the soldiers.

It is to be remarked that Ascalon was not among the cities that Joshua took, but we learn that the region submitted to the Hebrews (B. 103) and Ascalon was lost before 1360 B.C.

LETTERS FROM MAKKEDAH

These letters appear to be early. They have been supposed to come from Megiddo, but the topography (111 B. and 72 B. M.) cannot be reconciled with the latter, and applied exactly to the former town (now El Mughâr); in addition to which Megiddo appears as Makdani in the letter from Accho (95 B.).

113 B.—"To the King my Lord ... and my Sun by letter thus (says) Biridi a faithful servant, that I bow at the feet of the King my Lord and my Sun and my God, seven times and seven times. I have heard (literally, the servant has heard) the messages of the King my Lord and my Sun, and now they guard the city of Makidah, the chief city of the King my Lord." The text is broken, but seems to read probably "without rest, and is set right ... without rest they watch with chariots, and they guard with chariots of the King my Lord, from those who do injury. And now behold a battle of chiefs in (or from) the land (below Mizpah?).(307) The King is my Lord for his land."

114 B.—"To the King my Lord and my Sun by letter thus (says) Biridia, Chief of the city Makidda, a faithful servant of the King. At the feet of the King my Lord and my Sun seven times and seven times prostrated. I have been obedient then, zealous for the King ... thirty oxen ... they have gathered, and I (too) to fight."

115 B.— Biridia sends the usual salutation without mentioning his city. The text is rather worn and broken, but may be read as follows: "Let the King my Lord know this. Lo! since the Egyptian soldiers (bitati) have gone down (or away) Labaya makes war against me and (without cause?) coming angrily and (without cause?). Thereupon the entrance (of gate) has been closed through the appearance of Labaya. Behold learn this, and there are no men of the Egyptian soldiers with us. So now it is desired to see them sent into the city of Magiid (da) and let the King see accordingly whether (it is to be) done. Let not Labaya seize the city. If there is no word the city will open its gates. (For two years?) he rebels; and will not the King grant this also—chiefs of his guard as defenders of his chief city. Let not Labaya take her, though those who have fled from Labaya have failed in this. Moreover those who disgraced the city Ma ... are slain."

112 B.—"To the King my Lord and my Sun thus Labaya thy servant, and the dust of thy feet. At the feet of the King my Lord and my Sun seven times seven times I bow. I have heard the message which the King sent to me; and who am I? and the King will afflict his country before me. (I swear?) I am myself a faithful servant, and I have not sinned, and I have not murmured at my tribute, and I have not murmured at the wishes of my friends (or subjects). Lo! this province my destroyers eat up, and I have had no food. The King my Lord (says) it is my fault. Once more he makes it my fault. Lo! I strive with the city Gezer (Gazri)(308) and I complain of the young men. The King one hears will march. I restrained the band of Milcilu and my band desirous to fight. The quarrel of Milcilu against me is relinquished; as to Ben Zachariah the King has sent not to attack. Lo! Ben Zachariah with men of blood was known to us to march, and I marched, and we are conquering him. He gives up Abukasu. Once more he has made peace. The King has sent to my band (saying) 'I order peace.' I am desirous of peace, since the King has sent to me. Stay thy sword, ponder in thy heart, and is the peace hollow. Nay, the King's messages have been done."

59 B. M.—"To the King my Lord and my Sun and my God thus Yasdata a faithful servant to the King, and (he is) dust of the King's feet. At the feet of the King my Lord and Sun and my God seven times and seven times I bow. Let the King my Lord know this. Lo! all whatsoever things the King my Lord judges for his servant ... him ... the chiefs of the city of Tabu (309) have slain a hundred of my oxen, and they have wasted me. And with Biridia I have caused (men) to go forth. Let the King my Lord know this as to his servant."

This letter shows that the writer lived near Biridia, who was attacked by Labaya, and that the Hebron hills were inhabited by marauders.

72 B. M.—"Lo! a letter as to destruction of my brethren because of what the Gods of the King our Lord have done. And the people of Labaya are conquered; and so we have ordered Khaia (310) that this be borne by him to the King our Lord. And a (company?) of my horse was placed, and the people are sent out after him, and he rides with Yasdata also till I come. And he is gone away to smite him, and now Yasdata is thy servant, and he strives mightily with me in battle array, and has not he ... the rule of the King my Lord, and let there be ... to the King my Lord ... and Zurata is stopping the way of Labaya from the city Makidda. And he asked me to gather ships—my fleet, and it will go straight to inform the King; and Zurata marches on him and hinders him; from the city of 'Anana which is his. Zurata is damming the marshes. They have contrived a stoppage of the head (waters) from his drinking. Behold what thus I have done for the King my Lord. Lo! possession is possible for me, but it is difficult. My brethren (have become few?) but Zurata delays Labaya, and Zurata hinders Addumemur from them. And does not the King my Lord know this?"

This letter (confirmed by 154 B.) shows that a town near the sea, not like Megiddo, inland, is intended. Labaya had apparently taken Makkedah from Biridia, who had been afraid of it (115 B.). The writer of the present letter was probably Biridia and he was perhaps blockading the province by sea on the west, while Yasdata, who was on the east (which agrees with 59 B. M.), blocked up the stream near 'Anana. This site would be the Enam of the Bible (Josh. xv. 34), which is thus fixed at the ruin of Kefr 'Ain, by the numerous head springs which feed the river Rubîn, which passes close to Makkedah on the south. The marshes here between the hills would easily be dammed, and the water supply of Makkedah (el Mughâr) so cut off. Makkedah is close to the only stream of perennial water south of Joppa, and stands high on a cliff, not far from the sea. It is in the centre of the province, the boundaries of which Labaya's sons describe (154 B.).

149 B.—"(To the) King my Lord thus (says) Addu (urbilu) thy servant at the feet of my Lord I bow—to the King my Lord. And know thou, behold I have raised my ... what I desire as to Milcilu. Lo! my chiefs are going against his servants. As to Takanu a chief will march out to subject his servants for me.(311) And I have requited to this slave what they did to us." The letter then becomes broken, but refers to Milcilu, who was the King of Gezer. Takanu (or Tagi) is mentioned again in connection with Givti (B. 199).

61 B. M.—"To the King (my master?) by letter thus (says) Labaya thy servant. I bow at the feet of the King my Lord. Lo! a message as to me. Strong were the chiefs who have taken the city. As when a snake coils round one, the chiefs, by fighting, have taken the city. They hurt the innocent, and outrage the orphan. The chief man is with me. They have taken the city (and he receives sustenance?). My destroyers exult in the face of the King my Lord. He is left like the ant whose home is destroyed. You (will be displeased?), but I have extended to the hand of her chief that which is asked of him: like me he is ruined and unfortunate; and this same taking of my city had been stopped if you had spoken against it. This wickedness (or foolishness) you caused, and thou hast destroyed thy city. They have desired to throttle (or persecute) us—the chiefs who have taken the city from him. It is the city of my fathers also (that) they persecute."

154 B.—"To the King my Lord by letter thus (says) Addurbilu thy servant, at the feet of the King my Lord seven times and seven times I bow. The King my Lord will know the hate which is desired by the son of the sinful chief who hated me—the second son of Labaya. His face is estranged. I foresee estrangement of the land of the King my Lord. He has plotted as plotted (against me?) the chief who was his father; and the King my Lord shall know it. Lo! he has built a fort ... against me. The second son of Labaya (says) 'Why has a vain papyrus(312) taken from us the lowlands of the Gitties? ... thy Lord, O city of those who besieged the chief our father.' As I am saying speaks to us the second son of Labaya. He has made war for me with the chiefs of the Land of Gina (causing a chief our friend to be slain?). And when (there was) a battle he has not been confounded, and the fight was great, but he has made it his dwelling, bereaving me in the sight of the King my Lord: for he has made war in ... of Gina (with?) the servants of the King my Lord. And truly alone of the chiefs exceeding strong (is) Biruyapiza.(313) (And thou shalt hear?) what is said as to him." The text becomes broken, but still refers to the doings of the second son of Labaya, and continues with an important passage on the back of the tablet:

"And as I say speaks to us the second son of Labaya who is making war. 'As to our possessions from the King thy Lord, lo! this is the boundary: over against the city of Sunasu and over against the city Burku and over against the city Kharabu. And behold the boundary of the dwelling of my race. So it was defined by our Lord; and it includes the city of Giti Rimuna (Gath Rimmon). And the King thy Lord is (breaking the bond of our...?).' And I answered him. It is known that he deprives me of it in sight of the King my Lord. Because of his making wars with the King my Lord—my King my Lord—I and my brethren have gone down as you heard of us by me. And did not the messenger of Milcilu speak to him before the face of the second son of Labaya? It was made complete. I foresee estrangement of the land of the King my Lord. They disturb a peaceful region, and in vain I repeat the letter about me. The guard of my Lord ... to go down, and the King my Lord shall hear what the message says."

This letter settles the site of Gath Rimmon (the full name of Gath, so called as standing on a height)—now Tell es Sâfi. The land of Gina was near the present Umm Jîna—probably Engannim of Judah (Josh. xv. 34)—in the low hills about six miles to the northeast. Sunasu is Sanasin, a ruin in the hills east of the Valley of Elah. Burka is Burkah, in the plain northeast of Ashdod. Kharabu is el Khurab, a village east of Jaffa, and just north of the Valley of Jaffa. Gath stood over the Valley of Elah, and Burka close to the same. The province extended from the hills of Hebron to the sea, and from the Valley of Elah to the Valley of Jaffa; and just in the middle of this province was Makkedah.

111 B., a fragment of a letter from Biridia. He is a faithful servant, and sends the usual salutation. He has heard of (peace?), and he is marching. The son of Labaya is noticed, and there is a reference to gold. Biridia has already appeared as one of the enemies of Labaya.

73 B. M.—This seems to come from the same region on account of its topography. The letter is injured at the top, and probably not addressed to the King himself. "I say the dog is marching ... from their ravages against me. Now behold from (being loosed?) ... from the wastings against ... Lo! consider thou thyself my chief cities. Mighty against me ... he has made ... to the city Macdalim.(314) And soldiers of the city Cuuzbe (315) have destroyed east of me. And now there is no commander to lead me forth from their hands. Moreover, Abbikha (or Abbinebo) smites my western region. They have sinned against me and all the passes he marches against ... Abbikha..."

LETTERS FROM GEZER

63 B. M.—"To the King my Lord my God my Sun by letter thus (says) Milcili thy servant the dust of thy feet. At the feet of the King my Lord my God my Sun seven times seven times I bow. I hear what the King my Lord has sent to me, and the King my Lord despatches Egyptian soldiers (pitati) to his servants, and the King my Lord despatches (them) to dwell as guards. It is apportioned for my honor."

108 B., with the same salutation, is broken. It appears to refer to despatching six females, five chiefs, sons of ... and five trusty chiefs led to the King.(316)

109 B.—Begins with the same salutation as the preceding, and continues: "The message of the King my Lord my God my Sun to me being brought, now his command they have done for the King my Lord—the Sun from heaven; and truly the King my Lord my God my Sun knows, that peaceful is the land of the King my Lord which is with me."

110 B.—Begins with the same salutation, and continues: "The King my Lord shall know. Behold mighty is the war against me, and against Suārdatā;(317) but the King my Lord shall pluck his land from the hands of men of blood. Since there are none, the King my Lord shall despatch chariots to march to us ... you will restrain our slaves for us ... Yankhamu his servant..."

This may refer to the submission of Gezer to the Hebrews mentioned in a letter from Jerusalem (B. 103).

62 B. M.—Begins with the same salutation as the preceding, and continues: "Know O King my Lord the demands made to me by Yankhamu since my going forth from before the King my Lord. Lo! he ... let him take from my hands. And they say to me (give us?) thy wife and thy sons. And does the King know this? And does the King my Lord demand despatch of chariots, and that I shall go to his presence? Nay! Let it be brought to nothing by thee."

70 B. M., if not from Gezer, must come from near that town. It is written by Takanu, who is mentioned in connection with Milcilu (149 B.) in a letter from near Makkedah, which was the next great town to Gezer on the south.

"To the King my Lord thus (says) Takanu (318) thy servant: at the feet of the King my Lord seven times and seven times I bow. Lo! I am the King's servant, and the guard of the whole of my roads was in the hands of my people, but they are now without refuge: they have not come up to guard my roads for the King my Lord; and ask the chiefs thy Tarkas,(319) if they are not now without refuge for my people. Moreover, behold us. My eyes are toward thee when I beseech the God of heaven: for we are cast from the land, and have been needy. We have lacked at thy hand, and behold this now, the guard that guards my roads is in the hands of a chief who hates me because of the King my Lord, and the King my Lord shall instruct; behold send down a host and it shall watch."

Though the date is doubtful, within limits, this letter probably refers to the departure of the Egyptian soldiers mentioned in the Jerusalem letters.

155 B.—A much-damaged letter. The name of the writer is lost. He sends the usual salutation, and speaks of a letter: of transgression and sin; and mentions the city Gazri (Gezer). He speaks of the going down of the king (or casting down), and of the Paka. (See note.)

50 B. M.—"To the King my Lord my God my Sun, the Sun from the heavens, thus (says) Yapa'a(320) the chief of the city of Gazri (Gezer) thy servant, the dust of thy feet, a chief captain of thy horse. At the feet of the King my Lord—the Sun from the heavens, seven times and seven times bow indeed both this heart and this body; and whatever the King my Lord says to me I listen to exceeding much. I am the King's servant, the dust of thy feet. And the King my Lord shall learn. Behold the chief of my brethren; fellows foreign to me also strive for the city of Mu(ra)'azi;(321) and the delivery of the

same is the demand of men of blood; and now behold what has arisen against me, and counsel as to thy land. Let the King send to the chief who is his friend against one (who is a foe?)."

49 B. M.—After the same salutation from Yapa'a, chief of Gezer, master of the horse, the letter continues: "I hear the message of the messenger of the King my Lord exceeding much. And let the King my Lord, the Sun from heaven, counsel his servant as to his land. Now strong is the chief of the men of blood against us; and send thou to destroy him O King my Lord for me; and will not the King restore from the hand of the chief of bloody ones? We are not quite made an end of by the chief of the bloody ones."

51 B. M.—With the usual salutation from Yapa'a, the letter continues: "Whatever the King my Lord says to me I listen to him exceedingly. It is gracious. But as I fear what shall befall, help thou my region from the power of the people of the desert lands. And now I hear that the Pauri (chiefs; see the Jerusalem letter B. 103) of the King gather a multitude; and it suffices for me. And they have enlarged my heart very much."

From these letters we gather that there had been a withdrawal of the Egyptian troops about the time when the "desert people" attacked Yapa'a. That these desert people were the Hebrews under Joshua, who was the contemporary of Japhia, we learn more clearly from the Jerusalem letters. That Gezer submitted to them is also shown by the same.

LETTERS FROM JERUSALEM

105 B.—"To the King my Lord ... thus (says) Adonizedek (322) thy servant ... at the feet of my Lord ... seven times and seven times ... Behold Milcilu is not rid from the sons of Labaya, and from the sons of Arzaya, as to their desire of the King's land for themselves. A ruling man who makes demand thereof, why has he not asked it of the King? Lo! Milcilu and Takanu have desired the doing thereof. Lo! he has marched to it. Not having desired to strive ..." The lower half of the front is here lost, and the rest is on the back.

"So now, failing those who were chiefs of the garrison of the King, let me fly to the King.(323) Truly Ben Piru (or Ben Carru) has fled his being led captive by my destroyers, he goes from the city'Azati (Gaza): let him remind the King in his presence of a garrison to guard the land. All the King's land is rebellious. Yagu Balaam is sent, and let the King's land know from the King's scribe ... Thus says Adonizedek thy servant ... the messages."

102 B.—"To the King my Lord is mourning thus this Adonizedek thy servant. At the feet of my Lord, of the King, seven times and seven times I bow. What shall I ask of the King my Lord? They have prevailed, they have (taken the fortress of Jericho(324)) they who have gathered against the King of Kings, which Adonizedek has explained to the King his Lord. Behold, as to me, my father is not and my army is not.(325) The tribe that has ground me in this place is very rebellious to the King, the same is struggling with me for the house of my father. Why has the tribe sinned against the King my Lord? Behold O King my Lord arise! I say to the Paka (resident) of the King my Lord, 'Why should you tremble before the chief of the'Abiri (326) (Hebrews) and the rulers fear the end? So now they must send from the presence of the King my Lord.' Behold I say that the land of the King my Lord is ruined. So now they must send to the King my Lord, and let the King my Lord know this; behold the King my Lord has placed a garrison to stop the way ... (Bel'amu or Yankhamu?) ... of kings ... chiefs of the garrison ... the king as master to his land ... as to his land she has rebelled, the (lands) of the King my Lord—the whole of it. Ilimelec (327) cuts off all the King's land. And let one warn the King as to his land. I myself speak pleading with the King my Lord and (for once?) let the King my Lord behold the entreaties. And the wars are mighty against me, and (I am not receiving any pledge?) from the King my Lord. And let an order return from the King (my Lord). Whether will he not order chiefs for garrison? And let him be kind, and let the King my Lord regard the entreaties. This tribe behold O King my Lord has risen up. Lo the Paka they have expelled. I say the lands of the King my Lord are ruined. Dost not thou hear this same of me? They have destroyed all the rulers. There is no ruler now O King my Lord. Let the King give his countenance to the chiefs; and whether shall the chiefs of the Egyptian soldiers (pitati) remain at rest? They have lingered O King my Lord. The lands are failing to the King my Lord. The Hebrew chiefs plunder all the King's lands. Since the chiefs of the Egyptian soldiers (pitati) have gone away quitting the lands this year O King my Lord, and since there is no chief of the Egyptian soldiers (pitati) there is ruin to the lands of the King my Lord. They have ... O King my Lord, and Adonizedek (is) dust ... messages (are asked?) of the King my Lord, there is destruction by the foe of the lands of the King my Lord."

This letter, like others, clearly indicates a withdrawal of the Egyptian troops shortly before the appearance of the Hebrews.

106 B.—The salutation is broken, but is the same as before—from Adonizedek. The text continues: "... which have done for me Milcilu, and Suardata (328) for the land of the King my Lord. They have hired soldiers of the city of Gezer, soldiers of the city Givti (329) and soldiers of the city Kielti.(330) They have gone out to (or seized) the city of Rubute.(331) The King's land rebels to the chiefs of the Hebrews, and now against this capital city U-ru-sa-lim (Jerusalem) the city called Beth Baalath,(332) a neighbor of the city of the King—has rebelled, to delay the chiefs of the city of Kielti. Let the King hear as to Adonizedek; and will not he order Egyptian soldiers (pitati), and shall not the King's land turn to the King? And because there are no Egyptian soldiers (pitati) the King's land has rebelled to the chiefs of the tribe of the Hebrews. They have demanded to dwell in the same with me. They have gone out against (or seized) Milcilu ... and the city.... And let the King do justice to (or purify) his land."

104 B.—The same salutation from Adonizedek. He continues: "Lo! the King my Lord has established his law from the (rising?) of the Sun to the going down of the Sun. He is a flatterer who deceives as to me. Lo! am not I a ruler myself, a man allied to the King my Lord? Lo! I myself am a good chief of the King, and I have sent tribute to the King. There is no chief to join me, and my friends (or army) fail; they have been fighting for the King mightily. I remain ... in this Beth Amilla (333) ... from before me thirteen ... I am giving ten slaves ... Suuta the King's Paka (resident) takes charge from before me of twenty-one slave women. Twenty chiefs who remain trusty to my hand Suuta has led away to the King my Lord,(334) which the King advises to his country. The whole of the King's country, which is seized from me, is ruined. They have fought against me as far as the lands of Seeri (Seir)(335) as far as the city Givti Kirmil (Gibeah of Carmel?).(336) They have banded together against all the chiefs of the governments, and they have fought with me. Behold I, the chief of the lords (or of the Amorites), am breaking to pieces,(337) and the King my Lord does not regard entreaties, while they have fought against me (unceasingly?). Behold array O mighty King a fleet in the midst of the sea. Thou shalt march to our land, the land of Nahrima and the land of Cazib, and behold these are fortresses of the King.(338) Thou shalt march against the chieftains of the Hebrew. There is not a single ruler for the King my Lord. They have destroyed all. Lo Tuurbazu (339) (is slaughtered?...): in the great pass of the city of Ziluu (340) they have bowed down. Behold Zimridi of the city of Lachish. The slaves have subjected him; they have done as they chose(341).... The region of Rimmon (342) laments: slaughter (is) in the midst ... the fort of Zilu is overthrown ... let the King take heed ... let the King give his countenance to.... Egyptian soldiers (pitati) to the land.... Since there are no Egyptian soldiers (pitati) in this same year destruction has destroyed the people of all the lands of the King my Lord. Do not they say to the face of the King my Lord, 'Behold the land of the King my Lord has been ruined, and all the rulers have been slain, within this same year.' Will the King not order his Paka? And let the fleet come to me as helpers, and let them take care of the port (with the King commanding?) ... (to) the scribe of the King my Lord, (lo!) Adonizedek is his servant, at his feet (he bows). Translate the messages now to the King. I am thy ... myself."

103 B.—The salutation is much broken, but part of the name of Adonizedek is left. It then speaks of messages, and continues: "Let him know that they have fought all the lands that have been at peace with me; and let me warn the King as to his land. Lo! the land of the city of Gezer, and the land of the city of Ascalon, and the land of the city of (Lachish?) they have given (or settled) for themselves. Corn and oil (or fruit), and all things, this race has altogether gathered. And let me warn the King as to Egyptian soldiers (pitati). Will not he order Egyptian soldiers (pitati) against the chiefs who have done wrong to the King my Lord? Since within this year the Egyptian soldiers (pitati) have gone away, and quit the lands, the ruler of the King my Lord—since there were no Egyptian soldiers—(pitati) is brought to naught. Yea and the rulers of the King.... Behold the land of the city of Jerusalem.(343) No man is my subject. No people is subject to me. His tribe is arrayed (or prepared). They are not subject to me. Lo! my desire is the same as the desire of Milcilu and the desire of the sons of Labaya, that the chiefs of the Hebrews be subject to the King's land. Lo! the King my Lord will be just to me, because the chiefs are sorcerers.(344) Let the King ask his Pakas (or let one ask of the King's Pakas). Lo he is strong, very (determined?) and (men) have feared. The sinful fort (or camp) is very arrogant. They have burst forth from their pasture (or border) and ... to the land of the habitation of the people (night?).... Will not there be sent from the land (of Egypt?) ... (soldiers?): thou shalt come up with ... let the servants be defended ... to them. The tribe is pouring out ... lands from the city of As (calon). Let the King ask about them. Plenty of corn, plenty of fruit (or oil), plenty.... Up to the province of my Lord Pauru (345) the King's Paka for the land of the city of Jerusalem my foe is rebelling. Up to the chiefs of the garrison this chief has surged up. Let the King's (foe) perish by the King ... for me my foe ... revolted from me. Do not desert this ... send me a chief of garrison—a Paka of the King, despatched to this thy people. (The women?) are despatched(346) to the King my Lord (with) men who have been upright. Four messengers(347) ... to go out. The chiefs of the fort (or camp) are closing the roads of the pass ... the tribe who have caused the destruction of the city of Ajalon.(348) Let this be known to the King my Lord. Have not I shown the people despatched a road for the King, though it is not easy?(349) Lo! the King my Lord has established his law in the land of the city of Jerusalem forever, and is not the desertion of the lands of the city of Jerusalem manifest? To the scribe of the King my Lord this lamentation thus (speaks) Adonizedek thy servant—the afflicted. Translate the messages well to the King my Lord. O, scribe of the King my Lord (I am) afflicted, greatly am I afflicted. And thou shalt perform the desire of our people before the chiefs of the land of Cush(350) (Casi). Truly is not there slaughter with us? Thou shalt make it ... clear to the chiefs of the land of Cush (Casi) ... midst of my land the people to take ... the King to ... seven times and seven times ... my Lord to me..."

199 B. appears to be from Adonizedek, and speaks of Jerusalem. Only the lower third of the tablet remains. The clay is different to that of the preceding, and it may have been written after the city was left.

"And lo now! the city of Jerusalem when these went away from the land (was) faithful to the King. Lo! the city of Gaza has remained to the King. Behold the land of Harti Cirmiel (351) belonging to Takanu and the men of the city Givti,(352) they have bowed down, going away from the land quietly. And truly we do so (or but whether do we do so?). Behold Labaya! (353) and the land Salabimi (354) are inhabited by the Hebrew chiefs. Milcilu has sent for (tribute?)(355) and the fellows (say) 'Have we not indeed dwelt in (or spoiled?) this land?' They are adjudging all that they desire to the men of the city of Keilah. And truly we are leaving the city of Jerusalem. The chiefs of the garrison have left—without an order—through the wastings of this fellow whom I fear. These march to Addasi.(356) He has remained in his land (or camp) in the city of Gaza ... (women?) ... to the land of Egypt..."

This letter was written apparently after the defeat of Ajalon, perhaps from Makkedah, where the kings hid in the cave. It is clear from this correspondence that when they fled, after sending away their harems, the intention was to reach Egypt. Gaza is not mentioned as taken by Joshua, and it was here that they expected to find safety.

SUYARDATA'S LETTERS FROM (Keilah?)(357)

69 B. M.—"To the King my Lord my God my Sun by letter thus (says) Suyardata thy servant, the dust of thy feet. At the feet of the King my Lord my God my Sun seven times and seven times I bow. The message which is sent by the King my Lord the Sun from heaven (has come?). His order shall be done for the King my Lord the Sun from heaven."

67 B. M.—Is a broken letter. It appears to begin as follows: "To the King my Lord thus (says) this Suyardata thy servant: at the feet of the King my Lord seven times and seven times this soul and this body bow. An announcement to the King my Lord that I am causing one to make to bring all the soldiers of the King my Lord; and now this Ra (358) the overseer, my prince, has caused the countries of the King my Lord to be stripped. I am sending them to the King; to (inform myself?) of the King, I am sending to the King my Lord. Let him know this. Who are we ... of the King my Lord to the hands ... it is ruled. At the feet of the King my Lord seven times and seven times I bow."

100 B.—"... to the King my Lord ... my Sun ... letter thus (says) Suyardata thy servant, the dust of thy feet: at the feet of the King my Lord my God my Sun seven times seven times I bow. O King (the message?) is despatched by me, as to there having been made a war. With the city of Cielti (Keilah) I am warring.(359) My chief city has gathered and has turned to me: against which has sent Adonizedek who is greedy of silver—against the chiefs of the city of Keilah. And they have marched on me behind (or to the west of) me. And know O King my Lord lo! he is marching—Adonizedek—to remove my city from my hands. Let the King ask if he is marching—this chief; and if there is one ox or a beast before him.(360) And Labaya has deserted his faith. The weak (or the gate) he is marching against we have succored. But now Labaya is with Adonizedek. I march to a city of my brethren.... Know O King as to his servant. Order thou this my desire. And do they not gather? They have put all to shame. The news (is true?): let there be an order of the King for his servant."

107 B.—Begins with the same salutation from Suyardata. It is much injured, but the following words are clear: "Know O King my Lord lo! his land has ... the city of Keilah ... against me, chiefs ... the ... our ruler ... and truly we ... against them; and truly we guide the friendly chiefs from the land of the King my Lord."

It seems from this that the previous letter brought assistance to the writer.

68 B. M.—Perhaps earlier than the preceding; reads: "To the King my Lord my God my Sun thus (says) Suyardata thy servant: seven and seven times this soul and this body bow. Let the King my Lord learn. I am one (put to shame?). There shall be Egyptian soldiers (pitati) despatched of the King my Lord. I am hard pressed; and consider thou me (come out to me?) and I shall be established by the King my Lord."

101 B.—With the usual salutation is from Suyardata, and, though broken, appears to read: "It is my desire to approach, as taking refuge with the King my Lord. Who am I to regard (being seen?)? Let me approach the King my Lord with these things (articles) of silver—and the silver is pure. O King my Lord Yankhamu (is) thy right hand; and I am mourning for him, since, wholly having gone away, no Egyptian soldiers (bitati) will come back to me from the King my Lord. Let the King my Lord learn how thirty temples of the gods he has put to shame—he who fights against me. I am left alone. Mightily he has fought against.... Give me rest O King my Lord from his hand. The King my Lord shall send Egyptian soldiers (bitati). Now Yankhamu also has returned to the house of the King my Lord. He shall come back—soldiers of the King my Lord with him. Mighty is he who has fought against Suyardata and (men) fail."

The enemy must have been of another race to destroy the temples. The letter is valuable because it shows that Yankhamu was a contemporary of Suyardata, who was a contemporary with Adonizedek, for Yankhamu was also contemporary with Aziru, who was living about twenty years after the death of Thothmes IV.

LETTERS OF THE LADY BASMATH

137 B.—"To the King my Lord my God my Sun by letter thus (says) the Lady whose name is Basmatu,(361) thy handmaid. At the feet of the King my Lord my God my Sun, seven times seven times, I bow. Know O King my Lord behold! there has been war in the land, and the land of the King my Lord has been wearied by rebels, by men of blood. And know O King as to his land, and know my foolishness (or disgrace). Behold the men (or chiefs) of blood have sent to the city of Ajalon, and to the city of Zar'a (Zorah),(362) and (this is) to show that there is no place of refuge for the two sons of Milcilu; and know O King my Lord this request."

138 B.—"To the King my Lord my God my Sun by letter thus (says) the Lady whose name is Basmatu, thy handmaid, the dust of thy feet, and at the feet of the King my Lord my God my Sun seven times seven times I bow. Let the King my Lord pluck his land from the hands of the men of blood. Am not I tired marching to the town of Zabuba; and because of not resting O King my Lord?"

There is only one place in Palestine called Zabuba; it is the Sububa of the fourteenth century, the modern Ezbuba, south of Taanach, west of the plain of Esdraelon. Poor Basmath had to go some sixty miles by road to reach it from her home. This interesting little letter, which shows she was not one of the ladies sent to Egypt, though probably a person of importance, seems perhaps to indicate that the central part of the country, from which no appeals for help occur in the letters, was undisturbed. The Amorite-Hittite league came down to Bashan and to Tyre, but not apparently as far as Accho. The Hebrews, on the other hand, coming from Seir, are said to have gone as far north as Rimmon and Shiloh, but were mainly fighting southward from Ajalon. Between the two theatres of war lay the whole of Samaria and lower Galilee, in which Basmath found a refuge.

OTHER LETTERS FROM THE SOUTH OF PALESTINE

136 B.—"To the King my Lord (my God?), the Sun from heaven, by letter thus (says) Yamirdagan thy servant: at the feet of the King my Lord seven times seven times I bow. I hear the message of the King my Lord to me, and now I will guard the city of the King my Lord till the coming of a message of the King my Lord for me."

Comparing the name with that of Dagontacala of Ascalon, it appears that this writer was probably a Philistine.

151 B.—A letter from the "Chief of the town Naziba" to say he goes with his chariots and horses to meet the King's soldiers. This place must, therefore, have been in or near the plains. It may be the Nezib of the Bible (Josh. xv. 43), now Beit Nusîb, eight miles northwest of Hebron, close to Keilah. The chariots could easily reach this vicinity from the plain, by the broad flat highway of the Valley of Elah.

55 B. M.—With the usual salutation, Ben Addu, captain of the King's horse, says: "Now they watch the land of the King my Lord exceedingly. And who am I—a dog.... He will hear the messages of the King my Lord and of the Ka-pa (for Paka?) of the King my Lord. To (Sagusi Khasi?) ... thus (says) Ben Addu: I bow at thy feet. All is failing. So now those who are our friends are fleeing to the King; will not he despatch ... the road.... Now they guard the road: it is cleared for thee."

56 B. M.—The usual salutation from Ben Addu, of the city of Pitazza; continues: "Now they guard the city, and land of the King my Lord, the Sun from heaven: all that the King has said they watch—the allies. And the decree of the message of the King my Lord Bel Anapa (Baal Anubis) the Paka of the King my Lord has uttered. The King my Lord is mighty as the Sun in heaven. Whom I but a dog, and shall such a one not mind the message of the King my Lord the Sun from heaven?"

153 B.—From the same Ben Addu, of Pitazza, with the usual salutation, and to the same effect as the preceding, but too broken to read.

The only site which seems to be suggested by Pitazza is the important ruin of Futeis, southeast of Gaza. It is near the road to Egypt and in the plains. The letters probably refer to arrangements for the flight of the kings of Jerusalem and Gezer, or of their wives.

77 B. M.—A short broken letter by Satiya, who was apparently chief of the city (or chief town) of Eni-Saam (si), which is perhaps En-Shemesh, close to Zorah, in the Valley of Sorek, now 'Ain Shems. It is the Ir-Shemesh of the Bible (Josh. xix. 41), otherwise Beth-Shemesh (Josh. xv. 10). Here, again, we find an Egyptian station in an open valley, on one of the main roads to Jerusalem.

133 B.—"To the King my Lord by letter thus (says) the chief of Kanu thy servant: at the feet of the King my Lord seven times and seven times I bow. Thou thyself hast sent to me, to muster to meet the Egyptian soldiers (bitati); and now I with my soldiers and with my chariots (am) in sight of the soldiers of the King my Lord, as far as the place you will march to."

This town cannot well be any of the Kanahs of Palestine, since the word would then be "Kanatu." It is more probably the important ruin Kanya, close to Rabbath of Judah, immediately west of the Valley of Elah; chariots would be possible in this vicinity.

LETTERS FROM UNCERTAIN SITES

33 B. M.—"To the King my Lord by letter thus (says) Abd Istar (?)(363) the King's servant. At the feet of the King my Lord I bow, seven times at the feet of the King my Lord, and seven more, both heart and body. And this is to show the King my Lord how mightily he fights against me, and destroys the rulers from the presence of the King my Lord; and the great King shall give orders for my defenders. Moreover, it sends messages to the King my Lord as to me, and I shall hear all the messages of the King my Lord. I will listen. Now ten women (concubines?) I am retaining."

Perhaps these were some of the ladies on their way to Egypt: "tumiki" seems to come from the root "wamak," an Arabic root meaning "to love." The Amorite words with an initial "vau" are nearer to Arabic than to Hebrew or Aramaic. One of the commonest is "uras," "to desire" or "ask," whence one of the names of Istar, the goddess of desire.

34 B. M.—Is a short letter broken at the end; it merely acknowledges a message, and is from Abd Astati. There was a deity As, or Ast, apparently of Egyptian origin.

60 B. M.—"To the King my Lord my Sun my God thus Mayaya." The important part of this short letter is broken, but it appears to say: "Have not they devoured Yankhamu ... this conquest of all the lands from men of blood, and the devouring of thy land."

65 B. M.—(Sibtiaddu?) writes as a servant of the King with the usual salutation, and has heard the message. "Behold what Yankhamu (says). I am a faithful servant at the foot of the King. Let the King my Lord know it. I guard much the King's city which is with me."

147 B.—From (Khiziri?), the King's servant. He will meet the soldiers, and has received a message from Maya about a tax.

148 B.— Ruzbanya, of Taruna, is a servant of the King. The letter is broken. He was of old a servant of the King.

150 B.—From Nurtu.... He listens to the Paka, and will fortify until the King comes to his tribe. He fills a good-sized tablet, without giving any information of interest.

76 B. M.— Zidriyara writes, with the usual compliments, to acknowledge a message.

141 B.— Zidriyara is faithful, as of old, and a friend of the rulers, and listens to all the King's messages.

140 B.— Zidriyara hears the message of the King, whose servant he is—"the Sun from among the Heavenly Gods who has spoken"—and he will not neglect the messages of the King his lord, or of the Paka who is established with him.

135 B.—Apparently without a name. He is only a dog, but will march with chariots and horses to meet the Egyptian soldiers (bitati).

130 B.— Sutarnamu, of his city Zicaruenu,(364) bows to the King. He asks for soldiers of garrison, as they are obstructing the district of the King's land near him. Probably the site is the present village Dhikerîn, near Gath on the south, which was the Caphar Dikerin of the Talmud (Tal. Jer. "Taanith," iv. 8), in the region of Daroma (now Deirân), near Ekron (see Ekha ii. 2). He asks for soldiers.

131 B.— Samuaddu, of the town of Sama'una, listens to all the King's messages. Perhaps Sammûnieh, an ancient and important ruin immediately east of Kirjath Jearim ('Erma), on the way to Jerusalem, by the Valley of Sorek, is the place intended.

Nos. 79, 80, 81 B. M. are short and broken letters, which appear only to acknowledge messages received. No. 80 is from a certain Nebo...; in No. 79 there appears to be no personal name, and in No. 81 it is destroyed.

The names of these villages establish a regular chain of posts from Gaza, by Lachish, to the valleys of Sorek and Elah, which seem to have been the most eastern parts of the country in which chariots were to be found. There is no mention of chariots at Jerusalem, or at any village which was not accessible by a flat valley-road. By these posts communication was kept up, it would seem, with Jerusalem; and the messengers probably travelled by this route, avoiding Ajalon. It was by this route that Adonizedek proposed that Amenophis should come up to help him. Whether any such expedition was attempted, none of the letters seem to indicate. The troops had been withdrawn, and the Egyptian policy seems to have been to call out the native levies of the Amorite charioteers. Perhaps, when the five kings had been killed at Makkedah, no further steps were taken, but the lowlands remained unconquered till the time of Samuel and David. Even in Solomon's time Gezer was only received as the dower of the daughter of the Pharaoh (1 Kings ix. 16) who had burned the place and killed its Canaanite population. In Judges we read that Judah "could not drive out the inhabitants of the Shephelah (or lowlands) because they had chariots of iron" (i. 19). The coast road was still open when Dusratta was writing to his son-in-law Amenophis IV twenty years later; and all lower Galilee was, for some few years, with Philistia and Syria, reconquered by Rameses II, who, however, never entered the Judæan mountains.

***

This concludes the sum of 176 letters from Palestine, the translation of which has occupied me for nearly two years. I have no doubt that it may be improved upon in detail; but the general results seem to be too well corroborated, by comparison of the numerous epistles, which throw light on one another, to admit of any very important changes.

Royal Letters

DUSRATTA'S LETTERS

No. 9 B. M.—"To Neb-mat-ra (Amenophis III) King of Egypt my brother, by letter, thus Tuseratta (365) King of Mitani (366) thy brother. I am at peace. Peace be to thee; to Gilukhipa my sister be peace. To thy house, thy wives, thy sons, thy lords, thy terrible army, thy horses, thy chariots, and in thy land, be much peace. Since I have sat on my father's throne, and have conquered. But (Pirkhi?) made a lawless command in my land, and smote his Lord; and because of these things, they have striven to right me, with who so loved us well; and because my land submitted to this lawless order I was not afraid, but the chiefs who supported Artasu-mara my brother, with all that were theirs, I slew. As thou wast well with my father, and because of these things, I send this. I say to you, as my brother hears, and will rejoice; my father loved thee, and thou therefore didst love my father; and my father, as he saw this, gave thee my sister; and now ... as thou wast with my father. When my brother saw these things, he brought all those in the land of the Hittites as foes to my land; and Rimmon my Lord gave them to my hand; and I slew him among them, so that not one returned to his land.(367) Now I have sent thee a chariot with two horses, a young man and a young woman, of the spoil of the land of the Hittites. I have sent thee, as a present to my brother, five chariots, and five yoke of horses; and as a present to Gilukhipa (368) my sister, I have sent her (trinkets?) of gold, a pair of gold earrings, and ... of gold, and goodly stones, each(?). Now Gilia, a prudent man, and Tunipripi (369) I send to my brother; speedily let him reply to me; so I shall hear my brother's salutation, and shall rejoice. Let my brother wish me well; and let my brother send envoys: so my brother's salutation shall come to me, and I shall hear."(370)

22 B.—The salutation calls Amenophis III his "kinsman," but does not name his sister.

"Mani my brother's envoy has come to honor me: to take my brother's wife the Queen of Egypt;(371) and I received the letter that came: I learned the declaration of his (order?). My heart has been much gladdened by my brother's message, as my brother will see; and it rejoiced that day exceeding much: that day and night they made (rejoicings?).

"And, my brother, all the message that Mani came to bring has been performed. This same year behold, my brother, I will ... his wife, the Queen of Egypt, and I will send ... hence forth the land of Khanirabbe and the land of Egypt. And because of these things that Mani has spoken, I send back, my brother, Gilia and Mani with speed, to ... these things; and let not my brother blame them ... as to delay in being despatched; for there was no delay to ... for my brother's wife; and lo! delay is.... In the sixth month I have sent Gilia my envoy, and Mani my brother's envoy: I will send my brother's wife to my brother. So may Istar the Lady of Ladies my Goddess, and Amanu (372) my brother's God, give peace ... I have sent to my brother; and my brother as ... increased his (love?) very much, and ... as the heart of my brother was satisfied; and ... (for our children?) my brother ... more than before ... I have despatched Khai, my brother, trusting his ... and I give the letter to his hands ... and let him bear his message ... I have sent ... going to my brother ... my brother, are not his soldiers..."

The next five lines referring to the wife are too broken to read. The back of the tablet continues:

"... which my brother sent ... all that my brother has caused to be collected ... in presence of all of them they have been (given?) us ... all these things, beyond expectation thereof, and the gold ... which they have paid—and he has indeed lavished very much ... them, any or all these things; was not the gold ... They say 'In the land of Egypt there is plenty more gold for thee my brother, because he loves thee very much ... and will love (and being so?) is not there, behold, anything needful, anything beside, from the land of Egypt in addition? So send to me, accordingly, him by whom these are given, and there shall be no lack.' Thus indeed (said) I 'As to anything (further?) do not I say to your faces—He loves me, and my land, exceeding much, does this King of Egypt?'

"And my brother has taken me to his heart: all is as my heart desired; and is it not understood; when he sends shall not I hasten me for my brother: shall not I increase in longing toward my brother: as my brother does also? Mani, my brother's envoy, has brought my brother's ... which was with Mani. I have honored their ... and I have honored them very much. Now Mani will take this; and my brother we direct him to ... how I have received from him very much: he will tell my brother this, and my brother will hear what we have done (as I have sent list of gifts of this and that, and he shall not refuse it?).

"And may my brother send untold gold; and may my father's power increase with me, as my brother has increased my favor, as my brother has cherished me much, in the sight of my country, in the sight of the whole of my brethren. May Rimmon and Amanu appoint that my brother's wishes be ever fulfilled; and for myself, my brother, that my wishes may be fulfilled, as men whom the Sun-God loves. And so now the Gods shall indeed decree for us this prayer, ... we shall join as friends forever.

"For my brother's present I have sent to my brother a (double-edged weapon?) ... and (?) of emeralds, and pure gold ... enclosed in a box, and ... of alabaster, and pure gold, for a box ..."

21 B.—"To Amenophis III, the Great King, King of Egypt, my brother, my kinsman(373) whom I love, and who loves me, by letter thus Dusratta, the Great King, King of Mitani, thy brother, thy kinsman who also loves thee. I am at peace, etc.

"To my brother whom I love I have given his young wife.(374) May the Sun-God and Istar ... her face. As my brother desires: may ... and may my brother rejoice, in the day when ... the Sun-God and the God ... giving joy to my noble brother, ... let them grant it to be ... and may my brother ... forever.

"Mani my brother's envoy, and Khani(375) my brother's interpreter, as you cause them to be sent, plenty of (provisions?) I shall give them ... them much; as they performed their orders I made all the people protect them. If they do not may my Gods, and my brother's Gods, guard them. Now I have sent Nahramani who is careful in my brother's affairs, and I have sent (an ornament?) of precious stones—of precious stones and gold, as a present to my brother; and may my brother be granted to live a hundred years."

8 B. M.—The salutation is the same as before, but the writer's name is spelt "Tusratta" instead of Dusratta. The letter is the best preserved in the whole collection.

"Since your forefathers were friendly with my forefathers, thou therefore wast very greatly friendly with my father. So you love me: we are zealous friends. Ten times more you increase it than to my father. The heavenly Gods shall decree that we shall be friends. May Rimmon my God, and Amanu, so pronounce, even forever.

"And so my brother sent Mani his envoy. Thus indeed my brother (said) 'Does not my brother's heart desire that thy daughter (be) the wife of my young son(376)—as a princess of Egypt' and I spoke as to my intention about it; and my brother desiring that she should be made ready for Mani, and to show her, so he beheld her, and praised her much. And may they lead her in peace into the land of my brother. May Istar and Amanu make her agreeable to my brother's heart.

"Gilia, my envoy, set forth my brother's message before me. So I heard and it was very good; and so I rejoiced very much. Thus truly I say 'This is thus arranged between us so that we may be zealous friends.' Now with firm faith forever let us be friends.

"So I shall send to my brother, and I say thus myself, so let us be much more friendly; and do not you respond to us? And I say thus, that my brother has enriched me ten times more than my father.

"And I have asked much gold of my brother: so he has given me more than to my father. My brother indeed sent to me; and to my father you sent much gold: much (merchandise?) of gold; and besides all the gold you sent him you have sent me bricks of gold (lavished?) like copper.

"I sent Gilia (humbly?) to my brother, and asked for gold. Thus indeed I (said) 'Truly my brother has given me more than to my father, and may he send me untold gold.'

"May my brother send me more than to my father; and now I say thus to my brother: the (loan?) that my grandfather made, so I may (say), as (one thinking little of wealth?) he made it for thee; and now as regards (what) I say, the gold that my brother shall send, let him send it when he likes.

"Lo my brother has sent the gold saying 'It is due to you,' But no. No more was due; and he had satisfied the account; and when he had satisfied the account I was glad thereof exceedingly; and whatever my brother sends I have been very glad thereof.

"Now behold I sent to my brother—and may my brother extend his kindness to me more than to my father; now I asked gold of my brother, and whatever gold I asked of my brother, he has sent the double of what was asked. One (sum) for the (loan?), and a second of good-will.

"And may my brother send me untold gold; and may he send me more than to my father; and so may the Gods decree, that much more gold beside be in my brother's land, as there now is in my brother's land; and ten times more than there now is, may it increase.(377) And let not my brother refuse the gold that I ask by my brother's wish; and, as for me, let me not refuse my brother's wish; and may my brother send me very much gold uncounted; and whatever my brother needs let him send and take. Let me return the gift that my brother desires for his household. This land is my brother's land, and this house is my brother's house.

"Now I send Gilia my envoy to my brother. Let him not refuse him. Let him speedily command him: let him send him away. So hearing my brother's salutation let me rejoice exceeding much. Let me ever hear my brother's salutation. And these messages that we send, let my God Rimmon and Amanu decree that they may arrive through their mercy. And as now it is prayed therefor, so we are friends; and as now so forever may we be friends.

"Now as to the gifts for my brother: I have sent as my brother's gifts a quantity of solid gold, and precious stones: (its value?) includes the amount of twenty precious stones, and nineteen pieces of gold. The weight of precious stones and gold remaining includes the amount of forty-two precious stones and twenty pieces of gold Zuzas of Istar: (this is) the weight of precious stones and gold remaining; and ten yoke of horses, and ten chariots, with all that belongs to them, and thirty female slaves."

27 B.—This is the longest letter in the collection, including six lines in Aramaic, and 512 lines in Dusratta's native language (see "Journal Royal Asiatic Society," October, 1892, for my translation). The important passages of the letter appear to me to read as follows, and the meaning is confirmed by statements in other letters by this writer concerning his daughter's marriage. The letter was addressed to Amenophis III, and sent by the same two envoys, Mani and Gilias,(378) already noticed.

"Gilias the envoy, who takes the messages is ordered to utter it, his duty being to go out, because Amenophis III the Egyptian (ally?) rules a far off land, and I rule in the city Ikhibin(379) the city of the God Simigis(380) the paternal deity.

"To proceed: as Mani my brother's envoy says, it is understood that my brother is very desirous that it should be speedily completed.

"Brother, I gladly empower the envoy to take back this woman, whom Mani says my brother commanded him to bring, when he was ordered as an envoy.

"Understanding that my brother desires now to take her home, is it not necessary, understanding this decision to be preferred; as twenty-three months having gone by, is not her taking home to be hastened? My Court having decided to accept, and being satisfied as well as my wife, and resolved to accept the agreement; and the girl being heartily pleased—how happy she is words cannot tell—the decision is from the Gods, brother, for me the decision is from the mighty Gods, my brother. Surely you know whether I do not desire that she should be so brilliantly exalted, the girl being so fortunately (married): surely you know that I shall be glad.

"Proclaim thou for me that whatever people of Khalci,(381) west of the Minyan(382) country—whatever people of Khalci I have conquered, are made subject.

"I being the great chief of the power of the land of the Hittites taking to me, my brother, all the people that are conquered. Let it extend to the city of Harran(383) and let the land possessed by no king be taxed.

"My son-in-law being married in the city of Thebes in presence of the image of the deity."

"Is it not thus that Dusratta dwelling afar arranges the marriage of Tadukhipa(384)—Dusratta the favored (friend?) from the Minyan land, consenting to the wish of Amenophis III the Egyptian (friend) that the son of Amenophis III be so married to her, in the presence of the image of the deity."

As this letter is written in what is called by scholars an "unknown language," these renderings may be questioned. The dialect appears, however, to be closely related to the Akkadian and to other Mongol dialects of western Asia, and to be also the same used (B. 10) by the Hittites.

10 B. M.—Written, as the Egyptian docket at the bottom of the tablet on the back states, in the thirty-sixth year of Amenophis III which appears to have been probably the last of his reign.

"To Amenophis III King of Egypt my brother, my kinsman whom I love, and who loves me, by letter thus Dusratta King of Mitani who loves thee, thy kinsman. I am at peace. Peace be to thee, to thy house, to the woman Tachikhipa thy daughter to the wife thou lovest be peace.(385) To thy wives, to thy sons, to thy Lords, to thy chariots, to thy horses, to thy army, to thy land, and to all that is thine, be much, much, much peace.

"Thus (I say) Istar of Nineveh, the lady of the lands, is kind of heart to the land of Egypt. In the land that I love do not they walk after her?(386) Do not they cry aloud to her? Now behold it has brought thee prosperity.

"Now from the time of my father they have besought Istar in her land for thy prosperity; and, as of old so now, it continues. They honor her.

"And now may my brother receive of her ten times more than before. Let my brother receive with joy: let it be hastened for him: let it endure.

"Istar is the Lady of Heaven my brother, and as for me let me be guarded by her for a hundred years; and may great joy be given. Let it be granted by her that I may not fail; and as you desire may it (befall?).

"Is not Istar my God, and has not she (prospered?) my brother (or been with my brother?)."

24 B.—The second longest of Dusratta's letters, 185 lines in all, is unfortunately very much damaged, as it is perhaps the most important, giving as it does historical information extending over three generations, during which the kings of Egypt and of Mitani were allied by marriage.

"To ... ya(387) my kinsman, whom I love and who loves me ... the great King (King of) Mitani thy kinsman who loves thee. I am at peace ... to the Lady Teie ... to Tadukhipa my daughter thy wife be peace, to ... be peace. To thy sons, to thy Lords, to thy chariots, to thy horses, to thy ... and to all that is thine, be much, much, much peace ... of Amenophis III thy father he sent to me; he explained ... of all that he sent there was no message at all that I ... to your father as to what he sent to me; and Teie the chief wife of Amenophis III your mother knew all of them. All these have been seen by Teie your mother ... the messages that your father caused to be addressed to me.

"... and ten times more than with Amenophis III your father caused him to tell me whatsoever wish ... and whatever message I spoke, faithfully in the same day ... he himself did not turn away his heart from any message ... but faithfully in the same day he caused it to be done.

"... the father of Amenophis III sent to Sitatama(388) my grandfather, and ... a daughter. He sent to my grandfather five or six times, and he was not given her, when ... he sent; and at length he was given her. Amenophis III your father sent (humbly?) to Sut(tarna) my father ... and so for my father's daughter, my own sister, his heart was desirous; and five (or six) times he ... her: when he had sent five or six times at length he was given her. So Amenophis III ... sent to me, and so desired a daughter(389) and I ... I said in ... of his envoy 'Thus I say I have (sworn?) to give her: by our wish ... to take, and the ... which he has known: and she is a sister so it is lawful;' and I give ... Amenophis III thy (father's) ... if these are not truths ... heaven and earth bear witness ... to give her; and Khai(390) the envoy of my brother ... to the (Queen?) and to Amenophis III I sent with her ... in three months with the greatest speed ... and the gold ... truly was not ... which I sent.

"When you favored a daughter, and so (sent for) her, and as Amenophis III your father knew her ... I rejoiced being exceeding glad, and he said 'My brother, is not it thy wish thus to give the handmaid'; and he made public agreement with this his land, in presence of my envoy ... so men ... when they beheld; and I received from him; and Amenophis III established us ... for the future; and so receiving ... I was made great; and in the cities which for Tadukhipa ... in all of them he made us dwell as conquerors,(391) and among the envoys who went down ... none that Gilia ... the gold of one (limzu) was given by weight. Truly to Amenophis III for Tadukhipa it was given; and Tadukhipa ... was given ... and ... my envoys Amenophis III with ... I received; there was no one ... Amenophis III sent Nizik his envoy ... myself; and he ... (refusing?) to my face the ... of gold ... the gold which ... of Gilia and ... he established us ... my envoys ... to be despatched ... he did not cease to (deny?) ... and ... he took her... I was not able to refuse to please him ... he sent this to me ... they sent was wonderful, and then ... Amenophis III your father in every message ... the lord of the place to protect her. Did not he order all these as I say ... do not I say that Teie(392) ... has known ... and Teie is your mother, ask her if, among the messages that I spake, there is one message which is not vindicated by her, as to these (messages) to Amenophis III your father ... if to Amenophis III your father brotherhood was made by me: if it was said by Amenophis III your father 'If at all (there is) gold that ... in the land of Khani Rabbe I will despatch it; and order thou thus the ... do not I desire to cause it to be sent': the ... bore what was ordered to be given of Amenophis III your father; and Amenophis III said to me '... the treasures of gold ... all that my ... desires is sent ... and ... to do this I have sent to thee' ... there by Amenophis III with a message. Never was there a message without a reply. I never refused any of the messages.

"(And when) Amenophis III was obliged to be taken to his fate, and they told (me) ... I tore my cheeks, and I mourned on that same day; I sat (in the dust?); I (took) no food or water that same day; and I was grieved ... I said 'Let me perish myself from earth, and from my ... and that he loved me God knows, and he was loved' (and because of) these things we are cast down in our hearts."

"... to me the eldest son of Amenophis III by his wife Teie ... was made, and I said 'Has not Amenophis III died ... the eldest son of his chief wife Teie (is) in his stead ... shall not we be sent news ... from her abode as of old.'

"... I say thus Amenophis IV is my brother whom we shall love in our hearts ... the son of Amenophis III more than his father, because of Teie his mother, who was the wife ... as she desires a message to the presence of Amenophis IV (Abkhuriya) the son of Amenophis III her husband. I (rejoice) very exceeding much that we shall be friends

"(As they have sent me this message?) As they have ordered it, Gilias is humbly (sent?) ... they have sent Mani (as an envoy?), and treasures of woods (or trees) my brother has sent, and gold ... without gold and without..."

The next passage is too broken to read, but refers to the continuance of friendship since the time of the ancestors of both kings, and for the future. The back of the tablet is very much broken, the whole of one paragraph, and the greater part of the next, which refers to Teie as the mother of Amenophis IV being destroyed. It continues:

"... the message of your mother which to Gilias ... He has desired a message to be despatched and (as he desires) ... have not I sent my envoys, and have not I ... (and it is not my fault?) and the treasures ... which he asked of him I have caused to be given, not being desired ... my envoys four years since you(393) ..."

Eight lines are here almost entirely destroyed, referring to some speedy message, and to the former king, with a reference to certain persons, including the "father of Teie (your elders?) with me," with professions of friendship. The end of the paragraph (lines 40, 41) contains the words, "as thus he set us up over all her many lands ... all the lands are all hers in his sight."(394) The next paragraph continues:

"... the (treasures?) of gold (allowed to be despatched?) previously by Amenophis III ... he has sent. Lo! very exceedingly my brother has desired that treasures ... to us; and much of his gold ... very exceedingly my brother ... as intending for me ... whatever among ... and your father; was not he given by me; and lo! now let my brother see that I was not at all ... to your father: the treasures that he desired were given, and lo! ... I am sending back my message: there shall be nothing done to cause the heart to turn away ... all the messages ... Teie has been a witness, and Teie your mother ... plenty. Lo! I asked your father, and did not your father grant me? and ... let this gold be given, and let not my brother's heart ... let him not turn from my ... when the (loan?) ... was not made, and what had ...

"... Let Gilia know this day what my brother's heart desires. I have made Gilia travel ... thus I have made my brother's envoys to obey him, travelling with speed. If ever, my brother, my envoys ... if ever I send my envoys ... (the fault is not mine?) ... I have sent Mani and Gilia to my brother as before. If at all by my brother my envoys to him, and if by us they shall be received, I also shall so hasten him ... Lo! as regards messages from my brother, which he makes about anything as to my brother's intentions ... thence; and on the throne of his father he sits this day; and let me do my brother's will.

"I say thus, my brother, have not I sent my envoys, and much in their keeping which is for thee; and my brother let ... which is for thee. Mazipalali(395) my envoy is the paternal uncle of Gilia and for ... my brother I have sent him, and my brother am not I (the surer?) as Gilia is not ... And the other envoy whom I shall send to my brother is the brother of Gilia the son of his mother(396) ... I sent him. So my brother have not I despatched him speedily without stopping, and, my brother, as to my wishes that I wish (it is not my fault?) and because of these things did not I send Gilia ... for security, and for all this am not I the surer.

"Mazipalali whom I shall send to my brother is the uncle of Gilia; and the treasures (allowed to be despatched?) ... and plenty of untold gold of the (loan?) which I desire from my brother let my brother give ... and let him not refuse; and with my brother gold in addition ... ten times more may it increase to me exceedingly ... let these things be ordered; and Mani (with) my envoy my brother ... let be given of my brother; and let him send Gilia to me; and ... and all the news about my brother's mother that they shall speak, and (especially?) let me (hear?) ... that they did. And lo! as before I sent not to thee my brother, so let him ... me. Let not my brother ... and to my brother's pleasure ... and I meditate a message of consolation for my brother.

"Let both Artessupa(397) and ... thus relate in my brother's land this thing. I have been sent (under escort?) ... Mani (brought?) before me all my wicked slaves, who have dwelt in Egypt, and I examined them(398) as to ... and they said ... and I said before them 'Why is your insolence so great?' ... So they put them in chains, and ... one of my ... one from my city who has angered the land ... and another ... did not I slay because of these things? My brother, did not he say ... was not I wroth? Behold my brother they were wicked ... and ... my brother it was necessary and now let me (afflict them?).

"As to a present for my brother. My brother's presents (are)—a (weight?) of solid gold from the land Ris Burkhis, a weapon with a stone head(399) ... of precious stone ... (an ornament?) for the hands of precious stones, one part of gold: three cloths: three ... three ... (with fastenings?) of gold, ... of refined bronze (or copper) ... two ...

"As a present for Teie your mother an (ornament?) for the hands of precious stones ... earrings ... two cloths.

"As a present for (Tadukhipa) my (daughter) an ornament for the hands ... earrings ... two cloths."

23 B.—The salutation is the same as in the last, being addressed to Amenophis IV, to Teie and to Tadukhipa.

"Mani my brother's envoy (has come) to (me). I have heard. I liked much the gifts that my brother ... I saw, and I rejoiced very much. My brother utters this message and (says) 'As with my father Amenophis III you were friends, now behold this day be friends with me thy brother. You will continue to be kind,' and I have not delayed ... with my brother. Lo! ten times more than to your father I will be a friend.

"And your father Amenophis III spoke this message in his letter (by your ...) Mani, 'Continue thou the friendship,'(400) and when my brother Amenophis III said this, lo! what I had sent was nothing at all, and my brother shall not consider it anything. And I do not send this present, which behold I have sent to thee, as desiring to cause you to send; but (humbly?) whatever my brother desires to be given to his wife, they shall be made to take away. They shall see her,(401) and I will send ten times as much.

"And the treasures of gold (allowed to be despatched?) one treasure for me, and another treasure as the treasure of Tadukhipa my daughter, lo! I asked of Amenophis III your father. And your father said 'Send for the gold that (remains to be remitted?) let the (rest) be given, and the precious stones that are to be given thee, and the gold, because we have increased the gift, which is marvellous with treasure to be given to you.' And the gold of the treasures all my envoys who were in the land of Egypt beheld with their eyes; and your father lavishly increased the treasures in presence of my envoys. He welcomed them on their way; he maintained them! and lavishly expended the ... on my envoys. They gazed, and so truly they beheld with their eyes his favor poured out.

"And more gold beside, which was marvellous, which he sent to me, he piled up; and he said to my envoys 'Behold the treasures, and behold the gold in plenty, and the possessions which are marvellous,(402) which I shall send to my brother: behold them also with your eyes.' And my envoys beheld with their eyes.

"But now, my brother, the treasures remitted, which your father sent, you shall not send, but the woods (or trees) have been received.(403) You are sending the possessions that your father sent to me. You shall not send them, but shall store them up very much.

"And thinking of all that one has known, how I rejoiced because of my brother, none ever brought salutation from him at any time, my brother, but the same day return was made to him.

"And Khamassi my brother's envoy he sent (humbly?) to my presence, and (humbly?) he spoke my brother's message: I heard and then I said 'As I was friends with Amenophis III thy father, lo! now ten times more with Amenophis IV (Nabkhuriya) shall I be great friends.' So then I said to Khamassi your envoy.

"And lo! my brother: the treasures of gold to be remitted you shall not send; and there (shall be) respite of gifts which your father spoke of sending. It is desired that my brother shall not send them.

"Lo! my brother, the treasures of gold which I asked of your father I may say that half of them will be carried off (or stolen) ... The lands are at strife(404) ..."

The rest of this letter, including all the back, is too much broken to be read. It appears to go on to speak of "destruction" and to refer to a state of disturbance. It mentions the envoy Khamassi, and says, "Of what he has brought the fourth part has been robbed." On the back Gilia is mentioned with gold, and relations between the writer and Amenophis III. He refers again to the message from Amenophis IV and to Teie his mother; and invokes Rimmon and Amanu. The words "unless they are conquered" seem also to occur. This letter contained altogether 113 lines of writing.

26 B.—A list of presents. On the back, at the bottom of the left hand column, is the statement, "These are the things carried by the female slaves, all those things which Dusratta King of Mitani gave to Amenophis III his brother, his kinsman, when he sent his daughter Tadukhipa to the land of Egypt, to Amenophis III for marriage, he gave all these that day."

The list is a very long and difficult one. It begins with two horses, and a chariot plated with gold and silver, and adorned with precious stones. The harness of the horses was adorned in like manner. Two camel litters appear to be next noticed, and apparently variegated garments worked with gold, and embroidered zones and shawls. These are followed by lists of precious stones, and a horse's saddle adorned with gold eagles.(405) A necklace of solid gold and gems, a bracelet of iron gilt,(406) an anklet of solid gold, and other gold objects follow; and apparently cloths, and silver objects, and vases of copper or bronze. An object of jade or jasper (Yaspu), and leaves of gold, are noticed (both jade and leaves of gold have actually been found in the oldest ruins at Troy, the former being perhaps noticed as coming from Elam, by trade with central Asia, where jade was found. Five gems of "stone of the great light" (perhaps diamonds) follow, with ornaments for the head and feet, and a number of bronze objects, and harness for chariots. Boxes of strong wood to contain treasures follow next, and apparently a collar with disks and carved lions, objects of silver and gold and strong wood, bronze ornaments for horses. The last noticed objects may be written tablets, including some on the ritual of the gods.

25 B.—A list similar to the last, perhaps part of the same inventory, as it includes women's ornaments. The tablet is much injured. The objects noticed include an earring with gems, and others of gold, with a large number of precious stones, a necklace with 122 gems set in gold, including "green

stones"; bracelets and anklets of solid gold with jewels: an umbrella adorned with gold: boxes to hold treasures, and numerous objects of silver: horns of the wild bull, and wooden objects adorned with gold: cups of gold adorned with gems: other bracelets and anklets of gold with pendants and stars of jewels: a pair of gold earrings with pendants and stars of precious stones: silver anklets for women, and earrings with gold pendants. In each case the weight of gold and the numbers of the gems are stated.

These inventories of Tadukhipa's marriage outfit show how far advanced was the civilization of western Asia in the fourteenth century B.C., and indicate not only the native wealth of gold, silver, copper, and bronze, from Asia Minor and the Caucasus, but also a trade which brought jade from central Asia. The art of the age is similar to that of the objects found at Troy and Mycenæ, and represented on the Egyptian bas-reliefs, which give pictures of the tribute from Phœnicia. From other tablets in the collection we obtain similar information, including the use of ivory, as also from the records of tribute to Thothmes III in 1600 B.C.

11 B. M.—"To ... Princess of the Land of Egypt(407) thus Dusratta King of Mitani. I am at peace: Peace be to thee.... Peace be to thy son; peace be to Tadukhipa thy daughter-in-law. To thy land and to all that is thine be much, much peace.

"Thou hast known of me how I loved Amenophis III thy husband, and Amenophis III because he was thy husband how he loved me. As for Amenophis III thy husband he heard what I said; and Amenophis III because he was thy husband, sent messages to me; and what he said to thee my ... both Mani has known, and thou ... hast known all of these things—the messages we zealously uttered. There was nothing thus that he has not known of them.

"Now you said to Gilia, 'Say to your Lord, Amenophis III was friends with your father, and why should his favor be less than to your father? Nay, indeed, what he shall send to our place shall not ... will not you hasten to ... your friendship with Amenophis III ... making it greater; and assure him ... that you will gladly send ...'

"... to your husband friendship ... so now ... your son, ten times more ... and the messages....

"... why from ... our good faith, and ... is given to me ... thus I ... Amenophis IV (Nabkhuriya) ... and now behold ... to give is not....

"... when by your desire I ... and to the presence of Amenophis IV ... and you wished thus ... do not desire, and ... the treasures of gold to be remitted, let Amenophis IV receive. (There is nothing, indeed, he may not desire?) that is not ... ten times more than his father let him increase in friendship toward me, and in power."

"... you yourself, your envoys, with the envoys of Amenophis IV, with ... let them be sent to Yuni my wife,(408) for what is wished; and the envoys of Yuni my wife let them be sent to (thee) as to what is wished.

"Now as to thy present ... a goodly stone, also (a coronet?) and a ... of stones."

It seems clear from this letter, and from 24 B., that Teie (or Thi) the Queen of Egypt, was related to Dusratta, but it is not clear that she was his sister. Gilukhipa, the sister whom he names, is known from Egyptian sources to have been the daughter of Suttarna, Dusratta's father, and she came to Egypt with 317 ladies in her train.

It is also to be remarked that Dusratta invokes the Egyptian god Amen both when writing to Amenophis III and also when writing to Amenophis IV, so that there does not appear to have been any change of religion in Egypt during the reign of the latter—at least, at the time when he wrote.

Amenophis III also married at least one Babylonian princess, as will appear in the letters that follow.

RIMMON NIRARI'S LETTER

30 B.—"To the Sun God the King my Lord the King of Egypt, thus Rimmon-Nirari(409) thy servant. I bow at my Lord's feet. Lo! Manakhbiya (Thothmes IV) made my father King ... to rule in the Land of Markhasse (or Nukhasse), and established men to dwell with him; and as the King of ... was disputing for the kingdom, which has been made ... which he established for him ... he gave him..."

About twenty lines of the letter are here destroyed; the broken lines below continue thus:

"And lo! my Lord ... and the King of the land of the Hittites why ... my Lord the letters ... and fearing ... and lo! the King of Egypt ... and now my Lord against ... and to the hands ... to our Lord ... thy Lord in the years that may come.... Do not scorn, since the land was faithful in service to the King my Lord. And if God commands my Lord to go forth, let my Lord also send a chief, to be sent up to him with his soldiers and with his chariots."

CALLIMMASIN'S LETTERS

1 B.—"To Amenophis III the King of Egypt by letter thus (Cal)limmasin(410) the King of Carandunias (Babylonia) thy brother. I am at peace. To thee, to thy house, thy wives, thy land, thy chariots, thy horses, thy ... be much peace.

"Because of the youngest of my daughters, whom you send to wed, Irtabi whom you remember, they took this message. My father formerly sent a message. You collected many soldiers, you approved his message, and you sent making a present to my father.

"Now I send thee this envoy. In the sixth year you seek for this, and in the sixth year you send thirty manahs of gold (instead of?) silver for my present. I return the same gold. Casi your envoy has known its (value?) which he has seen. I send thy envoy well instructed as to our opinion. For I followed ... and the present that he is instructed to ... is thirty manahs of gold, which you ... a gift of alliance."

The rest is too broken to read. It mentions five women sent, and ten wooden chariots—the latter as presents. The next letter is from Egypt. Either a copy or an original never sent.(411)

1 B. M.—"To Callimmasin King of Carandunias my brother, by letter thus Amenophis III the great King, the King of Egypt thy brother. There is peace to my region. To thy region be peace: to thy house, to thy wives, to thy sons, to thy Lords, to thy horses, to thy chariots, and in thy hands be much peace. I am at peace. There is much peace to my house, to my wives, to my sons, to my Lords, my horses, my chariots, my army; and in my lands there is much peace.

"Now I heard the message you sent about her to me. Thus it was, 'Now you ask my daughter as your wife, but my sister whom my father gave thee, being good to you, has any seen her whether she has lived or whether she has died?' This is the message that you send in your letter. But did you ever send as your envoy, one who has known your sister, and who has spoken with her, and understood her? And let one speak with her. The chiefs you send are useless, your envoy Zakara is one who is a chief(?). There is not one among them related to your father, and ... concerning this my envoy is with thee, and has spoken to her ... her heart ... concerning this, and she has given ... to her mother. And lo! you send this, 'You spoke to my envoys, and they gathered your wives: a lady appeared before you (saying) thus, Behold your queen who is brought out before you all. But my envoys knew her not (to be) my sister.' Now satisfy yourself as to what you thus send, 'My envoys knew her not,' and you say, 'Who was it that was recognized by her?' Why do not you send as your envoy one who shall tell you a true message as to the salutation from your sister, I pray you? And you said that they disputed as to her appearance. But you can see her with the King. And lo! you send thus, 'Who was the princess—a daughter of one who was a native, or was she one of the land of (my neighbors?), or was she the daughter of the Land of Khani Rabbatu, or the princess of the Land of Ugarit, that my envoys so saw, and who was it that spoke to them to satisfy that nothing wrong was done?' And does not your message say all this? But if she has died—your sister, and I am concealing, as you pretend, her ... in former times, which we ... the God Amanu ... (I rejoice that the wife I love?) ... she has been made queen ... I deny that ... beyond all the wives ... that the Kings of Egypt ... in the land of Egypt. And lo! you send thus 'Both my daughters ... as wives of the Kings of the land of Carandunias.' But if the ... of my envoys is friendly, and they have said 'With these things our Lord has sent us, as a present, to satisfy thee concerning thy message: the princess salutes the Kings, and all her friends your daughters.' Take thou possession from him of whatever is with them, and send me a letter, and arrange with thy sister who is with me, and make sure of everything; and I have sent to thee an overseer, so to make known to your daughters, in order to perceive the evil that they teach you. And lo! you send 'The messages that my father has left, do not these messages of his say concerning this, that he established alliance between us?' This is the message you send. Now you and I have fulfilled the alliance, and the portion is before your envoys as they will say in your presence. Is not all to be given by us to her who (is) to come to the land of Egypt (whom) they shall bring before me? And (choose?) one of them. (Now) I have sent silver, gold, unguents, cloths, all whatsoever the land can give, and the overseer will say what is the value of that which he has brought—every gift to be weighed to you, that my envoy is to give. And we have been shamed by the evils that they speak. They have refuted the abominations—the evil things that they told you of us. And I was grieved when they ... us all these things. For is it not of their deceit that they told you thus? And I appointed them not to ... them about this. And lo! you send thus, you say thus to my envoys, 'There are no soldiers of my Lord, and is not (a young girl?) to be given them?' This is thy message: 'Thy envoys said for thee that none are going forth. It might be done safely if there were soldiers, if there be none it is impossible to arrange for us what I am asked by him. If there are soldiers I grant it you, if there are horses I grant you this.' This reason your envoy made use of with us, who put me to shame—the evil man whom you sent. I pray thee if they feared to be slain, and lamented evils when she went out, lo! all was in your hands. Thus let my chariots be granted from among the chariots of the ruling chiefs: do not you regard them as a possession? You can send them wherever you please. Are not they all a possession? Are not there, I pray you also, chariots, are not there I pray you horses with me? Demand all my horses: the chariots behold you shall send to meet you at the stations. As for me you shall send me the girl, and send out one to lead (her) to me."

3 B. M.—This is broken at the top, but supposed to be from Callimmasin.

"... my envoys ... the many ... that they send to me I ... Thou my brother without ... for thy daughter to wed, as I send ... (you say) thus, 'From of old a daughter of the King of Egypt was not given for anything.' Why so? Thou art a King, and doest thy will. As they spake this message to me I then sent thus, 'Many of (your) daughters are grown up. So send one who is grown up as (I ask for) her.' Who says thus, 'There is no daughter of the King to give.' Thou hast sent without enquiring as to this. Thou dost not rebuke alliance and good-will, as you send approaching me eagerly as to a taking to wife. And I sent to you because of these things, in brotherhood and good-will, because eagerly approaching me as to taking a wife. My brother, why not send a woman? Why am I repulsed? I myself have sent like thee, I have intrusted a woman. As there were daughters I did not refuse thee. Why associate by taking a wife as ... I have sent to thee to know this ... all your ... so ... they said your ... Lo! my daughter whom I have sent(412) ... you do not take unwillingly, consenting to whatever you desire ... and as for the gold that I send you, your envoy has agreed with me as to the amount of the gold I.... Behold speedily, within this year, whether in the month of June (Duzu) or in the month of July (Ab),(413) this message being taken away, let her whom I have taken be.... If within this year, in June or in July, I send you the gold, you shall send ... the daughter whom I am given by you, and you in return shall send the gold for your ... But if in June or in July the gold is not sent, do not cause her whom I have taken to be sent away. And in return for what will you send to be carried away her whom I have taken. Why, indeed, is it necessary to trouble about gold? Truly sending 3,000 (pounds?) of gold have not I completed the exchange for you, and have not I given my daughter to take to wife?"

ASSURUBALID'S LETTER

9 B.—"To Amenophis IV (the great King?) the King of Egypt my brother, thus Assurubalid,(414) King of Assyria the great King thy brother. Peace be to thee, to thy house, and to thy land. I was very glad when I saw your envoys. Let me send your envoys again with my message. I have sent as a present for you a chariot (of the royal forces?) of my ... and two horses swift and sure. A chariot (without harness?) and a precious stone.

"The sending of gold from your land that has formerly come across to the great King has ceased.(415) Why should he be repulsed from your sight? They have taken as much gold as there was; as much as I have received, which also I have needed, is caused to be sent.

"In the time of Assurnadinakhi(416) my ancestor they sent to the land of Egypt twenty (pounds?) of gold.

"In the time that the King of Khani-Rabbatu sent to your father, to the land of Egypt, they sent him twenty (pounds) of gold.

"... To the King of Khani-Rabbatu and to me ... you have sent gold. I sent ... and you ... from the hands of my envoys....

"If fortunately your face is favorable send gold, and let him who executes the message take what is needed. In return let our envoys be sent to thee from us. Your envoys who have tarried with me needing men to guide them it is granted, in order that I may send this. They took from me men to guide them as they went down. Do not disgrace my envoys, and do not delay them for me. Why should we not in future send out envoys? In future they will carry news, in future they will be sent out to the King to carry the news. And in future let it be declared 'Whosoever of us is treacherous let him be destroyed for the King.' I have received (envoys) thirteen times, why should not other envoys beside from the King in future again..."

LETTERS FROM BURNABURIAS

2 B. M.—"To Amenophis IV (Nibkhuarririya) King of Egypt, by letter thus Burnaburias King of Caradunias(417) thy brother. I am at peace. May there be much peace to thee, to thy house, thy wives, thy sons, thy land, thy Lords, thy horses, thy chariots.

"Since my fathers and thy fathers spoke good things zealously, sending eagerly to make presents, and making friends—and did not they speak eagerly—lo! now my brother has sent two manahs of gold as a present to me. Lo! there is much gold beside, which your father sent, and as this has increased beyond what your father gave, why should you send two manahs of gold? Lo! I have received much, even very much gold, which remains in the temple. Enough gold has been sent. Why should you send two manahs of gold? But as for thee, whatever is needed in thy land send for it, let it be taken of me for thee.

"In the time of Curigalzu(418) my father, all the Canaanites sent to him (saying) thus, 'What sayest thou as to the setting up of the land. It is weak. What sayest thou?'

"My father clave to thy (father). He sent to them thus, 'It has been sent to me as to your discontent. If you are foes with the King of Egypt my brother, you must cleave to some other. Shall not I go out against you for this? Shall not I destroy you, as if you were discontented with me?' My father heard them not because of your father. Now behold Assyria has arrayed against me. Did not I send to you, as to their thoughts about your land? Why do they send against me? If you have pity on me it will never be done. They will fail to win these things. I have sent to thee, as a present for thee, three manahs of precious stones, fifteen pairs of horses for five wooden chariots."

3 B. M.—The salutation is the same as in the preceding.

"Since the time of Caraindas, since your father's envoys to my father came to me, until now there has been good-will. Now I and thou are well with each other. Your envoys have come thrice to me, making also presents, whatever was sent. And I have sent to thee whatever present has been made. As for me, is it not all an honor, and as for thee have not I honored thee in all? Your envoy whom you send, has not he paid the twenty manahs of gold that he has brought? And as for the gifts that remainder, is not the amount five manahs of gold."

Five lines of the letter are here destroyed. On the back of the tablet it continues:

"... the forces of the land (of Egypt?) ... these let him gather within the year, which thy envoy says he has sent, and he shall cause the women of the princess to be guided to you, any time that you order. Let me ask for her that the speed may be greater; and having been delayed, when he has made speed let your envoy take (them), and he shall do more than they did before. So I have told my envoy Sindisugab to say. So let them both station the chariots speedily. Let them come to me, and let them make proper arrangements; so let my envoy and your envoy come to me, speedily conveyed.

"As a present for thee I have sent thee two manahs of precious stones; and (to enrich?) your daughter my son's wife(419) he gave a ... and (an amulet to cause safety?); and I have sent thee as a present precious stones to the number of one thousand forty and eight; and I sent, as your envoy was sent back with Sindisugab."

4 B. M.—With the same salutation as before, is very much broken. It contains a list of presents sent in connection with the same royal marriage of a daughter of the King of Egypt to the Babylonian prince. The envoy's name was Sutti; the presents included a throne of strong wood, ivory, and gold, and another of wood and gold, with other objects of gold and strong wood.

6 B.—The salutation is the same, but the Kings' names are spelled "Nabkhururia" and "Burnaburias." This tablet is very much injured. It refers to a daughter and a promise. It continues:

"He takes her people with (him in) seven chariots, with seven chariots which he took from me; all that belongs to her behold ... let me send her people to you. The Kings who ... of the daughter of the great King, in five chariots ... to your father ... three overseers ... us he (sent?)..."

About half the obverse of the letter is then lost, and about a quarter of the upper part of the back. It then continues:

"If (the arrangements) are already complete ... if there are no previous arrangements let ... to send Zalmu for the Royal Princess, for Zalmu(420) was your envoy whom I sent out, let him (come) ... let him take back the soldiers whom he has sought of me, and let him (take?) ... of the people of the neighborhood, who being speedily sent he may take back, and let them add as many as ...

"Khai(421) your chief, whom you send, is given soldiers and a chariot of our ... and send plenty of soldiers with Khai, for the King's daughter ... and otherwise do not send the King's daughter to travel.... Do not delay; send speedily ... in the course of this year you shall send a chariot and soldiers, so gathering ... let them unite as many as he says (are necessary?).

"Your father sent much gold to Curigalzu ... of Curigalzu, the quantity thereof increased in the palace ... so, because he heard the Kings (or great men) who gave advice, thus the gold ... the Kings, brotherhood, and good-will, peace, and fealty ... the ... increased the silver, increased the gold, increased....

"As thy present I have sent ... of precious stone. To the Lady of thy house twenty (?) of precious stones: so my wife causes me to send, because very greatly ... and as she desires shall it not be done, as I rejoiced being glad ... let them take of me much gold for thyself ... let them take of me according as I ... may it come quickly; and has not my lord ordered thus, that your envoy should bring to his brother much ... so let me send to thee..."

7 B.—The salutation from Burnaburias is the same as in the preceding letters. The letter continues:
"On the day that my brother's envoy arrived, and brought me this message, his envoy (came) wearied to my presence: he had eaten no food, and (had drunk) no strong drink ... the envoy you send told me the news, that he had not brought to me the caravan(422) on account of (wicked men?) from whom it was not (safe?). So he has not brought to me the caravan. The explanation of the (head man?) was, because of fear of being destroyed, which my brother has (known of). Thus as I desired explanation, not ... why the (chief?) did not ... his envoy, why he had not sent it, had not ... my brother's envoy he has caused to say this ... 'Is it not that the region was at strife?' thus ... your brother heard this. He has sent you salutation. Who is it that has told my brother thus that the land has risen? Your brother sends with speed to salute you, as wishing to hear this. Does not he send his envoy to thee? I have told him then to say to my brother, 'A great multitude has arisen, and the land is at strife: the thing is true that thy envoy has said. As thy brother heard not that the expedition has marched on thee, he has asked. Has not he sent to salute thee?' So as I asked my envoy he said, 'As the foe has arisen let him be destroyed.' My brother, have not I ordered this?(423) And so they told me all that has happened in my brother's country, and is not all this explanation necessary? And all has thus happened in my land, and as for me is it not all needful? 'The lawful command that was previously in the hands of our kingdom has been opposed,' he said. We have speedily sent salutation: an interchange of messages between us has been established ... to your presence ..."

Several lines are here missing at the top of the tablet on the back, and the letter then continues:

"... my salutation ... and your salutation with ... Thou thyself behold hast (sent?) thy envoy, to make known this message. So I made him wait for this. I have sent my messenger with speed, when he has rested sixty-one days, and as he said to me this 'I saw the foes (but not) at all was I afraid.' And to-day he is ... I have sent to thee making many presents. I have sent to my brother's hands, as a present for thee, (eighty?) precious stones; and I have sent to my brother five yoke of horses, which are brought this day by my envoy. I desired to send, making many presents to be sent to my brother. And whatever notification (is) needful let this notification be sent, let them take it for me from their home. I have claimed delay that they may send presenting much gold. I send notice to my brother: truly on account of my delay he has remained. The gold I notify I have sent. I return explanation to your presence. Have not I despatched everything to my brother? Let him behold the notice: let him sign for whatever is sent ... I was anxious lest when I sent a notice my brother did not see (it) ... thus I have returned that which my brother signed, I have sent (it) for the gold that they brought me. As for the gifts I so despatch thou shalt thus (reply?); does not ...

"Zalmu my envoy whom I send to you is responsible to us if ... have plundered. I have made Biriyamaza responsible for ... (If) again they have plundered, I have made Pamakhu responsible in part for ... to your land complete.

"... they have sworn ... let my envoy ... to the presence of my brother ... let him be sent back to me ... his message: let him salute ..."

8 B.—The same salutation from Burnaburias to Amenophis IV. The letter continues:

"For this also my brother we speak with good-will eagerly, and we cause this to be said thus with eagerness (or speed) in reply. As for us we have been troubled indeed. Lo! the merchants who have returned with a charge, from the land of Canaan, have spoken in my hearing. They were anxious on account of the charge from my brother's presence, as Sumatta(424) the son of Malumme from the city of Khinnatunu,(425) in the land of Canaan, and Sutatna son of Sarratu of the city of Acca(426) sent their soldiers: they perceived my merchants, and they spoiled our ... I sent to you ... let him tell you.

"The Canaanites in your country, and the Kings ... in your country have violently cut off ... the silver that they carried—a present ... And the men who are my servants ... has smitten them. He destroyed our (wealth?); and as these chiefs he has caused to be slain, it is clear that the man is, indeed, my foe. And, indeed, they are slaying a chief of your envoys: when he was an envoy between us he was slain, and his people have been hostile to you, and the chief my foe, Sumatta, dogging his steps, caused him to be slain; he saw him and slew him. And the other chief Sutatna the Acchoite (though at first they repelled him?) sent his chiefs against him ... he said thus. Behold this ... ask as to this, truly you know ... I have sent thee as a present one manah of precious stones ... my envoy speedily ... truly my brother has known ... do not (blame?) my envoy ... let him be speedily sent..."

These two last letters of Burnaburias are important as showing the disturbances in Syria, also mentioned by Dusratta (23 B.) early in the reign of Amenophis IV.

28 B.—A very broken tablet containing a long list of presents supposed to have been sent by Burnaburias, and consisting mainly of gold and gems.

LETTERS FROM ALASIYA

7 B. M.—"To the King of Egypt my brother by letter, thus the King of the Land of Alasyia(427) thy brother. I am at peace. Peace be to my brother. May there be much peace to his house, to his wives, to his son, to his horses, his chariots, and in his land. My brother's present (is) fifty (pounds of bronze?) five yoke of horses. I have sent my brother's present (and) my brother's envoy with speed, and let my brother despatch my messenger again with speed, and let me ask a gift which ... and.... In his letter it is directed what to send. He has sent silver. Let him send, not refusing the explanation of my envoy ... Cuniea, Ebiluna, Sirumma, Usbarra, Belraam,(428) the explanation which ... these things which are with ... my..."

12 B.—The salutation is the same, mentioning only one son of the King of Egypt.
"My brother has speedily sent my envoys (under escort?), and I heard your salutation. The chief (and) my merchants my brother has despatched speedily (under escort?): has not your chief approached with my merchants and my fleet (or ship)?"

15 B.—A much broken letter from the same, referring to the sending of copper. The last words appear to be "let him come returning year by year."

11 B.—The salutation is the same, including "thy house, thy concubines,(429) thy sons," etc. This is a very difficult letter, but appears to read: "Why, my brother, do you utter this message to me? My brother has known nothing at all that I have not done. As for me, behold the Chiefs of the land of the Lucci(430) whom you confounded in my land, I (was) glad should be conquered."

"My brother you say to me, 'Lo the Chiefs of thy land are with them,' but I (say) my brother has not known this that they are with them; (or) if they are Chiefs of my land. But send thou to me and do as I wish.

"Do not you know the Chiefs of my land? Do not make this message (even) if they are Chiefs of my land. But do as you wish.

"Lo! my brother, as you do not send my envoy, this letter will speak for me as a brother of the King. It is brought by your envoy.

"Moreover, I have perceived neither hinderance nor evil in what was done, and lo! my brother, are not you at rest in your heart?"

5 B. M.—The salutation is in the fullest form—nine lines. The letter is almost perfect, and continues:

"Lo I have sent to thy presence five hundred pieces of copper (or bronze) as a present for my brother; as brother, little copper is found (is it not so) in your midst. When the power of An-Amar-ut(431) my Lord smote the whole of the men of my land, and none made bronze, also my brother it has not been found in thy midst.

"Your envoy with my envoy I hope to despatch, and whatever my brother requires of copper I also have sent thee. A Brother thou art to me. Much gold and silver he has sent to me. My brother, God (Elohim) gives me also gold. And to my brother's presence I have sent thee whatever my brother desires. Moreover, my brother, do not you desire my envoy? And my brother has given me also men of his bosom. My brother has sent me two (precious vases?) and has despatched to me one of the Chiefs of illustrious birth.(432)

"Moreover, my brother, the Chiefs of my land say to me, that they have walked for me according to the letters of the King of Egypt; and, my brother, the decrees also, and the ...

"Moreover, as a Chief of the land of Alasyia has died in the land of Egypt, and his possessions are in your land, and his son and his wife are with me; and, my brother, the possessions of the Chiefs of Alasyia are ... Give them also, my brother, into the hands of my envoy. My brother, has not he abode in your midst, as your envoy abode three years in my land, because the power of An-Amar-ut is in my land; and with my family (and) my wife, is the son of him who has died even now, my brother. I hope to despatch (under escort?) your envoy with my envoy; and I have sent a present to thee, my brother. Moreover, my brother has sent the gold that I desired of thee—much gold, my brother. And let my brother send the possessions that I ask of thee. And, whatever were the messages, my brother has done all, and as for thee whatever messages you utter to me, I also have done. With the King of the Hittites, and with the King of Shinar, with these I am not familiar. Whatever gifts they have sent to me, and I have rendered twice the amount to thee. Thy envoy has been sent to me to serve, and my envoy has been sent to thee to serve."

6 B. M.—"Thus the King of Alasiya to the King of Egypt my brother. Let him learn: behold I have been at peace, and my land is mighty; and because of your salutation peace be to you, peace be to your house, your sons, your wives, your horses, your chariots, your land. May there be much peace forever, my brother.

"Lo! you shall send to me. Why do not you send your envoy to my city again; and I heard not. Lo! how much you afflict me, and I am not made acquainted with all in your midst, and I wonder at this. And now I have despatched my envoy to your city, and I have also despatched to you, by the hands of my envoy for you, one hundred (pounds?) of bronze again. And your envoy carries now gifts—a couch of strong wood, enriched with gold, and chariots enriched with gold, and two horses, and forty-two (vases?), and fifty gold (vases?), and two cups, and fourteen pieces of strong wood, and seventeen large vessels of good make ... from the (?); four (vases?), and four gold (vases?) ... the gifts of which none ..."

The next thirteen lines are almost entirely destroyed. The letter continues on the back of the tablet:

"... Alasiya my merchants with thy merchants, and ... with them; and truly there is good faith ... and my envoy will go to your city, and your envoy shall go to my city. Moreover, why will you not despatch for me (unguents and vases?) I (say), and I will order what you wish, and that which is useful (serving well?) in fulfilment of the decree, I order to be given thee. Behold you sit on the throne of your Kingdom."

13 B.—A short fragment, too broken to read, includes the names of the countries of Egypt and of Alasiya, with salutations. It includes a reference to merchants, and apparently to presents, nine lines in all.

14 B.—The writing and the clay appear to show that this also came from Alasiya. It included twenty-two lines, but is much broken. The following may be read:

"Lo! as a present to thee I have sent five pieces of copper, three (pounds) of good copper, one (?), one (weapon?)—a shipload. Also, my brother, these men of this royal ship ... and as for thee, the ship ... speedily ... is sent. Thou art my brother. You desire a salutation, and I have given it to thee. This man, the servant of the King my Lord, does not he approach before them? and thou, my brother, send him speedily (under escort?)."

16 B.—The ordinary salutation is much broken, but the writing, and the clay of the tablet, seem to show that the letter came from Alasiya. The second paragraph mentions countries called Umdhi ... and Tim ... possibly Hamath and Damascus. The third paragraph continues:

"And now behold why do you ... your fortress more than my fortress; and who is it that has vexed us? It is the abode of a hundred sons of violence. So now ... my brother, because of this, the city Khumme has meditated evil, and if ... why not gather, and ... to preserve, since it is necessary that they should be protected from what ..."

The remainder, including a note for the King's scribe, is too broken to read.

17 B.—A mere fragment, apparently from Alasiya, contains a list of presents, including five wooden thrones (or chairs), objects of silver, a wooden footstool, and a weight of one manah of some other substance.

CUNEIFORM INSCRIPTIONS AND HIERATIC PAPYRI

Translated by Various Egyptologists

The Great Tablet Of Rameses II At Abu-Simbel

Translated by Edouard Naville

In the great temple of Abu-Simbel, between two pillars of the first hall, there is a large tablet, which has been added, evidently, a long time after the completion of the temple. This tablet, which is the object of the present translation, is covered with a text of thirty-seven lines, containing a speech of the god Ptah Totunen to the King Rameses II, and the answer of the King.

It was very likely considered by the kings of Egypt to be a remarkable piece of literature, as it has been repeated, with slight alterations, on the pylons of the temple of Medinet-Habu, built by Rameses III. The tablet, which is decaying rapidly, has been published three times: first, by Burton, in the "Excerpta Hieroglyphica," pl. 60; then from the copies of Champollion, in the "Monuments de l'Egypte et de la Nubie," I, pl. 38; and, finally, by Lepsius, "Denkmäler," III, pl. 193. The inscription of Medinet-Habu has been copied and published by M. Duemichen, in his "Historische Inschriften," I, pl. 7-10, and by M. Jacques de Rougé, in his "Inscriptions recueillis en Egypte," II, pl. 131-138.

I am not aware that any complete translation of this long text has been made. The first part has been translated into German by Mr. Duemichen ("Die Flotte einer Ægyptischen Königin," Einleitung), from the text at Medinet-Habu; a portion of it is also to be found in Brugsch, "Ægyptische Geschichte," p. 538. The present translation I have made from the tablet, which, being more ancient than the inscription, is very likely to be the original. It contains an interesting allusion to the marriage of Rameses with a daughter of the King of the Kheta. The inscription at Medinet-Habu, which is written more carefully than the tablet, and with less abbreviations, has given me a clue to several obscure passages of the ancient text.

The tablet is surmounted by a cornice, with the winged disk. Underneath, the god Totunen is seen standing, and before him Rameses, who strikes with his mace a group of enemies whom he holds by the hair. Behind the god are the ovals of six foreign nations, most likely Asiatics: Auentem, Hebuu, Tenfu, Temuu, Hetau, Emtebelu.

The inscription above the god is as follows:

"Said by PTAH-TOTUNEN, with the high plumes, armed with horns, who generates the gods every day: (I am) thy father, I have begotten thee like a god, to be a king in my stead. I have transmitted to thee all the lands which I have created; their chiefs bring thee their tribute, they come bearing their presents because of their great fear; all foreign nations are united under thy feet, they are to thee eternally; thy eye is fixed on their heads forever."

TABLET OF RAMESES II

1 The 35th year, the 13th of the month Tybi, under the reign of Rā-Haremakhu, the strong bull, beloved of truth, the Lord of the Thirty Years, like his father Ptah, Totunen, the Lord of Diadems, the protector of Egypt, the chastiser of foreign lands, Rā, the father of the gods, who possesses Egypt, the golden hawk, the Master of Years, the most mighty sovereign of Upper and Lower Egypt.

2 Rā-userma-sotep-en-Rā, the son of Rā, the issue of Totunen, the child of the Queen Sekhet, Rameses, beloved of Amen, ever living.

Thus speaks Ptah-Totunen with the high plumes, armed with horns, the father of the gods, to his son who loves him,

3 the first-born of his loins, the god who is young again, the prince of the gods, the master of the thirty years, like Totunen, King Rameses.(433) I am thy father, I have begotten thee like a god; all thy limbs are divine. I took the form of the ram of

4 Mendes, and I went to thy noble mother. I have thought of thee, I have fashioned thee to be the joy of my person, I have brought thee forth like the rising sun, I have raised thee among the gods, King Rameses. Num

5 and Ptah have nourished thy childhood, they leap with joy when they see thee made after my likeness, noble, great, exalted.(434) The great princesses of the house of Ptah and the Hathors of the temple of Tem are

6 in festival, their hearts are full of gladness, their hands take the drum with joy, when they see thy person beautiful and lovely like my Majesty.

The gods and goddesses exalt thy beauties, they celebrate thee

7 when they give to me their praises, saying: "Thou art our father who has caused us to be born; there is a god like thee, the King Rameses."

I look at thee, and my heart is joyful; I embrace thee with my golden arms, and I surround thee with life, purity, and duration. I provide thee

8 with permanent happiness. I have fixed in thee joy, enjoyment, pleasure, gladness, and delight. I grant thee that thy heart may be young again like mine. I have elected thee, I have chosen thee, I have perfected thee; thy heart is excellent and thy words are exquisite; there is absolutely nothing

9 which thou ignorest, up to this day, since the time of old; thou vivifiest the inhabitants of the earth through thy command, King Rameses.

I have made thee an eternal king, a prince who lasts forever. I have fashioned thy

10 limbs in electrum, thy bones in brass, and thy arms in iron. I have bestowed on thee the dignity of the divine crown; thou governest the two countries as a legitimate sovereign; I have given thee a high Nile, and it fills Egypt for thee with the abundance of riches and wealth; there is

11 plenty in all places where thou walkest; I have given thee the wheat in profusion to enrich the two countries in all times; their corn is like the sand of the shore, the granaries reach the sky, and the heaps are like mountains. Thou rejoicest and thou art praised

12 when thou seest the plentiful fishing, and the mass of fishes which is before thy feet. All Egypt is thankful toward thee.

I give thee the sky and all that it contains. SEB shows forth for thee what is within him;(435) the birds hasten to thee, the pigeons of Horsekha

13 bring to thee their offerings, which are the first-fruits of those of Rā. Thoth has put them on all sides.

Thou openest thy mouth to strengthen whoever thou wishest, for thou art Num; thy royalty is living in strength and might like Rā, since he governs the two countries.

14 King Rameses, I grant thee to cut the mountains into statues immense, gigantic, everlasting; I grant that foreign lands find for the precious stone to inscribe(?) the monuments with thy name.

15 I give thee to succeed in all the works which thou hast done. (I give thee) all kinds of workmen, all that goes on two and four feet, all that flies and all that has wings. I have put in the heart of all nations to offer thee what they have done; themselves, princes great and small, with one

16 heart seek to please thee, King Rameses.

Thou hast built a great residence to fortify the boundary of the land, the city of Rameses; it is established on the earth like the four pillars

17 of the sky; thou hast constructed within a royal palace, where festivals are celebrated to thee as is done for me within. I have set the crown on thy head with my own hands, when thou appearest in the great hall of the double throne;(436) and men and gods have praised thy name

18 like mine when my festival is celebrated.

Thou hast carved my statues and built their shrines as I have done in times of old. I have given thee years by periods of thirty;(437) thou reignest in my place on my throne; I fill thy limbs with life and happiness, I am behind thee to protect thee; I give thee health and strength;

19 I cause Egypt to be submitted to thee, and I supply the two countries with pure life.

King Rameses, I grant that the strength, the vigor and the might of thy sword be felt among all countries; thou castest down the hearts of all nations;

20 I have put them under thy feet; thou comest forth every day in order that be brought to thee the foreign prisoners; the chiefs and the great of all nations offer thee their children. I give them to thy gallant sword that thou mayest do with them what thou likest.

21 King Rameses, I grant that the fear of thee be in the minds of all and thy command in their hearts. I grant that thy valor reach all countries, and that the dread of thee be spread over all lands; the princes tremble at thy remembrance, and thy

22 Majesty is fixed on their heads; they come to thee as supplicants to implore thy mercy. Thou givest life to whom thou wishest, and thou puttest to death whom thou pleasest; the throne of all nations is in thy possession. I grant thou mayest show all thy

23 admirable qualities and accomplish all thy good designs; the land which is under thy dominion is in joy, and Egypt rejoices continually.

King Rameses, I have exalted thee through such marvellous

24 endowments that heaven and earth leap for joy and those who are within praise thy existence; the mountains, the water, and the stone walls which are on the earth are shaken when they hear thy excellent name, since they have seen what I have accomplished for thee;

25 which is that the land of Kheta should be subjected to thy palace; I have put in the heart of the inhabitants to anticipate thee themselves by their obeisance in bringing thee their presents. Their chiefs are prisoners, all their property is the tribute in the

26 dependency of the living king. Their royal daughter is at the head of them; she comes to soften the heart of King Rameses; her merits are marvellous, but she does not know the goodness which is in thy heart;

27 thy name is blessed forever; the prosperous result of thy great victories is a great wonder, which was hoped for, but never heard of since the time of the gods; it was a hidden record in the house of books since the time of Rā till the reign of thy

28 living(438) Majesty; it was not known how the land of Kheta could be of one heart with Egypt; and behold, I have beaten it down under thy feet to vivify thy name eternally, King Rameses.

29 Thus speaks the divine King, the Master of the Two Countries, who is born like Khepra-Rā, in his limbs, who appears like Rā, begotten of Ptah-Totunen, the King of Egypt; Rā-userma-sotep-en-Rā, the son of Rā, Rameses, beloved of Amen, ever living, to his father who appears before him, Totunen,

30 the father of the gods:

I am thy son, thou hast put me on thy throne, thou hast transmitted to me thy royal power, thou hast made me after the resemblance of thy person, thou hast transmitted to me what thou hast created; I shall answer by doing all the good things which thou desirest.

31 As I am the only master like thou, I have provided the land of Egypt with all necessaries; I shall renew Egypt for thee as it was of old, making statues of gods after the substance, even the color of their bodies. Egypt will be the possession of their hearts, and will build them

32 temples. I have enlarged thy abode in Memphis, it is decked with eternal works, and well-made ornaments in stones set in gold, with true gems; I have opened for thee a court on the north side with a double staircase;

33 thy porch is magnificent; its doors are like the horizon of the sky, in order that the multitude may worship thee.

Thy magnificent dwelling has been built inside its walls; thy divine image is in its

34 mysterious shrine, resting on its high foundation; I have provided it abundantly with priests, prophets, and cultivators, with land and with cattle; I have reckoned its offerings by hundreds of thousands of good things; thy festival of thirty years is celebrated there

35 as thou hast prescribed it to me thyself; all things flock to thee in the great offering day which thou desirest; the bulls and calves are innumerable; all the pieces of their flesh are by millions; the smoke of their fat reaches heaven and is received within the sky.

36 I give that all lands may see the beauty of the buildings which I have created to thee; I have marked with thy name all inhabitants and foreigners of the whole land; they are to thee forever; for thou hast created them, to be under the command of thy son, who is on

37 thy throne, the master of gods and men, the lord who celebrates the festivals of thirty years like thou, he who wears the double sistrum, the son of the white crown, and the issue of the red diadem, who unites the two countries in peace, the King of Egypt, Rā-userma-sotep-en-Rā, the son of Rā, Rameses, beloved of Amen, living eternally.

Hymn To Osiris

(Stele of Amen-em-ha, Eighteenth Dynasty)

Translated by M. François Chabas

This stele is one of the usual funereal tablets which are found in the cemeteries at Memphis and Thebes. The upper part of the tablet is round, and has the two sacred eyes and symbolical signets, which, as well as the winged globe, almost invariably surmount these sacred inscriptions, and of which the meaning has not yet been satisfactorily determined.

Immediately below this emblem are two vignettes: in the first a functionary named Amen-em-ha ("Amen at the beginning") presents a funereal offering to his father Amen-mes ("Amen's son," or, "born of Amen") the steward of the deity's flocks,(439) beside whom is his deceased wife Nefer-t-aru and a young boy, his son, Amen-em-ua ("Amen in the bark"). In the second vignette, a principal priest (heb) of Osiris, dressed in the sacerdotal leopard's skin, offers incense to the lady Te-bok ("The servant-maid"); below is a row of kneeling figures, namely: two sons, Si-t-mau ("Son of the mother"), Amen-Ken ("Amon the warlike"), and four daughters, Meri-t-ma ("Loving justice"), Amen-Set ("Daughter of Amen"), Souten-mau ("Royal Mother"), and Hui-em-neter ("Food for god"). As there is no indication of relationship between the subjects of the two vignettes, it may be inferred that Te-Bok was a second wife of Amen-em-ha.

The lower portion of the tablet is filled up with the following Hymn to Osiris, written in twenty-eight lines of hieroglyphics which are very well preserved except wherever the name of the deity Amen occurs, which has been hammered out(440) evidently at the time of the religious revolution in Egypt under the reign of Amenophis IV, who, assuming the name of Chu-en-aten ("Splendor," or, "Glory of the solar disk"), overthrew the worship of the older divinities and principally that of Amen-Rā; a change which was again overthrown in the period of his successors, who restored the former letters. From the style of art and other indications it is almost certain that the monument was erected in the reign of Thothmes I of the eighteenth dynasty.

The stele is now deposited in the Bibliothèque Nationale, Paris, and has been published by M. Chabas in the "Revue Archéologique," May-June, 1857, after a paper stamp taken by the late M. Devéria.

A HYMN TO OSIRIS

1 Adoration of Osiris by the Steward of the flocks, Amen-em-ha, Son of the Lady Nefer-t-ari: he says,
   Welcome to thee(441) Osiris, Lord of length of times, King of the gods, of many names, of holy transformations, of mysterious forms in the temples, august being, residing in Tattu, Great One contained
   2 in Sokhem, Master of invocations in Ant.(442) Principle of abundance in On; who has the right to command in the place of double justice, mysterious soul, Lord of Kerer, Holy One of the White Wall, Soul of the sun, his very body reposing in
   3 Souten-Khnen; author of invocations in the region of the tree Ner: whose soul is existing for vigilance; Lord of the great dwelling in Sesennou(443) the very awful in Shashotep; Lord of the length of times in Abydos.
   The road to his dwelling is in the To-sar;(444) his name is stable in
   4 men's mouths. He is the paut-ti(445) of the world, Atum, feeder of beings among the gods, beneficent spirit in the abode of spirits.
   From him the heavenly Nile(446) derives its waters; from him comes the wind, and respirable air(447) is in his nostrils, for his satisfaction, and
   5 taste of his heart. For him, the ground brings forth to abundance; in obedience to him is the upper heaven and its stars, and he opens the great gates; he is the Master of invocations in the south heavens, and of adorations in the north heavens: the moving

6 constellations are under the place of his face, they are his dwellings, as also the reposing constellations. To him Seb orders offerings to be presented: the gods adore him; those who are in the lower heaven bow to him, the divine Chiefs(448) doing reverence, all supplicating.

7 They see him, those who are there, the august ones, and stand in awe from him; the whole earth glorifies him when his holiness proceeds [on the vault of the sky]: he is a Sahou illustrious among the Sahous, great in dignity, permanent in empire. He is the excellent master of the gods, fair and

8 beloved by all who see him. He imposes his fear to all lands so that they like to exalt his name to the first rank. Through him all are in abundance; Lord of fame in heaven and on earth. Multiplied (are his) acclamations in the feast of Ouak; acclamations are made to him by the

9 two worlds unanimously. He is the eldest, the first of his brothers, the Chief of the gods, he it is who maintains justice in the two worlds, and who places the son in the seat of his father; he is the praise of his father Seb, the love of his mother Nou; very valiant, he overthrows the impure; invincible, he strikes

10 his opponent, he inspires his fear to his enemy; he seizes the wicked one's boundaries; firm of heart, his feet are vigilant: he is the offspring of Seb, ruling the two worlds. He (Seb) has seen his virtues and has commanded him to conduct

11 the nations by the hand continually.(449) He has made this world with his hand, its waters, its atmosphere, its vegetation, all its flocks, all its flying things, all its fish, all its reptiles and quadrupeds. Justice is rendered to the

12 Son of Nou and the world is at quiet when he ascends the seat of his father like the sun: he shines at the horizon, he enlightens the darkness, he illuminates shades by his double plume:(450) he inundates the world like

13 the sun every morning. His diadem predominates at top of heaven and accompanies(451) the stars: he is the guide(452) of all the gods.

He is beneficent in will and words: he is the praise of the great gods and the love of the small gods.

His sister took care of him, by dissipating his enemies,

14 repelling (bad) luck; she sends forth her voice by the virtues(453) of her mouth: wise of tongue, no word of hers fails. She is beneficent in will and speech: It is Isis the beneficent, the avenger of her brother: she unrepiningly sought him:

15 she went the round of the world lamenting him: she stopped not till she found him: she shadowed with her wings; her wings caused wind, making the invocation of her brother's burial;

16 she raised the remains of the god of the resting heart: she extracted his essence: she had a child, she suckled the baby in (loneliness) secret; none know where that happened.

The arm (of the child) has become strong in the great dwelling

17 of Seb.(454) The gods are joyous at the arrival of Osiris, son of Horus intrepid, justified, son of Isis, heir of Osiris. The divine Chiefs join him: the gods recognize the Universal Lad himself. The Lords of justice there united

18 to watch over iniquity and sit in Seb's great dwelling are giving authority to its Lord.(455) The reign of justice belongs to him. Horus has found his justification; given to him is the title of his father, he appears with the royal fillet,

19 by the orders of Seb. He takes the royalty of the two worlds; the crown of the superior region is fixed on his head. He judges the world as he likes: heaven and earth are below the place of his face: he commands mankind; the intelligent beings, the race of the Egyptians, and the northern barbarians.(456) The circuit

20 of the solar disk is under his management, the winds, the waters, the wood of the plants and all vegetables. A god of seeds, he gives all herbs and the abundance of the ground. He affords plentifulness(457) and gives it to all the earth.

21 All men are in ecstasy, hearts in sweetness, bosoms in joy; everybody is in adoration. Everyone glorifies his goodness: mild is his love for us; his tenderness environs (our) hearts: great is his love in all bosoms. The

22 Son of Isis has justice rendered him: his foe falls under his fury, and the evil-doer at the sound of his voice: the violent is at his final hour, the Son of Isis, father avenger, approaches him.

23 Sanctifying, beneficent is his name; veneration finds its place: respect immutable for his laws: the path is open, the footpaths are opened: both worlds are at rest: evil flies and earth becomes fecundant peaceably under its Lord. Justice is confirmed

by its Lord who pursues iniquity.

24 Mild is thy heart, O Ounnefer, son of Isis! he has taken the crown of the Upper region: to him is acknowledged his father's authority in the great dwelling of Seb: Phra when speaking, Thoth in writing,

25 the divine Chiefs are at rest.

What thy father Seb has commanded for thee, let that be done according to his word.

(This Egyptian "So be it" ends the hymn. Below this is the usual formula.)

Oblation to Osiris living in the west, Lord of Abydos: may he allow funereal gifts: bread, liquor, oxen, geese, clothes, incense, oil, all gifts of vegetation:

To make the transformations, to enjoy the Nile, to appear as a living soul, to see the solar disk every morning: to go and to come in the Ru-sat: that the soul may not be repulsed in the Neter-Kher. To be gratified(458) among the favored ones, in presence of Ounnefer, to take the aliments presented on the altars of the great god, to breathe the delicious air and to drink of the rivers current. To the steward of the flocks of Ammon, Amen-mes, justified "Son of Lady Hen-t, justified, his consort, who loves him ..."

(The name of Nefer-t-aru, which ought to end the phrase, has been completely chiselled out.)

Travels Of An Egyptian In The Fourteenth Century B.C.

From a Papyrus in the British Museum

Translated by M. F. Chabas and M. C. W. Goodwin

The "Travels of an Egyptian" has first been translated into English by M. C. W. Goodwin ("Cambridge Essays," 1858, p. 267-269), from a hieratic papyrus in the British Museum, published in fac-simile by the trustees (Fo. 1842, pl. 35-61). In 1866, M. F. Chabas, availing himself of the collaboration of M. Goodwin, published a full translation of the same in French ("Voyage d'un Egyptien en Syrie, en Phenicie," etc., 4to, 1866), including a copy of the hieratic text with a double transcription into hieroglyphic and Coptic types, and a perpetual commentary. Objections were made by M. H. Brugsch ("Revue Critique," Paris, 1868, Août et Septembre). But M. Chabas strongly vindicated his views in an additional work, "Voyage d'un Egyptien—Réponse à la Critique," Châlons, 1868, 4to, since which the matter seems to be settled among Egyptologists. The debate was, however, unimportant in regard to geographical information, as it bore merely on the point to ascertain whether the narrative refers to an actual journey really effected by the Egyptian officer named a Mohar, or a model narrative of a supposed voyage drawn from a previous relation of a similar trip extant at the time.

TRAVELS OF AN EGYPTIAN

Section 1

18.3 Thy letter which is full of lacunæ is loaded with pretentious expressions: such is the retribution of those who wish to understand it; it is a charge

18.4 which thou hast charged at thy will. "I am a scribe, a Mohar," hast thou repeated: let us respect thy word and set off.

18.5 Thou hast put horses to the chariots; thy horses are as swift as jackals: their eyes flash; they are like a hurricane bursting; thou takest

18.6 the reins, seizest the bow: we contemplate the deeds of thy hand. I send thee back the Mohar's portrait: and make thee know

18.7 his actions. Didst thou not then go to the country of the Kheta? Hast thou not seen the land of Aup? Knowest thou not Khatuma, Ikatai

18.8 likewise? how is it? The Tsor of Sesortris, the city of Khaleb on its vicinity?—

19.1 How goes it with its ford? Hast thou not made an expedition to Qodesh and Tubakkhi? Hast thou not gone to the Shasous?

19.2 with the auxiliary body? Hast thou not trampled the road of Pamakar the sky(459) was dark on the day when

19.3 there flourished the cypresses, the oaks and cedars, which reached up to heaven: there are many lions, wolves, and hyenas

19.4 which the Shasous track on all sides. Didst thou not ascend the mountain of Shaoua? Hast thou not travelled, thy arms

19.5 placed on the back of thy car separated from its harness by the horses drawing it?

19.6 Oh! come to ... barta. Thou hastenest to get there: thou crossest

19.7 its ford. Thou seest a Mohar's trials. Thy car

19.8 is placed in thy hand: thy strength fails. Thou arrivest at the night: all thy limbs

19.9 are knocked up: thy bones are broken, thou fallest asleep from excess of somnolence: thou wakest up—

20.1 'Tis the hour when sad night begins: thou art absolutely alone. Comes there not a thief to rob the

20.2 things left aside: he enters the stable: the horses are agitated: the thief goes back in the night

20.3 carrying away thy clothes. Thy servant awakes in the night; he perceives the thief's actions: he takes away the rest,

20.4 he goes among the bad ones; and joins the tribes of the Shasous: and transforms himself to an Asiatic.

20.5 The enemy comes to plunder, he finds only the wreck: Thou wakest, dost thou not find them
20.6 in their flight? They take thy baggage. Thou becomest an active and quick-eared Mohar?

Section 2

20.7 I also describe to thee the holy city, whose name is Kapaon (Gabal). How is it? Of their goddess (we will speak) another time. Therein
20.8 hast thou not penetrated? Come then to Berytus, to Sidon, to Sarepta. The ford
21.1 of Nazana, where is it? Aoutou, how is it? They are neighbors of another city on the sea. Tyre the
21.2 port is its name: water is carried to it in barks, it is richer in fish than in sands.

Section 3

21.3 I will speak to thee also of two other small chapters. The entrance of Djaraou, and the order thou hast given to set this city in flames. A Mohar's office is a very painful one.
21.4 Come, set off to return to Pakaïkna. Where is the road of Aksaph?
21.5 In the environs of the city; come then to the mountain of Ousor: its top,
21.6 how is it? Where is the mountain of Ikama? Who can master it? What way has the Mohar
21.7 gone to Hazor? How about its ford? let me go to Hamath,
21.8 to Takar, to Takar-Aar, the all-assembling place of the Mohars; come
22.1 then, on the road that leads there. Make me to see Jah. How has one got to Matamim?
22.2 Do not repel us by thy teachings; make us to know them.

Section 4

22.3 I will speak to thee of the towns other than the preceding ones. Wentest thou not to the land of Takhis, to Cofer-Marlon, to Tamena,
22.4 to Qodesh, to Dapour, to Adjai, and to Harnemata? Hast thou not seen Keriath-Anab, near to
22.5 Beith-Tuphar? Knowest them not Odulam and Tsidphoth? Knowest thou not the name of
22.6 Khaouretsa, which is in the land of Aup? 'Tis a bull on his frontier, the place where one sees the battle (mêlée)
22.7 of the brave ones. Come then to the image of Sina: let me know Rohob;
22.8 represent to me Beith-Sheal as well as Keriathaal. The fords of the
23.1 Jordan, how does one cross them? let me know the passage to enter Mageddo, whereof it remains to speak. Thou art a Mohar,
23.2 expert in courageous deeds. Is there found a Mohar like thee to march at the head of the soldiers, a Marina
23.3 superior to thee to shoot an arrow! Take care of the gulf in the ravine 2,000 cubits deep, full of rocks and rolling stones.
23.4 Thou makest a détour: seizest thy bow; preparest the iron in thy left hand; showest thyself to the good chiefs.
23.5 Their eye looks down at thy hand: "Slave, give camel for the Mohar to eat." Thou makest thy name of Mohar known,
23.6 master of the captains of Egypt; thy name becomes like that of Kadjarti, the Chief of Assur, after his encounter with
23.7 the hyenas in the wood, on the defile infected by the wood-hidden Shasous.
23.8 Some of these were four cubits from the nose to the heel: fierce without mildness, not listening to caresses.
23.9 Thou art alone, no guide with thee, nor troop behind thee. Didst thou not meet the Marmar? He makes thee
24.1 pass: thou must decide on departing, and knowest not the road. Anxiety seizes thee, thy hair bristles up:
24.2 thy soul places itself in thy hand: thy way is full of rocks and rolling stones, no practicable passage; the road is obstructed by
24.3 hollies, nopals,(460) aloes and bushes called "dog-wolf's shoes." On one side is the precipice, on the other rises the vertical wall of the mountain.
24.4 Thou must advance going down. Thy car strikes the wall and thy horses are startled by the rebound:
24.5 they stop at the bottom of the harness; thy reins are precipitated and left behind; all fall down, thou passest on.

24.6 The horses break the pole and move it out of the path; you cannot think of refastening them, cannot repair
24.7 them. The seats are precipitated from their places; the horses refuse to be loaded with them. Thy heart fails thee. Thou beginnest to
24.8 reel; the sky is clear: thirst torments thee: the enemy is behind thee, thou beginnest to quake;
25.1 a thorny bush hinders thee; thou placest it aside; the horses wound themselves.
25.2 At this moment thou art stretched flat and beholdest the sad satisfaction (of thy state?). Entering Joppa
25.3 thou seest a verdant enclosure in a ripe state. Thou makest an opening for eating the fruit. Thou findest a pretty
25.4 young girl who takes care of the gardens: she yields herself to thee as a companion, and yields to thee her secret charms.
25.5 Thou art perceived: thou art subjected to an interrogatory; thou art recognized as a Mohar. Thy tie of
25.6 sweet servitude, is settled by a compromise. Each night thou liest down; a rug of hair
25.7 is on thee: thou imprudently fallest asleep, a robber takes away thy bow, thy dagger,
25.8 and thy quiver: thy reins are cut in the night, and thy horses run away. Thy valet takes a sliding path: the road mounts before him, he breaks
26.1 thy car in pieces ... thy armor-pieces fall on the ground.
26.2 They sink in the sand. Thou must have recourse to prayers, and thou gettest puzzled in thy address. Give me victuals and water, and I
26.3 shall reach my safety. They pretend to be deaf, they do not listen: they do not consent. Thou orderest:
26.4 "Pass to the forge! Pass through the workshops!" Workmen in wood and metals and workmen in leather come before thee: they do
26.5 all thou wishest. They repair thy car, leaving aside all unserviceable pieces: they nail on again
26.6 a new pole: they replace the fittings: they replace the leathers of the harness, and at the back
26.7 they consolidate thy yoke: they replace the metallic ornaments: they incrust the marquetry:
26.8 they put on the handle of thy whip and arrange the thongs. Thou leavest very hastily
26.9 to fight at the perilous post; to perform valiant deeds.

Section 5

27.1 Mapou, O chosen scribe! Mohar, who knows his hand, conductor of the Arunas, chief of Tsebaou, explorer of the most distant limits of the land of Pa ... thou dost not
27.2 answer me anyhow: thou givest me no account; come let me tell all that happened to thee at the end of thy road. I begin
27.3 for thee at the dwelling of Sestsou (Rameses): hast thou not forced thy way therein? Hast thou not eaten fishes of...?
27.4 Hast thou not bathed therein? Oh, come, let us describe Atsion to thee: where is its fortress?
27.5 Come to the house of Ouati; to Sestsou-em-paif-nakhtou-ousormara;(461) to Sats ... aal,
27.6 also to Aksakaba? I have pictured to you Aïnini. Knowest thou not its customs? Nekhai,
27.7 and Rehoboth, hast thou not seen them since thy birth, O eminent Mohar? Raphia,
27.8 how about its entrenchment? It covers the space of an aour going toward Gaza.
27.9 Answer quickly, and speak to me of what I have said of a Mohar concerning thee. I have thunderstruck
28.1 the strangers at thy name of Marina: I have told them of thy fierce humor, according to which word thou saidst: "I am fit for all works; I have been taught by my father, who had verified his judgment millions of times. I
28.2 can hold the reins, and also am skilful in action. Courage never forsakes my limbs; I am of the race Mentou."
All that issues from thy tongue is very thwarting: thy phrases
28.3 are very puzzling: thou comest to me enveloped in difficulties charged with recrimination. Thou cuttest off the discourse of those who come in thy presence; thou dost not disgust thyself with fumbling, and
28.4 with a stern face sayest: "Hasten ye: and desist not! How to do not to be able to succeed in it, and how to do to succeed in it?"(462) No! I stop not, for I arrive; let thy preoccupation get calmed:
28.5 tranquillize thy heart: prepare not privations for him who offerest himself to eat. I have mutilated the end of thy book, and I send it to thee back, as thou didst request; thy orders accumulate on my tongue, they rest on my lips:

28.6 but they are difficult to understand; an unskilful man could not distinguish them; they are like the words of a man of Athou with a man of Abou. Yet thou art a scribe of Pharaoh; whose goodness reveals the essence of the universe.

28.7 Be gracious when seeing this work, and say not, "Thou hast made my name repugnant to the rabble, to all men." See I have made for thee the portrait of the Mohar: I have travelled for thee through foreign provinces. I have collected

28.8 for thee nations and cities after their customs. Be gracious to us: behold them calmly: find words to speak of them when thou wilt be with the prince Ouah.

Dirge Of Menephtah

Translated by S. Birch, LL.D.

The following short poetical eulogium of a king, apparently of Menephtah or Seti II of the nineteenth dynasty, is found in Papyrus Anastasi 4 of the British Museum. It is published in "Select Papyri," pl. lxxxiv, l. 2-9; lxxxv, l. 1. Although not divided by red dots it is clearly poetic in style, and is accordingly given in paragraphs. From the final line it appears to be addressed to the monarch after his death. Although the titles do not exactly correspond with those of Rameses II, or Menephtah, it appears to relate to him, as the papyrus is of his reign and that of Seti II of the same dynasty. It may indeed refer to this later monarch; but as no cartouche is given and the titles after the palatial or so-called Horus ones are doubtful, it is uncertain whom the monarch is to whom it refers. It has been translated by M. Chabas ("L'Egypt aux temps de l'exode," Chalons, 1873, p. 118).

DIRGE OF MENEPHTAH

1 Amen gave thy heart pleasure,
2 he gave thee a good old age,
3 a lifetime of pleasure followed thee
4 blessed was thy lip, sound thy arm
5 strong thy eye to see afar
6 thou hast been clothed in linen.(463)
7 Thou hast guided thy horse and chariot
8 of gold with thy hand
9 the whip in thy hand, yoked were the steeds
10 the Xaru,(464) and Nahsi,(465) marched before thee
11 a proof of what thou hadst done
12 thou hast proceeded to thy boat of as(466) wood
13 a boat made of it before and behind
14 thou hast approached the beautiful tower which
15 thou thyself made
16 thy mouth was full of wine, beer, bread and flesh
17 were slaughtered cattle and wine opened:
18 the sweet song was made before thee
19 thy head anointer anointed thee with kami(467)
20 the chief of thy garden pools brought crown
21 the superintendent of thy fields brought birds
22 thy fisherman brought fish
23 thy galley came from Xaru(468) laden with good things
24 thy stable was full of horses(469)
25 thy female slaves were strong(470)
26 thy enemies were placed fallen
27 thy word no one opposed
28 Thou hast gone before the gods the victor the justified!(471)

Hymn To The Nile

Translated by Rev. F. C. Cook

    This hymn is important as bearing witness to the state of religious thought in Egypt in the time of Merneptah, the son of Rameses II, nineteenth dynasty, according to the generality of Egyptologers, contemporary with Moses. It is extant in two papyri, "Sallier," ii, p. 11, "Select Papyri," pls. xx-xxiii, and "Anastasi," vii. "Select Papyri," pls. cxxxiv-cxxxix, published by the trustees of the British Museum.

    The name of the author Enna is well known. He wrote the "Romance of the Two Brothers" and other works preserved in the "Select Papyri," and partially translated by Mr. Goodwin, in "Cambridge Essays," 1858, p. 257, and M. G. Maspero, in "Genre épistolaire chez les anciens Egyptiens," Paris, 1872.

    A translation of this hymn was published by Maspero ("Hymne au Nil"), in 1868, with an introduction and critical notes of great value.

    The attention of the reader is specially called to the metrical structure of this poem. The stanzas, containing upon an average ten couplets, are distinctly marked in the original, the first word in each being written in red letters; hence the origin of rubricated MSS. Each clause also has a red point at the close. The resemblance with the earliest Hebrew poems has been pointed out by the translator in the "Introduction to the Book of Psalms," and in the "Notes on Exodus," in the "Speaker's Commentary on the Bible."

HYMN TO THE NILE

I. Strophe
Adoration of the Nile

    1 Hail to thee O Nile!
    2 Thou showest thyself in this land,
    3 Coming in peace, giving life to Egypt:
    4 O Ammon, (thou) leadest night unto day,(472)
    5 A leading that rejoices the heart!
    6 Overflowing the gardens created by Rā.(473)
    7 Giving life to all animals;
    8 Watering the land without ceasing:
    9 The way of heaven descending:(474)
    10 Lover of food, bestower of corn,
    11 Giving light to every home, O Ptah!

II.

    1 Lord of fishes, when the inundation returns
    2 No fowls fall on the cultures.(475)
    3 Maker of spelt; creator of wheat:
    4 who maintaineth the temples!
    5 Idle hands he loathes(476)
    6 For myriads, for all the wretched.
    7 If the gods in heaven are grieved,(477)
    8 Then sorrow cometh on men.

III.

    1 He maketh the whole land open to the oxen,(478)
    2 And the great and the small are rejoicing;
    3 The response of men at his coming!(479)

4 His likeness is Num!(480)
5 He shineth, then the land exulteth!
6 All bellies are in joy!
7 Every creature receives nourishment!
8 All teeth get food.

IV.

1 Bringer of food! Great lord of provisions!
2 Creator of all good things!
3 Lord of terrors(481) and of choicest joys!
4 All are combined in him.
5 He produceth grass for the oxen;
6 Providing victims for every god.
7 The choice incense is that which he supplies.
8 Lord in both regions,
9 He filleth the granaries, enricheth the storehouses,
10 He careth for the state of the poor.

V.

1 He causeth growth to fulfil all desires,
2 He never wearies of it.
3 He maketh his might a buckler.(482)
4 He is not graven in marble,(483)
5 As an image bearing the double crown.
6 He is not beheld:
7 He hath neither ministrants nor offerings:
8 He is not adored in sanctuaries:
9 His abode is not known:
10 No shrine is found with painted figures.(484)

VI.

1 There is no building that can contain him!(485)
2 There is no counsellor(486) in thy heart!
3 Thy youth delight in thee, thy children:
4 Thou directest(487) them as King.
5 Thy law is established in the whole land,
6 In the presence of thy servants in the North:(488)
7 Every eye is satisfied with him:(489)
8 He careth for the abundance of his blessings.

VII.

1 The inundation comes, (then) cometh rejoicing;
2 Every heart exulteth:
3 The tooth of the crocodiles, the children of Neith(490)
4 (Even) the circle of the gods who are counted with thee.
5 Doth not its outburst water the fields,
6 Overcoming mortals (with joy):
7 Watering one to produce another.(491)
8 There is none who worketh with him;
9 He produces food without the aid of Neith.(492)
10 Mortals he causes to rejoice.

VIII.

1 He giveth light on his coming from darkness:(493)
2 In the pastures of his cattle
3 His might produceth all:
4 What was not, his moisture bringeth to life,

5 Men are clothed to fill his gardens:
6 He careth for his laborers.
7 He maketh even and noontide,
8 He is the infinite Ptah and Kabes.(494)
9 He createth all works therein,
10 All writings, all sacred words,
11 All his implements in the North.(495)

IX.

1 He enters with words the interior of his house,(496)
2 When he willeth he goeth forth from his mystic fane.
3 Thy wrath is destruction of fishes.(497)
4 Then(498) men implore thee for the waters of the season.
5 "That the Thebaid may be seen like the Delta.
6 That every man be seen bearing his tools,
7 No man left behind his comrade!
8 Let the clothed be unclothed,
9 No adornments for the sons of nobles,
10 No circle of gods in the night!"
11 The response (of the god) is refreshing water,
12 Filling all men with fatness.

X.

1 Establisher of justice! men rejoice
2 With flattering words to worship(499) thee,
3 Worshipped together with the mighty water!
4 Men present offerings of corn,
5 Adoring all the gods:
6 No fowls fall on the land.(500)
7 Thy hand is adorned with gold,(501)
8 As moulded of an ingot of gold,
9 Precious as pure lapis lazuli,(502)
10 Corn in its state of germination is not eaten.(503)

XI.

1 The hymn is addressed to thee with the harp;
2 It is played with a (skilful) hand to thee!
3 The youths rejoice at thee!
4 Thy own children.
5 Thou hast rewarded their labor.
6 There is a great one adorning the land;
7 An enlightener, a buckler in front of men,
8 Quickening the heart in depression.
9 Loving the increase of all his cattle.

XII.

1 Thou shinest in the city of the King;
2 Then the householders are satiated with good things,
3 The poor man laughs at the lotus.(504)
4 All things are perfectly ordered.
5 Every kind of herb for thy children.
6 If food should fail,
7 All enjoyment is cast on the ground,
8 The land falls in weariness.

XIII.

1 O inundation of Nile, offerings are made to thee:
2 Oxen are slain to thee:
3 Great festivals are kept for thee;
4 Fowls are sacrificed to thee;
5 Beasts of the field are caught for thee
6 Pure flames are offered to thee;
7 Offerings are made to every god,
8 As they are made unto Nile.
9 Incense ascends unto heaven,
10 Oxen, bulls, fowls are burnt!
11 Nile makes for himself chasms in the Thebaid;(505)
12 Unknown is his name in heaven,
13 He doth not manifest his forms!
14 Vain are all representations!(506)

XIV.

1 Mortals extol (him), and the cycle of gods!
2 Awe is felt by the terrible ones;
3 His son(507) is made Lord of all,
4 To enlighten all Egypt.(508)
5 Shine forth, shine forth, O Nile! shine forth!
6 Giving life to men by his oxen:
7 Giving life to his oxen by the pastures!
8 Shine forth in glory, O Nile.

The Solemn Festal Dirge Of The Egyptians

Translated by C. W. Goodwin, M.A.

  This dirge or hymn, which is that alluded to by Herodotus,(509) is contained in one of the "Harris Papyri" (No. 500), the same from which I have already translated the "Story of the Doomed Prince." The first line of the hymn ascribes it to the authorship of King Antuf, one of the Pharaohs of the eleventh dynasty. The papyrus itself is, however, of the time of Thothmes III, eighteenth dynasty, but that is no reason why all the texts in the MSS. should be of the latter date. The translation here given was printed by myself for the first time in the "Transactions of the Society of Biblical Archæology," Vol. III, part 1, but the hieroglyphic text remains yet to be published. A fragment of another copy of this identical hymn is to be found in the "Monumens du Musée de Leide," part iii, pl. 12, and from it several words which were wanting in the Harris papyrus have been restored.

FESTAL DIRGE

 1 (Wanting.)

 2 The song of the house of King Antuf, deceased, which is (written) in front of

 3 the player on the harp.(510)
   All hail to the good Prince,
   the worthy good (man),
   the body is fated(?) to pass away,
   the atoms(511)

 4 remain, ever since the time of the ancestors.
   The gods who were beforetime rest in their tombs, the mummies

 5 of the saints likewise are enwrapped in their tombs.
   They who build houses, and they who have no houses, see!

 6 what becomes of them.
   I have heard the words of Imhotep(512) and Hartatef.(513)
   It is said in their sayings,

 7 After all, what is prosperity?
   Their fenced walls are dilapidated.
   Their houses are as that which has never existed.

 8 No man comes from thence
   who tells of their sayings,
   who tells of their affairs,
   who encourages our hearts.
   Ye go

 9 to the place whence they return not.(514)
   Strengthen thy heart to forget how thou hast enjoyed thyself,
   fulfil thy desire whilst thou livest.

 10 Put oils upon thy head
   clothe thyself with fine linen adorned with precious metals

 11 with the gifts of God

multiply thy good things,
yield to thy desire,
fulfil thy desire with thy good things

12 (whilst thou art) upon earth,
according to the dictation of thy heart.
The day will come to thee,
when one hears not the voice
when the one who is at rest hears not

13 their voices.(515)
Lamentations deliver not him who is in the tomb.(516)

14 Feast in tranquillity
seeing that there is no one who carries away his goods with him.
Yea, behold, none who goes thither comes back again.

Hymns To Amen

Translated by C. W. Goodwin, M.A.

These beautiful poems are contained in the "Anastasi Papyri" in the collection at the British Museum. They have been mostly translated in French by M. F. Chabas, from whose interpretation I have occasionally found reason to differ.

The papyrus itself is considerably mutilated, and bears no date, but from the character of the script there can be little doubt that it is of the period of the nineteenth dynasty.

These hymns have been published by myself with exegetical notes in the "Transactions of the Society of Biblical Archæology," vol. II, part 2, 1873, p. 353; and, as before mentioned, in French by M. Chabas in the "Mélanges Egyptologiques," 1870, p. 117.

HYMN TO AMEN(517)

1 "O Amen, lend thine ear to him
2 who is alone before the tribunal,
3 he is poor (he is not) rich.
4 The court oppresses him;
5 silver and gold for the clerks of the book,
6 garments for the servants. There is no other Amen, acting as a judge,
7 to deliver (one) from his misery;
8 when the poor man is before the tribunal,
9 (making) the poor to go forth rich."

HYMN TO AMEN(518)

1 "I cry, the beginning of wisdom is the way of Amen,(519)
2 the rudder of (truth).
3 Thou art he that giveth bread to him who has none,
4 that sustaineth the servant of his house.
5 Let no prince be my defender in all my troubles.
6 Let not my memorial be placed under the power
7 of any man who is in the house ... My Lord is (my) defender;
8 I know his power, to wit, (he is) a strong defender,
9 there is none mighty except him alone.
10 Strong is Amen, knowing how to answer,
11 fulfilling the desire of him who cries to him;
12 the Sun the true King of gods,
13 the Strong Bull, the mighty lover (of power)."

HYMN TO AMEN(520)

1 "Come to me, O thou Sun;
2 Horus of the horizon give me (help);
3 Thou art he that giveth (help);
4 there is no help without thee,
5 excepting thou (givest it).
6 Come to me Tum,(521) hear me thou great god.
7 My heart goeth forth toward An(522)
8 Let my desires be fulfilled,
9 let my heart be joyful, my inmost heart in gladness.
10 Hear my vows, my humble supplications every day,
11 my adorations by night;
12 my (cries of) terror ... prevailing in my mouth,

13 which come from my (mouth) one by one.
14 O Horus of the horizon there is no other beside like him,
15 protector of millions, deliverer of hundreds of thousands,
16 the defender of him that calls to him, the Lord of An.(523)
17 Reproach me not(524) with my many sins.
18 I am a youth, weak of body.(525)
19 I am a man without heart.
20 Anxiety comes upon me(526) as an ox upon grass.
21 If I pass the night in ...(527) and I find refreshment,
22 anxiety returns to me in the time of lying down."

Hymn To Pharaoh

[The previous hymns are addressed to the Supreme Being, under the names of Amen, Horus, and Tum, all identical with the Sun. But for the old Egyptians the ruling Pharaoh of the day was the living image and vicegerent of the Sun, and they saw no profanity in addressing the King in terms precisely similar to those with which they worshipped their god. The following address or petition, which also is found in the "Anastasi Papyri," is a remarkable instance of this:]

HYMN TO PHARAOH(528)

1 "Long live the King!(529)
2 This comes to inform the King
3 to the royal hall of the lover of truth,
4 the great heaven wherein the Sun is.
5 (Give) thy attention to me, thou Sun that risest
6 to enlighten the earth with this (his) goodness.
7 The solar orb of men chasing the darkness from Egypt.
8 Thou art as it were the image of thy father the Sun,
9 who rises in heaven. Thy beams penetrate the cavern.
10 No place is without thy goodness.
11 Thy sayings are the law of every land.
12 When thou reposest in thy palace,
13 thou hearest the words of all the lands.
14 Thou hast millions of ears.
15 Bright is thy eye above the stars of heaven,
16 able to gaze at the solar orb.
17 If anything be spoken by the mouth in the cavern,
18 it ascends into thy ears.
19 Whatsoever is done in secret, thy eye seeth it,
20 O Baenra Meriamen,(530) merciful Lord, creator of breath."

[This is not the language of a courtier. It seems to be a genuine expression of the belief that the King was the living representative of Deity, and from this point of view is much more interesting and remarkable than if treated as a mere outpouring of empty flattery.]

The Song Of The Harper

Translated by Ludwig Stern

    The text of the following song, found in the tomb of Neferhetep at Abd-el-Gurnah, is a good specimen of Egyptian poetry of the eighteenth dynasty. It was first copied by Mr. Dümichen ("Historische Inschriften," ii. 40), and subsequently by myself. In addition to a translation in the "Zeitschrift für ägyptische Sprache," 1873, p. 58, I gave some critical observations in the same journal of 1875. Professor Lauth of Munich translated it in an appendix to his essay on the music of the ancient Egyptians.
    The song is very remarkable for the form of old Egyptian poetry, which like that of the Hebrews delights in a sublimer language, in parallelisms and antitheses, and in the ornament of a burden; no doubt it was sung, and it seems to be even rhythmic, forming verses of equal length—

> "Ured urui pu mā,
> Pa shau nefer kheper
> Khetu her sebt ter rek Rā
> Jamāu her at r ast-sen."

    Though part of the text is unhappily much mutilated, we yet may gather the general ideas of the poem from the disjecta membra which remain.
    It is a funeral song, supposed to be sung by the harper at a feast or anniversary in remembrance of the deceased patriarch Neferhetep, who is represented sitting with his sister and wife Rennu-m-ast-neh, his son Ptahmes and his daughter Ta-Khat standing by their side, while the harper before them is chanting. The poet addresses his speech as well to the dead as to the living, assuming in his fiction the former to be yet alive. The room of the tomb, on the walls of which such texts were inscribed, may be thought a kind of chapel appointed for the solemn rites to be performed by the survivors. The song which bears a great resemblance to the "Song of the House of King Antef," lately translated by the eminent Mr. Goodwin, affords a striking coincidence with the words which Herodotus (ii. 78) asserts to have been repeated on such occasions, while a wooden image of the deceased, probably the figure called "usheb," was circulating among the guests. "Look upon this!" they said; "then drink and rejoice, for thou shalt be as this is."

THE SONG OF THE HARPER

[Chanted by the singer to the harp who is in the chapel of the Osirian, the Patriarch of Amen, the blessed Neferhotep.]

He says:

> The great one is truly at rest,
> the good charge is fulfilled.
> Men pass away since the time of Rā(531)
> and the youths come in their stead.
> Like as Rā reappears every morning,
> and Tum(532) sets in the horizon,
> men are begetting,
> and women are conceiving.
> Every nostril inhaleth once the breezes of dawn,
> but all born of women go down to their places.
>
> Make a good day, O holy father!
> Let odors and oils stand before thy nostril.
> Wreaths of lotus are on the arms and the bosom of thy sister,
> dwelling in thy heart, sitting beside thee.

Let song and music be before thy face,
and leave behind thee all evil cares!
Mind thee of joy, till cometh the day of pilgrimage,
when we draw near the land which loveth silence.
Not ...(533) peace of heart ...(534) his loving son.

Make a good day, O blessed Neferhotep,
thou patriarch perfect and pure of hands!
He finished his existence ... (the common fate of men).
Their abodes pass away,
and their place is not;
they are as they had never been born
since the time of Rā.
(They in the shades) are sitting on the bank of the river,
thy soul is among them, drinking its sacred water,
following thy heart, at peace ...(535)
Give bread to him whose field is barren,
thy name will be glorious in posterity for evermore;
they will look upon thee ...(536)
(The priest clad in the skin)(537) of a panther will pour to the ground,
and bread will be given as offerings;
the singing-women ...(538)
Their forms are standing before Rā,
their persons are protected ...(539)
Rannu(540) will come at her hour,
and Shu will calculate his day,
thou shalt awake ...(541) (woe to the bad one!)
He shall sit miserable in the heat of infernal fires.

Make a good day, O holy father,
Neferhotep, pure of hands!
No works of buildings in Egypt could avail,
his resting-place is all his wealth ...(542)
Let me return to know what remaineth of him!
Not the least moment could be added to his life,
(when he went to) the realm of eternity.
Those who have magazines full of bread to spend,
even they shall encounter the hour of a last end.
The moment of that day will diminish the valor of the rich ...(543)

Mind thee of the day, when thou too shalt start for the land,
to which one goeth to return not thence.
Good for thee then will have been (an honest life,)
therefore be just and hate transgressions,
for he who loveth justice (will be blessed).
The coward and the bold, neither can fly, (the grave)
the friendless and proud are alike ...
Then let thy bounty give abundantly, as is fit,
(love) truth, and Isis shall bless the good,
(and thou shalt attain a happy) old age.

Hymn To Amen-Ra

Translated by C. W. Goodwin, M.A.

This hymn is inscribed upon a hieratic papyrus, No. 17, in the collection of papyri at the Museum of Boulaq. A fac-simile of the papyrus has been published by M. Marriette ("Les papyrus Egyptiens du Musée de Boulaq," fo. Paris 1272, pls. 11-13). It is not a very long composition, being contained in eleven pages of moderate size, and consisting of only twenty verses. It has the advantage of being nearly perfect from beginning to end, written in a legible hand, and free from any great difficulties for the translator.

From the handwriting of the papyrus it may be judged to belong to the nineteenth dynasty, or about the fourteenth century B.C. It purports to be only a copy, and the composition itself may be very much earlier.

In the original the beginning of each verse is indicated by rubricated letters; each verse is also divided into short phrases by small red points; these are indicated in the translation by colons.

This translation has just been published with exegetical notes in the "Transactions of the Society of Biblical Archæology," vol. ii, p. 250.

HYMN TO AMEN-RA

1 Praise to Amen-Rā:
    the Bull in An(544) Chief of all gods:
    the good god beloved:
    giving life to all animated things:
    to all fair cattle:
    Hail to thee Amen-Rā, Lord of the thrones of the earth:
    Chief in Aptu:(545)
    the Bull of his mother in his field:
    turning his feet toward the land of the South:
    Lord of the heathen, Prince of Punt:(546)
    the Ancient of heaven, the Oldest of the earth:
    Lord of all existences, the Support of things, the Support of all things.

2 The ONE in his works, single among the gods:
    the beautiful Bull of the cycle of gods:
    Chief of all the gods:
    Lord of truth, Father of the gods:
    Maker of men, Creator of beasts:
    Lord of existences, Creator of fruitful trees:
    Maker of herbs, Feeder of cattle:
    Good Being begotten of Ptah, beautiful youth beloved:
    to whom the gods give honor:
    Maker of things below and above, Enlightener of the earth:
    sailing in heaven in tranquillity:
    King Rā true speaker, Chief of the earth:
    Most glorious one, Lord of terror:
    Chief creator of the whole earth.

3 Supporter of affairs above every god:
    in whose goodness the gods rejoice:
    to whom adoration is paid in the great house:
    crowned in the house of flame:
    whose fragrance the gods love:
    when he comes from Arabia:
    Prince of the dew, traversing foreign lands:

benignly approaching the Holy Land.(547)

4 The gods attend his feet:
    while they acknowledge his Majesty as their Lord:
    Lord of terror most awful:
    greatest of spirits, mighty in ...:
    bring offerings, make sacrifices:
    salutation to thee, Maker of the gods:
    Supporter of the heavens, Founder of the earth.

5 Awake in strength Min(548) Amen:
    Lord of eternity, Maker everlasting:
    Lord of adoration, Chief in ...:
    strong with beautiful horns:
    Lord of the crown high plumed:
    of the fair turban (wearing) the white crown:
    the coronet(549) and the diadem(550) are the ornaments of his face:
    he is invested with Ami-ha:
    the double crown is his head-gear, (he wears) the red crown:
    benignly he receives the Atef-crown:
    on whose south and on whose north is love:
    the Lord of life receives the sceptre:
    Lord of the breastplate armed with the whip.

6 Gracious ruler crowned with the white crown:
    Lord of beams, Maker of light:
    to whom the gods give praises:
    who stretches forth his arms at his pleasure:
    consuming his enemies with flame:
    whose eye subdues the wicked:(551)
    sending forth its dart to the roof of the firmament:
    sending its arrows against Naka to consume him.

7 Hail to thee Rā Lord of truth:
    whose command the gods were made:
    Athom Maker of men:
    supporting their works, giving them life:
    distinguishing the color of one from another:
    listening to the poor who is in distress:
    gentle of heart when one cries unto him.

8 Deliverer of the timid man from the violent:
    judging the poor, the poor and the oppressed:
    Lord of wisdom whose precepts are wise:
    at whose pleasure the Nile overflows:
    Lord of mercy most loving:
    at whose coming men live:
    opener of every eye:
    proceeding from the firmament:
    causer of pleasure and light:
    at whose goodness the gods rejoice:
    their hearts revive when they see him.

9 O Rā adored in Aptu:(552)
    high-crowned in the house of the obelisk:(553)
    King (Ani) Lord of the New-moon festival:
    to whom the sixth and seventh days are sacred:
    Sovereign of life health and strength, Lord of all the gods:
    who art visible in the midst of heaven:
    ruler of men ...:
    whose name is hidden from his creatures:
    in his name which is Amen.(554)

10 Hail to thee who art in tranquillity:
　　Lord of magnanimity strong in apparel:
　　Lord of the crown high plumed:
　　of the beautiful turban, of the tall white crown:
　　the gods love thy presence:
　　when the double crown is set upon thy head:
　　thy love pervades the earth:
　　thy beams arise ... men are cheered by thy rising:
　　the beasts shrink from thy beams:
　　thy love is over the southern heaven:
　　thy heart is not (unmindful of) the northern heaven:
　　thy goodness ... (all) hearts:
　　love subdues (all) hands:
　　thy creations are fair overcoming (all) the earth:
　　(all) hearts are softened at beholding thee.

11 The ONE maker of existences:
　　(creator) of ... maker of beings:
　　from whose eyes mankind proceeded:
　　of whose mouth are the gods:
　　maker of grass for the cattle (oxen, goats, asses, pigs, sheep):
　　fruitful trees for men:
　　causing the fish to live in the river:
　　the birds to fill the air:
　　giving breath to those in the egg:
　　feeding the bird that flies:
　　giving food to the bird that perches:
　　to the creeping thing and the flying thing equally:
　　providing food for the rats in their holes:
　　feeding the flying things in every tree.

12 Hail to thee for all these things:
　　the ONE alone with many hands:
　　lying awake while all men lie (asleep):
　　to seek out the good of his creatures:
　　Amen sustainer of all things:
　　Athom Horus of the horizon:(555)
　　homage to thee in all their voices:
　　salutation to thee for thy mercy unto us:
　　protestations to thee who hast created us.

13 Hail to thee say all creatures:
　　salutation to thee from every land:
　　to the height of heaven, to the breadth of the earth:
　　to the depths of the sea:
　　the gods adore Thy Majesty:
　　the spirits thou hast created exalt (thee):
　　rejoicing before the feet of their begetter:
　　they cry out welcome to thee:
　　father of the fathers of all the gods:
　　who raises the heavens who fixes the earth.

14 Maker of beings, Creator of existences:
　　Sovereign of life, health, and strength, Chief of the gods:
　　we worship thy spirit who alone hast made us:
　　we whom thou hast made (thank thee) that thou hast given us birth:
　　we give to thee praises on account of thy mercy to us.

15 Hail to thee Maker of all beings:
　　Lord of truth father of the gods:
　　Maker of men creator of beasts:

Lord of grains:
making food for the beast of the field:
Amen the beautiful Bull:
beloved in Aptu:(556)
high crowned in the house of the obelisk:(557)
twice turbaned in An:
judge of combatants in the great hall:
Chief of the great cycle of the gods:

16 The ONE alone without peer:
Chief in Aptu:
King over his cycle of gods:
living in truth forever:
(Lord) of the horizon, Horus of the East:
he who hath created the soil (with) silver and gold:
the precious lapis lazuli at his pleasure:
spices and incense various for the peoples:
fresh odors for thy nostrils:
benignly come to the nations:
Amen-Rā Lord of the thrones of the earth:
Chief in Aptu:
the Sovereign on his throne.

17 King alone, single among the gods:
of many names, unknown is their number:
rising in the eastern horizon setting in the western horizon:
overthrowing his enemies:
dawning on (his) children daily and every day:
Thoth raises his eyes:
he delights himself with his blessings:
the gods rejoice in his goodness who exalts those who are lowly:
Lord of the boat and the barge:
they conduct thee through the firmament in peace.

18 Thy servants rejoice:
beholding the overthrow of the wicked:
his limbs pierced with the sword
fire consumes him:
his soul and body are annihilated.

19 Naka(558) saves his feet:
the gods rejoice:
the servants of the Sun are in peace:
An is joyful:
the enemies of Athom are overthrown and Aptu is in peace, An is joyful:
the giver of life is pleased:
at the overthrow of the enemies of her Lord:
the gods of Kher-sa make salutations:
they of the Adytum prostrate themselves.

20 They behold the mighty one in his strength:
the image of the gods of truth the Lord of Aptu:
in thy name of Doer of justice:
Lord of sacrifices, the Bull of offerings:
in thy name of Amen the Bull of his mother:
maker of men:
causing all things which are to exist:
in thy name of Athom Chepra:(559)
the great Hawk making (each) body to rejoice:
benignly making (each) breast to rejoice:
type of creators high crowned:
... (Lord) of the wing:

Uati(560) is on his forehead:
the hearts of men seek him:
when he appears to mortals:
he rejoices the earth with his goings forth:
Hail to thee Amen-Rā Lord of the thrones of the world:
beloved of his city when he shines forth.(561)

Finished well as it was found.(562)

Hymn To Ra-Harmachis

Translated by E. L. Lushington, LL.D., D.C.L.

The hymn to Amen-Rā-Harmachis (the Sun identified with the Supreme Deity), of which a translation is here attempted, is found, with other compositions of a similar nature, among the Berlin papyri. (No. 5, published in Lepsius, "Denkmäler," Abth. vi. Bd. 12, pp. 115-117.)

It probably belongs to the Ramesside period; the writing is careful and for the most part very distinct; some lacunæ are met with toward the end, and in a few passages the characters baffle the present translator's skill in deciphering.

Citations from this hymn occur not unfrequently in the writings of eminent Egyptian scholars, as Brugsch, Devéria, and others; compare especially Chabas, "Le Nom de Thèbes," p. 16, where the long antithesis of epithets bestowed on Rā and his adversaries is described as "furnishing a page of the Egyptian dictionary."

As far as I am aware, no complete translation of it was published till the appearance of Professor Maspero's "Histoire Ancienne," Paris, 1875; where the whole is rendered into French, pp. 32-35. My own translation was made before I had the opportunity of seeing this work; since consulting it I have modified my version of one or two passages in accordance with M. Maspero's views.

HYMN TO RA-HARMACHIS

Adoration to Rā-Harmachis at the front of the morning.(563) Say:
Thou wakest beauteous Amen-Rā-Harmachis, thou watchest in triumph,
Amen-Rā, Lord of the horizon. O blessed one beaming in splendor,
towed by thy mariners who are of the unresting gods, sped by thy
mariners of the unmoving gods. Thou comest forth thou ascendest,
thou towerest in beauty, thy barge divine careers wherein thou
speedest, blest by thy mother Nut each day, heaven embraces thee,
thy foes fall as thou turnest thy face to the west of heaven.
Counted are thy bones, collected thy limbs, living thy flesh, thy
members blossom, thy soul blossoms, glorified is thy august form,
advanced thy state on the road of darkness. Thou listenest to the
call of thy attendant gods behind thy chamber; in gladness are the
mariners of thy bark, their heart delighted, Lord of heaven who
hast brought joys to the divine chiefs, the lower sky rejoices,
gods and men exult applauding Rā on his standard, blest by his
mother Nut; their heart is glad. Rā hath quelled his impious foes,
heaven rejoices, earth is in delight, gods and goddesses are in
festival to make adoration to Rā-Hor, as they see him rise in his
bark. He fells the wicked in his season, the abode is inviolate,
the diadem mehen in its place, the urœs hath smitten the
wicked.

O let thy mother Nut embrace thee,(564) Lord Rā, those who are
with her tell thy glories. Osiris and Nephthys have uplifted thee
at thy coming forth from the womb of thy mother Nut. O shine
Rā-Harmachis, shine in thy morning as thy noonday brightness, thy
cause upheld over thy enemies, thou makest thy cabin speed onward,
thou repellest the false one in the moment of his annihilation: he
has no rest(565) in the moment when thou breakest the strength of
the wicked enemies of Rā, to cast him into the fire of
Nehaher,(566) encircling in its hour the children of the profane.
No strength have they, Rā prevails over his insensate foes, yea,
putting them to the sword thou makest the false one cast up what
he devoured.

Arise O Rā from within thy chamber, strong is Rā, weak the foes:
lofty is Rā, down-stricken the foes: Rā living, his foes dead: Rā
full of meat and drink, his foes ahungered and athirst: Rā bright,
his foes engulfed: Rā good, his foes evil: Rā mighty, his foes
puny: Rā hath despoiled Apap.

O Rā thou givest all life(567) to the King, thou givest food for
his mouth, drink for his throat, sweet-oil for his hair. O blessed
Rā-Harmachis thou careerest by him in triumph, those in thy bark
exult to quell and overthrow the wicked. Cries of joy in the great
seat, the divine cabin is in gladness, acclamation in the bark of
millions of years. Rā's sailors are charmed at heart to see Rā
hailed as supreme of the order of great gods, they gain delight in
doing adoration to the great bark, homage in the mysterious
chamber. O shine Amen-Rā-Harmachis self-sprung, thy sister
goddesses stand in Bech,(568) they receive thee, they uplift thee
into thy bark, which is perfect in delights before Lord Rā, thou
begettest blessings. Come Rā, self-sprung, thou lettest Pharaoh
receive plenty in his battlemented house, on the altar of the god
whose name is hidden.

Glory to thee, Prince coming forth in thy season, Lord of many
faces, diadem producing rays, scattering darkness, all roads are
filled with thy splendors, apes make to thee salutations with
their arms, they praise thee, they cry aloud to thee, they tell
thy glories, their lips exalt thee in heaven, in earth; they
conduct thee at thy splendid arising, they open or drive back the
gate of the western horizon of heaven, they let Rā be embraced in
peace and joy by his mother Nut; thy soul is approved by the
tenants of the lower heaven, the divine spirits rejoice at the
twofold season of brightness: thou turnest gloom into repose,(569)
thou sweetenest pain of Osiris, thou givest breezes in the valley,
illuminest earth in darkness, sweetenest pain of Osiris. All
beings taste the breath, they make to thee acclamations in thy
changes, thou who art Lord of changes, they give adoration to thy
might in thy forms of beauty in the morn. Gods hold their arms to
thee, those whom thy mother Nut bore.

Come to the King O Rā, stablish his glories in heaven his might on
earth.

O Rā heaven rejoices to thee, O Rā earth trembles at thee, O
blessed Rā-Harmachis thou hast raised heaven to elevate thy soul,
the lower sky has hidden thee in thy mystic forms. Thou hast
uplifted heaven to the expanse of thy outstretched arms, thou hast
spread out earth to the width of thy stride. Heaven rejoices to
thee at thy greatness of soul, thy terror fills earth at thy
figure, princely hawk of glittering plume, many colored frame,
mighty sailor god, self-existing, traversing paths in the divine
vessel, thou roarest in smiting thy foes, making thy great bark
sweep on, men hail thee, gods fear thee, thou hast felled thy foes
before it. Courier of heaven outstripped by none, to illumine
earth for his children, uplifted above gods and men, shining upon
us; we know not thy form when thou lookest on our faces, thy bulk
passes our knowledge.

O blessed Rā-Harmachis thou penetratest ... Bull at night,
Chieftain by day, beauteous orb of mafek, King of heaven, Sovran
of earth, great image in the horizon of heaven. Rā who hast made
beings, Tatanen giving life to mankind, Pharaoh son of Rā has
adored thee in thy glories, he has worshipped at thy gracious

rising brightness on the Eastern horizon, he makes tranquil thy path, he beats down thy foes before thee in his turning back all thy adversaries, he assigned to thee the Uta on her seat, he makes them ... he assigned to thee honors ... he cleared the way for thee, he established thy rites in Abydos; he opens to thee roads in Rusta, he beats down evil.

The Lamentations Of Isis And Nephthys

Translated by P. J. De Horrack

This papyrus was found by the late Mr. Passalaqua, in the ruins of Thebes, in the interior of a statue representing Osiris. It is divided into two parts, very distinct. The first contains chapters of the funeral ritual in the hieroglyphic writing; the second, of which a translation here follows, consists of five pages of a fine hieratic writing of the lower epoch (probably about the time of the Ptolemies).

This manuscript now belongs to the Royal Museum of Berlin, where it is registered under the No. 1425.

A partial translation of it was published in 1852 by M. H. Brugsch ("Die Adonisklage und das Linoslied"). He translated the second page and the beginning of the third, but without giving the hieratic text. I have since published and completely translated this interesting document ("Les Lamentations d'Isis et de Nephthys," Paris, 1866), and now give the English translation revised.

The composition has a great analogy with the "Book of Respirations," a translation of which will be added here. Both refer to the resurrection and renewed birth of Osiris (the type of man after his death), who, in this quality, is identified with the sun, the diurnal renewal of which constantly recalled the idea of a birth eternally renewed. The object of the prayers recited by Isis and Nephthys is to effect the resurrection of their brother Osiris, and also that of the defunct to whom the papyrus is consecrated.

LAMENTATIONS OF ISIS AND NEPHTHYS

Recital of the beneficial formulæ
made by the two divine Sisters(570)
in the house of Osiris who resides in the West,
Great god, Lord of Abydos,
in the month of Choiak, the twenty-fifth day.
They are made the same in all the abodes of Osiris,
and in all his festivals;
and they are beneficial to his soul,
giving firmness to his body,
diffusing joy through his being,
giving breath to the nostrils, to the dryness of the throat;
they satisfy the heart of Isis as well as (that) of Nephthys;
they place Horus on the throne of his father,
(and) give life, stability, tranquillity to Osiris-Tentrut(571)
born of Takha-aa, who is surnamed Persais the justified.
It is profitable to recite them,
in conformity with the divine words.

Evocation By Isis.(572) (She says:)

Come to thine abode, come to thine abode!
God An,(573) come to thine abode!
Thine enemies (exist) no more.
O excellent Sovereign, come to thine abode!
Look at me; I am thy sister who loveth thee.
Do not stay far from me, O beautiful youth.
Come to thine abode with haste, with haste.
I see thee no more.
My heart is full of bitterness on account of thee.
Mine eyes seek thee;
I seek thee to behold thee.
will it be long ere I see thee?
Will it be long ere I see thee?

(O) excellent Sovereign,
will it be long ere I see thee?
Beholding thee is happiness;
Beholding thee is happiness.
(O) god An, beholding thee is happiness.
Come to her who loveth thee.
Come to her who loveth thee.
(O) Un-nefer,(574) the justified.
Come to thy sister, come to thy wife.
Come to thy sister, come to thy wife.
(O) Urt-het,(575) come to thy spouse.
I am thy sister by thy mother;
do not separate thyself from me.
Gods and men (turn) their faces toward thee,
weeping together for thee, whenever (they) behold me.
I call thee in (my) lamentations
(even) to the heights of Heaven,
and thou hearest not my voice.
I am thy sister who loveth thee on earth;
no one else hath loved thee more than I,
(thy) sister, (thy) sister.

Evocation By Nephthys. (She says:)

O excellent Sovereign, come to thine abode.
Rejoice, all thine enemies are annihilated!
Thy two sisters are near to thee,
protecting thy funeral bed;
calling thee in weeping,
thou who art prostrate on thy funeral bed.
Thou seest (our) tender solicitude.
Speak to us, Supreme Ruler, our Lord.
Chase all the anguish which is in our hearts.
Thy companions, who are gods and men,
when they see thee (exclaim):
Ours be thy visage, Supreme Ruler, our Lord;
life for us is to behold thy countenance;
let not thy face be turned from us;
the joy of our hearts is to contemplate thee;
(O) Sovereign, our hearts are happy in seeing thee.
I am Nephthys, thy sister who loveth thee.
Thine enemy is vanquished,
he no longer existeth!
I am with thee,
protecting thy members forever and eternally.

Invocation By Isis.(576) (She says:)

Hail (O) god An!
Thou, in the firmament, shinest upon us each day.
We no longer cease to behold thy rays.
Thoth is a protection for thee.
He placeth thy soul in the bark Ma-at,
in that name which is thine, of God Moon.
I have come to contemplate thee.
Thy beauties are in the midst of the Sacred Eye,(577)
in that name which is thine, of Lord of the sixth day's festival.
Thy companions are near to thee;
they separate themselves no more from thee.
Thou hast taken possession of the Heavens,
by the grandeur of the terrors which thou inspirest,
in that name which is thine, of Lord of the fifteenth day's festival.

Thou dost illuminate us like Rā(578) each day.
Thou shinest upon us like Atum.(579)
Gods and men live because they behold thee.
Thou sheddest thy rays upon us.
Thou givest light to the Two Worlds.
The horizon is filled by thy passage.
Gods and men (turn) their faces toward thee;
nothing is injurious to them when thou shinest.
Thou dost navigate in the heights (of Heaven)
and thine enemy no longer exists!
I am thy protection each day.
Thou who comest to us as a child each month,
we do not cease to contemplate thee.
Thine emanation heightens the brilliancy
of the stars of Orion in the firmament,
by rising and setting each day.
I am the divine Sothis(580) behind him.
I do not separate myself from him.
The glorious emanation which proceedeth from thee
giveth life to gods and men,
reptiles and quadrupeds.
They live by it.
Thou comest to us from thy retreat at thy time,
to spread the water of thy soul,
to distribute the bread of thy being,
that the gods may live and men also.
Hail to the divine Lord!
There is no god like unto thee!
Heaven hath thy soul;
earth hath thy remains;
the lower heaven is in possession of thy mysteries.
Thy spouse is a protection for thee.
Thy son Horus is the king of the worlds.

Invocation By Nephthys. (She says:)

Excellent Sovereign! come to thine abode!
Un-nefer the justified, come to Tattu.
O fructifying Bull, come to Anap.
Beloved of the Adytum, come to Kha.
Come to Tattu, the place which thy soul prefers.
The spirits of thy fathers second thee.
Thy son, the youth Horus, the child of (thy) two sisters,(581)
is before thee.
At the dawn of light, I am thy protection each day.
I never separate myself from thee.
O god An, come to Sais.
Sais is thy name.
Come to Aper; thou wilt see thy mother Neith.(582)
Beautiful Child, do not stay far from her.
Come to her nipples; abundance is in them.(583)
Excellent Brother, do not stay far from her.
O son, come to Sais!
Osiris-Tarut, surnamed Nainai, born of Persais the justified,
come to Aper, thy city.
Thine abode is Tab.
Thou reposest (there) by thy divine mother, forever.
She protecteth thy members,
she disperseth thine enemies,
she is the protection of thy members forever.
O excellent Sovereign! come to thine abode.
Lord of Sais, come to Sais.

Invocation By Isis.(584) (She says:)

Come to thine abode! come to thine abode.
Excellent Sovereign, come to thine abode.
Come (and) behold thy son Horus
as supreme Ruler of gods and men.
He hath taken possession of the cities and the districts,
by the grandeur of the respect he inspires.
Heaven and earth are in awe of him,
the barbarians are in fear of him.
Thy companions, who are gods and men,
have become his, in the two hemispheres
to accomplish thy ceremonies.
Thy two sisters are near to thee,
offering libations to thy person;
thy son Horus accomplisheth for thee the funeral offering:
of bread, of beverages, of oxen and of geese.
Toth chanteth thy festival-songs,
invoking thee by his beneficial formulæ.
The children of Horus are the protection of thy members,
benefiting thy soul each day.
Thy son Horus saluteth thy name
(in) thy mysterious abode,
in presenting thee the things consecrated to thy person.
The gods hold vases in their hands
to make libations to thy being.
Come to thy companions,
Supreme Ruler, our Lord!
Do not separate thyself from them.
When this is recited,
the place (where one is)
is holy in the extreme.
Let it be seen or heard by no one,
excepting by the principal Khereb-heb(585) and the Sam.(586)
Two women, beautiful in their members,
having been introduced,
are made to sit down on the ground
at the principal door of the Great Hall.(587)
(Then) the names of Isis and Nephthys
are inscribed on their shoulders.
Crystal vases (full) of water
are placed in their right hands;
loaves of bread made in Memphis
in their left hands.
Let them pay attention to the things done
at the third hour of the day,
and also at the eighth hour of the day.
Cease not to recite this book
at the hour of the ceremony!

It is finished.

The Litany Of Ra

Translated by Edouard Naville

The following Litany of Rā is the translation of a long text which is to be found at the entrance of several of the largest tombs of the kings, in the valley called Biban el Moluk at Thebes. It is a kind of introduction to the long pictures which adorn the walls of the royal sepulchres, and which generally represent the course of the sun at the different hours of night.

Although very nearly connected with the "Book of the Dead," this text has not yet been found complete in any funereal papyrus; the second section of the fourth chapter only is contained in a papyrus of the British Museum.

The importance of this text consists in this, that it gives us an idea of the esoteric doctrine of the Egyptian priests, which was clearly pantheistic, and which certainly differed from the polytheistic worship of the common people.

The present translation has been made from the book "La Litanie du Soleil" (Leipzig, 1875, avec un vol. de XLIX planches), where this text has been first translated in French, with a commentary. Among the different tombs where this inscription was collected, that of Seti I, commonly called Belzoni's tomb, has been chosen as the standard text.

THE LITANY OF RA

CHAPTER I

Title. The beginning of the book of the worship of Rā in the Ament(588) of the worship of Temt(589) in the Ament. When anyone reads this book, the porcelain figures are placed upon the ground, at the hour of the setting of the Sun, that is of the triumph of Rā over his enemies in the Ament. Whoso is intelligent upon the earth, he is intelligent also after his death.

1 Homage to thee, Rā! Supreme power, the master of the hidden spheres who causes the principles to arise, who dwells in darkness, who is born as(590) the all-surrounding universe.

2 Homage to thee, Rā! Supreme power, the beetle that folds his wings, that rests in the empyrean, that is born as his own son.

3 Homage to thee, Rā! Supreme power, Tonen(591) who produces his members,(592) who fashions what is in him, who is born within his sphere.

4 Homage to thee, Rā! Supreme power, he who discloses the earth and lights the Ament, he whose principle has (become) his manifestation, and who is born under the form of the god with the large disk.

5 Homage to thee, Rā! Supreme power, the soul that speaks, that rests upon her high place, that creates the hidden intellects which are developed in her.

6 Homage to thee, Rā! Supreme power, the only one, the courageous one, who fashions his body, he who calls his gods (to life), when he arrives in his hidden sphere.

7 Homage to thee, Rā! Supreme power, he who addresses his eye, and who speaks to his head,(593) he who imparts the breath of life to the souls (that are) in their place; they receive it and develop.

8 Homage to thee, Rā! Supreme power, the spirit that walks, that destroys its enemies, that sends pain to the rebels.

9 Homage to thee, Rā! Supreme power, he who shines when he is in his sphere, who sends his darkness into his sphere, and who hides what it contains.

10 Homage to thee, Rā! Supreme power, he who lights the bodies which are on the horizon, he who enters his sphere.

11 Homage to thee, Rā! Supreme power, he who descends into the spheres of Ament, his form is that of Tum.

12 Homage to thee, Rā! Supreme power, he who descends into the mysteries of Anubis, his form is that of Chepra (Atmu).

13 Homage to thee, Rā! Supreme power, he whose body is so large that it hides his shape, his form is that of Shu.

14 Homage to thee, Rā! Supreme power, he who leads Rā into his members, his form is that of Tefnut.

15 Homage to thee, Rā! Supreme power, he who sends forth the plants in their season, his form is that of Seb.

16 Homage to thee, Rā! Supreme power, the great one who rules what is in him, his form is that of Nut.

17 Homage to thee, Rā! Supreme power, he who goes always toward him who precedes him, his form is that of Isis.

18 Homage to thee, Rā! Supreme power, he whose head shines more than he who is before him, his form is that of Nephthys.

19 Homage to thee, Rā! Supreme power, the urn(594) of the creatures, the only one, that unites the generative substances, its form is that of Horus.

20 Homage to thee, Rā! Supreme power, the brilliant one who shines in the waters of the inundation, his form is that of Nun.

21 Homage to thee, Rā! Supreme power, he who creates the water which comes from within him, his form is that of Remi.(595)

22 Homage to thee, Rā! Supreme power, the two vipers that bear their two feathers, their form is that of the impure one.

23 Homage to thee, Rā! Supreme power, he who enters and comes forth continually from his highly mysterious cavern, his form is that of At.(596)

24 Homage to thee, Rā! Supreme power, the spirit that causes his disappearance, his form is that of Netert.(597)

25 Homage to thee, Rā! Supreme power, the spirit that sets up (those whom he has created), that creates(598) his descendants, his form is that of Ntuti.(599)

26 Homage to thee, Rā! Supreme power, he who raised his head and who lifts his forehead, the ram, the greatest of the creatures.

27 Homage to thee, Rā! Supreme power, the light that is in the infernal regions, its form is that of Ament.

28 Homage to thee, Rā! Supreme power, the penetrating spirit who is in the Ament, his form is that of Kerti.(600)

29 Homage to thee, Rā! Supreme power, the timid one who sheds tears, his form is that of the afflicted.

30 Homage to thee, Rā! Supreme power, he who raises his hand and who glorifies his eye(601) his form is that of the god with the hidden body.

31 Homage to thee, Rā! Supreme power, the spirit who is raised upon the two mysterious horizons, his form is that of Chentament.(602)

32 Homage to thee, Rā! Supreme power; the god with the numerous shapes in the sacred dwelling, his form is that of the beetle.

33 Homage to thee, Rā! Supreme power, he who puts his enemies into their prison, his form is that of the lion.

34 Homage to thee, Rā! Supreme power, the ray of light in his sarcophagus, its form is that of the progenitor.

35 Homage to thee, Rā! Supreme power, the covering of the body, which develops the lungs, its form is that of Teb-ati.(603)

36 Homage to thee, Rā! Supreme power, he who calls the bodies into the empyrean, and they develop, who destroys their venom, his form is that of the transformer.

37 Homage to thee, Rā! Supreme power, the being with the mysterious face, who makes the divine eye move, his form is that of Shai.

38 Homage to thee, Rā! Supreme power, the supremely great one who embraces the empyrean, his form is that of the spirit who embraces (space).

39 Homage to thee, Rā! Supreme power, he who hides his body within himself, his form is that of the god with the hidden body.

40 Homage to thee, Rā! Supreme power, he who is more courageous than those who surround him, who sends fire into the place of destruction, his form is that of the burning one.

41 Homage to thee, Rā! Supreme power, he who sends destruction, and who causes the development of his body in the empyrean, his form is that of the inhabitant of the empyrean.

42 Homage to thee, Rā! Supreme power, the wonderful one who dwells in his eye,(604) who lights the sarcophagus, his form is that of Shepi.(605)

43 Homage to thee, Rā! Supreme power, he who unites the substances, who founds(606) Amto, his form is that of one who joins substances.

44 Homage to thee, Rā! Supreme power, he who invents(607) secret things, and who begets bodies, his form is that of the invisible (progenitor).

45 Homage to thee, Rā! Supreme power, he who furnishes the inhabitants of the empyrean with funeral things, when he enters the hidden spheres, his form is that of Aperto.(608)

46 Homage to thee, Rā! Supreme power, his members rejoice when they see his body, the blessed spirit who enters into him, his form is that of the joyful one.

47 Homage to thee, Rā! Supreme power, the adult who dilates his eyeball, and who fills his eye,(609) his form is that of the adult.

48 Homage to thee, Rā! Supreme power, he who makes the roads in the empyrean, and who opens pathways in the sarcophagus, his form is that of the god who makes the roads.

49 Homage to thee, Rā! Supreme power, the moving spirit who makes his legs stir, his form is that of the moving one.

50 Homage to thee, Rā! Supreme power, he who sends forth the stars and who makes the night light, in the sphere of the hidden essences, his form is that of the shining one.

51 Homage to thee, Rā! Supreme power, he who makes the spheres and who creates bodies; from thy person emanating from itself alone, thou hast sent forth, Rā, those who are and those who are not, the dead, the gods, the intellects; his form is that of creator of bodies.

52 Homage to thee, Rā! Supreme power, the mysterious, the hidden one, he whom the spirits follow as he conducts them, he gives the step to those surrounding him, his form is that of Ameni.

53 Homage to thee, Rā! Supreme power, the horn, the pillar of the Ament, the lock of hair that shines in ...(610) its form is that of the horn.

54 Homage to thee, Rā! Supreme power, the eternal essence who penetrates the empyrean, who praises the spirits in their spheres, his form is that of the eternal essence.

55 Homage to thee, Rā! Supreme power, when he arrives in the good Ament, the spirits of the empyrean rejoice at sight of him, his form is that of the old man.

56 Homage to thee, Rā! Supreme power, the great lion that creates the gods, that weighs words, the chief of the powers inhabiting the holy sphere, his form is that of the great lion.

57 Homage to thee, Rā! Supreme power, when he speaks to his eye and when he addresses his eyeball, the bodies shed tears; his form is that of the being who speaks to his eye.(611)

58 Homage to thee, Rā! Supreme power, he who raises his soul, and who hides his body, he shines and he sees his mysteries, his form is that of Herba.(612)

59 Homage to thee, Rā! Supreme power, the high spirit who hunts his enemies, who sends fire upon the rebels, his form is that of Kaba.(613)

60 Homage to thee, Rā! Supreme power, the substance which hides the intestines and which possesses the mind and the limbs, its form is that of Auai.(614)

61 Homage to thee, Rā! Supreme power, the great eldest one who dwells in the empyrean, Chepri who becomes two children, his form is that of the two children.

62 Homage to thee, Rā! Supreme power, the great walker who goes over the same course, the spirit who anoints the body, Senekher, his form is that of Senekher.(615)

63 Homage to thee, Rā! Supreme power, he who creates his body and who detaches his members by the sacred flame of Amto, his form is that of the flame of Amto.(616)

64 Homage to thee, Rā! Supreme power, the master of the hooks (who struggles) against his enemies, the only one, the master of the monkeys, his form is that of Anteti.(617)

65 Homage to thee, Rā! Supreme power, he who sends the flames into his furnaces, he who cuts off the head of those who are in the infernal regions, his form is that of the god of the furnace.

66 Homage to thee, Rā! Supreme power, the parent who destroys his children, the only one who names(618) the earth by his intelligence, his form is that of Tonen.

67 Homage to thee, Rā! Supreme power, he who sets up the urshi(619) themselves upon their foundation, no one sees their mysteries, his form is that of the urshi.

68 Homage to thee, Rā! Supreme power, the vessel of heaven, the door of the empyrean, he who makes the mummy come forth, his form is that of Besi.

69 Homage to thee, Rā! Supreme power, the monkey ...(620) the being in his nature, his form is that of the monkey of the empyrean.

70 Homage to thee, Rā! Supreme power, he who opens the earth and who shows the interior of it, the speaking spirit who names his members, his form is that of Smato.(621)

71 Homage to thee, Rā! Supreme power, he who is armed with teeth, who consumes his enemies, the flame that lights the wick, his form is that of Nehi.(622)

72 Homage to thee, Rā! Supreme power, the walker, the moving luminary, who makes darkness come after his light, his form is that of the walker.

73 Homage to thee, Rā! Supreme power, the master of souls who is in his obelisk, the chief of the confined gods, his form is that of the master of souls.

74 Homage to thee, Rā! Supreme power, the double luminary, the double obelisk, the great god who raises his two eyes, his form is that of the double luminary.

75 Homage to thee, Rā! Supreme power, the master of the light, who reveals hidden things, the spirit who speaks to the gods in their spheres, his form is that of the master of the light.

76 Homage to thee, Rā! Supreme power, O Rā of the sphere, O Rā who speakest to the spheres, O Rā who art in thy sphere, homage to thee, Rā Keschi, four times. They sing praises to the spirit Keschi,(623) the spheres honor his spirit, they glorify thy body which is in thee, saying, Homage to thee, great Keschi! four times. They sing praises in thy honor, spirit Keschi in thy seventy-five forms which are in thy seventy-five spheres. The royal Osiris knows them by their names, he knows what is in their bodies, all their hidden essences. The royal Osiris speaks to them in their forms, they open to the royal Osiris, they display the hidden doors to his spirit which is like thy spirit, thou creates them, thou createst the royal Osiris; the development of his body is like thine because the royal Osiris is one of thy companions, who are in their spheres, and who speak in their caverns, those who are blessed through thy creation and who transform themselves when thou commandest it. The royal Osiris is like one of those who speak in their hidden spheres. Ha! he has arrived, he advances in the train of the spirit of Rā. Ha! he has completed the journey from Chepri.(624) Hail! he has arrived. The royal Osiris knows all that concerns the hidden beings. Hail! he has arrived in the midst of you; homage to his spirit Keschi! four times.

77 O Rā of the Ament, who hast created the earth, who lightest the gods of the empyrean, Rā who art in thy disk, guide him on the road to the Ament, that he may reach the hidden spirits; guide him on the road which belongs to him, guide him on the Western road; that he may traverse the sphere of Ament, guide him on the road to the Ament, that the King may worship those who are in the hidden dwelling, guide him on the road to the Ament, make him descend to the sphere of Nun. Hail, Rā! the royal Osiris is Nun. Hail Rā! the royal Osiris is thyself and reciprocally. Hail, Rā! thy spirit is that of Osiris, thy course is his in the empyrean. Hail, Rā! he dwells in the empyrean, he traverses the good Ament. Such as thou art, such is the royal Osiris. Thy intellect, Rā, is his. Osiris worships the hidden gods, he praises their spirits, these latter say to one another that thy course (Rā!) is that of Osiris, that thy way is his, great god who dwellest in the empyrean. Hail! god of the disk with the brilliant rays, praise be to the spirit Keschi! four times.

78 Hail to thee, universal covering, who createst thy soul and who makest thy body grow; the King traverses the most secret sphere, he explores the mysteries contained in it. The King speaks to thee like Rā, he praises thee with his intelligence, the King is like the god; and reciprocally. He moves by himself, he moves by himself. The all surrounding universe says: Ah, guide him unto the interior of my sphere; four times.

79 This chapter is said to the most mysterious god, these words are written like those upon the two sides of the door of the empyrean ...(625) this book is read every day, when he has retired in life, according to custom, perfectly.

CHAPTER II

1 Worship of the Spheric Gods, when Rā sets in life. Hail, gods of the spheres, gods who are in the Ament, perfect gods ...(626) the enemies of Rā, you make the universal covering(627) grow ...(628) you worship the god who is in his disk ...(629) thou commandest thy enemies, great god who art upon the horizon; four times. Thou commandest thy enemies, Osiris Temt; four times.

2 The royal Osiris commands his enemies in heaven and upon earth, by authority of all the gods and all the goddesses, by authority of Osiris Chentament, because the royal Osiris is Rā himself, the great inhabitant of the heavens, he speaks in the presence of Ament. The King governs by favor of the great powers. The royal Osiris is pure, what is in him is pure, the royal Osiris governs the two worlds, the royal Osiris commands his enemies; four times.

3 He is powerful, Rā in the empyrean, he is powerful, Rā in the empyrean. He traverses the empyrean with joy, for he has struck Apap;(630) there is joy for thee, god of the horizon, Osiris, King of the Ament, there is joy for thy triumphant spirit, for thou destroyest his enemies; thou art delighted, Tesherti, red spirit who openest the Ament. Thou givest thy hand to Osiris, thou art received in the good Ament, and the gods rejoice over thee. Osiris gives thee his hand, thou art received by Chentament. He is brilliant, the spirit of Rā in the empyrean, he is brilliant, the body of Teb Temt. Rā commands in the empyrean, because he has struck Apap. Teb Temt commands; he worships the spirit of the two horizons; the spirit of the two horizons worships him.

4 The royal Osiris receives dominion over his enemies from the great powers of the mysterious avenger, he who reveals the mysterious empyrean, who dissipates the darkness, who chases away the rain, he who hurries, and who makes the blessed servants of Rā come forth. He(631) sees the body of the god when he assumes forms with a mysterious name, when he sheds his rays in obscurity, and when

he hides the uncovered bodies; when he traverses the mysterious spheres and when he gives eyes to their gods; they themselves see him, and their spirits are blessed.

5 Hail, Rā! give eyes to the royal Osiris, give him divine eyeballs, and may they guide the royal Osiris. Hail, Rā! give a heart to the royal Osiris; he traverses the earth, he traverses the world like Rā.

6 Thou takest care that what thou commandest to exist, exists; thou rulest the royal Osiris like Chuti(632) and the King honors thy spirit, he glorifies thee.

7 Thou commandest Osiris to be like Khuti, the brilliant triangle which appears in the shining place.

8 Thou commandest Osiris to be like the mysterious spirit which comes forth from the mysterious place.

9 Thou commandest Osiris to be like the blessed spirit which comes forth from the blessed place.

10 Thou commandest Osiris to be like the destructive spirit which comes forth from the place of destruction.

11 Thou commandest Osiris to be like the revealing spirit which comes forth from the opening.

12 Thou commandest Osiris to be like the elevated spirit which comes forth from the high place.

13 Thou commandest Osiris to be like the hidden spirit which comes forth from the Ament.

14 Deliver him from the crocodiles which frighten the spirits, like geese; let them not do their work upon the royal Osiris, in the presence of the gods armed with swords; may Osiris never fall into their furnaces, may their nets never entangle him; his spirit flies away and soars into the heavens, his spirit returns and enters into the empyrean, because the royal Osiris knows the mysteries which are in the empyrean, the secret forms of Osiris, that none of his servants know, in the secret of his hidden dwelling. Hail! the royal Osiris knows thy form, great and mysterious god.

15 Deliver the royal Osiris from the agile demons furnished with legs, from the cruel gods who pluck out hearts and who throw them into their furnaces. May they never do their work upon the royal Osiris, may they never put him in their furnaces, because Osiris is Rā; and reciprocally. His soul is that which is in the disk. His body is in the middle of the hidden gods; they make Osiris rule, Osiris makes them rule; he commands, and he rests as you rest in the Ament.

16 The soul of Rā shines in his shape, his body rests amid the invocations which are addressed to him; he enters into the interior of his white disk, he lights the empyrean with his rays, he creates it, he makes the souls remain in their bodies, they praise him from the height of their pedestal. He receives the acclamations of all the gods who open the doors, the hidden essences who prepare the way for Rā's soul, and who allow the King of souls access to the fields. He traverses his disk himself; he calls (to life) the body of Kat;(633) he places the gods of the stars upon their legs; these latter make the god An(634) come at their hours; the two sisters join themselves to him, they decorate his head, as a spirit worthy of adornment.

17 O, Rā, place the royal Osiris in thy train; he is the divine key which opens his haunts, he knows admirable means of obtaining the great victory over his enemies; Osiris is powerful through thy two eyes; walking god, the course of Osiris is thy course. Rā, the journeys of Osiris are thy journeys, Osiris makes thee rule over thy enemies, thou makest Osiris rule over his enemies, by means of the great splendor which is the splendor of Rā in the empyrean, they cry to him: Bull of the country of the dead, thou art Rā, thy body rests in peace, thou art blessed in thy mysteries.

CHAPTER III

1 O, Rā, come to the King! truly. Highly glorious Teb Temt.

2 O, Rā, come to the King! truly. Thou makest thy soul young again and thou givest birth to thy body.

3 O, Rā, come to the King! truly. Lead him into the holy dwelling.

4 O, Rā, come to the King! truly. Guide him on the good ways.

5 O, Rā, come to the King! truly. Guide him on the roads of Nun.

6 O, Rā, come to the King! truly. Guide him on the roads of Nut.

7 O, Rā, come to the King! truly. He restores the body of Osiris.

8 O, Rā, come to the King! truly. He places the corpse upon its foundation, in its place that no one knows.

9 O, Rā, come to the King! truly. He calls his body Osiris.

10 O, Rā, come to the King! truly. He sees him who is in the sarcophagus.

11 O, Rā, come to the King! truly. The rays of Aten(635) are upon his person.

12 O, Rā, come to the King! truly. He has taken the good ways.

13 O, Rā, come to the King! truly. He worships thy soul upon the horizon.

14 O, Rā, come to the King! truly. Thou speakest to him as to the god who is upon the ground.

15 O, Rā, come to the King! truly. He is one of thy Nine Gods.

CHAPTER IV

Section I

1 Thou art what he is, Rā, thou givest birth to the royal Osiris, thou makest him exist like thyself, god of the two horizons; the birth of Osiris is the birth of Rā in the Ament, and reciprocally; the birth of Osiris in the heavens is the birth of the soul of Rā in the heavens, and reciprocally; the life of Osiris is the life of Rā, and reciprocally; the development of his body is the development of Rā's body. Rā conceived, Tum gave birth to Osiris; it is the young Chepra; Nut brings Osiris into the world, she nourishes Osiris, like Rā's soul which issued from her.

2 O, Rā who art in the Ament ...(636) who art in the empyrean, deliver Osiris from thy conductors who separate souls from their bodies, the agile beings who move quickly in thy places of torment. May they never seize Osiris, may they never take him, may they never quicken their steps toward him, may they never put him in their places of torture, may they never cast their toils round him, may they never place him upon their altars, may he never tremble in the land of the condemned, may he never be lost in the Ament. He walks as the god of the horizon walks, he takes Rā's steps, he worships the god who is on the earth, he honors the mysterious bodies ...(637) they say to Osiris: Hu and Sa; they call him this, because he is like the spirit of Hu and Sa(638) in his creations; he makes the sacred tree grow he is not ignorant of it. There are cries of joy in the mysterious region, for Rā sets under the form of Osiris, and reciprocally. Rejoice, you the dead, render praises to Rā, and Rā renders praises to you. Rā comes forth from the cow Mehur,(639) he sets in Netur;(640) Osiris comes forth from Nehur like the sun, he sets in Netur like Temt. The name of the King is the name of Rā, Ammehur,(641) the setting of Osiris, it is his setting, Amnetur.(642)

3 The gods of the empyrean bless him, the hidden gods rejoice over him; they say to him: thy person is the god of the country of the dead, thy form is Teb Temt. The hidden gods speak to the royal Osiris, they rejoice on seeing him; (they say to him:) Hail, blessed and perfect one, who comest forth from Tonen, the god who destroys the forms; it is great, thy essence, spirit, shadow that no one destroys, that lives where you live. He knows the essences of the primitive beings, he knows the mysterious flames of the empyrean, for he attains to holy and mysterious things.

4 The two gods speak to the royal Osiris, they rejoice on seeing him, this blessed, perfect spirit; (they say to him:) This is one of us. The gods speak to the royal Osiris, they rejoice when they see him, him, the splendor of Rā, the splendor of the two goddesses that appears in Heset,(643) the supplicant Heset addresses the guardians who watch over the doors, who devour souls and who swallow the shades of the dead; when they approach them, they are led by them to the place of destruction: O guardians who watch over your doors, who swallow souls and devour the shades of the dead; when they approach you, you lead them to the place of destruction; Oh! allow this blessed this most holy spirit, to be in the dwelling of the Akher;(644) it is a spirit like Rā glorious like Osiris. This is what Heset the supplicant says before the royal Osiris.

5 O Heset, make him come, O Heset, guide the royal Osiris, O Heset open to him the empyrean, give him the lot of the god of the empyrean; he puts the veil nems(645) upon his head at the bottom of the dwelling of the Ament. Hail to thee, he has reached thee; Heset, guide him on the good way, he speaks to thee, he glorifies thee by his invocations, and thou rejoicest on seeing his spirit; Heset, the supplicant, open the doors which are in the empyrean, open his spheres to him, for the club is in the hand of Osiris, and he grasps his lance; his club strikes the enemies, and his lance destroys the rebels; his dwelling is that of the god of the two horizons; his throne is Rā's throne; for he is the Horus of the two horizons.(646) He is beautiful, this spirit, he is perfect, he is powerful in both his hands.

6 The two great gods speak to the royal Osiris; they rejoice on his account; they celebrate his victorious strength, they give him their protection, they send him their spirit of life; (they say to him:) He is brilliant like the spirit of the horizon that is the dwelling of Rā in the heavens;(647) they communicate their words to him, they give him the power by their authority. He opens the door of heaven and earth like his father Rā; a spirit shining in the place where they burn the offerings, in the arms of Osiris. The royal Osiris rests in the mysterious dwelling, he shines like the god of the luminary, the dwelling of Rā of the horizon.(648) The royal Osiris is Rā; and reciprocally, he is the spirit of Osiris, he rests (in him).

7 He reaches the gods of the pyramid; these latter praise him on seeing the happy arrival of Osiris; they address him as Rā of the horizon; praise be to Rā! cheers for the spirit of the horizon, praises to the spirit of Rā! Praise his spirit that inhabits the empyrean, invoke him who is in his disk, bear him to him who created you, carry him unto the pyramid, since you are the gods who accompany Rā Osiris. Here is Osiris, carry him into the hidden sanctuary of Osiris, the lord of years(649) who is under the care of the two Rehti. Carry him into the hidden dwelling where Osiris resides, carry him into the funeral monument which is in the Ament, the mysterious sanctuary of the god who is at rest; bear him, open your arms to him, stretch out your hands to him, take off your veils before him, for he is the great

essence whom the dead spirits do not know; it is Rā, the god of the two horizons, and Osiris, the King of the Ament, who send him.

8 The royal Osiris is one of you, for his diadem is a vulture; his face is a sparrow-hawk, his head is Rā; his eyes are the Rehti, the two sisters; his nose is Horus of the empyrean; his mouth is the King of the Ament; his lungs are Nun; his two hands are the god Secheni;(650) his fingers are the gods who seize him; his body is Chepra; his heart is Horus, the creator; his chest is the goddess of life; his spleen is the god Fenti;(651) his lungs are the goddess Heti; his stomach is Apu; his intestines, the god with the mysterious names;(652) his back is the corpse-god; his elbows are Makati; the nape of his neck, Horus Thoth; his lips Mehur; his phallus is Tonen;(653) ...(654) the goddess of Cher; ...(655) the two hidden gods; his sitting posture the two goddesses; his legs, he who traverses the hidden places; his shin-bones are uræus. His members are gods, he is throughout a god, no one of his members is without a god, the gods are of his substance. The royal Osiris is an intelligent essence, his members guide him, his flesh opens the way to him, those who are born of him create him, they rest when they have given birth to him. The royal Osiris is he who gives them birth, it is he who begets them, it is he who makes them exist; his birth is that of Rā in the Ament, Rā gives birth to the royal Osiris, he causes his own birth.

Section II

1 O Rā, open to his spirit, for the royal Osiris knows what there is in the empyrean, he is the great mummy, Osiris, the King of the Ament; he is Osiris, he is perfect like Osiris, he is blessed like Osiris, his club is that of Osiris, his sword is that of Chentament, his sceptre is that of Sahou, he is the great one, the King of the blessed, for he is the original one, he who knows the mysteries, the greatest of the holy ones in the empyrean. He is happy, the spirit Keschi who makes his own law in the Ament, he speaks to what is born of him,(656) Osiris Chentament.

2 Hail to thee, inhabitant of the empyrean, praised be what is in thee; hail to thee, inhabitant of the empyrean, the weeping gods cut their hair in honor of thee, they clap their hands, they revere thee, they weep before thee, thy spirit rejoices in their fear, thy body is blessed.

3 Hail to thee, inhabitant of the empyrean, god seated upon his throne, who boldest the sceptre hik,(657) King of the empyrean, Prince of the Aker, great Prince crowned with the urer,(658) great god who hides his dwelling, Lord of wisdom, Chief of the powers.

4 Hail to the inhabitant of the empyrean, thy son Horus rests in thee, thou communicatest thy orders to him, thou permittest him to shine like An of the empyrean, the great star who creates his names,(659) who knows the empyrean and who traverses the interior of it, he, the son of Rā, proceeding from Tum. The royal Osiris is thy son, thou communicatest thy orders to him, thou permittest him to shine like An of the heavens, the great star who creates his names,(660) who knows the empyrean and who traverses the interior of it, he the son of Rā, proceeding from Tum. He rests in the empyrean, he rejoices in the dusk, he enters in there and comes forth, the arms of Tonen receive him, the blessed lift him, they stretch out their hands toward him, the ...(661) guide him. Praise him ye blessed, exalt the royal Osiris, ye blessed! Rejoice over him, as over Rā, extol him like Osiris, he has placed your offerings before you, he accords you the favor of receiving your portion as his father Rā commanded. He is his darling, he is his descendant upon the earth, and the blessed show him the way. Let him arrive in the empyrean, and let him penetrate into the good Ament. The royal Osiris fixes the crown upon the head of Osiris, he offers his casket to Seb, he presents Sah with the sceptre, he gives the royal diadem to him whose name is Ammon.

5 Look at him, ye blessed, let him receive a perfect intelligence, let him shine like the god of mysteries, deliver him from the gods of the pillory who fasten to their posts. May they never bind Osiris to their posts, may they never put him in the place of destruction, for he is the descendant of Osiris who permits him to receive the diadem in the empyrean.

6 He is sublime, the spirit of Rā in the Ament, his body is blessed there, the spirits rejoice when they develop their forms in the zones of the empyrean, before the soul of Rā, the inhabitant of the empyrean, and Teb Temt who rests in his covering. Hail, yes, hail! Hail spirit of Rā, hail, spirit of the royal Osiris like Temt! Hail, royal Osiris who art Rā, and reciprocally! O Temt who art Rā, and reciprocally, hail!

7 The royal Osiris is one of you. He gives birth to you, he gives you your names, he makes you perfect; ha! he sends his body into you; ha! he is your creator. Look at him, he shines like him who proceeds from you; he honors his father, perfect, blessed, blessing his mother; look at him, make his essence sublime and make him like him who destroys his forms;(662) show the way to his spirit, set him upon your pedestals, make him rest in his members, show him his dwelling in the midst of the earth, open your doors to him, unfasten the bolt.

8 O Rā, O Teb-Temt, guide the royal Osiris following the direction of the spirits, following the course of the gods. The royal Osiris is in his gateway (in presence of the) navigating gods; the royal Osiris is the only one, the guardian of his doors, he who puts the gods in their places. He is upon his

pedestal in the empyrean, he is the possessor in the midst of the possessors, he is at the extremities of the empyrean, he is blessed in the infernal regions. He rests in the Ament among the spirits who are in the members of the Ament. The royal Osiris is Rā's darling, he is the mysterious phœnix, he enters in peace into the empyrean, he leaves Nut in peace; the royal Osiris has his throne in heaven, he traverses the horizons in Rā's train, he is at peace in the heavens, in Rā's fields, his share is upon the horizon in the fields of Aalu; he traverses the earth like Rā, he is wise like Thoth, he walks at will, he hastens in his course, like Sahu with the mysterious names, who becomes two divinities. The royal Osiris becomes two divinities. What Rā produces, the royal Osiris produces; he gives a spiritual existence to what he loves; he does not give it to what he hates. The royal Osiris is the Chief of the gods who make offerings to the spirits, he is powerful in his course, he is the courageous being who strikes his enemies.

9 O ye gods, O ye blessed who precede Rā and who escort his spirit, do to the royal Osiris as to Rā, tow him with you in the same way that you conduct Rā and the two navigating gods in the heavens; the royal Osiris is Rā himself, and reciprocally; he is the Chief of his worshippers who gives life to the forms.

Section III

1 O Ament, O Ament, O good, O good, O strong, O strong, O powerful, O powerful, O protecting, O protecting, O mysterious, O mysterious (Ament), the royal Osiris knows thee, he knows thy form, he knows the name of thy companions. Ament, hide my corpse, good Ament, hide my body. O resting-place, let me rest in thee; O strong one, may the royal Osiris be strong with thy strength; O powerful one, may he be powerful with thy power! O Ament, open thy arms to him; O protectress, cover his body; O mysterious being, stretch out thy hand to him. Hail, holy Ament of Osiris with the mysterious names, the most holy of the gods, thou who art the most hidden of all mysteries. Hail! the royal Osiris worships thee; he addresses the great god who is within thee. Hail! he worships thee; open thy mysterious doors to him. Hail! he worships thee; (open to him) thy hidden spheres, for he has his dwelling in the heavens like Rā, and his throne is upon the earth like Seb; he is seated upon the throne of Seb, upon the seats of Horchuti; his spirit soars into the heavens, it rests there; his body descends to the earth in the midst of the gods. He walks with Rā, he follows Tum, he is like Chepra, he lives as thou livest in truth.

2 When this book is read he who reads it purifies himself at the hour when Rā sets, who rests in the Ament of the Ament, when Rā is in the midst of hidden things, completely.

The Book Of Respirations

Translated by P. J. De Horrack

The manuscript a translation of which here follows belongs to the Museum of the Louvre, in Paris, where it is registered under the No. 3284 (Devéria, Catalogue des MS. égypt., p. 132). It probably dates from the epoch of the Ptolemies. It is in hieratic writing and generally known by the name of "Book of Respirations" or "Book of the Breaths of Life," according to Mr. Le Page Renouf's ingenious interpretation. This book seems to have been deposited exclusively with the mummies of the priests and priestesses of the god Ammon-Rā, if we may judge from the titles inserted into the manuscripts.

Dr. Brugsch, in 1851, first directed the attention of Egyptologists to this curious work, by publishing a transcription in hieroglyphics of a hieratic text in the Berlin Museum, with a Latin translation, under the title of "Shaï an Sinsin, sive liber Metempsychosis," etc. He added to this a copy of a hieratic text of the same book found in Denon ("Voyage en Egypte," pl. 136).

A full analysis of this literary composition has also been given by Dr. Samuel Birch, in his Introduction to the "Rhind Papyri," London, 1863.

The Paris manuscript is as yet unpublished, but a copy of it will be produced ere long by the present translator. A few passages corrupted by the ancient scribe have been restored from copies of the same text, which are in the Egyptian Museum of the Louvre.

The "Book of Respirations" has a great analogy with that of the "Lamentations of Isis and Nephthys." It not only makes allusion to the formulæ and acts by means of which the resurrection is effected, but also treats of the life after death, thus greatly increasing our knowledge of the religious system of the ancient Egyptians.

THE BOOK OF RESPIRATIONS

1 Commencement of the Book of Respirations
    made by Isis for her brother Osiris,
    to give life to his soul,
    to give life to his body,
    to rejuvenate all his members anew;
    that he may reach the horizon with his father, the Sun;
    that his soul may rise to Heaven in the disk of the Moon;
    that his body may shine in the stars of Orion on the bosom of Nu-t;(663)
    in order that this may also happen
    to the Osiris, divine Father, Prophet of Ammon-Ra, King of the gods,
    Prophet of Khem, of Ammon-Ra, bull of his mother,
    in his great abode,
    Asar-aau, justified,
    Son of the Prophet of the same order, Nes-paut-ta-ti, justified,
    Conceal (it), conceal (it)!
    Let it not be read by anyone.
    It is profitable to the person who is in the divine Nether-World.
    He liveth in reality millions of times anew.

2 Words spoken:
    Hail to the Osiris N!(664) thou art pure;
    thy heart is pure,
    thy fore-part is purified,
    thy hind-part is cleansed,
    thy middle is in Bat(665) and natron.
    No member in thee is faulty.
    The Osiris N is (made) pure by the lotions
    from the Fields of Peace, at the North of the Fields of Sanehem-u.(666)
    The goddesses Uati (and) Suben have purified thee

at the eighth hour of the night
and at the eighth hour of the day.
Come Osiris N!
Thou dost enter the Hall of the Two Goddesses of Truth.
Thou art purified of all sin, of all crime.
Stone of Truth is thy name.

3 Hail to the Osiris N!
Thou, being very pure, dost enter the Lower Heaven.
The Two goddesses of Justice have purified thee in the Great Hall.
A purification hath been made to thee in the Hall of Seb.
Thy members have been purified in the Hall of Shu.(667)
Thou seest Rā in his setting,
(as) Atum(668) in the evening.
Ammon is near to thee, to give thee breath,
Ptah, to form thy members.
Thou dost enter the horizon with the Sun.
Thy soul is received in the bark Neshem(669) with Osiris.
Thy soul is divinized in the Hall of Seb.
Thou art justified forever and ever.

4 Hail to the Osiris N!
Thine individuality is permanent.
Thy body is durable.
Thy mummy doth germinate.
Thou art not repulsed from heaven, (neither from) earth.
Thy face is illuminated near the Sun.
Thy soul liveth near to Ammon.
Thy body is rejuvenated near to Osiris.
Thou dost breathe forever and ever.

5 Thy soul maketh thee offerings, each day,
of bread, of drinks, of oxen, of geese, of fresh water, of condiments.
Thou comest to justify it.
Thy flesh is on thy bones,
like unto thy form on earth.
Thou dost imbibe into thy body.
Thou eatest with thy mouth.
Thou receivest bread, with the souls of the gods.
Anubis doth guard thee.
He is thy protection.
Thou art not repulsed from the gates of the Lower Heaven.
Thoth, the doubly great, the Lord of Sesennu, cometh to thee.
He writeth for thee the Book of Respirations, with his own fingers.
Thy soul doth breathe forever and ever.
Thou dost renew thy form on earth, among the living.
Thou art divinized with the souls of the gods.
Thy heart is the heart of Rā
Thy members are the members of the great god.(670)
Thou livest forever and ever.

6 Hail to the Osiris N!
Ammon is with thee each day
to render thee life.
Apheru openeth to thee the right way.
Thou seest with thine eyes;
thou hearest with thine ears;
thou speakest with thy mouth;
thou walkest with thy legs.
Thy soul is divinized in Heaven,
to make all the transformations it desireth.
Thou makest the joy of the sacred Persea in An.

Thou awakenest each day.
Thou seest the rays of Rā.
Ammon cometh to thee with the breath of life.
He granteth to thee to breathe in thy coffin.
Thou comest on earth each day,
the Book of Respirations of Thoth being thy protection.
Thou breathest by it each day.
Thine eyes behold the rays of the disk.
Truth is spoken to thee before Osiris.
The formulæ of justification are on thy body.
Horus, the defender of his father, protecteth thy body.
He divinizeth thy soul as well as (those) of all the gods.
The soul of Rā giveth life to thy soul.
The soul of Shu filleth thy respiratory organs with soft breath.(671)

7 Hail to the Osiris N!
Thy soul doth breathe in the place thou lovest.
Thou art in the dwelling of Osiris, who resideth in the West.
Thy person is most pure.
Thou dost arrive in Abydos.
He (Osiris) filleth thy dwelling Hotep with provisions.

8 Hail to the Osiris N!
The gods of all Egypt come to thee.
Thou art guided toward the end of centuries.
Thy soul liveth.
Thou dost follow Osiris.
Thou breathest in Rusta.
Secret care is taken of thee by the Lord of Sati(672)
and by the great god.(673)
Thy body liveth in Tattu (and in) Nifur.
Thy soul liveth in Heaven forever.

9 Hail to the Osiris N!
Sechet prevaileth against what is injurious to thee.
Har-aa-hetu taketh care of thee.
Har-shet doth form thy heart.
Har-maa doth guard thy body.
Thou continuest in life, health (and) strength.
Thou art established upon thy throne in Ta-ser.
Come, Osiris N!
Thou appearest in thy form.
Strengthened by thine ornaments(674)
thou art prepared for life.
Thou remainest in a healthful state;
thou walkest, thou breathest everywhere.(675)
The Sun doth rise upon thine abode.
Like unto Osiris, thou breathest, thou livest by his rays.
Ammon-Ra giveth life to thee.
He doth enlighten thee by the Book of Respirations.
Thou dost follow Osiris and Horus, Lord of the sacred bark.
Thou art as the greatest of the gods among the gods.
Thy beautiful face liveth (in) thy children.
Thy name doth always prosper.
Come to the great temple in Tattu.
Thou wilt see him who resideth in the West,
in the Ka-festival.
Delicious is thy perfume as that of the blessed;
great thy name among the elect.

10 Hail to the Osiris N!
> Thy soul liveth by the Book of Respirations.
> Thou unitest thyself to the Book of Respirations.
> Thou dost enter the Lower Heaven;
> thine enemies are not (there).
> Thou art a divine soul in Tattu.(676)
> Thy heart is thine;
> it is (no longer) separated from thee.
> Thine eyes are thine;
> they open each day.

11a Words spoken by the gods who accompany Osiris, to the Osiris N:
> Thou dost follow Ra.
> Thou dost follow Osiris.
> Thy soul livest forever and ever.

11b Words spoken by the gods who dwell in the Lower Heaven (like) Osiris of the West, to the Osiris N:
> Let them open to him at the gates of the Lower Heaven.
> He is received(677) in the divine Nether-World,
> that his soul may live forever.
> He buildeth a dwelling in the divine Nether-World.
> He is rewarded.(678)
> He hath received the Book of Respirations,
> that he may breathe.

12 Royal offering to Osiris who resideth in the West,
> great god, Lord of Abydos,
> that he may give offerings
> of bread, of hak, of oxen, of geese, of wine, of the liquor aket, of bread Hotep,
> of good provisions of all kinds,
> to the Osiris N.
> Thy soul liveth.
> Thy body doth germinate,
> by order of Rā himself,
> without pain, without injury,
> like unto Ra forever and ever.

13 O Strider, coming out of An,(679)
> the Osiris N hath not committed any sin.
> O Mighty of the Moment, coming out of Kerau,
> the Osiris N hath not done any evil.
> O Nostril, coming out of Sesennu,(680)
> the Osiris N hath not been exacting.
> O Devourer of the Eye, coming out of Kerti,
> the Osiris N hath not obtained anything by theft.
> O Impure of visage, coming out of Rusta,
> the Osiris N hath not been angry.
> O Lion-gods, coming forth from heaven,
> the Osiris N hath not committed any sin by reason of hardness of heart(?)
> O Fiery-Eyed, coming out of Sechem,
> the Osiris N hath not been weak.

14 O ye gods who dwell in the Lower Heaven,
> hearken unto the voice of Osiris N.
> He is near unto you.
> There is no fault in him.
> No informer riseth up against him.
> He liveth in the truth.
> He doth nourish himself with truth.
> The gods are satisfied with all that he hath done.
> He hath given food to the hungry,

drink to the thirsty,
clothes to the naked.
He hath given the sacred food to the gods,
The funeral repasts to the pure Spirits.
No complaint hath been made against him before any of the gods.
Let him enter (then) into the Lower Heaven
without being repulsed.
Let him follow Osiris, with the gods of Kerti.
He is favored among the faithful,(681)
(and) divinized among the perfected.
Let him live!
Let his soul live!
His soul is received wherever it willeth.
(He) hath received the Book of Respirations,
that he may breathe with his soul,
(with) that of the Lower Heaven,
and that he may make any transformation at his will,
like (the inhabitants) of the West;(682)
that his soul may go wherever it desireth,
living on the earth forever and ever.

He is towed (like) Osiris into the Great Pool of Khons.
When he has retaken possession of his heart(683)
the Book of Respirations is concealed in (the coffin).
It is (covered) with writing upon Suten,
both inside and outside (and)
placed underneath his left arm,
evenly with his heart;...
When the Book has been made for him
then he breathes with the souls of the gods forever and ever.(684)

It is finished.

THE EPIC OF PENTA-OUR

Translated by C. W. Goodwin, M.A.

The commencement of the epic of Penta-our is wanting in the papyrus, and the end is also defective, but the date of the composition and the name of the writer have fortunately escaped. It appears to have been written in the ninth year of the King whose valor it celebrates. Champollion saw this papyrus, and had formed some notion of the nature of its contents, but to M. de Rougé belongs the honor of having first given a complete translation of it. This was published in the "Revue Contemporaine," 1856, p. 389. The scene of the exploit lies in the neighborhood of the city of Katesh,(685) the capital of the Hittites, which stood on the banks of a river named Anrata (or Aranta, as it is sometimes written), perhaps the Syrian Orontes. It appears, from the sculptures and inscriptions of Ibsamboul and the Theban Ramesseum, that Rameses II, in the fifth year of his reign, made an expedition into Asia to suppress a revolt of the Asiatic tribes headed by the Prince of Heth. Arrived near Katesh, upon the south side of the city, certain wandering Arabs came to inform him that the forces of the Hittites had retired toward the south, to the land of the Khirbou. These Arabs were, however, in the service of the enemy, and were sent with the intention of entrapping the Egyptians, the fact being that the Hittites and their allies were assembled in force to the north of the town. Rameses fell into the trap, and advanced to the northwest of Katesh while the body of his army proceeded to the south. Shortly after two Hittite spies were caught and brought to the King, and under the pressure of the bastonnade, confessed the true state of the affair. The prince of the Hittites had in the meantime executed a movement to the south of the city, and thus the King was cut off from the body of his troops, and only escaped destruction by the dashing exploit which his admiring subjects seem to have been never weary of commemorating, and which furnished Penta-our, the court poet, with a brilliant theme. A few extracts from the recital shall be given, based upon M. de Rougé's version, from which I venture in a few respects to deviate. The papyrus begins in the middle of a sentence, at the moment when the King had discovered his mistake.

"[The Prince of] Heth advanced with men and horses well armed [or full of provender?]: there were three men to each chariot.(686) There were gathered together all the swiftest men of the land of the vile Hittites, all furnished with arms ... and waited stealthily to the northwest of the fortress of Katesh. Then they fell upon the bowmen of Pharaoh, into the middle of them, as they marched along and did not expect a battle. The bowmen and the horsemen of his Majesty gave way before them. Behold they were near to Katesh, on the west bank of the river Anrata. Then was [fulfilled?] the saying of his Majesty. Then his Majesty, rising up like the god Mentou [Mars], undertook to lead on the attack. He seized his arms—he was like Bar [Baal] in his hour. The great horse which drew his Majesty his name was Nekhtou-em-Djom, of the stud of Rameses-Meiamen ... His Majesty halted when he came up to the enemy, the vile Hittites. He was alone by himself—there was no other with him in this sortie. His Majesty looked behind him and saw that he was intercepted by 2,500 horsemen in the way he had to go, by all the fleetest men of the prince of the base Hittites, and of many lands which were with him—of Artou [Aradus], of Maausou, of Patasa, of Kashkash, of Aroun, of Kadjawatana, of Khirbou, of Aktra, Katesh, and Raka. There were three men to each chariot, they were ... but there were neither captains, nor squires, nor leaders of bowmen, nor skirmishers [with the King], 'My archers and my horsemen forsook me, not one of them remained to fight with me.' Then said his Majesty, 'Where art thou now, my father Amen? Behold, does a father forget his son? But do I confide in my own strength? Walking or standing, is not my face toward thee? Do I not inquire the counsels of thy mouth? Do I not seek for thy mighty counsels, O thou great lord of Egypt, at whose approach the oppressors of the land are scattered? What now is the hope of these Aamou? Amen shall abase those who know not god. Have I not made for thee many and great buildings of stone? have I not filled thy temple with my spoils, building for thee a temple to last myriads of years? ... The whole earth unites to bring thee offerings ... [to enrich] thy domain. I have sacrificed to thee 30,000 oxen, with all kinds of sweet-scented herbs. Have I not put behind me those who do not thy will? ... I have built thee a house of great stones, erecting for thee eternal groves; I have brought for thee obelisks from Abou [Elephantine]; I have caused the everlasting stones to be fetched, launching for thee boats upon the sea, importing for thee the manufactures of the lands. When was it ever before said that such a thing was done? Confounded is every one who resists thy designs; blessed is every one who obeys thee, O Amen. That which thou doest is dear to my heart[?] I cry to thee, my father, Amen. I am in the midst of many unknown people gathered together from all lands. But I am alone by myself; there is none other with me. My bowmen and my horsemen have forsaken me; they were afraid; not one of them listened when I cried to them. Amen is more helpful to me than myriads of bowmen, than millions of horsemen, than tens of thousands of chosen youths, though they be all gathered together in one place. The arts of men prevail not, Amen is more powerful than they; they follow not the commands of thy mouth, O sun! Have I not sought out thy commands? have I not invoked thee from the ends of the earth?' "

This invocation is heard, and the King proceeds to make a vigorous charge against the enemy, who are scattered in all directions. The prince of the Hittites rallies, and succeeds in bringing them again to the combat, but they are repulsed by the King. It will be observed that sometimes the writer himself speaks, but generally the narrative is put into the mouth of the King—a poetical artifice which gives a certain liveliness to the composition—

" 'I ran toward them, like the god Mentou, I fleshed my hand upon them in the space of a moment[?]. I smote them, I slew them, so that one of them cried to another, saying, "It is no man" [superhuman]. Mighty was he who was among them, Soutech, the most glorious. Baal was in my limbs; why was every enemy weak? his hand was in all my limbs. They knew not how to hold the bow and the spear. As soon as they saw him, they fled far away with speed, but his Majesty was upon them like a greyhound. He slew them, so that they escaped not.' "

The King's squire or armor-bearer is seized with terror, and conjures his master to fly. The King comforts him; and after charging the enemy six times, returns victorious from the field. Rameses, on rejoining his troops, addresses a long tirade to his captains upon their cowardice, and enlarges upon his own valor without any modest scruples. In the evening the rest of the troops came dropping in, and were surprised to find the whole country strewed with the bodies of the dead. The whole army joins in singing the praises of the courageous leader—

" 'Hail to the sword, thanks to the bold warrior, strengthener of hearts, who deliverest thy bowmen and thy horsemen, son of Toum, subduing the land of the Hittites with thy victorious sword. Thou art King of victories; there is none like thee, a King fighting for his soldiers in the day of battle. Thou art magnanimous, the first in battle. The whole world joined together cannot resist thee. Thou art the mighty conqueror, in the face of thy army. The whole earth falls down before thee saying homage. Thou rulest Egypt, thou chastisest the foreigners, thou crushest, thou bowest the back of these Hittites forever.' Then said his Majesty to his bowmen and his horsemen, likewise his captains, 'Ye who did not fight, behold none of you have done well, in that ye left me alone among the enemy. The captains of the vanguard, the sergeants of the infantry, came not to help me. I fought against the myriads of the land alone. I had the horses Nechtou-em-Djom and Becht-herouta; they were obedient to the guidance of my hand, when I was alone by myself in the midst of the enemy. Therefore I grant to them to eat their corn in the presence of Ra continually, when I am in the gate of the palace, on account of their having been found in the midst of the enemy: and as for the armor-bearer who remained with me, I bestow upon him my arms, together with the things which were upon me, the habiliments of war.' Behold his Majesty wore them in his great victory, overthrowing myriads assembled together with his conquering sword."

The battle is renewed the next day, and the Hittites are thoroughly routed. An envoy from the chief is now announced, suing for mercy. Rameses acts the part of a magnanimous conqueror, and grants pardon to the repentant rebels. He then returns peaceably to Egypt, leaving the terror of his arms in all the countries of the East.

At the end of the last page of the manuscript are the date and dedication, unfortunately somewhat mutilated. The writer Penta-our dedicates it, not to the King, but to a chief librarian, probably Amen-em-an, with whom he carried on a correspondence. This poem was so highly appreciated by the King that he caused it to be engraved in hieroglyphics upon the walls of one of his palaces, where some remains of it may be still seen. If the date be correctly read, it would appear to have been written four years after the event it celebrates, and, notwithstanding the exaggerated style of adulation which pervades it, there can be little doubt that some such occurrence as that which it represents really took place.

FOOTNOTES

1 I.e., the mountain of sunset.
2 I.e., Maāt.
3 The following petition, "Oh, grant thou unto me a path," etc., is written once only, and at the end of the Litany, but I think it is clear that it was intended to be repeated after each of the nine addresses. This is proved by the Saïte Recension (see Lepsius, op. cit, Bl. 5) where the words, "Grant thou the sweet breath of the north wind to the Osiris Auf-ānkh," are written in two places and are intended to be said after each of the ten addresses above them.
4 I.e., "the place where nothing groweth," the name of a district in the underworld.
5 The name of the sanctuary of the goddess Nekhebet in Upper Egypt, the Eileithyiapolis of the Greeks.
6 I.e., the two lands Atebui, which were situated one on each side of the celestial Nile.
7 I.e., the land on each side of the Red Sea and on the coast of Africa.
8 I.e., "Lady of life," a name of Isis.
9 I.e., the mountain of the sunset.
10 I.e., the mountain of the sunset.
11 I.e., An-rut-f, the place where nothing groweth.
12 I.e., the mountain of sunrise, but the scribe appears to have written "Baakha" instead of "Manu."
13 I.e., the Sun and the Moon.
14 I.e., the Sun and Moon.
15 I.e., the dead.
16 The name of the deceased is wanting.
17 I.e., "Osiris, Governor of Amentet."
18 Pe and Tepu were two famous sanctuaries of northern Egypt.
19 I.e., An-rut-f.
20 "Ab" is undoubtedly the "heart," and "hat" is the region wherein is the heart; the word may be fairly well rendered by "breast," though the pericardium is probably intended.
21 "Erpat," i.e., "tribal chief."
22 The Papyrus of Mes-em-neter (Naville, "Todtenbuch," Bd. II. p. 92) adds: "His heart goeth forth to take up its abode in his body, his heart is renewed before the gods, and he hath gained the mastery over it."
23 The words within brackets are from the Papyrus of Mes-em-neter.
24 I.e., the god of the "Large Face."
25 I.e., the deceased.
26 The words within brackets are translated from the Papyrus of Nebseni (sheet 4).
27 I.e., Mycerinus, a king of the fourth dynasty.
28 I.e., "He of two teeth" (or two horns); the Saïte Recension (Lepsius, op. cit., Bl. 16) reads "Bent," i.e., "ape."
29 I.e., "Thy face is of right and truth."
30 We should probably add the word "tep" and read "Tep tu-f," "He that is upon his hill," i.e., Anubis.
31 The Theban texts mention four crocodiles only.
32 So far back as 1867 the late Dr. Birch identified the animal "maftet" with the lynx.
33 Read, "the lord of the city of Shennu" i.e., of Kom Ombos.
34 Or, "I report [my] message to Nebes" (or Nebses).
35 The two opponent goddesses, or Isis and Nephthys(?).
36 These words are from the Papyrus of Ra.
37 The words within brackets are supplied from the Papyrus of Mes-em-neter.
38 I.e., The "land of cold and refreshing water."

39 Literally, "eat."
40 A king of the first dynasty. See also the rubric to the longer version of the 64th from the Papyrus of Nu, infra, p. 47.
41 These words are added from the Papyrus of Nebseni.
42 From the Papyrus of Nu, sheet 13.
43 From Papyrus of Nu, sheet 21.
44 He was the son of Cheops, the builder of the Great Pyramid at Gîzeh.
45 Here follows the text of Chapter of "Preserving the Heart," page 25.
46 I.e., the souls of Horus and Rā.
47 This Rubric is taken from the Papyrus of Thenna (see Naville, op. cit., Bd. II. p. 153).
48 From the Papyrus of Ani (Brit. Mus. No. 10,470, sheet 6).
49 The words in brackets are supplied from Naville, op. cit., Bd. II. p. 158.
50 Literally, "Thou hast given unto me."
51 The variants are Aahet At, Aahet Ateh, and one papyrus gives the words, "I am the great god"; see Naville, op. cit., Bd. II. p. 167.
52 Literally, "I flew."
53 I believe that "Turtle" is the correct translation.
54 Literally, "dilated with years."
55 Added from the Papyrus of Nebseni.
56 Added from the Papyrus of Nebseni.
57 The Papyrus of Nebseni has, "make thou me to see my soul and my shade."
58 This rubric is taken from the Papyrus of Ani, sheet 17.
59 The Papyrus of Ani contains what are, apparently, two versions of this chapter.
60 I.e., the "Governor of Amenti," or Osiris.
61 This title is taken from the Saïte Recension.
62 I.e., the four pillars at the south, north, west, and east of heaven upon which the heavens were believed to rest.
63 In the Saïte Recension this chapter is about twice as long as it is in the Theban Recension.
64 The words in brackets are from the Papyrus of Nebseni.
65 Or, "I am at peace with the god of the city."
66 I.e., "Existence in Peace," the name of the first large section of the Elysian Fields.
67 The name of a pool in the second section of the Elysian Fields.
68 The name of a pool in the first section of the Elysian Fields.
69 The name of a pool in the second section of the Elysian Fields.
70 The name of a district in the third section of the Elysian Fields.
71 The name of a pool in the first section of the Elysian Fields.
72 The name of a pool in the third section of the Elysian Fields.
73 The name of a pool in the third section of the Elysian Fields.
74 A name of the city of Mendes, the metropolis of the sixteenth nome of Lower Egypt.
75 I.e., he lost his temper and raged.
76 I.e., Cusæ, the metropolis of the fourteenth nome of Upper Egypt.
77 The words in brackets are from the Papyrus of Neb-qet (sheet 3).
78 A fuller title of this chapter is, "The Chapter of knowing the name of Osiris, and of going into and of coming forth from Re-stau."
79 For the text see Naville, op. cit., Bd. I. Bl. 130.
80 The words in brackets are from the Papyrus of Amen-em-heb. See Naville, op. cit., Bd. II. p. 267.
81 The Papyrus of Mes-em-neter adds, "bringing right unto thee the divine being who loveth her."
82 I.e., Heliopolis, Mendes or Busiris, Heracleopolis, Abydos, Panopolis, and Sennu (a city near Panopolis).
83 The words in brackets are from the Saïte Recension (see Lepsius, op. cit., Bl. 46).
84 I.e., the "Land of the inundation," a name of Egypt.
85 In other papyri this chapter is called: (1) "The Chapter of going into the Hall of double Maāti;" (2) "The Chapter of [the Hall of] double Maāti and of knowing what is therein;" and (3) "The Book of entering into the Hall of double Maāti." See Naville, op. cit., Bd. II. p. 275.
86 Variant, "I have not caused misery, I have not caused affliction."
87 The words in brackets are added from the Papyrus of Amen-neb (Brit. Mus. No. 9,964). See Naville, op. cit., Bd. II. p. 282.
88 Variant, "I have not defrauded the gods of their chosen meat offerings."
89 I.e., the month called by the Copts Mekhir, the sixth month of the Egyptian year.
90 These words are added from the Papyrus of Nebseni.
91 These words are added from the Papyrus of Ani.

92 A city near Memphis.

93 The "Qerti," or caverns out of which flowed the Nile, were thought to be situated between Aswān and Philæ.

94 Variant, Neha-hra.

95 Variant, "like fire."

96 I.e., the ninth nome of Lower Egypt, the capital of which was Per-Ausar or Busiris.

97 The "City of the Sycamore," a name of a city of Upper Egypt.

98 The thirteenth nome of Lower Egypt.

99 The metropolis of the nineteenth nome of Upper Egypt.

100 I.e., "lost my temper and become angry."

101 These words are added from Brit. Mus. No. 9,905. Other papyri introduce the address with the words: (1) "To be said when [the deceased] cometh forth victorious from the Hall of double Maāti;" (2) "To be said when he cometh forth to the gods of the underworld;" (3) "The words which [are to be said] after the Hall of double Maāati."

102 The ordinary reading is, "For I have heard the word which was spoken by the Ass with the Cat."

103 A people who dwelt, probably, on the northeast frontier of Egypt, and who have been by some identified with the Phœnicians.

104 These words are added from the Papyrus of Nebseni.

105 The Papyrus of Nu continues: " 'I will not open unto thee and I will not let thee pass by me,' saith the Guardian of this door, 'unless thou tellest [me] my name'; 'Ox of Seb' is thy name." See above, l. 30.

106 Here the Papyrus repeats a passage given above.

107 The words "sema-kua" are superfluous.

108 After "Osiris" a Paris papyrus adds, "He shall come forth in whatsoever form he is pleased to appear as a living soul forever and ever."

109 This chapter has no title either in the Theban or in the Saïte Recension.

110 The words in brackets are added from Brit. Mus. No. 9,913.

111 I.e., districts or divisions of the underworld.

112 A name of the city of Abydos.

113 "The Book of making the soul to live forever. [To be recited] on the day of embarking in the boat of Rā to pass over to the chiefs of flame." See Naville, op. cit., Bd. II. p. 338.

114 Read "Shu" instead of "maat."

115 Or, "images."

116 Or, "The chapter of making the way into heaven nigh unto Rā."

117 In the Saïte Recension (see Lepsius, op. cit., Bl. 54) the house is said to be "in the underworld."

118 Another papyrus adds the words, "I have advanced, and behold, I have not been found light, and the Balance is empty of my affair."

119 The Papyrus of Nebseni has, "The Osiris Nebseni is the lord of transformations in the presence of the hawk of gold."

120 The Papyrus of Ani has "seven cubits."

121 The words "or thy father" are from the Papyrus of Ani.

122 These words are from the Brocklehurst Papyrus (see Naville, op. cit., Bd. II. p. 334). There are three copies of this rubric extant, and no one of them is complete!

123 In the Papyrus of Nebseni the title of this chapter reads: "The Chapter of embarking in the boat of Rā and of being with those who are in his following."

124 Read "god Osiris"?

125 Added from the Papyrus of Nebseni.

126 In the Papyrus of Nebseni the deceased is here addressed.

127 This name, frequently found in the letters, is the Egyptian "Neb-mat-ra," or Amenophis III.

128 As the Amorite "z" or "s" seems sometimes to represent the Hebrew "sh," this name might be compared with the Philistine "Achish."

129 "Katna" is the present Katanah, on the south of Hermon, west of Damascus.

130 Others read "Nuhasse." It was a Hittite country, and appears to be that of Mer'ash, under the Taurus, where a number of important Hittite remains are found (see especially B. 31, 32).

131 Throughout the letters the enemy is always called a "slave," a "slave dog," or "son of a dog," as also in Egyptian texts.

132 Where breaks occur they are due to fractures of the tablet.

133 This appears, as throughout the letters, to apply to the King of Egypt. All the Egyptian kings were regarded as descendants of gods, and are so addressed in Egyptian records.

134 "Aidugama" does not appear to be a Semitic name, but, as we should expect in Hittite, it is Mongol, and compares with "Akkadian," as meaning "the victorious lord." He is called "Edagama" by the King of Tyre (B. M. 30), who mentions his fighting with Neboyapiza, and Aziru's also.

135 Probably "Lapana" is Lybo, now Lebweh, north of Baalbek.

136 Probably R'aith (or R'ais), on the east side of the Buka'ah plain, east of Zahleh, on the way from the Hittite country.

137 Perhaps should read "Zinaar" for "Senaar," the Shinar of the Bible. Merash and Ni have been noted above.

138 This word "bitati" always applies (and it is used very often) to Egyptian soldiers. It seems to be an Egyptian word. Compare "pet" ("foot") and "petet" ("to invade or march") in Egyptian.

139 Huba is identified by Dr. Bezold with the land of Hobah (Gen. xiv. 15), which was at the "entering in" north of Damascus. The "entering in" here and at Hamath means a pass between hills leading to the city. It has been objected that Hobah would be "Ubatu" in Assyrian; but this fails in view of the detailed topography, which shows that Dr. Bezold was right. The Hebrew heh is often replaced by Aleph or vau in Aramaic.

140 The land Am or Amma, several times mentioned, appears to be the Old Testament land of Ham, in northern Bashan, near Damascus (Gen. xiv. 5). The Hebrew is spelled with the soft aspirate, not the hard guttural. It may perhaps be connected with the name of the "Amu" of Egyptian records.

141 Damascus according to Dr. Bezold.

142 This name can be read "Namyapiza" or "Zimyapiza," but probably means "Nebo is holy," Nebo being a well-known deity.

143 Gidisi or Cidisi is apparently Kadesh of the Hittites—now Kades on the Orontes—north of the city of Neboyapiza. It is called "Cidsi" by the King of Tyre (B. M. 30), and "Ciidsa" in the proclamation (92 B.).

144 "Paka" is one of the words used to designate Egyptian residents or generals. It seems to be Egyptian, and simply means "Pa-ka" ("chief man").

145 Ammusi might be the ancient name of Emesa, now Homs, immediately north of Kadesh.

146 "Elohim" is in the plural, as several scholars have remarked. It often applies to the King of Egypt.

147 "Khazi" is evidently Ghazzeh, near the south end of the Baalbek plain, south of the Damascus road.

148 This is doubtful, as the text is broken, and only gives "Belgi ..." Baal Gad was, as I have attempted recently to show, probably near 'Ain Ju-deideh, on the north of Hermon, and close to the great pass.

149 "Maguzi," or Mukhzi, is probably Mekseh, on the Damascus road, west of Stora.

150 May be read "Yanuamma." It seems to be M'araba, north of Damascus, which agrees with the context. The great pass mentioned here in connection with Damascus was apparently that by which the main road from the west came down the Barada at Abila. This is the "entering in" to Damascus, which (Gen. xiv. 15) was in the land of Hobah. This agrees with the position of Neboyapiza's town Kamid, west of Baal Gad, and to the west of the pass. The scribe here wrote "east of me," and corrected to "behind me."

151 Probably not Ashtoreth Carnaim, which is mentioned in another letter, but rather Stora, in the Baalbek plain, northwest of Baal Gad. Arzaya's town seems to have been Mekseh, west of Stora (125 B. M.).

152 "Buzruna" is probably Batruna, on the mountain west of the west end of the pass, and immediately east of Baal Gad (perhaps mentioned again in the fragment 205 B.).

153 "Khalavunni," or Halabunni, is the Helbon of the Bible (Ezek. xxvii. 18), now Helbon, north of Damascus, and five miles north of the middle of the pass. It must have been an important city because of the term "King." It was noted for wine, not only in Ezekiel's time, but, as Strabo mentions, the kings of Persia brought wine from Chalybon.

154 "Gizza" is perhaps the important town Jezzin, in the Lebanon, southwest of Kamid, unless it be Jizeh, in Bashan, between Edrei and Bozrah.

155 "Saddu" is perhaps Nebi Shit, south of Baalbek, or possibly, though less probably, Sh'ait, south of Kamid, on the southwest slope of Hermon.

156 "Cumidi," or Kamid, was important as a central station between Damascus and the coast cities of Sidon and Beirut.

157 Or, perhaps, "hard-pressed."

158 "Mikhiza," perhaps the same as Maguzi, written by another scribe—the modern Mekseh, as given above. "Maguzi" might be otherwise transliterated as "Mukhzi."

159 "Tubakhi" is the Tabukhai of the "Travels of an Egyptian" in the reign of Rameses II (Chabas, p. 313), mentioned with Kadesh on Orontes, and is the Tibhath of the Bible (1 Chron. xviii. 8), otherwise Berothai. It may perhaps be the present Kefr Dubbeh, west of Baalbek, and south of Kadesh,

while Berothai is thought to be the present Brithen (see 2 Sam. viii. 8), a few miles south of Baalbek. The letter shows Aziru in league with the Hittites. David conquered these cities from the King of Damascus.

160 Dr. Sayce calls this "the fields of Bashan"; probably, when taken with the next letters, we may place the site at Zora, in Bashan, now Ezra. De Rougé and Mariette showed that Thothmes III conquered Bashan.

161 "Gubbu" is perhaps Jubbata, on the south side of Hermon, near the places mentioned in the next letter.

162 Yankhamu, an Egyptian commander, appears in these letters in all parts of the country, from the extreme south to the north, and in Phœnicia as well as in Bashan. His name does not seem to be Semitic.

163 This letter does not say who the enemies were or in which direction they advanced. Perhaps "Bikhisi" may be regarded as the present "'Abbaseh" (by inversion of the guttural), which is fifteen miles southwest of Damascus, near the main road to the town of Jabesh, whence the letter comes.

164 The word "rabizi," which is here made equivalent to "zukini," gives great difficulty. In Hebrew the root means "to rest," and the word is still applied in Palestine to resting of flocks. "Zukini" appears, as Dr. Bezold points out, to be the same as the Phœnician word "Soken" (which has exactly the required letters); but the meaning of this also is doubtful. Renan translates it either "inhabitant" or "senator." The word occurs in the Bible (1 Kings i. 2, 4; Ezek. xxviii. 14), with the meaning also doubtful, but the root means "to cherish." Perhaps "friends" suits best the various recurrences.

165 This word seems to mean "glory of the sun," the Egyptian "Khu-en-Aten." The explanation throws light on a difficult passage in a letter from Elishah (B. M. 5). If "Khu-en-Aten" (Amenophis IV) is intended, he may have been commander while still only a prince, since the events seem to belong to the reign of Amenophis III.

166 "Astarti" seems here to be Ashtoreth Carnaim, the present "Tell Ashterah."

167 "Udumu," now Dameh, the Dametha of Maccabean times.

168 "Aduri"—Edrei in Bashan, now Edhr'a.

169 "Araru"—'Ar'ar, nine miles southeast of Ashtoreth.

170 "Meispa"—Ramath-Mizpah of Basnan, now Remtheh.

171 "Macdalim," probably Mejdel Shems, east of Banias.

172 "Khini"—Hineh, south of Hermon, near the last.

173 "Zaar"—Zora of Bashan, now Ezra.

174 "Yabisi"—Yabis, a few miles northwest of the last.

175 The Egyptians would cross the Jordan near Megiddo, and come from the southwest to oppose an enemy on the north and east, and reach 'Abbâseh, on the north, later than Yabis.

176 Saskhi is probably S'as'a, east of Banias, and northwest of Yabis.

177 Lupackhallu, a non-Semitic Hittite name. As a Mongol word, "the very swift."

178 Zitatna was King of Accho—a somewhat similar name; but probably the King of Arvad is meant, as appears later.

179 This letter belongs to a late period in the war, since Ullaza has been taken. It is given here as referring to the land of Ham. It may very well have been written after Ribadda, the King of Gebal, left the city (see 71 B.).

180 "Ammia," mentioned again, appears to be Amyun south of Simyra.

181 "Ardata" is Ardi, near the last.

182 Kefr Khullis, north of Gebal, agrees with the required position for Ullaza, which is mentioned often.

183 Nariba is Nereb, on the Euphrates, in the Hittite country.

184 An Egyptian name; perhaps to be compared with "han" ("kind") in Egyptian. An envoy of this name was sent to Dusratta, King of Armenia, by Amenophis III, as an "interpreter" (21 B.).

185 Perhaps the Hittite King of Kadesh, or some other city.

186 Or perhaps "oil."

187 Dodo in the Bible (1 Chron. xi. 12), from the same root as "David." He was not really Aziru's father, but apparently a friend in Egypt.

188 "Beiti beitac" is still a polite phrase of welcome in Palestine.

189 The text is clear, but the epigram is not. He appears to mean the King of Egypt when speaking of his gods, as also a few lines lower.

190 Meaning the King of Egypt.

191 "Khai" is also an Egyptian name, meaning "distinguished" in that language. He is perhaps the "Khaia" of another letter by Ribadda (57 B.). It would seem that his embassy to Aziru had occurred between the first and second visits of the envoy Khanni.

192 Mer'ash was in the west of the Hittite country, seventy-five miles northwest of Tunep. The distance fits well, since thirty-seven and one-half miles may be considered a forced march.

193 We cannot rely on Aziru's protestations. If Khatib was a Hittite King, it is certain that both were intriguing against Egypt.

194 Probably the pass in the valley of the 'Afrin River, near Kyrrhus, twenty miles north of Tunip, is meant, being on the direct road to Mer'ash.

195 "Abuca" ("your father") might be understood in the sense in which it is used every day in the East, where abûc means, "God curse your father!"

196 Ni was to the east of Aziru's country near Tunip.

197 "Khat-ib" may mean "Hittite hero." The name of the Hittites means probably "the confederates"; and the sign used on Hittite monuments for the nation seems to be that which represents two allies facing each other.

198 Abdasherah, as Dr. Sayce points out, means the servant of the goddess Asherah ("the grove" of the Bible), and this is rendered certain by the sign for Deity prefixed in one instance. It has no connection with the name of Ashtoreth.

199 An Egyptian name, "Pa-Khemt" or "Pa-Khent," meaning "very strong" (see B. M. 24, Pakhamnata). It appears from Ribadda's letter that the station of this Paka was Simyra, and apparently the Amorites killed him later on.

200 The word "Gur" is used in these letters as in the Bible, and, like the Arab "Jâr," to mean a man of one tribe or race protected by a powerful tribe or person of another country.

201 In each case "gate" might be rendered "port," as both of the cities had famous ports.

202 The word "Khazanu," commonly used in these letters for a ruling class, apparently native, and in communication with the "Paka," or "head man," who was Egyptian, appears to come from a root which means "to treasure." The word "Khazanutu" appears to mean "a government."

203 "Canaan" in these letters, as on the Phœnician coins and in the Bible, is used in its strict sense as a geographical term for the "lowlands" of Phœnicia and Philistia.

204 "Pisyari" appears to be a Hittite name, like the "Pisiris" of an Assyrian inscription (Schrader), being the Mongol "bisir" ("rich"), with the indefinite nominative in s, which marks the Hittite as a non-Semitic tongue. The other names are also apparently non-Semitic, and may refer to Hittites.

205 "Pabahaa" is perhaps the "Papaa," conquered by Thothmes III (Karnak List, No. 296), which was somewhere in North Syria, not far from Tunip. The wickedness of this chief is said to have caused the war.

206 Gutium, mentioned in Assyrian texts, was a country on the northeast, near the Caucasus. It has been compared with the word "Goim," for "Gentiles," in Hebrew. Perhaps "Jebel Judi" ("Ararat") is intended, being Dusratta's country allied to Egypt.

207 Probably 'Arkah, a well-known Phœnician city north of Tripoli, but south of Simyra (Gen. x. 17). Aziru killed its king (91 B.).

208 "Yapaaddu" ("Adonis is beautiful") is often mentioned again. He (see 61 B.) fell into the hands of Aziru, and seems to have been a king of one of the cities near Simyra, apparently Sigata. This letter was probably written about the time of the siege of Tyre, at a late period in the war.

209 Ugariti is mentioned in a letter from Tyre (B. M. 30) in a connection which shows that it was the present Akrith, between Tyre and Accho.

210 "Sigata" appears to be Shakkah, north of the great pass of Shakkah (Theouprosopon), where the King of Gebal was defeated by Aziru.

211 "Ambi" is now 'Aba, immediately east of Shakkah.

212 Simyra was on the low hills above the sea-plains, by the river Eleutherus.

213 The last words explain how the letter got to Egypt.

214 These ships of the men of Misi are mentioned by Ribadda as failing in an attempt to assist him. We may, perhaps, understand Egyptian ships, and compare the Egyptian name "Mesti" applied to part of the Delta.

215 From Dusratta's great Hittite letter (27 B.) it appears that the King of the Minyans, whose country was called Mitani, west of Lake Van, in Armenia, claimed to be King of all the Hittites; and this is what appears to be here intended. In other letters he is mentioned among the invaders.

216 Arada, a city mentioned again as assisting Aziru with ships, appears to be Aradus, the Arvad of the Bible, now Er Rûad, the island town north of Simyra.

217 "Gula" is perhaps the town of Jûneh, north of Beirût, on the way to Gebal.

218 "Ammiya" is Amyun, north of Gebal; and "Ardata" is Ardi near the preceding.

219 Arpad is the city close to Tennib, which is mentioned in the Bible in several passages (2 Kings xvii. 34; xix. 13; Isa. x. 9; Jer. xlix. 23, etc.), now Tell Erfûd. It is remarkable that Aleppo is not mentioned in this correspondence, for it is referred to in Egyptian texts.

220 "Ribadda" (as the name is spelled in some of the letters in syllables) may mean "child of Adonis." Compare the Chaldee "Ribah" for "girl," in the feminine. That "Adda" was Adonis seems to be derivable from the name "Adoram" (2 Sam. xx. 20), otherwise Adoniram (1 Kings iv. 6).

221 "Gebal," now "Jubeil," was apparently the chief city of Phœnicia. Its goddess Baalath is mentioned in the famous inscription of Yehumelec (about 800 B.C.), found in the ruins of Gebal. She is also mentioned in the "Travels of an Egyptian" (Chabas, p. 312).

222 Hamath was half-way from Aziru's country to that of Ribadda.

223 A name very like Jeremiah.

224 "Mitana," the later Matiene, Dusratta, its king, claimed to rule the Hittites. The Amorites joined this league.

225 The region called "Casi" in the inscription of Usurtasen I (Brugsch, "Hist.," i., p. 139) was in Upper Egypt, and the Cush of the Bible is apparently intended—a very vague term for the southern deserts from the Euphrates to Nubia. There were, however, Cushites also in Babylonia. In the present case the Cassites who lived on the Euphrates, east of the Hittites, and who were Mongols, are probably intended.

226 Literally "boys." It seems often in these letters to be used as the word "weled" ("a boy") is still used in Syria to mean "a fellow," applied often to very old men.

227 This letter shows that the war lasted several years, over which the Gebal letters (written by three or four different scribes) extend; that the attack on Sidon preceded the taking of Gebal; and that Ribadda was not deceived by Amorite promises, knowing their co-operation with their Mongol allies of Armenia and the Hittite country.

228 The letter in question may have been the proclamation against Aziru given above.

229 "Milukha," or Meroe, in Assyrian inscriptions means, according to Dr. Brugsch, Nubia.

230 This perhaps refers to Khanni's proclamation already given, and to the Khai who had been sent at an earlier period to Aziru. The rebels are named in the proclamation of the later embassy, which we thus see to have had no effect. An envoy without a military force behind him usually fails.

231 Durubli is probably the city which the Greeks called Tripoli, the largest town between Simyra and Gebal. There is a village called Turbul, on the northeast of Tripoli (Trâblus).

232 "Kau Pa-ur," Egyptian words in the plural. "Kau" signifies "men," and "Pa-ur" (as in the letter from Jerusalem, B. 103) means "very important."

233 Probably the "Pakhanata" (97 B.) who was the "Paka," or chief, of whom Abdasherah speaks in the letter about the town of Ullaza, near Gebal. He seems to have been the resident in Simyra (B. 80).

234 "Abur" is perhaps Beit-Abura, in the valley north of the great pass Theouprosopon, between Gebal and Tripoli. The enemy had not as yet forced the pass.

235 The second sign is doubtful, and the place does not suggest identification (see 60 B.).

236 This agrees with the Jerusalem letters, as showing that the troops had been withdrawn to Egypt. Amenophis sent commissioners and summoned native levies, but does not appear to have been able to send Egyptian forces.

237 The name "Saarti" perhaps survives in that of the Sha'arah district of Lebanon, immediately south of Simyra, and near Yapaaddu's town of Sigata (Shakkah).

238 In Assyria we find the "measure of Istar."

239 The Berbers are mentioned in Egyptian texts as inhabitants of Upper Egypt.

240 "Khaia," now in Egypt, had no doubt already become known to Ribadda as an envoy.

241 A god Sausbe is mentioned in Dusratta's Hittite letter.

242 Sigata (Shakkah) was just outside the great pass between Batrûn and Tripoli.

243 Ambi ('Aba) was close to the last.

244 Only—rari is left, which Dr. Bezold thinks refers to Amenophis IV; but it is doubtful if this letter can be placed so late.

245 "Kappa" is Keffa. The plain of Keffa is close to Amyun, north of the great pass of Theouprosopon (Shakkah). Amyun follows at once.

246 "Batruna" is the well-known town Batrûn, the "Botrys" of classical writers, which lies south of the wild pass of Râs Shakkah, where apparently one of the battles of the war occurred (22 B. M.). When the pass was taken, Batrûn seems still to have held out with Gebal, being no doubt provisioned by sea.

247 "Kalbi" is Kelbata, in the heart of the great pass. I visited all these places in 1881.

248 In this case the modern name "Akka" is nearer to the spelling of these letters than is the Hebrew. This is the case with Shiloh and other important towns, showing the Canaanite extraction of the modern peasantry in Palestine. The Hebrews hardly ever renamed towns, and the nomenclature preserves the ancient Canaanite forms found in the lists of Thothmes III a century earlier than these letters. Many towns were named from Canaanite and Philistine gods (Shamash, Dagon, etc.), and the forms of the names in the Karnak lists are Aramaic, and not Hebrew.

249 "Patzil" I understand to be equivalent to the Arabic "Fadl," meaning to do pleasure or honor to a person.

250 The Amorite chief had more than one son, as is clear in some cases. Benmabenat (or Bumabuat) was Aziru's brother.

251 Perhaps the name survives in that of the river Kadisha, near Tripoli.

252 Ardata (Ardi), Ambi ('Aba), and Sigata (Shakkah) were north of the pass; Yahlia, representing I'al, rather farther north than the others.

253 Ullaza (Kefr Khullis) was close to Batrûn, on the south.

254 "Caphar Yazu," or Alu-yazu, seems to be Kefr Yashit, near the others.

255 Perhaps "Takheda" of another letter (58 B.).

256 See letter 71 B. The sign has the meaning "oracle," "prophet." No doubt Ribadda had his diviners, like the kings of Assyria in later times.

257 No. 53 B. is another short letter, much injured, which mentions Batrûn; and in this a town called "Sina" is apparently noticed, which, if the broken tablet can be so read, would be "Kefr Zina." In 54 B. a city "Zina" occurs, but seems to be a clerical error for "Sidon." The land of Mitana is also mentioned in 53 B.

258 Neboyapiza had his own difficulties, as appears from his letters (96 B., 142 B., 43 B. M.).

259 Zimridi of Sidon is mentioned as a fugitive, while Gebal still held out. Aziru marched from (ina) Gebal, no doubt, to attack the south. In later ages the shore cities often held out while invaders from the North marched on Egypt.

260 Amanabba was not really his father; it is a title of courtesy. His father was Rabzabi (81 B., 82 B.), and Amanappa is an Egyptian name. A certain captain Amenemhib has left an account of his services in North Syria, at Aleppo, Carchemish, Kadesh, and at Ni, where he hunted elephants; but this is supposed to have been a century earlier. The site of Ni is settled by these letters and by the Karnak lists as being in Mesopotamia, and there is a picture of an elephant among the Asiatic spoils of Thothmes III. It is very curious to find elephants so far west in Asia at this period.

261 Probably "outside" means north of the pass, and Ribadda made the serious military mistake of defending his pass from outside instead of inside.

262 This would seem to have been about the time of the proclamation against Aziru, or rather earlier.

263 "Sapi" is probably the famous fortress Safita, northwest of Simyra.

264 The reinforcements were expected by sea, no doubt in the ships of the Misi, or Delta men, the soldiers being Nubians from near Tell Amarna, which was 180 miles south of Memphis.

265 Or Zabanba. Perhaps this is the Subandi, who writes letters from an unknown town.

266 King of Beirût (B. M. 26, 27).

267 This translation is confirmed by the independent letter of Ribadda's friend Ammunira (B. M. 36).

268 Egada is no doubt the land of Ikatai mentioned in the "Travels of an Egyptian" (Chabas, p. 312); it there occurs with Aleppo and the country of the Hittites. In the letter of the Hittite Prince of Rezeph (north of Palmyra) we hear of his country as Egait (B. 10). Rezeph was not far south of Tiphsah, on the Euphrates, and southeast of Aleppo. Bikhuru is, however, mentioned (18 B. M.) in connection with the town of Cumidi.

269 I misread this name at first. The Amorite chief seems to have had five sons including Aziru and (p. 224) Ben-mabenat (or Bumabula).

270 The paragraphs are marked off in many of the letters by the word "sacunu" ("pause").

271 "Taratzi" may perhaps be Tarsus. Baal Tarzi is the legend on Phœnician coins of that city. Its king naturally would have a common border with Abdasherah on the north, if his fortresses (or land) were outside the northern Lebanon, which was the Amorite country, and he was therefore regarded as a possible ally.

272 Comparing the letters from Beirût and Sidon (27 B. M., 90 B.) it will be seen that the city whose freemen were on the side of Aziru was Sidon.

273 If Ukri be the right reading, the town of 'Akkar in Lebanon, east of Tripoli, would be probable. It gives its name to the district of Jebel 'Akkâr, and is at the source of the river 'Akkâr, which agrees with the mention of the "waters."

274 "Maar"(ah) is probably the Mearah of the Bible (Josh. xiii. 4), now "el Mogheiriyeh," six miles northeast of Sidon. This conquest may have just preceded the fall of Sidon.

275 Gebal and Batrûn are ten miles apart. Ribadda's kingdom had extended at least twenty miles along the coast; and if Beirût and Tripoli were not independent, his land would have reached much farther—to Simyra and Sidon.

276 This letter shows very clearly that the taking of Sidon preceded the fall of Byblos (Gebal).

277 From 75 B. it seems that Amanabba had been sent to Gebal (probably in consequence of the former letters from Ribadda), but it seems he fled again.

278 In later times the small mina of Palestine was £8 6s. 8d., and the large was £16 13s. 4d. (see Conder's "Handbook to the Bible," p. 81). This represents, therefore, at least £500 or perhaps £1,000; but in this early age the value of money was probably higher.

279 Ribadda has said (63 B.) that his sons fell into the power of the enemy when in ships. He also sends a list of property to Egypt (85 B.). Probably when these ships were sent his father went to Egypt, whence he wrote (82 B.), and a copy was sent to the King. There is one other letter in the collection, which was written from Egypt, by Amenophis III to the King of Babylon (B. M. 1), which seems to be a copy, unless in both cases the letters were not sent. (See Appendix.)

280 Gebal was celebrated for its papyrus. It grew in the river Adonis, close to the city. The enemy were now closing in.

281 The salutations in the last letters are very curt as compared with the earlier ones.

282 The King of Babylon refused to help the Canaanites in the reign of Amenophis III.

283 The younger brother was not the one left in charge.

284 "Buruzizi" probably Beit Ziza, east of Batrûn, in the range which runs out to the great pass of Ras Shakkah. Batrûn was perhaps still holding out, and the town was a refuge high up in the wild mountains. "Buru" means "well"; and "Beit" "house" of Ziza.

285 As regards the final outcome of these wars in the north we obtain light from the letters of Dusratta, King of Mitani. He was a younger man than Amenophis III, and his sister married the said King of Egypt. His daughter Tadukhipa married Amenophis IV, and there were friendly relations with Egypt in the latter as well as in the former reign. In his Hittite letter (27 B.) Dusratta speaks of the boundaries of a region which seems to have been conceded to him as his daughter's wedding-gift. He calls himself "Great Chief of the Hittites," and the border was to run to Harran, Chalcis (south of Ieppo), and the "Phœnician West." Thus Dusratta, who says in another letter (apparently his first) that he has conquered the Hittites, would seem to have swallowed up the Hittite King of Mer'ash and part, if not the whole, of Aziru's country; and the Mongol populations were thus to be ruled from Armenia, which was much nearer than Egypt. What became of the King of Kadesh these letters do not say; but he was independent in later times, when Seti I went up "to conquer the city of Kadesh in the land of the Amorites" (Brugsch, Hist., ii. p. 15), and Kadesh was taken by Rameses II, the successor of Seti I, after which a commercial treaty was made with Kheta Sar, the King of Kadesh, whose daughter Rameses II married. There was thus, perhaps, Hittite blood in the veins of the Pharaohs of the nineteenth dynasty. In the treaty papyrus (see Chabas' "Voyage," p. 336), it is mentioned that the same terms—of quality— had existed in the time of the writer's father and grandfather that were claimed of Rameses II, and that war had occurred later. This seems to show that Kadesh was independent shortly after the time of the rebellion detailed in the Tell Amarna letters. The relations with the Hittites were still friendly in the reign of Rameses III, when the Aryan hordes from Asia Minor overran the Hittite country, and came down even to Egypt. In David's time, the border between his kingdom and those of the Hittites and Phœnicians was drawn from Hermon to Danjaan, south of Tyre (2 Sam. xxiv. 6), and Solomon married Hittite princesses. The Hittite independence was only finally destroyed about 700 B.C. by the Assyrians.

286 The mulberry is still found in large gardens at Beirût and throughout the Lebanon. Since Justinian's time it has been the food of silkworms.

287 This repetition may perhaps be regarded as only a phonetic explanation of the preceding ideograms; but perhaps the words were added to show with certainty that by the terms God and Sun he meant the King of Egypt.

288 The name "Abimelech" at Tyre is interesting. It occurs as the name of a Phœnician king in the time of Assurbanipal (885-860 B.C.). The chief deity of Tyre was Moloch, or Melkarth; and the name means "my father is Moloch," claiming a divine descent. The son of Gideon and certain Philistine kings are so named in the Bible.

289 Huzu is probably the modern el Ghazîyeh, near Sidon. It is at the foot of the hills, and there is a stream (Nahr ez Zahrâny, "flowery river") four miles to the south, which accounts for the notice of the waters. It seems clearly to have been in the direction of Sidon.

290 "Belu amil neru," literally "a lord, a chief man of the yoke (or government)."

291 See the letters from Hazor after those from Tyre. This petty monarch was an enemy to the southern possessions of the King of Tyre.

292 The site of Zarbitu is probably the Sarepta, or Zarephah, of the Bible (1 Kings xvii. 9, etc.), which is now Sarafand, half way between Tyre and Sidon. The decision was therefore just; but though apparently satisfied Abimelec did not get what he asked in the preceding letter—if that demand was really the earlier one. There is a fine fountain ('Ain el Kantarah, "spring of the arch") to the north of Sarepta, and the region generally is well watered. The town was famous in the Byzantine age for wine.

293 "Danuna" is probably the Danjaan of the Bible, now the ruin Dâniân, four miles north of Achzib, and on the border between Tyre and Accho (see 2 Sam. xxiv. 6).

294 "Hugarit" is probably 'Akrîth, eight miles east of Danjaan. It has been mentioned as taken by Aziru, in Yapaaddu's letter (128 B.). Perhaps the attack was from the east; and the King of Hazor seems to have joined the Hittites (see 99 B.).

295 Edagama has been mentioned as "Aidugama" in Akizzi's letter from Katna, which was east of Neboyapiza's city Cumidi (Kamid). See B. M. 37.

296 In the former letters (B. M. 31, B. 99) Abimelec has spoken of the Paka as distinct from himself. Perhaps the Egyptian residents withdrew when the troops were withdrawn.

297 Irib is probably 'Arab Salim, fourteen miles southeast of Sidon, on the highest part of the mountains. It stands on a precipice 400 feet above the gorge of the Zahrany River (Robinson, "Later Bib. Res.," p. 47), and was a stronghold.

298 Aziru's allies from Arvad no doubt attacked Tyre by sea.

299 Dr. Bezold has remarked that want of water was always the weakness of Tyre. In the reign of Rameses II the Egyptian traveller (Chabas, p. 313) speaks of water sent to the island of Tyre in boats. Tyre is called by him the city of "two ports," one being on the north, called the Sidonian, and one on the south, called the Egyptian.

300 This letter agrees with others preceding. Neboyapiza's town Kamid, in Lebanon, was about sixty miles to the northeast of Accho, and Ziza was perhaps his sister or daughter, married to the king of an adjoining kingdom. The soldiers to be sent to Megiddo would obtain news, perhaps, of his fate, from a force on its way to Yabis, in Bashan, which his enemies reached after taking Damascus. Makdani is probably the Megiddo of the Bible, on the way to Bashan, at the great ruin of Mujedd'a, near Beisân. The situation agrees with that of the city of Makta, or Megiddo, mentioned by the Egyptian traveller near the Jordan fords (Chabas, p. 207). The Magid— of the previous passage is probably another spelling of the same name. The lady seems to have intended to go there with a guard, and perhaps to obtain a detachment to go to Kamid. In the lists of Thothmes III, Megiddo (Makdi) stands second, after Kadesh of the Hittites; and it was at Megiddo that the chief victory of Thothmes was won. It was then already a fortress which stood a siege, and was the key to the road from Accho to Damascus. The form "Makdani" is explained by the Megiddo of Zechariah (xii. II); and this final "n" is represented by the guttural "'Ain" of the modern Arabic "Mujedd'a." There is no reason at all for placing the site at Legio, west of the plain of Esdraelon, a site which does not agree with any monumental notice, or with the Biblical accounts (see "Memoirs of the Survey of Western Palestine," vol. ii.).

301 There were several Hazors in the north of Palestine. Perhaps the most likely site is the Hazor of the Egyptian traveller. It is mentioned as on a mountain (Chabas, p. 313), between Aksap (Achzib, north of Accho) and the Sea of Galilee. This might be the Hazor which Joshua took (Josh. xi. 1) from Jabin, which was above the Hûleh. The name only remains, west of the probable site, in the Arabic "Jebel Hadireh," a high mountain of Upper Galilee. The King of Hazor's name is unfortunately not quite clear in the text, but seems to be either Abdebaenu, or more probably Iebaenu (Jabin). There was another Jabin of Hazor later on in history (Judges iv. 2). It was no doubt a family name.

302 The nearest places to Hebron seem to have been Nezeb in the valley of Elah, easily reached by a broad, flat road, and on the south Kanana (Kana'an), a fortress taken by Seti I, which is only two miles southwest of Hebron. This was (if the identification be accepted) the limit of conquest (see Brugsch, "Hist.," vol. ii., p. 13), when Seti (about 1366 B.C.) conquered the Beersheba plains, dvancing by Rehoboth and Bethlebaoth. The land of Zahi was south of Hebron, and famous for its wine and trees (Brugsch, vol. i., p. 330), Hebron still possessing fine vineyards. But the Amorites of Hebron were never apparently disturbed by the chariots, and appear in these letters as marauders of Egyptian stations. There is no mention of any advance of the Egyptians into Moab, though Seir and Edom are noticed very early, when the Sinaitic copper-mines were being worked, and before chariots came into use. In the time of the twelfth and thirteenth dynasties, however, the political conditions in Syria were different. The Akkadian King Kudea—a Mongol—was ruling in 2500 B.C. in North Syria, and sent for granite to Sinai. At this time also, according to the Bible, there were Hittites in Hebron, who had been driven to the north by Ahmes about 1700 B.C. So that the population in 1500 B.C. seems to have been entirely Semitic.

303 Gulata is an interesting name to find in the south, as it may have some connection with that of Goliah.

304 The sign of deity is attached to this name, showing that Dagon, the Philistine god, is intended; and it appears to mean "Thou, Dagon, art a shield." Compare Yamirdagan (B. 136).

305 The word "Khazanu" is here used of an Egyptian official, but with the qualification "chief Ka" introducing the Egyptian word. This agrees with the view that "Pa-ka" means "principal man."

306 The sign meant originally "cup." It is remarkable that wine is not mentioned in the letters, unless the drink here noticed was wine. There was plenty of wine in Syria and in Hebron as early as 1600 B.C.

307 The text is damaged. It seems perhaps to read "Citam Mizpi." If this is right, Mizpah near Jerusalem might be intended, or it may mean "below the heights."

308 Gazri is the Gezer of the Bible, now Tell Jezar, at the foot of the Jerusalem hills.

309 Tabu is probably Taiyibeh, seven miles northwest of Hebron, on a hill at the head of the valley of Elah. This fits in with the rest of the topographical notices.

310 Probably the same Khaia who appears in the north as an envoy to the Amorites—an Egyptian official.

311 Takanu (see B. 199, 70 B. M.) lived near Givti, and perhaps was the chief of that town, which may be Gibeah of Judah, near the valley of Elah, south-east of Makkedah. It is mentioned with Hareth, which was close by Gibeah.

312 Referring to the King's order on papyrus. In Dusratta's Hittite letter a royal decree on papyrus is also mentioned.

313 Biruyapiza was probably the second son of Labaya.

314 Macdalim may be Mejdel, in the Philistine plain, which is still a place of importance, with a market.

315 Cuuzbe is probably the Chezib of the Bible (Gen. xxxviii. 5), in the low hills east of Gath, now 'Ain Kezbeh. The marauders seem to issue from the mountains, destroying the commerce of the plains (compare 59 B. M.). Chezib is again mentioned (104 B.).

316 This letter is perhaps explained by another (104 B.), in which the King of Jerusalem sends his wives to Egypt with the Egyptian envoy, on account of the war with the Hebrews.

317 Chief of Keilah, whose letters follow.

318 If Takanu's town was Givti, and Givti was Gibeah of Judah, he is referring to the southern route by the Valley of Elah.

319 "Tarka" instead of "Paka." In Egyptian the word "tar" means "to drive" or "compel," preceding the sign of a man with a stick. "Tarka" is thus apparently an "overseer" of the people.

320 "Yapa'a" is the same name as "Japhia," mentioned as the King of Lachish (Josh. x. 3), who was the enemy of Joshua. He appears here as King of Gezer, and the King of Gezer is called in the Bible Horam (x. 33). The words Gezer and Lachish would not look unlike in the writing of the earlier Hebrew (about the Christian era), but it is not impossible that the two towns may have had the same king. Indeed, the letter seems to show this, as Mer'ash is near Lachish.

321 "Mu(ra)'azi" seems clearly to be "Mer'ash," the Hebrew "Moresheth Gath" (Micah i. 14). The modern name is nearer to the Amorite than to the Hebrew, having a guttural at the end; and, as in other cases, the Amorite "z" stands for a Hebrew "s." The site is south of Gath, and not far from Lachish, close to Beit Jibrîn.

322 The name of the King of Jerusalem is rendered "Abdhiba" by Dr. Winckler, and "Abd Tobba" by Dr. Sayce. The second reading is possible in all cases but one (B. 102), when the sign used was not the syllabic value "Tob," but only "Khi" or "Hi." This would mean "servant of the Good One." Adonizedek was the name of the King of Jerusalem killed by Joshua (x. 3). It is to be remembered that many of the names in these letters are written, not in syllables, but by ideograms. Ribadda's name is hardly ever spelled syllabically, though it is rendered certain by the cases in which it is so spelled. I am inclined, therefore, to suppose that we have to deal, not with an unusual name, like Abdhiba or Abdtobba, which is unknown in history, but with the name of Joshua's contemporary, spelled "US" (= "Adoni" "Lord"), and "KHI" × "BA," "good do" = "zedec" ("justice"). There must, however, always be some doubt as to personal names, unless checked by variant readings.

323 Adonizedek is meditating flight. His letters speak of a raid on Gezer, Ascalon, and as far as Lachish, after the taking of Ajalon by the Hebrews, but they say nothing of Makkedah. From the book of Joshua we learn that after the battle of Ajalon the Hebrews pursued to Azekah, perhaps the ruin of Zak, east of Gaza, and to Makkedah (x. 11), and then returned to Gilgal (15). An interval of unstated duration occurred, while the five kings, Adonizedek, Japhia, Hoham, Piram, and Debir (ver. 3), fled to Makkedah, where they were found hid in a cave. It was during this interval, apparently, that these Jerusalem letters were written.

324 The sign is unusual. The words are "icalu, ca-ar (Irhu) zabbatu," or perhaps "icalu-ca ar(unu) zabbatu." The latter would mean "They prevail over thee; they have been swift to seize."

325 "I have no father and no army." It either means this or "Have I no father and no friend?" It might refer to his father's death, or to the King of Egypt not being his father and friend. Dr. Sayce renders "neither father nor mother" ("SAL um" for "rag um"); but it is very unusual for orientals to refer to their female relations or wives, though in the case of the King of Accho (95 B.) the writer speaks of his wife; but this is for a special reason (see also 104 B.).

326 "'Abiri." This is read by others "Habiri" ("allies"); but the political circumstances do not agree with this explanation, and the sign is used throughout the letters for the guttural "'Ain" (as, for instance, in the name of Azzah or Gaza). There is no mention in the southern letters of Aziru, Abdasherah, Aitugama, or any of the northern allies; and the sign for "allies" or "helpers" in the northern letters is quite different. On the other hand, the 'Abiri are never mentioned, except in the south, near Jerusalem. They are called people of the "blood" or "tribe" of the 'Abiri (B. 106), and of the "land" of the 'Abiri (B. 199), showing that the term is derived from the 'Abarim, or mountains east of Jordan. The Abiru chiefs are mentioned in the singular (B. 102, 104), and none of these facts can be reconciled with the view that they were "allies." They are distinctly said to have come from Seir (Edom) in one

letter (B. 104), and to have left their pastures (B. 103), and are probably the "desert people" of the Gezer letter (51 B. M.). Their actions are those recorded of Joshua's first campaign, and the date agrees, as does also the notice in the letters of Jabin, Japhia, and Adonizedek, the contemporaries of Joshua. Another suggestion has been that they were Hebronites; but in such case the "n" would not be absent, and the sign for city would no doubt occur. They have also been supposed to be Babylonians, but this is indirect contradiction to the relations noticed in the letters between Egypt and Babylon at this time.

327 Ilimelec is a name found in the Bible (Ruth i. 2; ii. 1) as the name of Ruth's father-in-law, a native of Bethlehem, in the time of the Judges. It is therefore a Hebrew name.

328 Milcilu was the King of Gezer, and Suardata of Keilah; his letters follow. This represents the league of kings before the battle of Ajalon.

329 Givti is probably one of the Gibeahs, perhaps Gibeah of Judah, now Jeb'a, southwest of Jerusalem, in the direction of Keilah (Josh. xv. 57), eight miles west of Bethlehem; unless we should read Gimtzi, in which case it would be Gimzu (2 Chron. xxviii. 18), now Jimzu, east of Lydda, and north of Gezer. The former reading seems the better (see 199 B.).

330 "Kielti" is "Keilah" (Josh. xv. 44), now Kilah, east of the Valley of Elah, in the direction of Hebron.

331 Rubute is Rabbah of Judah, now the ruin Rubba, in the same district, four miles east of Beit Jibrîn (Josh. xv. 60).

332 "Beth Baalath" is probably Baalath of Judah, the old name of Kirjath Jearim, now Erma, in the Valley of Sorek. The word "gur" may either mean that the city was "near" Jerusalem, or that it had been an ally of Jerusalem. It is clear that if the forces of the lowlands were marching to assist Jerusalem by the highway, past Kirjath Jearim, the revolt of that town would delay the forces from Gezer, which would naturally take that route.

333 "Beth Amilla" is evidently the "Beth ham Millo" of the Bible (2 Sam. v. 9); "house of the chief," as we now know. It was the royal palace in the lower city (Akra), north of Zion. There was also a Millo in Shechem (Judges ix. 6, 20), evidently the palace of that city.

334 When Adonizedek sent away his women he was preparing for his own flight, by the advice, it would seem, of Egypt. The Egyptian resident also retired. Suta has already been mentioned as an Egyptian official in the north (48 B.); he is also mentioned in a letter from Babylon (4 B. M.), and by the King of Accho, who was a contemporary of Neboyapiza and of Aziru (95 B.), which with other indications shows that Aziru's revolt was contemporary with the Hebrew invasion—at least, within a few years.

335 This shows the enemy as coming from Mount Seir or Edom.

336 This "Givti" would seem to be one of the Gibeahs, unless we should read "Gimtzi" as before.

337 Perhaps this is capable of being rendered, "I am breaking to pieces; the chief is becoming master."

338 What is meant is that the Egyptians, having come by sea to Ascalon or Gaza, are to march to Jerusalem by the Valley of Elah, the highway by which the Philistines came up against Saul. "Cazib" ("Chezib") is in this valley, now 'Ain Kezbeh; and north of it is a valley with the unique name "Naheir" ("the little river"). The road becomes difficult when the Valley of Elah turns to the south, which is alluded to in the next letter (B. 103). (For Chezib see also 73 B. M.)

339 "Tu-ur ba-zu" appears to be spelled phonetically, but does not sound like a Semitic name. If it were taken as an ideogram it might be rendered "Ben Zicaru."

340 "Zelah" has been proposed (Heb. "Zel'a"), but the final sign does not seem to be used to represent the "'Ain." There were two Zelahs, one being Petra, the other north of Jerusalem (now probably the ruin of Salah); it appears to me more probable that Shiloh is intended. The Amorite "z" or "s" occasionally stands for a Hebrew "sh"; and the modern name "Seilûn" has always presented the difficulty that the "s" is not the proper representative of the Hebrew "sh." Perhaps, as in other cases, the peasant pronunciation represents the Amorite rather than the Hebrew sound. Shiloh is remarkable for the great pass it commands.

341 There was a siege of Lachish by Joshua (Josh. x. 33).

342 Rimmon is probably the Rimmon of Benjamin, not far south of Shiloh, now the village of Rummon (Judges xx. 45, etc.).

343 The name spelled in other cases "U-ru-sa-lim" is here spelled "Uru-sa-lim," showing that the usual explanation, "city of peace," is probable. It has been proposed to translate "city of the god Salim," a deity who is not known otherwise; but in these letters the names of gods have the prefix AN ("deity"), which does not occur in any instance in the name of the city. The word "salim" for "peace" has just been used in the letter, and occurs elsewhere in these letters.

344 "Casipi." It has been read "Casia" ("Cushites"), but the word before is in the plural, and the plural could not end in "a." Any great success is still attributed to sorcery in the East. It may, however, only mean "malicious," according to its use in Hebrew.

345 There was an Egyptian known to history who bore the name of Paur (Brugsch, "Hist." i. p. 462); he was a governor in Nubia, somewhat later than the present events. The name, however, must have been common, since "Paur" stands for "Paka" in some cases. It has been already explained as an Egyptian word.

346 The participle is feminine.

347 There had been four previous letters, agreeing with my arrangement.

348 Ajalon (now Yâlo) is at the foot of the Bethhoron Pass, where the battle against the five kings occurred. The women were apparently sent away before the battle of Ajalon, after which the easiest road to the plains, by Bethhoron and Ajalon, was closed. The flight of Adonizedek took place, according to the Biblical account, after the battle of Ajalon, while Joshua was at Gilgal, where the news was brought.

349 This appears to be the meaning, and refers to the road, mentioned in the last letter, by the Valley of Elan—less easy than that by Ajalon.

350 "Casi," or Cush, as in Egyptian records, appears to mean upper Egypt. See what has been said as to this name in Ribadda's letter (61 B.).

351 "Harti Cirmiel" is evidently Hareth Carmel, representing the Hebron country from Hareth (Kharas), on the northwest, above the Valley of Elah, to Carmel of Judah on the southeast. This would agree with placing Givti at Jeb'a.

352 Apparently the southern Gibeah of Judah, mentioned before (106 B.). Dr. Sayce reads Gath, but when Gath is mentioned it it called Giti (154 B.).

353 "Labaya" may mean, according to a common form of expression, the land of Labaya.

354 "Salabimi," Shaalbim (Judges i. 35; 1 Kings iv. 9) or Shaalabbin (Josh. xix. 42), is probably Selbît, lying southeast of Lydda, near Ajalon.

355 In Judges i. 35 we read of the Amorites remaining in this district.

356 This name may be read various ways, as "Addamaru" or "Abu Amaru." Perhaps the name "Ithamar" may be compared (Exod. vi. 23; xxviii. 1). See also Yabitiri of Joppa (Abiather?).

357 The only difficulty in identifying this place, "Ci el-ti," with Keilah lies in the spelling with "Caph" instead of "Koph." The name contains the required guttural found in the Hebrew; this has disappeared from the modern name, "Kilah." The sign for "Ki" does not seem to be used in these letters; and there are several other instances of confusion of the two letters, as when "Ka" is written for "Ca" ("thee") in a few cases.

358 "Ra" is apparently an Egyptian name. The order for withdrawal of the troops appears to have arrived.

359 This quarrel between the King of Jerusalem, the King of Makkedah, and the King of Keilah is probably early, before the appearance of the Hebrews; for Adonizedek says that the sons of Labaya (103 B.) were his contemporaries at that time, and Suyardata becomes his ally (106 B.) in presence of the common danger. If "behind" means to the west (the front being always the east), the attack was from the Valley of Elah. Keilah has very rough mountains on the east, and is easily reached on the west.

360 The meaning seems to be that Adonizedek had seized the flocks and herds.

361 "Basmath," meaning "balsam" or "sweet," was no doubt a common woman's name. It occurs as the name of Ishmael's daughter whom Esau married (Gen. xxxvi. 3, 4, 13), and as that of one of Solomon's daughters (1 Kings iv. 15). She may have been the wife of Milcilu, King of Gezer, and pleads for her sons after her husband's death. He had apparently been seized by the Hebrews (106 B.).

362 Zorah, now Sur'ah (Josh. xix. 41; Judges xiii. 2, etc.), was not far south of Ajalon, and near Gezer on the southeast.

363 This name cannot be identified, as has been proposed, with that of Abdasherah, since "Ashtoreth" and "Asherah" are different words.

364 If it is to be read simply as a syllabic name, it would be perhaps "Musi-huna." There is a "Mes-hah" ("place of unction") in lower Galilee. I have here supposed "huna" to come from the root "hana" (Heb. "hanah"), "to inhabit."

365 "Tuser Atta," a Mongol name, "father of conquest." "Arta Sumara" appears to mean "destroying hero."

366 "Mitani" or Matiene (Herod, i. 72, 189, 202; iii. 94; v. 49, 52; vii. 72) extended from the sources of the Araxes to the Halys River, and thus included all Armenia west of Lake Van: other names for the region were, the "Land of Khani Rabbe" (or Khani Rabbatu) and the "Land of the Minyans." (See 27 B.)

367 The Hittites clearly did not live in Matiene, but in the adjacent country of northern Syria.

368 "Gilukhipa," a Mongol name, "possessing glory."

369 "Gilia" and "Tunipripi," Mongol names, "glorious" and "very reliable."

370 This may be dated late in the reign of Amenophis III, as Dusratta survived him.

371 Possibly Queen Teie or Thi.

372 Amanu, the Egyptian god Amen.

373 The word "Khatanu" means any kinsman by marriage, and "emu" is still used generally of any "kinsman" or even for "friend." Some have translated "son-in-law" and "father-in-law," but the latter word would be "khamu," not "emu." Dusratta was the father-in-law of Amenophis IV, but brother-in-law of Amenophis III.

374 "Binti," not "Bintiya" ("my daughter"). The word "Bint" is still used generally for "a young woman." Perhaps Queen Teie is intended.

375 "Targumanu" ("interpreter") is the modern "dragoman." Khani (see p. 201) was sent to Aziru, showing that the Canaanite rebellion may have occurred in the reign of Amenophis III.

376 "Assat mariya elme," or perhaps "Assutti elme" ("in marriage to the youth"). There is no statement that shows Dusratta's daughter to have married Amenophis III. She married his son, and is called "daughter-in-law" of Queen Teie (11 B. M.).

377 The gold came from Nubia and Abyssinia. (See Brugsch, "Hist. Egypt," i. pp. 287, 310.)

378 In Aramaic "Gilia," in the native tongue "Gilias," with the Mongol termination of the nominative indefinite.

379 "Ikhibin," possibly Kaban Maden in Armenia.

380 "Si-migi-s" is apparently a Mongol title for some deity, "the eye of night" (or "of sunset"), either the moon or the evening star.

381 "Khalci," either Chalcis near Aleppo, or the "Land of the Khal" or "Phœnicians." (Karnak list, No. 140.)

382 The Minyans (Jer. li. 27; and in Ps. xlv. 8, Targum) lived west of Lake Van. The Hyksos are called Men, or Menti in Egyptian texts. Apepi, the Hyksos King, adored Set, or Sut, who was adored also by the Hittites, and from whom Dusratta's father, Sut-tarna ("Set is his lord") was probably named. It would appear that the Hyksos, Hittites, and Armenians, were of the same race. The land of the Men is said to have been near Assyria, and east of Syria, which agrees. (See Brugsch, "Hist. Egypt," i. pp. 210, 233, 234, 239.) The Minyæ of Herodotus (i. 146; iv. 145-148) are noticed as mixed with Aryans in Ionia, and in Lacedæmon were regarded as descendants of sailors in the Argo—perhaps from Colchis and the Caucasus. See what is said as to the similarity of the presents from Armenia (26 B.), and the art of Mycenæe and Troy, which is of Asiatic origin.

383 Harran (Gen. xi. 31, etc.), now Harrân, was on the south border of Dusratta's kingdom, marching with Assyria. (Compare 24 B.)

384 "Tadukhipa," a Mongol name, "possessing sweetness."

385 Probably Teie is here meant, as there is no notice of Gilukhipa. She may have died.

386 "Walk after" for "obey" or "worship," is used just as in Biblical Hebrew.

387 The broken name was "Nabkhuriya," or Amenophis IV, as is clear from the next paragraph. He was also the husband of Tadukhipa, as here stated. (See 11 B. M.)

388 "Sitatama," a Mongol name, apparently "fair-faced." "Suttarna," also Mongolic, "Sut is his Lord."

389 As Gilukhipa was married during the reign of Suttarna (apparently from Egyptian sources in the tenth year of Amenophis III, or about 1490 B.C.), it is possible that "Teie" is here intended; but her father's name was Iuaa, or Ivaa, and it is not clear what relation she was to Dusratta. From 11 B. it seems clear that they were related, and later in the present letter he mentions the "father of Teie," apparently as living with him after his own father's death. The syllables "Ivve" (perhaps for "Ivaa") precede the father's name, but as the text is here broken, it is not certain that these syllables represent a personal name. Perhaps Teie was Dusratta's cousin. She was certainly of royal birth, and is represented as very fair, but with dark hair. The words "a daughter" may mean only "a young woman."

390 Khai was sent to Aziru (31 B.), which again shows the date of the Canaanite rebellion to have been early.

391 This agrees with 27 B. as regards Dusratta's conquests in the Hittite country.

392 As Amenophis IV was married already in the reign of Amenophis III, his mother's marriage evidently took place some twenty years at least before the date of this letter.

393 Apparently this was written at least four years after the death of Amenophis III, or about 1450 B.C. at earliest.

394 The lands given when Tadukhipa was married.

395 "Mazipalali," a Mongol name, "hero with the sword."

396 Indicating that these Mongols were not monogamists.

397 Mongol name, "Ar-Tessupas," "worshipper of Tessupas" (Rimmon). Other Mongol names occur in 27 B. (in the native speech) including Asali ("joyful") and Artatan ("strong soldier"). If Teie's name was Mongolic, it would mean "bright."

398 Similar extradition is noticed in the treaty between Rameses II and Kheta Sar, the Hittite king, a century later.

399 The signs IZCU, SAK, TAK ("weapon, stone, head") seem to indicate a stone axe such as the Carians used. Battle-axes of flint are noticed in the time of Thothmes III. (Brugsch, "Hist. Egypt," i. p. 342.)

400 This letter may, perhaps, be earlier than the preceding.

401 From a later letter (1 B. M.) it seems that the foreign ladies were shown to envoys from their parents, to enable them to report as to their health.

402 Or "the curious things."

403 Or, perhaps, "but letters are received."

404 This agrees with the letters from Babylonia in showing the disturbed state of the countries between Armenia and Egypt early in the reign of Amenophis IV, due to the revolts of Hittites, Amorites, and Hebrews.

405 The two-headed eagle was a Hittite emblem; it is also found at Mycenæ.

406 Iron from Asia is believed to have been known yet earlier (Brugsch. "Hist. Egypt," i. pp. 342, 354). It was known in the fourteenth century B.C. by its Semitic name, "berzil."

407 Clearly written to Teie, as Amenophis IV is mentioned as her son.

408 "Yuni," as a Mongol name, would mean "true."

409 "Rimmon Nirari" is an Assyrian name, but the king so called lived a good deal later. The rank of this writer is evidently inferior, but not as inferior as that of the Canaanite chiefs. He may have been an Assyrian prince, and perhaps wrote to Amenophis III. "Nukhasse" Dr. Bezold supposes to be the "Anaugas" of the records of Thothmes III, an unknown region in Syria. I have supposed it to be Merash, reading "Markhasse."

410 This king, unknown before, was probably older than Amenophis III, who married his daughter, who was marriageable before the writer's father died.

411 As in the previous case (82 B.). See p. 236.

412 Probably Irtabi (1 B.).

413 The month names are written in ideograms of Accadian origin.

414 This King's date has been placed as late as 1400 B.C., but the dates are not accurately fixed. His daughter appears to have married Burnaburias of Babylon before 1450 B.C. ("Trans. Soc. Bib. Arch." i. p. 69). His predecessor, Buzur, Assur, had settled the Assyrian boundary with Burnaburias. (Ibid., p. 68.)

415 This interruption (see also the letter from Chaldea, 18 B., in the later reign of Horus) was probably due to the Syrian revolt (compare 23 B., 7 B., and 8 B.), showing that the power of Egypt, broken in 1480 B.C., was still unrecognized as late as 1400 B.C., which brings us near the time when Rameses II recognized the independence of the Hittites, about 1360 B.C. (See p. 241.)

416 Supposed to have reigned about 1550 B.C.: presents from Assyria were received by Thothmes III even earlier (Brugsch, "Hist. Egypt," i. p. 328), including chariots and cedar-wood.

417 Burnaburias appears to have reigned about 1450 B.C., or a little later. As regards the dates of Egyptian kings, they rest on the statement (see Brugsch, "Hist.," i. p. 395) that the star Sothis rose on the 28th of Epiphi, in the reign of Thothmes III, and on the date of the new moon of various months in the same reign. The Egyptian year was a year of 365 days, and therefore vague as regarded the sidereal year. The risings of Sothis (Sirius) are recorded ("Decree of Canopus") in the later Ptolemaic times as they occurred in connection with the Egyptian year, changing one day every four solar years; and the Rosetta stone fixes the calendar. From the rising of Sothis we should obtain a date about 1598 B.C. as falling in the reign of Thothmes III; and from the coincidences of the new moon we should obtain 1574 B.C. as the thirty-fourth and 1585 B.C. as the twenty-third years of his reign. He would, therefore, accede 1608 B.C. Dr. Brugsch places his accession about 1600 B.C.

418 This indicates the beginning of the Syrian wars in the reign of Amenophis III.

419 Apparently a Babylonian princess was to be sent to Egypt, and an Egyptian princess to Babylon. The two royal families were already allied by the marriage of Irtabi, and yet earlier of the sister of Callimmasin (1 B. M.), even if no Egyptian princess had been granted to the latter. The writer's son was probably Carakhardas, who succeeded him.

420 Zalmu was a Babylonian. See the next letter.

421 Khai was still living in the reign of Amenophis IV.

422 "Siiri," "a company of merchants," as in Hebrew.

423 Or "advised this." The foes attacking Egypt were at some distance from Babylonia, and the news only came by the envoy from Egypt.

424 "Sumatta." Compare "Shammah" (Gen. xxxvi. 13-17), a proper name, perhaps, from the same root.

425 "Khinna tuni" would mean "inhabiting Khinna," see Khini (64 B. M., p. 25), but more probably Hannathon in lower Galilee, east of Accho, is intended, now Kefr' Anân.

426 See Zatatna and Surata, kings of Accho (93 B., 95 B.), p. 249. This, taken with the name of Neboyapiza in the latter letter, indicates a date early in the reign of Amenophis IV.

427 Alasiya was apparently a maritime region beyond the tributary Egyptian States, and not either in Babylonia (Shinar) nor in the Hittite country (5 B. M.); probably it is the Elishah of the Bible on the south shores of Asia Minor. (See my note "P. E. F. Quarterly Statement," January, 1892, p. 44.) Elishah (Gen. x. 4; Ezek. xxvii. 7) was a maritime region. The diffusion westward of a Semitic population in Cilicia has long been suspected to have occurred early.

428 Semitic personal names, showing the worship of Ea and Baal in Elishah.

429 The signs SAL US indicate "female servants."

430 "Lukki," perhaps the Lycians, or perhaps the Ligyes of Herodotus, on the borders of Matiene (vii. 72). They appear to be the Laka who lived in the Taurus, the Leku of Egyptian records (Brugsch, ii. pp. 44, 54, 116, 124) mentioned with other tribes of north Syria, and with the Shakalisha—perhaps Cilicians.

431 "An-Amar-ut" ("sun-disk") I have supposed to be the name of Khu-en-Aten ("glory of the sun-disk"), a title apparently of Amenophis IV (Brugsch, "Hist. Egypt," i. p. 441); but it may, of course, refer to the god so called (see note, p. 198). The King of Egypt is called the sun-god in many of the letters in this collection.

432 The sign KHU means "bird," but also "glory" and "prince." "Ilid KHUMES" I take to mean "born of princes." Others have rendered it "who trains birds," but it would rather mean "who gives birth to birds," which is impossible.

433 The name of the King is everywhere written in full, with the two cartouches.

434 Here and in other places a gap in the tablet has been filled up by the corresponding sentence in the inscription of Medinet Habou.

435 The plants.

436 Allusion to the festival of the coronation.

437 The τριακονητηρις here and in the title of the King has been employed as we should say a "century."

438 Literally, life, health, and strength.

439 I.e., the flocks of the temple's estates.

440 The defaced passages ran thus, "Adoration of Osiris by the steward of the flocks (Amen-mes), son of the Lady Nefer-t-ari."

441 Ave!

442 Vide Goodwin, in Chabas; Mélanges III, Tom. I, pl. 257.

443 Hermopolis magna.

444 The entrance to the dwelling of the dead.

445 The words "paut" and "paut-ti," or double-paut, are connected with the idea of "creation."

446 NOYN, νουν, abyssus.

447 "Mesess," sky, vault, and veil.

448 Ritual, ch. XVIII. Lepsius, "Todtenbuch," xi. ch. XVIII. ix. e. 17. I. 62.

449 Literally, "for a number of times."

450 The two long feathers which adorn the head-attire of the Sun-god.

451 "Sensen," fraternize.

452 Sam.

453 Beneficent force.

454 The great dwelling of Seb is the earth itself.

455 I.e., To the lord of justice.

456 The entire north.

457 Or, satiating abundance.

458 The exact meaning is the French "combler."

459 The papyrus is much worn here. The name of the place is perhaps "Pamakar of the sky."

460 Indian fig.

461 "Sestsou-em-païf-nakhtou Ousormara" is the name of a fortress built by Rameses II, in Syria or Palestina, and different from Ouati. The name means "Rameses II in his victories."

462 The order is quite contradictory. How can it be disobeyed, and how obeyed?

463 Or, gone to the gap to which the dead went in the Sun-boat.

464 Syrians as prisoners of war.

465 Negroes.

466 Cedar or acacia.

467 A kind of balsam.

468 Syria.

469 Or cattle.

470 Or industrious, "rut."

471 Dead or departed.

472 If this rendering is correct, the meaning must be that the god of the Nile is the secret source of light; see § 3, l. 5, and § 8, l. 1. The attributes of Egyptian gods, who represent the unknown under various aspects, are interchangeable to a great extent; here the Nile is Ammon, doing also the work of Ra. Dr. Birch suggests that the rendering may be, "hiding his course night and day."

473 Ra, the Sun-god, who is represented as delighting in flowers; see Ritual, c. lxxxi, "I am the pure lily which comes out of the fields of Ra."

474 The Nile-god traverses heaven; his course there corresponds to that of the river on earth.

475 See x. 6. This is obscure, but it may mean that the Nile-god protects the newly sown fields from the birds.

476 I.e., he sets them at work. Thus Ritual, c. xv. 20, "Ra, the giver of food, destroys all place for idleness, cuts off all excuse."

477 As they are by idleness; see Ritual, cxxv. p. cclv. (Birch).

478 I.e., he makes it ready for cultivation.

479 Their joy and gratitude respond to his advance.

480 Num is the Nile-god regarded as giving life.

481 The Egyptian word corresponds to Αρσαφης, which, according to Plutarch, signifies τὸ ἀνδρεῖον. (Isis et Osiris, c. 37.) The Egyptians, like all ancient people, identify terror with strength or greatness.

482 This scriptural phrase comes in abruptly. It is probably drawn from some older source.

483 The true Deity is not represented by any image. This is a relic of primeval monotheism: out of place as referring to the Nile, but pointing to a deeper and sounder faith. Compare the laws of Manu, i. 5-7.

484 See last line of § 13. There are no shrines covered, as usual, with colored hieroglyphics. The whole of this passage is of extreme importance, showing that, apart from all objects of idolatrous worship, the old Egyptian recognized the existence of a supreme god, unknown and inconceivable, the true source of all power and goodness. Compare the oldest forms of the 17th chapter of the funeral Ritual in Lepsius's "Aelteste Texte."

485 1 Ki. viii. 27.

486 Is. xi. 13, 14.

487 Or "thou givest them counsels, orderest all their goings."

488 I.e., "all magistrates are the servants of the deity, and administer his law from South to North."

489 Maspero "par lui est bue l'eau (les pleurs) de tous les yeux," i.e. "he wipes away tears from all eyes."

490 Dr. Birch, to whom I am indebted for this rendering, observes that the goddess Neith is often represented with two crocodiles sucking her breasts.

491 I.e., "The Nile fills all mortals with the languor of desire, and gives fecundity."

492 I.e., "without needing rain, the gift of the goddess of heaven." Such seems to be the meaning of a very obscure passage.

493 See note on § 1.

494 The meaning is, evidently, that he combines the attributes of Ptah the Demiurge, and Kabes, an unknown god.

495 All things serviceable to man—arms, implements, etc.

496 This seems to mean, "he gives oracles at his shrine." Observe the inconsistency of this with § 5.

497 Causing scarcity of food in the land. See Ex. viii. 18, 21.

498 In a season of scarcity prayers are offered for supply of water. The following lines seem to describe great haste when the inundation comes on; none wait for their clothing, even when valuable, and the nightly solemnities are broken up: but the passage is obscure.

499 Literal answer, "i.e., with thanks and prayers, when thou bringest the water in abundance."

500 See II. 2.

501 The gold represents the preciousness of the gift of food.

502 This is often mentioned in the inscriptions among the most precious stones.

503 See note on II. 4.

504 Which he ate when he could get nothing else.

505 An allusion to the legend that the Nile comes forth from two openings in the South.

506 See V, last line.

507 The Pharaoh.

508 The two regions.

509 "At the entertainments of the rich, just as the company is about to rise from the repast, a small coffin is carried round, containing a perfect representation of a dead body; it is in size sometimes of one, but never more than two cubits, and as it is shown to the guests in rotation the bearer exclaims, 'Cast

your eyes on this figure; after death you yourself will resemble it: drink, then, and be happy.' "—Herodotus, "Euterpe," xxviii.

510 "The Song of the Harper" in the tomb of Nefer-hotep bears a great resemblance to this composition. See Dümichen, "Historische Inschriften," ii. pl. 40.

511 Or, perhaps, "the little ones, the children."

512 Imhotep, the son of the primeval deity Ptah, was the mythical author of various arts and sciences. The Greeks spelled the name Ἰμούθης, Imouth, but more frequently substituted the name Ἀσκλήπιος, Asclepios.

513 Hartatef was the son of King Menkera (Mycerinus), to whom the discovery of part of the Ritual, cap. lxiv. is attributed, and who was the author of a mystical work.

514 Compare the Assyrian phrase "The land men cannot return from," "Descent of Ishtar," "Records of the Past," Vol. i. p. 143, p. 5.

515 I.e., "of the mourners."

516 Here follows a lacuna.

517 2 Anastasi, p. 8, l. 5, to p. 9, l. 1.

518 2 Anastasi, p. 9, l. 2, to p. 10, l. 1.

519 The phrase which I have translated "the way of Amen" is literally "the water of Amen." In Egypt the river Nile was the great road or highway, hence by an easy metaphor the water was used to signify "the way"; that is, the will, command, or rule

520 2 Anastasi, p. 10, l. 1.

521 Tum or Atum (the setting sun), Lord of Heliopolis.

522 Heliopolis, the city of Tum.

523 Heliopolis, the city of Tum.

524 Or, "do not censure me."

525 Literally, "without his body." It seems to mean weakness, mutilation, or disability.

526 Literally, "upon my mouth."

527 Lacuna.

528 2 Anastasi, p. 5, l. 6.

529 Literally, "in health, life, and strength"; but the King being the subject of the wish, I have ventured to Anglicize the phrase as above.

530 The King Meneptah, son of Rameses II, and his immediate successor.

531 The Sun.

532 A form of the Sun-god of the West, the chief god of Heliopolis.

533 Lacuna.

534 Lacuna.

535 Lacuna.

536 Lacuna.

537 The panther's skin was the special characteristic of the dress of the priest of Khem the Vivifier.

538 Lacuna.

539 Lacuna.

540 Rannu, an Egyptian goddess who presided over the harvest.

541 Lacuna.

542 Lacuna.

543 Lacuna.

544 An or On, "the house of the Obelisk," or Heliopolis.

545 Thebes.

546 Arabia.

547 Palestine or Arabia.

548 Chem.

549 Mahennu.

550 Uati.

551 Frequent allusions are made in the papyri to the production of created things from the eyes of Ra or of Horus. Noxious things were supposed to be produced from the eye of Set or Typhon.

552 Thebes.

553 Heliopolis.

554 The name Amen means "secret," or "hidden."

555 Harmachis.

556 Thebes.

557 Heliopolis.

558 The serpent

559 Creator.

560 The diadem.

561 Many of the phrases in this beautiful hymn are ambiguous, even where the original text is perfect.

562 This note is subscribed in the original papyrus.

563 "At the front of the morning." Some prefer rendering the words "every morning."

564 Perhaps "Approach thou thy mother Nut." "Neb Ra," "Lord Ra," seems clearly the reading of the text given in Lepsius, unless the scribe has twice put the hieratic character for "nuter" instead of the usual form of "h"; "neb heh," "lord of eternity," as Maspero renders it, is what might rather have been expected. In the following, "Isis and Nephthys" is the version of M. Maspero; the text appears to me to give Osiris.

565 Perhaps, "he cannot advance."

566 Nehaher, "ghastly faced," an infernal demon, sometimes represented as a serpent.

567 "Thou givest life;" this may be understood also as imperative, "give life."

568 Bech, the Eastern hill of sunrise. Its opposite height was called Manu.

569 "Thou turnest gloom into repose." I am not confident that the meaning of the original, "ta-k neshen enti ster," is correctly given in these words; perhaps "thou makest the adversary prostrate" may more truly convey the sense.

570 Isis and Nephthys.

571 The name of Osiris is invariably prefixed to that of the deceased, the latter being always assimilated to this god.

572 The first two sections are evocations addressed to Osiris defunct, expressing the grief of his two sisters at the loss of their brother, and referring to the search made by them after him.

573 One of the names of Osiris.

574 Surname of Osiris.

575 Surname of Osiris.

576 The following sections are invocations addressed to Osiris under the forms of the Moon and the Sun, expressing the joy of his two sisters at having thus perceived him.

577 The Sacred-Eye here indicates the disk of the moon.

578 The sun in all his power.

579 The setting sun.

580 The star of Sirius, where the soul of Isis dwelt.

581 Isis having with the aid of her sister Nephthys reunited the parts of Osiris's body, dispersed by Set, formed of them the infant Horus.

582 Neith personified the Lower Hemisphere, whence Osiris, the Rising Sun, appeared under the form of Horus.

583 The sun nightly sinks into the bosom of his mother Neith, who personifies the Lower Hemisphere of heaven.

584 Osiris, again coming forth under the form of Horus-conqueror (or the Rising Sun), becomes the Lord of the Universe.

585 The high-priest, reader in the panegyrics.

586 The high-priest presiding over funeral ceremonies and rituals.

587 The Great Hall wherein the Judgment-scene was painted.

588 The heavenly region.

589 The universal being.

590 "Under the form of."

591 The earth.

592 Gods.

593 "Who speaks to himself."

594 Crater.

595 The weeper.

596 A fish, most likely the "phagros," the appearance of which was connected with the inundation.

597 The divine eye.

598 Vivifies.

599 The meaning of this name is doubtful.

600 The god of the spheres.

601 Glorifies himself.

602 A title of Osiris, literally "He who resides in the West."

603 The covering of Ati, the air(?).

604 Solar disk.

605 The splendid one.

606 Gives a body to.

607 Creates.

608 Perhaps Anubis.
609 Solar disk.
610 Lacuna.
611 Who speaks to himself.
612 "He who raises his soul."
613 "The high spirit."
614 Flesh, or substance.
615 Literally, "the shining face."
616 "He who is on the ground."
617 Doubtful meaning.
618 "Creates," "fashions."
619 The genii of the watches of the night.
620 Lacuna.
621 He who opens the earth.
622 He who is armed with teeth.
623 Doubtful meaning.
624 Ra under the form of a scarab.
625 Lacuna.
626 Lacuna.
627 Teb Temt.
628 Lacuna.
629 Lacuna.
630 Apophis, the great serpent of evil.
631 The royal Osiris.
632 The god of the two horizons.
633 Unknown constellation.
634 The moon.
635 The solar disk.
636 Lacuna.
637 Lacuna.
638 Hu, the creative life; Sa, the intelligence.
639 The water of the East.
640 The water of the West.
641 He who comes forth from Mehur.
642 He who is in Netur.
643 One of the halls of the empyrean, which is here personified as a goddess.
644 The lower region.
645 The striped headdress generally worn on the statues of the kings.
646 The planet Mars.
647 Thoth.
648 Thoth.
649 The eternal being.
650 He who embraces.
651 The God of the Nose. Each part of the body of the deceased becomes a god. The same is found in the funereal texts, and especially in the "Book of the Dead," ch. xlii.
652 Osiris.
653 The Osiris is an hermaphrodite being.
654 Lacuna.
655 Lacuna.
656 His own form.
657 The sceptre which has the form of a hook, and commonly held in the hand of Osiris.
658 The white and red crown, which is the emblem of dominion over both Upper and Lower Egypt.
659 His existences.
660 His existences.
661 Tonen.
662 Tonen.
663 Nut personified the Upper Hemisphere of heaven.
664 Here was written the name of the deceased.
665 Probably a substance used for purifying and perfuming.
666 The earth.
667 Heaven.

668 The setting sun.
669 The solar bark.
670 Osiris.
671 Another version: uniteth itself (to) the breath of thy nostrils.
672 Another version, "by thy Lord, Ra."
673 Osiris.
674 Those of the mummy.
675 This is the acknowledgment of the resurrection effected by the ceremonies of the mummification. I am indebted to the friendly aid of M. Chabas for the translation of this and one or two other passages.
676 Corrupted passage restored by means of the manuscripts of the Louvre.
677 Another version: "thou art received."
678 Corrupted passage: translation uncertain.
679 Heliopolis.
680 Hermopolis.
681 Another version: "the living."
682 Literally, "the Westerners."
683 Illegible passage restored by means of the manuscripts of the Louvre.
684 Another version: "this volume of the Book of Respirations is made for him and the souls of the gods."
685 M. de Rougé reads "Atesch," but there are very strong reasons for believing that the first syllable in this word is to be read "Kat," not "At." Of this opinion is M. Brugsch. The Syrian name was probably "Kadesh" (the Holy City), which the Egyptians, not having the letter "d," wrote "Katesh." There were several places so called in the East, but the Kadesh here mentioned has not been satisfactorily identified with any of them.
686 The word "horse" is used in the original for a chariot, Homer uses the plural ippoi in a similar manner.

www.ingramcontent.com/pod-product-compliance
Lightning Source LLC
Chambersburg PA
CBHW031309150426
43191CB00005B/148